John Heyl Vincent

Curiosities of the Bible

pertaining to Scripture persons, places, and things including prize questions and answers, enigmas, acrostics, facts and statistics, with many valuable ready reference tables, founded upon and answered in the Bible

John Heyl Vincent

Curiosities of the Bible

pertaining to Scripture persons, places, and things including prize questions and answers, enigmas, acrostics, facts and statistics, with many valuable ready reference tables, founded upon and answered in the Bible

ISBN/EAN: 9783744685078

Printed in Europe, USA, Canada, Australia, Japan

Cover: Foto ©Thomas Meinert / pixelio.de

More available books at **www.hansebooks.com**

CURIOSITIES

OF THE

BIBLE

PERTAINING TO SCRIPTURE

PERSONS, PLACES AND THINGS

INCLUDING

PRIZE QUESTIONS AND ANSWERS, ENIGMAS, ACROSTICS,
FACTS AND STATISTICS, WITH MANY VALUABLE
READY REFERENCE TABLES

Founded upon and Answered in the Bible

DESIGNED TO INCITE IN OLD AND YOUNG A GREATER DESIRE TO

"Search the Scriptures." John v 39

WITH

BLACKBOARD OR SLATE ILLUSTRATIONS, BIBLE
STUDIES, CONCERT EXERCISES AND
PRAYER MEETING OUTLINES

BY A NEW YORK SUNDAY-SCHOOL SUPERINTENDENT

WITH AN INTRODUCTION

BY

REV. J. H VINCENT, D.D.

Revised, Enlarged and Illustrated

NEW YORK
E. B. TREAT, 757 BROADWAY
CHICAGO: R. C. TREAT   CINCINNATI: FORSHEE & McMAKIN
KANSAS CITY: F. PROTHERO.

1884.

COPYRIGHT,
E. B. TREAT,
1875—1879.

NOTE.—*The more difficult and prize questions are indicated by bold-face figures in numbering.*

NOTE.—*The blank pages following each section are designed as memoranda pages for entering additional curiosities and facts as they occur in Bible reading or study.*

Among the attractive features of this enlarged edition are the Illustrations, for which we are chiefly indebted to S. W. Clark, publisher of the "Blackboard," and in part to J. Fairbanks & Co., and to them also we tender acknowledgments for suggestions and outlines from "HAND-BOOK OF BIBLE READINGS."

We are also under obligations to Rev. H. H. BIRKINS for valuable services in editorial work.

INTRODUCTION.

THERE is no saving power in the mere letter of the word, even though it be the word of God. It is the Spirit that giveth life.

We should not, however, despise the letter. It is the body; and the body is of some worth as a medium for the soul.

He who knows most of the word of God, though it be with but an intellectual knowledge, will be that much richer when the Holy Spirit of God touches the dry bones and bids them live. The dry bones in the "Valley of Vision" were better than so many stones, when the time came for the miracle of resurrection.

We cannot give to our children too much Bible knowledge. They cannot know too much Bible history, nor too much Bible geography, nor be too well able to explain the obscure passages, nor too familiar with the true solution of the common difficulties which all Bible students sooner or later encounter, and which they should be able to explain.

CURIOSITIES OF THE BIBLE.

In view of this need, I do most sincerely thank the industrious and ingenious "New York Sunday-School Superintendent," who has compiled the valuable little manual of biblical curiosities now presented to the public.

Let it be used wisely. Let the circle of friends, old and young, who may gather about table or fireside to spend an hour or an evening in the profitable recreation which it may furnish—let them all remember that cheerfulness and generous rivalry are allowable here, but that irreverence and impatience, out of place always and everywhere, are especially inappropriate, while we hold in our hands the most holy word of God, or busy ourselves with the truths which are to be found in it.

May the students of the "Curiosities of the Bible" become skilled in the interpretation of that Divine Book, and, enjoying its spiritual illumination, may they prove its divinity by pure and unselfish lives.

J. H. VINCENT.

PREFACE.

This collection of treasures, new and old, is the outgrowth of eighteen years experience in devising methods and incentives to interest children and those of older growth in bible study; and thus aid them in fulfilling the injunction—"search the scriptures."

It has been a part of every Sunday's programme in our school, for the past eight years, to propose a bible question or exercise to be answered the following Sunday upon cards distributed by the secretary and collected at the call of the bell; the correct and incorrect answers being announced from the desk, with appropriate comments and explanations.

By this method, if an incorrect answer was given, the unsuccessful seeker after truth was not exposed to ridicule in consequence of failure, but was ready for the next proposition with as much zeal as at the outset.

Such questions only were given as were founded upon the bible and answered in it, and such as would excite in the mind of bible readers and seekers after truth a curiosity to know how, when, where, and under what circumstances they occurred.

To secure these, a vast range of bible literature has been searched. Among the most prominent aids may by mentioned the very excellent London periodicals, "The Sunday at Home," "The Quiver," and "Band of Hope Review." My

PREFACE.

associates—officers, teachers, and scholars—have jointly interested themselves with me in solving many of the intricate problems herein contained.

A large number of these are *prize questions* and puzzles, which have elicited a wide correspondence, and the deep interest manifested in them gives the assurance that the benefit derived from these exercises can never be estimated.

In verification of this statement, selections are given from the testimony of a large number who, in their researches, have not only been stimulated by the hope of winning an earthly reward, but have been led to deeper thought and richer experience, which of itself is a matchless prize.

EXTRACTS FROM LETTERS.—"I cannot tell you how pleasant and happy have been the hours spent in studying the bible for this purpose. Time and trouble have been repaid with interest in the enlargement of biblical knowledge, and the increase of love for the bible."

"I have derived lifelong benefit from the close communion with the book of books and the author of it, finding new beauties in the scriptures, and obtaining a priceless treasure which neither the world nor time can take away."

"I can thankfully say, reading the bible for these answers has shown me the truth in a way I never saw before."

"I read the entire book of psalms through five times for one answer."

This volume has a two-fold mission: to increase our knowledge of all biblical facts, and beget and intensify in all hearts a greater love for the Book of Life. That the number of those who may be thus benefitted may become *legion* is the hope of the compiler.

T. B. E.

Washington Heights, New York City,

CONTENTS.

	PAGE
INTRODUCTION	5
PREFACE	7
CONTENTS	9
THE BIBLE LEGACY	13

CURIOSITIES OF THE BIBLE PERTAINING TO—

First Things of the Bible	Page	13	Key, Part II., Page		3
Old Testament Persons	"	19	"	"	9
New Testament Persons	"	49	"	"	31
Old Testament Places	"	61	"	"	41
New Testament Places	"	67	"	"	47
Old Testament Things	"	71	"	"	51
New Testament Things	"	85	"	"	63
Bible Time	"	91	"	"	69
Bible Pictures	"	214	"	"	68
Familiar Bible Quotations	"	93	"	"	68
Scripture Metaphors	"	95	"	"	71
Scripture Enigmas	"	101	"	"	79
Scripture Anagrams	"	213	"	"	144
Bible Characters	"	215	"	"	146

BLACKBOARD OR SLATE ILLUSTRATIONS:

	PAGE
The Young Bible Reader	226
Light on our Pathway	228
The Spider's Web	230
The Door open or shut	232
The Vine and its Branches	234
Sin and Salvation	236
The Bow in the Cloud	238
Light from the Bible	240
The Great Ship and the Little Helm	242
Figs or Thistles—Which?	244
The Uplifted Saviour	246
Signals of Danger	248

CONTENTS.

PAGE

Gaining and Losing 250
The Christian's Defence. 252
The Two Ladders... 254
The Yoke of Christ... 256
The Christian's Crown.. 258
The Full Surrender.. 260
The Cross of Christ.. 262
The Two Paths... 264
The Family in the Ark. 266
Love not the World.. 268
Steps in Sin 270
The Door of the Heart.. 272
God's Promise in the Rainbow 274
The Ascending Lord... 276
What Jesus says.. 277
Triumphs of the Cross... 279
Jacob's Ladder.. 279
The World for Jesus... 280
Christians the Light of the World................................ 283
Heaven by the Way of the Cross................................ 283
Christ our Guiding Star.. 284
Lessons from the Lion.. 286
Searching the Scriptures.. 287
The Wine Cup.. 288

CONCERT EXERCISES:

The Lord's Prayer—Bible Proofs................................. 223
The Nine Attributes of God.. 224
The Life and Times of St. Paul................................... 225
Wanted for the Lord's Service.................................... 265
The Blood of Christ.. 271
What Christians should be.. 443

BIBLE STUDIES AND READINGS:

How to Search the Scriptures 227
Why we should take God for our Guide........................ 229
What is Heaven according to the Bible 229
What we are by Nature... 231
God's best Gifts... 235
What the Bible says of the Fool.................................. 237
What Christians have... 239
Come to Jesus for what ?.. 239

CONTENTS.

	PAGE
The Bible Mirror	241
How may we get to Heaven?	241
Six Commands of Christ	243
Indispensable Things	243
Prayers offered in Danger, and by whom	245
What Christ is to us	247
The Christian's Dedication	247
The Gospel Railroad	249
God is able	253
The Path to Eternal Life	255
"Comes" of the Old Testament	257
"Comes" of the New Testament	257
God's Way and our Ways Contrasted	259
Temperance—demijohn and jug	261
Sowing and Reaping	265
The Six one Things	267
What the Christian Soldier must do	267
What it is to be a Christian	269
What we do by Faith	273
New Things of the Bible	273
The Apostles' Creed	275
He leadeth us	281
"Comes" of Christ	285

PRAYER-MEETING OUTLINES:

What a Prayer Meeting should be	289
Characteristics of God's People	289
The Two Masters	289
How shall I approach the Mercy-Seat?	290
What shall I do with Jesus?	290
How shall I find Jesus?	290
To whom shall we go for Safety?	290
Seven Confessions of the Bible	291
God's Providence	291
The Atoning Saviour	291
All Things through Christ	291
Seven Things to Hold Fast	292
The Seven "Musts"	292
Things to which we should take heed	293

What Christians should be	443
Curious Facts about the Bible	449

CONTENTS.

	PAGE
Chronological Index of the Bible	450
Prominent Events in Ecclesiastical History	455
Chronological Table of Patriarchs, from Adam to Moses, 2,500 years.	456
Special Prayers of the Bible	457
Old Testament Miracles	458
Miracles of Christ	459
Miracles of the Apostles	459
Parables of the Old Testament	460
Parables of Jesus	460
Discourses of Jesus	461
Tables of Scripture Measures, Weights, and Money	462
Names and Titles applied to Our Saviour	464

THE BIBLE.*

A nation would be truly happy if it were governed by no other laws than those of this blessed book.

It contains everything needful to be known or done.

It gives instruction to a senate, authority and directions to a magistrate.

It cautions a witness, requires an impartial verdict of a jury, and furnishes the judge with his sentence.

It sets the husband as the lord of his household, and wife as mistress of the table—tells him how to rule, and her how to manage. [dren.

It entails honor to parents, and enjoins obedience on chil-

It prescribes and limits the sway of the sovereign, the rule of the ruler, and the authority of the master; commands the subjects to honor and the servant to obey, and the blessings and the protection of the Almighty to all that walk by this rule.

It gives directions for weddings and burials.

It promises food and raiment, and limits the use of both.

It points out a faithful and eternal Guardian to the departing husband and father; tells him with whom to leave his fatherless children, and whom his widow is to trust—and promises a father to the former, and a husband to the latter.

It teaches a man to set his house in order, and how to make his will; it appoints a dowry for his wife, and entails the rights of the first born, and shows how the young branches shall be left.

---

* This description of the Bible was found in Westminster Abbey, nameless and dateless. It is invaluable for its wise and wholesome counsel to the race of Adam.

It defends the rights of all, and reveals vengeance to every defaulter, over-reacher, and trespasser.

It is the first book, the best book.

It contains the choicest matter, gives the best instruction, affords the greatest degree of pleasure and satisfaction that we have ever enjoyed.

It contains the best laws and most profound mysteries that were ever penned ; and it brings the very best comforts to the inquiring and disconsolate.

It is a brief recital of all that is to come.

It settles all matters in debate, resolves all doubts, and eases the mind and conscience of all their scruples.

It reveals the only living and true God, and shows the way to Him, and sets aside all other gods, and describes the vanity of them and all that trust in such—in short, it is a book of laws, to show right and wrong, of wisdom that condemns a folly and makes the foolish wise, a book of truth that detects all lies and confronts all errors, and it is a book of life that shows the way from everlasting death.

It contains the most ancient antiquities and strange events, wonderful occurrences, heroic deeds, unparalleled wars.

It describes the celestial, terrestrial, and infernal worlds, and the origin of the angelic myriads, the human tribes, and the devilish legions. [critic.

It will instruct the accomplished mechanic and most profound

It teaches the best rhetorician, and exercises every power of the most skilful arithmetician, puzzles the wisest anatomist, and exercises the wisest critic.

It is the best covenant that ever was agreed on, the best deed that ever was sealed, the best that ever will be signed.

Patrick Henry's Legacy.—Patrick Henry, a great statesman of Virginia, before he died made a *will* bequeathing all his property to his relatives; and at the close he wrote this true sentiment. "There is one thing more I wish I could leave you all, *the religion of Jesus Christ*—with this, though you had nothing else, you *could be* happy; without this, though you had all things else, you *could not* be happy."

BIBLE CURIOSITIES

PERTAINING TO

First Things.

[Answers page 3.]

1. What was the first command of God?
2. What was the first prophecy?
3. Who built the first city?
4. Who was the first sacred historian?
5. Who was the first judge according to the Bible?
6. Who was the first pilgrim?
7. Who was the first shepherd mentioned in the Scriptures?
8. Who told the first lie as recorded in the Scriptures?
9. What was the first of the ten plagues of Egypt?
10. What was the first recorded song of the angels?
11. Who was the first Jewish high priest?
12. Who was the first transgressor?
13. Who was the first gardener?
14. Who first wore the bridal veil?
15. Who was the first machinist in brass and iron?
16. Who was the first exile in Bible times?
17. Of what did the first wedding present consist?
18. What was the first thing engraved?
19. Who first held the office of scribe?
20. By whom and for whom was the first burying ground bought?
21. According to sacred history who was the first hunter?
22. Who built the first ship?
23. Who was the first outcast and vagabond?

24. Who first suffered martyrdom?
25. Who is the first person known to have worn a ring on his finger and a gold chain on his neck?
26. Who first used a saddle as recorded in the Bible?
27. Who was the first man born that was named by the Lord before his birth?
28. Who was the first to weep, according to the Scriptures?
29. Who was the first person that broke all the commandments?
30. Who was the first person that died after the creation?
31. Who was the first person that died a natural death?
32. What was the first Scriptural song?
33. Who made the first confession to the Lord, as recorded in the Bible?
34. Who was first guilty of theft, aside from Eve?
35. What was the first offering of woman recorded in the Bible?
36. Who was the first shepherdess?
37. Who was the first recorded person raised from death to life?
38. Who erected the first monument to the memory of the dead?
39. Who was the first Jew to marry a Gentile, according to the Scriptures?
40. What is the first mountain mentioned in the Bible?
41. What were the first words spoken to man?
42. Who was the first negro convert to Christianity mentioned in the Bible?
43. Who was the first that was called "the Hebrew" or Jew?
44. What is the first Bible record of the use of a navy?
45. Where was the ferry-boat first used, and by whom?
46. When was the Sabbath first instituted, and by whom observed?
47. Where have we an account of the first missionary meeting?
48. Where is mention first made of the purchase of land?

49. Where is the first mention of printing in the Bible?
50. What is the first recorded use of current money?
51. What was the text of our Saviour's first sermon?
52. Give the occasion on which man first exercised the power of speech.
53. What was the occasion of the first voluntary fast recorded in the Bible?
54. How does the first sermon delivered by man (who?) resemble the modern style of discourses?
55. Who was the first president appointed in sacred history, and by whom appointed?
56. When was the use of flesh as food first allowed to man?
57. What is the first recorded account of female government?
58. Which of the tribes marched first in their journeyings through the wilderness?
59. What was the first miracle performed by Christ?
60. Where are the wicked first spoken of as sinners, in the Bible?
61. Who first took an oath or affidavit?
62. Where is mention first made of a library?
63. Give the first Scripture reference made to God as a King.
64. What was the first prayer for a king?
65. Where is the first mention of beggars?
66. Where is the first prophecy of the millennium recorded?
67. Where is recorded the first act of surveying?
68. Where do we read of the first Christian letter of recommendation?
69. When and by whom were temperance societies first formed?
70. Where were moles first found and by whom?

OLD TESTAMENT CURIOSITIES

PERTAINING TO

Persons.

[Answers page 9.]

1. To whom did God promise that his children should be in numbers as the stars in heaven?
2. How many examples does the Scripture give of ungodly men desiring the prayers of the righteous?
3. What queen was deprived of her throne by her son because of her idolatry?
4. By whom were the Jews delivered according to prophecy?
5. Why were the Levites scattered over the face of the earth?
6. What king beat down a city and sowed it with salt?
7. Who was the father-in-law of Moses?
8. A man was driving his oxen in the field, and another man came and threw his mantle over him. Who were these men?
9. What prophet was himself the subject of prophecy?
10. In what famine do we read that women ate their own children?
11. The legal heir to the throne of Judah was hid by his aunt for six years in the House of God to escape a murderous band. Who was the woman and who was the future King?
12. In what cave did David seek refuge when pursued by Saul?
13. What did Solomon name the two pillars in the porch of the temple?
14. What cave was the hiding-place of five Kings of Israel?

15. Of whom does the Bible speak as plowing with twelve yoke of oxen?

16. Which of the Kings of Israel built an ivory house?

17. Who alone escaped the massacre of the priests of Nob.

18. Of whom does the Bible say, when frightened, his hair stood on end?

19. What King of Babylon put out the eyes of a captured King of Judah?

20. Who was the last King of Judah?

21. Who was the last King of the ten tribes of Israel?

22. On what mountain was Josiah slain in battle?

23. What King of Israel commanded eighty-five priests to be slain with a sword?

24. What woman upon the death of her son, king of Judah, murdered her grandchildren and usurped the kingdom?

25. When was the feast of tabernacles celebrated for the first time after the death of Joshua?

26. What was the name of the King of Judah that had his eyes put out and then imprisoned for life?

27. On what mountains was a King commanded to gather a whole nation?

28. What prophetess dwelt under a palm tree?

29. Who was the left-handed judge that delivered Israel?

30. Who slew his seventy brothers and proclaimed himself King of Israel?

31. Of whom does the Bible give an account as highway robbers?

32. The life of what King was endangered by a stone from he hand of a woman?

33. Whose life was lengthened fifteen years in answer to prayer?

34. Who wished to " die the death of the righteous?"

35. Who are the only three persons mentioned in the Bible whose names commence with the letter V?

36 What King in besieging a city set an example to his people and said · " What ye have seen me do, make haste and do as I have done?"

OLD TESTAMENT PERSONS.

37. Who was made King of Judah at seven years of age having been hid for six years?

38. What King shut up the temple of God?

39. Of whom and by whom was it said, they had "written bitter things against him?"

40. What High Priest stood between the living and the dead and averted a plague that had already slain 14,700?

41. What King of Judah was smitten with leprosy as a judgment of the Lord for his pride?

42. What Canaanite King cruelly cut off the thumbs and great toes of seventy conquered Kings and was subsequently captured and made to suffer the same cruelty?

43. What rebel General gave the blood of a Queen to the dogs?

44. What King was wounded in battle and to avoid the reproach of being killed by a woman ordered his armor-bearer to slay him?

45. What book of the Bible was written without mentioning the name of God?

46. What King of Israel established an itinerant Ministry?

47. By whom and to whom was it said "Come with us and we will do thee good?"

48. What King had two sons that were lovely and pleasant in their lives and in death they were not divided?

49. Who delivered Israel by killing 600 Philistines with an ox goad?

50. From whom did Moses the leader of Israel receive his name, and why?

51. Who was King of Sodom at the time of its destruction?

52. Who was King of Gomorrah at the time of its destruction?

53. What was Aaron's conduct when his two sons were destroyed by fire from the Lord?

54. Who attempted to escape from the presence of the Lord and paid his fare on a ship to another port?

55. Where was Moses buried?

56. What was the early Bible name for Prophet?
57. How many were the Songs of Solomon?
58. What is the shortest song in the Bible?
59. A certain King was smothered by his servant, who was he?
60. Who had for a possession 23 cities of Gilead?
61. By whom were the children of Israel carried captive into Babylon.
62. What ancient King employed dromedaries as mail carriers?
63. Who was the founder of the Hebrew nation?
64. What King of Israel committed suicide, and how?
65. What laboring men were so honest in their dealings that no accounts were kept?
66. Name two persons that saved their lives by hiding in a well.
67. Of what defeated King does the Bible say, "How are the mighty fallen?"
68. What two young men of the Bible were swifter than eagles and stronger than lions?
69. What King lost a thousand chariots in battle and who captured them?
70. Who was Melchizedek?
71. What Jewish King displayed his zeal for the Lord in destroying idolaters?
72. What King and what punishment was inflicted upon him for attempting to lay hold on a prophet of God?
73. What was the name of Moses' wife?
74. What leader of a rebellion among the children of Israel was swallowed by an earthquake and all his host?
75. Who prayed "Give me neither poverty nor riches?"
76. Who said though He slay me yet will I trust Him?
77 Who is the shortest man mentioned in the Bible?
78. What five instances does the Bible give of caves being used as places of refuge?
79. How were the Israelites commanded to treat strangers?
80. What tribe was condemned to perpetual bondage, and by whose order?

OLD TESTAMENT PERSONS.

81. What employment did Joshua give the Gibeonite bondmen?

82. With what people was the first battle fought by the Israelites after leaving Egypt?

83. Who hid one hundred prophets in a cave?

84. In whose funeral possession do we find the first mention of horsemen?

85. Who prophesied that the Jews should eat their own children?

86. Who did the Lord make a terror to himself and his friends, and why?

87. Who prophesied that Judah should be carried captive into Babylon and where is it recorded?

88. Where do we first read of a collection being taken, and for what purpose?

89. What woman said " I am weary of my life?"

90. What criminal in his confession said I saw, I coveted, I took?

91. Of what old man do we read who felt none of the infirmities of age?

92. Six women once took a journey which resulted in a wedding. Who was the bride and groom.

93. Who expressed a desire to be " where the wicked cease from troubling and the weary be at rest?"

94. What two instances do the Scriptures give of *deceit* being employed by good men for their own preservation?

95. What woman ridiculed a King for rejoicing, and suffered by it?

96. What did Job say at the loss of his children and all his possessions?

97. What was the name of Aaron's wife?

98. What was the language of Eli when sore afflicted?

99. Which of the prophets was carried captive to Babylon?

100. Who was the prophet of Israel in the time of Saul?

101. Which of the prophets was a herdsman?

102. Who was Maher-shalal-hash-baz?

103. What High Priest made and worshipped idols?

104. What victorious army took as trophies of war two hundred thousand captives and much spoil?

105. Upon the advice of what prophet was a captive host returned to their own country by their victors?

106. What king in his vain glory took a census of his people?

107. What four persons does the Bible mention as being engaged in a legitimate, remarkable, and profitable oil speculation?

108. What king traded in apes and peacocks?

109. Who, when bereft of his best earthly friend, did not weep in compliance with the command of God?

110. What two prophets reproved King David?

111. What King of Israel followed heathen practices by burning his children in the fire?

112. What haughty king, and in what way did God punish him for his pride and arrogance?

113. Who is greater than he that taketh a city?

114. Who sang a song of lamentation over the death of Saul and Jonathan?

115. What is the longest word in the Bible?

116. What prophet was confined in a dungeon?

117. Who in time of trouble preferred to fall into the hands of God than into the hands of men?

118. Of what prophet is it recorded that he ate a book?

119. How many prophetesses are there mentioned in the Bible?

120. In whose time was the great Jewish reformation?

121. What is the most noted instance of devoted friendship?

122. Why was Joab promoted to be captain over David's army?

123. What pious King of Israel before going into battle sought help from God?

124. What three servants of God, during trial, wished to die?

125. From whence was fire originally obtained which was kept perpetually burning on the golden altar?

126. How many instances does the Bible mention of adopted children?

127. Who was the most wicked King of Israel?

128. To which son of Jacob was the birthright given when taken from Reuben?

129. To whom did God promise an early death as a special favor?

130. What nation was famed for skill in hewing timber?

131. What distinguished female character was buried under an oak?

132. In answer to whose prayer was rain witheld and afterwards granted?

133. Who refused to seek refuge in the temple in a time of danger?

134. Who was forbidden to eat anything made from the vine?

135. What King of Israel was a shepherd in his youth?

136. What was Balaam's wish concerning his death?

137. Who was the last King of Israel?

138. Prove from the Scriptures, that Moses had a pattern of the tabernacle shown him?

139. To what King of Israel did the Lord appear in a dream by night?

140. What people was always employed day and night?

141. What tribe was so fond of jewelry as to put golden chains on their camel's necks?

142. What three persons where swallowed alive in a pit, and why?

143. Who are now the children of Abraham?

144. By whom was the first temperance society organized?

145. By whom was a water test once used to prove soldiers?

146. Whose army was compared to " grasshoppers for multitude," and their camels were without number?

147. What king was smitten with leprosy, and why?

148. What was the name of Elisha's father?

149. What leader of Israel demanded of a conquered tribe their golden ear-rings as a trophy of his victory?

150. Who built an altar unto the Lord at Mount Ebal?

151. What king shut up the temple of God?

152. Who did the Lord help in battle with hail-stone, which slew more than the sword?

153. Who did the Lord send as spies by night to the Midianite's camp and secured to them the victory?

154. What was Joshua's inheritance in Canaan?

155. What prophet speaks of children playing in the streets when describing Jerusalem in prosperity?

156. Who built the first city, according to the Scriptures?

157. Who was punished with death for touching the Ark of God?

158. What are the names of the five kings who made war against Gideon and were hanged?

159. To whose house was the Ark taken when brought to Jerusalem, and how long did it remain?

160. Whose house was taken by the authorities for a prison, and what prophet was secured in it?

161. By whom was the prophet Jeremiah arrested and put in prison?

162. Who mortgaged their farms in time of drouth to buy corn?

163. What governor of Judea refused a salary from his people and treated them with princely hospitality?

164. Who was the first person that died after the creation?

165. Who was the first person that died a natural death?

166. What was the name and rank of the officer under Nebuchadnezzar that set fire to the temple at the first destruction of Jerusalem?

167. Unto whom was it said "set thine house in order for thou shalt surely die"?

168. How many were the Proverbs of Solomon?

169. What prophet wore a veil, and why?

170. What were the names of the twelve men, one from each tribe of Israel, sent to search out the land of Canaan?

171. What was the manner of Saul's death, and why?

172. Who was the mighty man of valor afflicted with leprosy?

173. A boy was once sent to carry to his brothers some loaves and some parched corn. The army to which his brothers belonged gained a great victory in consequence of this visit What was name of the boy? How was the victory won?

174. What distinguished Bible personage was arrayed in scarlet and gold with a chain about his neck?

175. What aged prophet's hands where upheld by two persons and caused the armies of Israel to be victorious?

176. Who entertained an angel unawares by offering a burnt offering, and the angel ascended in the flames thereof?

177. Who was successor to David, King of Israel?

178. Who was Samson's father?

179. Who was Manoah?

180. Who partook of a meal prepared by an angel, and was sustained forty days and nights while in the mountain?

181. The birth of how many distinguished Bible characters were announced by angels?

182. Whose life was saved by giving heed to the warnings of an angel?

183. Unto whom did an angel appear with a drawn sword?

184. What names were given to angels, and how many?

185. How many Canaanite kings did the children of Israel destroy on the taking of the promised land?

186. Who slew three hundred Philistines with a spear?

187. Who was chief of the mighty men of David?

188. Who wrested a spear from a giant's hands and slew him in self-defence?

189. Who made the first confession to the Lord as recorded in the Bible?

190. Who was the first Jew that married a Gentile, according to the Bible?

191. Who preferred to "abide in the street all night, than partake of the hospitatity of a prophet?

192. Who wrote of being a witness to the swift flight of an angel?

193. What mighty man had his robe torn in twelve pieces by a prophet?

194. Of whom was it foretold by an angel that his beard should never be shaved?

195. On how many occasions were angels sent to destroy men?

196. For whom did an angel prepare a dinner?

197. Who was chief among the captains of David?

198. Of whom does the Bible mention as having met and killed a lion in a snow storm?

199. What office will the angels perform at the judgment day?

200. Who entertained angels unawares?

201. What three persons does the Bible mention as being mighty in strength and each slew a lion?

202. What two persons were commanded by an angel to take off their shoes?

203. What heroic act of one of the captains of David made him chief among them?

204. Who was Moses' father-in-law?

205. Who had giant sons, and preserved their land forty years from a foreign invasion?

206. What was the fate of the ten spies that brought a false report from Canaan?

207. What prophet tore the robe of a mighty man in twelve pieces?

208. Who was borne away by angels after his death?

209. Who hid a linen girdle in a rock by the river Euphrates?

210. Which of the prophets was a gatherer of sycamore fruit?

211. Who plundered the temple and took away the shields of gold?

212. Who carried a little coat to her son every year?

213. Unto whom did God say, "I am thy shield?"

214. By whom was Solomon's temple first destroyed?

215. Of whom was it said he prayed by an open window?

216. Who does the Bible say is greater than he that taketh a city?

OLD TESTAMENT PERSONS.

217. Who could say of the Lord from sad experience "those that walk in pride he is able to abase?"

218. What wicked King was punished by the Lord till his hairs were grown like eagles' feathers and his nails like birds claws.

219. What builders worked with a sword girded at their side and armed men standing beside them? Who were these and why were they armed?

220. What King showed to the messengers of another King all his silver and gold and treasures?

221. Who restored the vessels taken from the first temple?

222. What prophet broke the yoke and bonds off the neck of another prophet, and what was his name?

223. What general lay in ambush with his army and succeeded in capturing it and destroyed its inhabitants and burnt the city?

224. The King of what city was taken alive in battle and hung to a tree until dead?

225. What was Joshua's name up to the time he was chosen one of the twelve to spy out the land of Canaan?

226. What King was guilty of idolatry in making two golden calves and commanding the people to worship them?

227. Who boastfully said, "Is not this the great Babylon that I have built?"

228. Who, to avoid being captured, was let down from a house top by a scarlet cord?

229. What vision did Ezekel see by the river Chebar?

230. Who dedicated the temple?

231. How was the prophecy fulfilled that the glory of the second temple should be greater than the glory of the first?

232. Who sought retirement in a field for meditation?

233. Of what King is it said "that he was driven from men and did eat grass as oxen?"

234. Who put out Zedekiah's eyes?

235. What captive was appointed ruler over all that his master had?

236. What prophet put bonds and yokes on his neck, and why?

237. Who prepared the material for building the temple?

238. By whom was the foundation of the second temple laid?

239. Who prophesied that the glory of the second temple should be greater than the glory of the first?

240. Who beheld a vision in the valley of dry bones?

241. In answer to whose prayers was rain sent; also prevented?

242. Who buried Saul's body after he had committed suicide?

243. Who said "To obey is better than sacrifice, and to hearken, than the fat of rams?"

244. Who burned incense on an altar before idols of gold?

245. Who was afflicted with insanity as a punishment from the Lord for his pride and arrogance?

246. Who built Tadmor (Palmyra) in the desert?

247. Which prophet acted the part of a physician by giving a medical prescription?

248. Who proved themselves the servants of God by partaking only of vegetables and water?

249. Why were the Ammonites and the Moabites prohibited from coming into the congregation of the Lord forever?

250. Which of the prophets was called from the plow?

251. Who in deep affliction was forsaken by all his friends and afterward in the time of prosperity visited him, each one bringing a piece of gold and an ear-ring?

252. Who rent his mantle and plucked off his hair?

253. Who were the bride and groom of the first bridal procession that entered the land of Canaan?

254. Who prophesied the destruction of a city and its doom was averted by the repentance of its people?

255. The destruction of Ninevah was the fulfilment of whose prophecy?

256. Who built a monument in the middle of a river? What river, and why?

257. By whom and on what occasion was a monument used as a table in eating?
258. What was Belshazzar's last official act before his death?
259. Who was Belshazzar's successor as King of the Chaldeans?
260. What commander refused to lead his army to battle unless a prophetess accompanied him?
261. What prophetess played upon a musical instrument?
262. What Jewish captives were promoted to positions of honor in Babylon?
263. Who was reigning King of Babylon at the time of its capture by the Medes?
264. Who was the first president mentioned in Sacred History and by whom appointed?
265. What exile returned and rebuilt the walls of the city of his fathers?
266. What aged person waited in Jerusalem the coming of the Messiah?
267. Why did God permit the children of Israel to be removed from their land?
268. What King was carried captive to Babylon and brought back to Jerusalem?
269. What was the height of the giant Goliath?
270. Who does the Bible say had six fingers and six toes on each hand and foot?
271. What prophet mentions by name three men eminent for piety and prayer? Who were they?
272. What was the total number of the children of Israel that went down to Egypt?
273. How many were there of the children of Israel that came out of Egypt 430 years afterward?
274. Who slew eighty-five priests, and by whose command?
275. Who was very near being killed for eating a little honey?
276. What King of Judah had not seen a copy of the Law till he was twenty-six years old?
277. What treasurer built for himself a sepulchre in which he was never laid?

278. Who built a pillar to make himself remembered because he had no son?

279. What two false prophets of the same names as a King of Israel and a King of Judah were burned by Nebuchadnezzar?

280. How many instances are recorded in the Old Testament of the dead being raised to life?

281. Who was in command of the largest army recorded in the Bible?

282. What wicked King delayed the punishment due to his evil deeds by humbling himself? [battle?

283. What King of Israel disguised himself before entering

284. Who was the mother of Jehoshaphat, King of Judah?

285. Who was pronounced a ready scribe in the law?

286. What King of Israel sold himself to work wickedness?

287. What prophet shared the fate of a criminal by being placed in the stocks?

288. Why was the name of Pashur, a governor of Judah, changed to Magor-missabib?

289. What King released Jehoiachim, King of Judah, after he had been in prison thirty-seven years, and nourished and honored him till the day of his death?

290. What captive Jew grieved so bitterly over the downfall of Jerusalem that he was permitted by the King, whom he served, to return and rebuild the holy city?

291. How many instances are given of laying hold on the horns of the altar for refuge?

292. What prophet called for music before delivering his prophecy?

293. Under whose reign was silver as plentiful as stones in Jerusalem?

294. What King of Israel was slain in battle and the dogs licked up his blood?

295. What Scriptural examples are there of early piety?

296. Who was the brother of Goliath, and who slew him?

297. What dead man was restored to life by touching the bones of another?

OLD TESTAMENT PERSONS.

298. What tribe had no inheritance in the land of promise, and why?

299. What King of Israel was told by a dying prophet to take a bow and arrow and shoot out the window and smite the ground?

300. Who hid a hundred prophets in a cave?

301. By whom and to whom was the question asked. "How old art thou?" and what answer was given?

302. Who employed a wandering Levite as a family priest, paying him a yearly salary, besides his board and clothes?

303. What "mighty man of valor" was restored to health by means of a captive servant?

304. What two remarkable prayers were answered before the petition was concluded?

305. Who followed a father's advice, "To drink no wine?"

306 Who stole money from his mother, and upon its return was melted into idols?

307. What was Samson's riddle, and where is it recorded?

308. Who prayed all night till break of day?

309. By whose order were seventy brothers slain and their heads put in a basket?

310. What king had an iron bedstead?

311. Who filled up the wells that Abraham had dug, and who dug them out?

312. What woman wandered seven years in a land of strangers, during a famine in her own country?

313. When was prayer once offered from the depths of the sea?

314. Who calls the grave "the house appointed for all living"?

315. What Jewish prince was found suspended in the branches of an oak?

316. What young man listened to the counsel of his companions with disastrous results, rather than heed the advice of his father?

317. Who was King of Assyria at the time the children of Israel were first carried into captivity?

318. What two men were prophesied of by name long before their birth?

319. Who built Nineveh?

320. Which tribes of Israel were first carried into captivity?

321. What man wept when those that had injured him asked his forgiveness?

322. Among the men born after the flood, who attained the greatest age?

323. What women are mentioned in the Bible as taking part in the religious services?

324. Mention the name of the only female whose full name is given in the Bible.

325. What king visited a dying seer, and from restricted faith injured his own fortunes?

326. What warrior fought so long and desperately that his hand clave to the hilt of his sword?

327. Give instances of a single person being called by different names in the Bible.

328. What prophecy was fulfilled by Sampson becoming a judge?

329. The tribe of Dan is omitted from one of the lists of the tribes of Israel and that of Simeon from another, where are these lists found?

330. On what three occasions is the destroying angel mentioned?

331. How was it that Ahaziah, the youngest son of Jehoram King of Israel, came to the throne upon the death of his father?

332. By what means did Rahab aid the escape of the spies sent to Jericho?

333. What disciples of our Lord wished to command fire to come down from heaven upon the Samaritans?

334. For what purpose did Jeremiah use the type of good and bad figs?

335. What special law was given to Moses in reference to cases where property was left to the daughters of a family?

336. For what purpose did Jeremiah hide stones in the clay nearest to the house of Pharaoh, King of Egypt, in Taphanhes?

OLD TESTAMENT PERSONS.

337. What price did Amaziah, King of Judah, pay for the hire of one hundred thousand of Israelites?

338. Who was the founder of Samaria?

339. Mention a passage where old clouts are mentioned as used in helping a prophet out of a dungeon.

340. What King of Judah "did that which was evil in the sight of the Lord," and reigned but three months and ten days?

341. What man of Israel was stoned for blaspheming God?

342. For what purpose was Aaron's rod, which budded, kept in the tabernacle? [and by whom?

343. Where were the bones of Saul and Jonathan buried.

344. What two kings disguised themselves before going into battle, and were both slain by archers?

345. Who is it likens the ungodly to chaff?

346. What relation was David to Joab?

347. By what means did Michal, the daughter of Saul deceive her father as to the absence of David?

348. What king was on the throne of Judah when he was only eight years old?

349. What were the names of the sons of Samuel?

350. Quote the words used by Moses at the commencement and termination of the journeyings of the Israelites.

351. What king was smitten with leprosy for burning incense?

352. What women helped to build the walls of Jerusalem?

353. Which of David's relatives acted as a scribe for him?

354. What was the name of the nurse of Rebakah, the wife of Isaac?

355. Who was the captain of the guard appointed to look after Jeremiah and remove him from prison?

356. What miracle did God work to enable a widow to pay her debts?

357. What was the total number of captives who returned from the Babylonish captivity with Ezra?

358. When God sent an angel in the days of David to destroy Jerusalem, who was said to have seen the angel and hid themselves?

359. Who is mentioned as having dwelt in the college of the prophets?

360. Quote the passage in which Elisha calls Ahab a murderer.

361. What persons are mentioned as being able to use both the right hand and the left in hurling stones and shooting arrows?

362. What judgment fell upon the two eldest sons of Aaron, and why?

363. Where do we find it recorded of Moses that he was leprous?

364. What king's body was fastened to the wall of Beth shan?

365. Of what people is it said that they could " fling a stone at a hair's breadth?"

366. Of whom is it recorded that he went down and slew a a lion in a pit on a snowy day?

367. What king visited a dying prophet's bed and wept over him?

368. Which was the learned tribe of Israel?

369. Who was the Ethiopian who trusted in the Lord and his life was given him for a prey?

370. Who was hypocrite enough to weep with some mourning worshippers, thus decoying them into the city and then slew them?

371. Who predicted that an evading king should pitch his tent over the spot indicated?

372. What other nation besides Israel is to be scattered to every people?

373. In Ezek. xii. 13, it is said to Zedekiah, I will bring him to Babylon, yet he shall not see it, how could that be?

374. Who was the young man that was jealous of his master's honor?

375. Which was the honest tribe in Israel?

376. Name the man and his four sons who hid themselves from an angel.

377. What relation was Esther to Mordecai?

OLD TESTAMENT PERSONS.

378. What prophet waited for a good man to say grace before they sat down to their feast?

379. What King of Israel loved farming?

380. Who did a brave deed upon a "snowy day?"

381. Whom did the Lord seek to kill in an inn as he was on a journey with his wife and child?

382. What woman was won by the bravery of a warrior and became his wife, after the husband had fled from his country, she married another man, but when he became great he sent to the king of the country he had left and demanded his wife, the king took her from her husband and sent her under a soldier's escort, her husband followed weeping until sent back by the captain?

383. Who was the heathen priest whose grandsons are frequently mentioned in scripture?

384. What very old man, the oldest since the flood, was kind to a boy who afterwards repaid his kindness by killing his son?

385. What king's name meant peaceable?

386. What man, although warned, invited his murderer to a feast?

387. What tribe furnished the counsellors of Israel?

388. Where is the destroying angel mentioned three times in the Old Testament?   [death?"

389. Who said "there is but one step between me and

390. The Lord once asked a man if he sought great things for himself, and told him not to do so, who was it?

391. How many men were sent to take up Jeremiah from the dungeon?

392. Where do we read that certain postmen were mocked and jeered at when they delivered the news?

393. What king did God smite with leprosy?

394. What king offered to covenant with the men of a city, provided he might thrust out their right eyes?

395. Name the man to whom an angel spake as he stood on a hill top, at whose foot lay one hundred and two men, scorched to death.

396. Name the seven persons whose names were predicted before their birth.

397. In the Jewish polity, who might not marry a widow?

398. What two young men fell victims to a curse which had been pronounced five centuries previously, a curse which probably their fathers, who were the cause of the judgment, never knew or had forgotten?

399. Give instances of possessing the assurance of forgiveness of sin.

400. Where are tinkering gipsies mentioned in the Bible?

401. Who was David's companion and counsellor at an early part of his reign?

402. What king had eighty-eight children?

403. Prove from the Old and New Testament that David was inspired.

404. What tribe of Israel was noted for the possession of practical wisdom?

405. The Tree of Life mentioned in the revelations is also spoken of by which of the prophets?

406. Quote the passage in which Isaiah expressly foretells the resurrection of the dead.

407. Who, in Bible times, preached from a pulpit?

408. Name two Hebrew leaders whose strength did not abate with age.   [kingly manner?

409. Who, though not a King, was said to have acted in a

410. Name the King that was slain by conspirators and was brought on horses to his grave.

411. Name a King who was an extensive farmer and loved husbandry.

412. When Ezra the scribe expounded the Book of the Lord, what posture did the people assume?

413. What King applied the very same words to a prophet as that prophet had previously applied to another prophet?

414. Who was the youngest son of the Patriarch Jacob?

415. Who was it said "let all thy wants lie on me?"

416. Mention the circumstances under whch a prophet declared himself to be no prophet.

OLD TESTAMENT PERSONS.

417. What judgment fell on one who was highly exalted and prosperous in consequence of his arrogating to himself spiritual functions?

418. Of whom was it said that baldness was produced artificially, as indicative of mourning?

419. What were the three principal promises that God made to Abraham?

420. In what language did Moses foretell the terrible consequences of rejecting the Messiah?

421. What reason is assigned for King Solomon passing sentence of death upon his brother Adonijah?

422. We read in John xix. 17, " And Jesus bearing his cross went forth," &c. Where do we find its antitype in the Old Testament?

423. Whatsoever hath a blemish, said Moses, that shall ye not offer. What exception was there to this rule?

424. To what three persons was the second prophesy of the Messiah made?

425. By whom and to whom was the first letter written, according to the Scriptures?

426. Give a complete list from the Old Testament of those who were raised from the dead.

427. Why did God forbid the Israelites obtaining horses from Egypt?

428. Who was it caused the destruction of the city of Nob?

429. From the head of what King did David take a crown, and it was placed on his own head?

430. Who rebuilt Jericho and what prophecy was then fulfilled?

431. Where is it recorded that Elisha called Ahab a murderer?

432. How many instances of suicide are recorded in the Bible? Name the persons and the manner of their death?

433. How many cities were given to the Levites for their use?

434. Of whom did Jeremiah prophesy that he should be buried with the " burial of an ass?"

435. To whom did God promise that he should beget twelve princes?

436. What were Solomon's other names, and by whom were they given? [adder?"

437. Who are compared in the Scriptures to "a deaf

438. Who was the man the prophet Jeremiah said "would be a terror to himself and to all his friends?"

439. Give the name of a King of Judah to whom it was revealed, several hundred years beforehand, that the Redeemer should be born of a virgin.

440. What two persons are mentioned in the Old Testament as fasting 40 days?

441. Whose seven sons were hanged on account of their father's perfidy?

442. Why was the brazen serpent "that Moses made" destroyed, and by whose order?

443. What two persons lost their lives by using "strange fire in burnt offering?

444. We read that according to the Mosaic law, a Jew, when he came into his neighbor's vineyard, might eat "his fill of grapes." What restriction was imposed on one so doing?

445. Who was the Apollo of the Greeks and inventor of string and wind instruments?

446. Who was guilty of worldly cunning in the hope of a reward?

447. What King mentioned in the Old Testament and another in the New who made the same offer?

448. Quote the instance in which a man was slain in a city of refuge. Who was he?

449. What King and prophet both refer to slavery of the Israelites in Egypt in the very same terms?

450. What three Kings were denounced in exactly the same words?

451. What judgment befell the two sons of Aaron, and why?

452. Of whom did God say "I will make him a mighty nation?"

453. What is the most ancient war on record?

OLD TESTAMENT PERSONS.

454. In what manner, and by whom, was Benhadad put to death?

455. For what reason were the Israelites forbidden by God to procure horses in Egypt?

456. With what two fearful commissions from God were entrusted to Jehu, the son of Hanani the seer?

457. The names of but two of the seventy elders elected by Moses are mentioned in the Bible; who were they?

458. What two ungodly persons recorded in Genesis were gainers by having god-fearing servants?

459. What King of Moab fought against two of the grandsons of Omri, King of Israel? [Israel?

460. What prophet foretold the result of the ten tribes of

461. By the deceit and falsehood of a woman the lives of what two men were saved?

462. How many times is it recorded that God appeared to Solomon?

463. Give two reasons recorded in Deuteronomy why God delivered the Jews from Egyptian bondage.

464. Show that Job attributed his troubles to the Almighty

465. What prophet was told by God not to mourn when his wife died?

466. What two wicked persons, one in the Old and one in the New Testament were once possessed of the prophetic spirit?

467. By whose advice were the women of Moab and of Midian instigated to turn the Israelites to idolatry?

468. On what occasion did Solomon petition God to be favorable to his people in case they were ever carried captive by their enemy?

469. Which of the tribes quarrelled with Gideon because they were not summoned to join him in the fighting against the Midianites?

470. The names of only three women besides Eve who lived before the flood are recorded in the Bible; give them and state who they were.

471. Where do we read of a colored woman aiding and abetting the escape of two fugitives?

472. Mention the names of a few individuals whose violent deaths may be regarded as a consequence of their covetousness.

473. In what part of the Old Testament do we read of the interment of a Jewish King in his own garden?

474. Prove from Scripture, 1. That the Bible must be referred to; 2. That it should be searched; 3. That it must be obeyed on all points.

475. In what reign and for what reasons was the brazen serpent " that Moses had made " destroyed?

476. Where were the children of Israel encamped when the spies were despatched to " search the land of Canaan? "

477. Who was allowed the choice of three punishments in consequence of his vain glory? [salem?

478. What man was forbidden by the king to leave Jeru-

479. What queen sent a message under a false signature?

480. What prophet was suspended between earth and heaven by a lock of his hair?

481. What king feigned insanity in an enemy's country?

482. Who told his life's secret to a woman with disastrous results?

483. Three men, in different periods, stood almost alone in their godliness, among a crooked and perverse generation—name them.

484. What words of Shechaniah may be used by every sinner *this side* the grave?

485. The Almighty condescended so far as to take a name f om certain men by which He might be known among their posterity; give their names and Christ's comment upon it.

486. From the language used by the daughters of Zelophehad, show that they understood how death entered the world.

487. What mother looked out of a window and cried for the return of her son from battle?

488. What blind prophet received a disguised queen?

490. What prophet was sent as a missionary to the Gentiles?

491. To which of the prophets does Christ relate the circumstances of his martyrdom?

492. What exiled mother, in distress for want of water, threw her child under a bush to die; the cry of the boy brought relief from God?

493. To whom did an angel announce the birth of a deliverer of Israel?

494. What king was declared by his people to be worth ten thousand of them?

495. What captured King had his thumbs and great toes cut off?

496. To whom was applied the military title of general?

497. What king, during a sleepless night, recalled an unremembered act of faithful service?

498. What prophet was the recipient of an open letter, and by whom sent?

499. Who in the midst of starvation prophesied plenty on the morrow?

500. What king was slain by a prophet?

501. The mourning of a king was employed as a designation of the deepest grief by a prophet; name the king and prophet.

502. Give in one verse from the book of Job, a most significant description of the weakness and vanity of man.

503. When was it plainly shown to the heathen, that the faith of one man is stronger than the united might of many ungodly nations?

504. Name a king who specified the God he served by an appellation which is nowhere to be found except in his history.

505. Which of the prophets attests the statement of Moses as to the duration of the march of the Israelites through the wilderness?

506. When was a great reformer disregarded by those he wished to help, and obliged to wander, fearing punishment as a murderer?

507. One and the same way was a way of life and a way of death; prove this by a fact described in the Old Testament.

508. Name a child whom God heard and answered when crying

509. Whose confession of sin was followed by forgiveness, and attested through a heavenly sacrament, and conveyed through the medium of seraphic absolution?

510. Which of the prophets is it asserts that thirsty cattle call to God?

511. To whom was applied the epithet "mad fellow," and by whom?

512. What accident was the occasion of King Ahaziah's death?

513. What nation threw off the yoke of Israel upon the succession to the throne of an idolatrous king?

514. What prophecy was fulfilled in the death of Ahab?

515. What were the names and fate of two servants that attempted to lay violent hands on a King of Judah?

516. How many and what are the names of the queens that reigned over Judah?

517. What king was sick two years of an incurable disease and died according to prophecy?

518. What king on the eve of a battle was encouraged by the words of a prophet :—"Be not afraid, for the battle is not your's, but God's?"

519. What prophet was slain in the house of the Lord? How? Why? And by the order of what king?

520. But one of the Kings of Israel was annointed, who was he, and by whom annointed?

521. Dark days were at hand for the ten tribes of Israel. They had forsaken God, and He had given them over to their own ways. A succession of idolatrous kings led them farther and farther from God. And now their enemies are permitted to ravage their country. What tribes suffered first? And what geographical reason can be assigned for this?

522. What queen of Bible times is described by the epithet "that wicked woman?"

523. What wicked King of Israel died an ignominious death, and was not permitted a burial in the sepulchre of the kings?

524. What distinguished titles were given to the descendants of Esau and to no other Bible characters?

525. What servant of a prophet was smitten with leprosy for having obtained money and goods under false pretenses?

526. What were the names of the three handsomest women in all the land?

527. What prophet refused to obey the command of the Lord; concerning whom a miracle was wrought, and he afterwards repented and went?

528. What king forced into his service every strong and valiant man he saw?

529. What prophet declared himself to be "old and grayheaded?"

530. What king, by the advice of his wife, appropriated the fruits of a poor man's vineyard?

531. What king disguised himself in battle and was slain?

532. What king was cursed and grossly insulted, and by whom?

533. Who in his prayer said "I am but dust?"

534. Who are the only two women whose ages are recorded in the Bible? [judge?

535. Of whom does the Bible speak as being a circuit

536. What two persons witnessed the death of Aaron and performed the burial service?

537. On what occasion did the prophet Samuel express a fear that Saul would kill him?

538. What peculiar ceremony was performed by Moses in the consecration of Aaron and his sons to the office of priesthood?

539. Why was Joab made the captain of David's army?

540. Why did not Ezra have a band of soldiers to protect him and the Jews on their journey from Babylon to Jerusalem?

541. What prophet gave a prescription to a king that healed a painful disease?

542. What king, in sickness, trusted in physicians rather than in the Lord for recovery?

543. What King of Judah was overtaken by an invading army and had his eyes put out?

544. To whom did Aaron transfer his robes of office at death?

545. What people suffered torture, equaled only by the inquisition of the dark ages?

546. Who said "This is none other but the house of God and this is the gate of heaven?"

547. What are the names of Job's three friends that came to mourn with him?

548. What prophet erected a monument commemorative of a great victory? What did he name the monument?

549. The appeal of five orphan girls to a judge caused a new law to be made in favor of woman's rights. Name the parties, and what was the law?

550. What two kings were driven from their dominions by hornets?

NEW TESTAMENT CURIOSITIES

PERTAINING TO

Persons.

[Answers page 31.]

1. Who are the only three persons mentioned in the Bible whose names commence with the letter F?
2. Who was the first Christian convert in Europe?
3. Who carried the Epistle of St. Paul from Corinth to Rome?
4. What unrighteous judge trembled before a prisoner in chains?
5. For whom did a band of men lie in wait, bound by an oath that they would neither eat nor drink till they had killed him?
6. What New Testament orator preferred charges against St. Paul?
7. Who accused St. Paul as being a ringleader?
8. What prisoner in chains addressed a multitude from the stairs of a castle?
9. Where may we find in St. Paul's own words an account of his conversion?
10. What is the name of the only person mentioned in the Bible whose name commences with the letter Q?
11 To whom is promised the hidden manna?
12. Who in preaching prolonged his sermon till midnight?
13. Which Apostle told Christ he had left all to follow him?
14. Which of the Apostles first suffered martyrdom?
15. Where in the Bible is St. Paul first mentioned?

16. Which of the Apostles cut off the right ear of a man with a sword, and what was his name? [Philip.

17. What are the only two recorded acts of the Apostle

18. What city claims the birth-place of St. Paul?

19. To what religious sect did St. Paul belong?

20. Of whom and by whom was it said they were neither cold or hot spiritually?

21. In what one point did Christ as man differ from mankind in general?

22. What was our Saviour's last command to his disciples?

23. Of whom was it said he was mighty in the Scriptures?

24. Who said if all the things which Jesus did were recorded the world itself could not contain the books that would be written?

25. What test of discipleship did Jesus give?

26. What words of Moses are quoted in the New Testament which are not found in the Old?

27. On what two occasions was the displeasure of Jesus excited. [death?

28. What intimation was given to Peter of the manner of his

29. What was the parting promise of our Saviour to his disciples?

30. Who being overcome with sleep during a sermon, and fell out of a third story window, was taken up for dead?

31. Who was called a ringleader?

32. Who read the writings of a prophet while riding in a chariot?

33. What prophet bound his feet and hands with a girdle?

34. What woman continued in prayer day and night in the temple?

35. Who is called the light of the world?

36. What was Saul's errand to Damascus when arrested and converted?

37. What was the Apostle Paul's first prayer?

38. Who did the Lord send to restore sight to Paul?

39. To what converts does St. Paul refer as the "seal of his apostleship?"

NEW TESTAMENT PERSONS.

40. Of whom was said their zeal was without knowledge?

41. What scripture examples have we of Christian zeal being attributed to madness?

42. Who was St. Paul's teacher?

43. How many years subsequent to the event did Christ say "Remember Lots wife"?

44. What great honor was conferred upon Mary Magdalene by our Saviour after his resurrection?

45. To whom did our Saviour appear the second time after his resurrection?

46. To whom did our Saviour appear the third time after his resurrection?

47. When and where, by whom and to whom was the command given, "Go to all the world and preach the gospel?"

48. Who was the only person, according to the sacred record, that raised a voice against the mock trial and crucifixion of our Saviour?

49. Who is mentioned as coming to Jesus by night?

50. Who was compelled to bear the cross of Christ to the place of crucifixion?

51. How many and what are the recorded expressions of our Saviour on the cross?

52. At the trial of our Saviour upon the charge of treason and sedition, what was the first question asked him?

53. What three Apostles were regarded by St. Paul as pillars in the church?

54. By whom are we told to search the Scriptures?

55. Who wrote the last book in the Bible?

56. With whom did our Saviour spend his last Sabbath?

57. Whose sermon was adorned with poetical quotations?

58. Who was commanded by an angel to bind on his sandal?

59. On what occasion and where were St. Paul and Barnabas taken for gods?

60. The name of what heathen god was applied to St. Paul, by whom, and why?

61. The name of what heathen god was applied to Barnabas?

62. What Athenian judge was converted under Paul's preaching?

63. What New Testament character forsook Christ for the love of the world?

64. Who said "At the name of Jesus every knee should bow?"

65. What Christian was commended by the Apostles for hospitality?

66. Who will be the guests at the marriage supper of the lamb?

67 Who was Diotrephes, and what was his character?

68. Who predicted the famine in the days of Claudius Cæsar?

69. Whom did a high priest command to be smitten on the mouth?

70. Who had a coat woven without seam?

71. On the foundation of the walls of what city are the names of the twelve Apostles written?

72. Who escaped arrest by being let down from the walls of a city in a basket?

73. What was St. Paul's occupation?

74. What Athenian woman is mentioned as being converted under Paul's preaching?

75. Who on one occasion kept back part of what they had devoted to the cause of God?

76. Sick persons were once placed where the shadow of a good man might pass over them. Why was this done? Who was the man?

77. Who had power divine to handle serpents unharmed?

78. Whose face in preaching shone like an angel?

79. How many instances have we of Christ raising the dead to life?

80. How many instances have we of the Apostles raising the dead to life?

81. What instance is recorded of the dead being raised to life without the interposition of the Prophets, Christ or the Apostles?

82. How long did St. Paul live in his own hired house at Rome?

NEW TESTAMENT PERSONS.

83. Whose life was endangered by a conspiracy of 40 men?
84. Who took Judas' place among the twelve?
85. The Apostle James suffered martyrdom. How? By whom?
86. Who came to prove Solomon with hard questions?
87. What member of the primitive church tried the patience of even the loving disciple?
88. Who, when cruelly put to death, prayed like his Lord for his murderers?
89. On what two occasions did the Lord Jesus receive the assistance of angels?
90. In which of the Gospels is the mission of the seventy alone recorded?
91. Who charged the Gentiles as being a "foolish nation?"
92. To what country did Trophimus (one of St. Paul's missionary companions) belong?
93. By whose order was the Apostle James martyred?
94. What three portions of the Holy Scriptures did the Saviour say contained predictions concerning himself?
95. On what three occasions is mention made of Nicodemus?
96. What Levite sold his land and laid its price at the Apostle's feet?
97. How many times did the Lord Jesus cleanse the Temple?
98. In which of our Lord's miracles is reference made to the custom of employing professional mourners?
99. Prove St. James' assertion (James ii. 9) "The devils also believe" in the Saviour's divinity.
100. Before how many tribunals was the Saviour brought after his apprehension?
101. Who was called Mercurius, by whom, and why?
102. Who called Jesus "the shepherd and bishop of our souls?"
103. To whom did St. Paul write "prepare me also a lodging?"
104. What was the cause of the quarrel between Paul and Barnabas?

105. How many times is it recorded, and by whom used, the words " Be not weary in well doing ? "

106. The words "Jesus Christ" are placed together once only in the Gospels. Where?

107. Show both from the Old and New Testaments that the custom of celebrating birthdays is a very ancient one.

108. Quote the precise words of the Saviour when for the first time he was smitten in the face.

109. By whom is Noah mentioned as a preacher of righteousness?

110. Who was the wife of Felix, the Governor of Cæsarea?

111. Why was Zacharias, the father of St. John the baptist, struck dumb?

112. What prophet, in the New Testament, foretells a famine which afterwards occurred in the days of Claudius Cæsar?

113. What does St. Paul say was a stumbling block to the Jews?

114. To what king did our Lord refer when he said "Go ye and tell that fox?"

115. Where does St. Paul tell us how to know his epistles?

116. Quote a passage in which St. Paul says he was hindered in his work by Satan.

117. On what occasion did St. Paul conform to the Jewish ceremonial law in order to conciliate the Jewish converts?

118. Which of St. Paul's fellow workers does he say "was sick unto death?"

119. What apostle is it speaks of journeying into Spain?

120. What lawyer is mentioned as being one of St. Paul's workers?

121. Who was the chief man in the island of Melita, where St. Paul was shipwrecked?

122. Upon what occasion did our Lord check the undue curiosity of one of his disciples?

123. What epistle does St. Paul state he wrote with his own hand?

124. Who are mentioned by St. Paul as his kinsmen?

NEW TESTAMENT PERSONS.

115. Which was the last appearance of the Virgin Mary?

126. Why did Christ so forcibly press his personal identity on his disciples after his resurrection?

127. What two distinct promises did our Saviour make his disciples when about to leave them?

128. How often does St. Paul quote heathen writers, and who are they?

129. Where is our Lord's first recorded act of intercession?

130. What three persons (not including our Saviour) are called Jesus?

131. Give an instance from the Bible of each of the following characters:—
   (1) Those who believe in eternity and live for it.
   (2) Those who believe in the world and live for it.
   (3) Those who believe in eternity but live for the world.

132. Who were certain men who perceived the power of God, and attained to exercise it independent of his grace, and suffered for their presumption?

133. What prophet used the girdle of another when foretelling his death?

134. What king's son was lamed by falling from his nurse's arms?

135. An Ephesian Christian who accompanied St. Paul to Jerusalem.

136. Quote the first and last words of our Saviour while on earth.

137. Of whom did our Saviour say "I will make you fishers of men?"

138. Who is it called Jesus "the shepherd and bishop of souls?"

139. To whom does St. Paul write "Prepare me also a lodging?"

140. Where do we find our Lord's answer to a question by asking another?

141. What man, in the days of the Apostles, tried to usurp such pre-eminence in the church as to cast out those with whom he disagreed?

142. Who was reigning in Judah when Joseph returned from Egypt with the infant Jesus ?

143. Give an instance, in the New Testament, where a man was dependent for his recovery upon human help and sympathy.

144. Define the individual creeds of the Pharisees and Sadducees, as they are in the words of Scripture.

145. What text proves that our Lord on earth had body, " soul and spirit ? "

146. How many times is it recorded of our Saviour as standing on the right hand of God, and how many times is seated ?

147. Give instances to prove that our Lord's body, after his resurrection, though material, was endowed with other powers than it exercised before.

148. Give in one phrase Peter's description of the world since sin came into it.

149. In seven words give a very beautiful speech made by a woman to servants respecting Christ.

150. What does "the divine" Apostle style those who would not let themselves be illuminated ?

151. In one verse Christ is spoken of as a successor and declared to be a predecessor.

152. Which of the sacred writers debars a heretic from the house and home of a believer ?

153. Name the person introduced by our Lord to three Apostles.

154. Describe in four words a journey every Christian has accomplished.

155. The inhabitants of heaven and the heavens, are called upon to rejoice ; on what occasion ?

156. What true and distinguished preacher lost himself entirely in the substance of his message ?

157. Name one who saw a sight, whereof he was to testify on earth for one short moment and then enter upon its full and eternal contemplation.

158. Quote a verse in which the name of Jehovah is paraphrased.

NEW TESTAMENT PERSONS.

159. Give a solemn declaration made by our Saviour to one who led a wicked life under a false reputation of piety.

160. We have in Scripture a very short history of two men, which shows the great difference between dying *in* sin, and dying *because* of sin ; both died because of *their* sins, but only one *in* his sins ;—who were the men ?

161. What emperor banished all Jews from Rome ?

162. Who went up to Rome to carry contributions to Paul while he was a prisoner there, and carried back with him the epistle to the Philippians ?

163. Who was captain of the guard while Paul was taken prisoner to Rome ?

164. Who shook his raiment, and to whom did he say " your blood be on your own heads " ?

165. What test does the Apostle John give by which we may know the children of God ?

166. On what three occasions are we expressly told that Jesus wept ?

167. Prove from the Bible that devils have faith.

168. What converts did St. Paul baptize at Corinth ?

169. By what expression did the Virgin Mary acknowledge herself a sinner ?

170. Who requested that her two sons might sit one on the right and one on the left of our Saviour in the kingdom of Heaven ?

171. What young preacher on the occasion of his first sermon witnessed the largest number of conversions on record ?

172. Our Saviour in four words, and in three words, gives a most awful description of what city ?

173. When did two hundred and seventy-six distressed persons, before day-break, partake of a joyful meal ?

174. What singular expression does the Apostle Paul on one occasion employ when speaking of food ?

175. On what occasion did our Lord command those who loved him to mourn ?

OLD TESTAMENT CURIOSITIES

PERTAINING TO

Places and Localities.

(Answers page 41.)

1. What is the name of the city to which Lot escaped at the destruction of Sodom?
2. Where was the voice of God first heard by human ear?
3. In what city was a forty-day fast proclaimed?
4. What is illustrated by a dish wiped and turned up side down?
5. What Bible city was known as the city of palm trees?
6. Where was Rachel buried?
7. What city was destroyed and never again inhabited, according to prophecy?
8. Where, in Scripture language, is the land of Canaan located?
9. Where is it recorded that the Jews were to be God's chosen people forever?
10. Where in the Bible is the only reference to ferry-boat mentioned?
11. At what seaport town were assembled the largest navy of Bible times?
12. What city was saved from massacre by the strategy of its people?
13. In what city, and when does the Bible say that gold and silver were as plentiful as stones?
14. What city, for its beauty, was once known as "the glory of kingdoms"?

15. At what place did King David eat the shew-bread ?
16. Upon what mountain was Israel cursed for disobedience ?
17. What is the oldest city in the world ?
18. On what mountain was King Josiah slain in battle ?
19. On what mountain did a king command a whole nation to be gathered ?
20. What cave was the hiding-place of five kings ?
21. What battle was fought on Mount Tabor?
22. Where can the prophetical account be found of the mode in which Babylon was taken by the Medes and Persians ?
23. What reward does the Bible promise a man diligent in business ?
24. What wild beast was employed by God to punish a disobedient servant ?
25. What birds were used in sacrifice ?
26. Prove from the Scriptures that confession of sin to God is a duty.
27. Prove from Scriptures that afflictions sent to the people of God are a mark of their heavenly Father's love.
28. How many instances can be found in the Bible when a blessing was granted to a number of individuals on account of the presence among them of one man of God ?
29. What birds are referred to in Scripture as birds of passage ?
30. What is a nation's glory ?
31. What bird was employed to convey a token of peace to a servant of God ?
32. Where is the promise recorded that the children of Israel (Jews) should possess the land of Canaan ?
33. The inhabitants of what four cities were reduced to perpetual bondage by the order of a victorious General ?
34. What city was taken by strategem and burned, with 12,000 women and children ?
35. On what mountain was Solomon's temple built ?
36. Who built Nineveh ?
37. What is the origin and meaning of the word Mizpah ?

PLACES AND LOCALITIES.

38. On what condition could Sodom have been saved from destruction ?

39. How many, and what were the cities known as the cities of refuge ?

40. At what age were the Levites no longer allowed to work in the Tabernacle ?

41. What stone, according to the Scriptures, heard all the words of the Lord which he spoke unto the people ?

42. At the destruction of what city were "all her great men bound in chains?"

43. At what place was the last revelation of God to Abraham ?

44. What celebrated edifice was erected on the spot which was the scene of the greatest instance of human obedience ?

45. Where were 10,000 people cast down from a precipice and killed ?

46. What inheritance had the children of Caleb ?

47. What conquered city became a field of salt ?

48. Where, at the touch of a staff, fire rose out of a rock and consumed a feast ?

49. What thirty neighboring cities were ruled over by thirty brothers ?

50. The Mount of Olives, now so blessedly associated with so many epochs in the life of our Lord, had once a very evil name —what was it ?

51. What two prophecies refer to the taking of Jerusalem by the Romans ?

52. How many cities were given to the Levites for their use ?

53. By whom was Jericho rebuilt, and what prophecy was then fulfilled ?

54. Why was Zion (Jerusalem) called the City of David ?

55. What mountain was purchased by a King of Israel, upon which he built a city ?

56. On what mountain was a blessing for obedience promised upon the children of Israel ?

57. On what mountain was curses pronounced upon the children of Israel ?

58. On what mountain did a King of Israel commit suicide?

59. How many cities, with their kings and inhabitants, were destroyed by an invading army of Israel?

60. What Bible city suffered the horrors of a famine by a besieging army?

61. Why was the ancient city of Luz changed to Bethel, and subsequently to Bethaven?

62. On what occasion was a firmly fortified place taken by a mere ceremony?

63. What place of eminent sacredness in Jewish history, and what prophet, in five words, sadly and solemnly predicted its ruin?

NEW TESTAMENT CURIOSITIES

PERTAINING TO

Places and Localities.

[Answers page 47.]

1. What remarkable event took place at Atad?
2. What was the first name given to the country of the gesenes?
3. What place is said to have been a Sabbath day's journey from Jerusalem?
4. Where did the Apostle dwell of whom our Lord stated that he was an Israelite indeed, in whom is no guile?
5. Our Saviour bade his disciples shake the dust off their feet against those cities who refused to receive them. Where did they do this?
6. In what town did our Lord spend his last Sabbath?
7. What mountain was Christ's abode by night?
8. On what island was a ship ran aground for safety?
9. Where did the Apostles hold their first missionary meeting?
10. At what place was St. Paul stoned?
11. At what place was Elymas struck blind?
12. What was the prophet Jonah's native town?
13. What city was exalted to heaven yet brought to destruction?
14. Where was it said and of whom, "they have turned the world upside down?"

15. What was the ruling nation of the world in the time of Christ?

16. What city was popularly supposed to produce nothing good?

17. Where was an altar erected "to the unknown God?"

OLD TESTAMENT CURIOSITIES

PERTAINING TO

Things.

[Answers page 51.]

1. With what was the Garden of Eden guarded to prevent the return of our first parents?
2. Upon what did God pronounce the first curse?
3. Of what wood was Noah's Ark made?
4. What news did the first carrier pigeon bring?
5. What presents did Jacob send into Egypt?
6. Of what wood was the Ark of the Covenant?
7. What is the whole duty of man, according to the Scriptures?
8. What is harder to be won than a strong city?
9. What is good news from a far country like?
10. With what was the sin of Judah written?
11. Upon what were epistles and documents written in Bible times?
12. What is the meaning of the word Ichabod. By whom and to whom was it applied?
13. In what book of the Bible does the name of God nowhere occur?
14. On what four occasions were savage beasts employed as instruments of God's anger?
15. What price was paid for horses by the King of Israel?
16. How long was the temple building, and in what year was it commenced?
17. What was Elijah's dying gift to Elisha?

18. How did God manifest his presence at the dedication of the temple?

19. How many instances are there on Bible record of rain being sent in answer to prayer?

20. Where is it recorded that rain was prevented in answer to prayer?

21. How were the children of Israel guided in their forty years' wanderings in the wilderness?

22. Of what did the first wedding present consist?

23. What miracle led to the dispersion of mankind over all the world?

24. What men refused to give bread to fainting soldiers?

25. What army fled in confusion when none pursued?

26. What is the Bible list of a lady's wardrobe?

27. What article of clothing was the token of a father's partiality?

28. What garment was hid in a rock on the bank of a river?

29. What departing nation borrowed garments of their enemies?

30. What kind of trees were the Israelites forbidden to cut down for use in a siege, and why?

31. What was the last of the ten plagues of Egypt?

32. What warnings do the Scriptures give to avoid bad company?

33. How many camels had Job?

34. What is the Bible inventory of the Christian's treasure?

35. How many instances are recorded in the Bible of embalming the dead?

36. What does the Old Testament mention as being sanctified?

37. For what three things was Bashan renowned?

38. The temple tax, according to Exodus xxx. 13, was half a shekel, what was the amount after the captivity?

39. What was the origin of the fire with which the Jews offered their burnt offerings?

40. What Old Testament example have we of miraculous darkness?

OLD TESTAMENT THINGS.

41. Where, in Scripture language, do we find a beautiful description of spring time?

42. Prove from Scripture the sin and folly of leaning on human help in time of trouble.

43. How many instances are recorded that sailors called upon God to avert a storm?

44. Where in the Bible do we find God's promises to supply the temporal wants of his people?

45. On what occasion were messengers despatched in vessels made of bulrushes?

46. How were the vast number of presents conveyed to King Solomon?

47. What was the value of gold presented to Solomon in one year?

48. What was the special avocation of the Gibeonites?

49. How was a miracle once wrought to recover a borrowed axe?

50. What words were once spoken to man by a beast of burden?

51. What King was killed by his own sons?

52. By whom were two sticks miraculously united and became one?

53. What is the year of Jubilee mentioned in the Bible?

54. What was the punishment threatened the man who should rebuild Jericho?

55. Prove from the Bible that God alone (and not priests) can forgive sin.

56. When did curiosity of the eye, through the mercy of God, lead to the belief of the heart?

57. How was the timber used in building Solomon's Temple conveyed to Jerusalem?

58. Where in the Scripture do we find the grandeur of a thunder storm depicted?

59. What two miracles were wrought upon the sun?

60. What instances have we in the New Testament of affliction being the cause of joy to the believer in Christ?

61. What Scripture examples can you give of choosing by lot?

62. How many examples does the Old Testament give of weak things being employed to confound the mighty?

63. What does the Bible declare to be the whole duty of man?

64. What is called in the Bible the "*royal law?*"

65. In what instance did God send rain as a sign of his displeasure against Israel?

66. What does the Bible say is better than precious ointment?

67. What is it which makes its possessor truly rich?

68. What is a greater conquest than taking of a city?

69. What was found in the Ark of the Covenant when first brought into the temple?

70. How many times has it been noticed that the Sabbath has been impressed on the observance of man?

71. What was the divinely appointed punishment for blasphemy?

72. Can there be found in God's Word a promise to the wicked?

73. How many witnesses were required among the Jews to establish a charge?

74. How many Old Testament prophesies are there of the time when Christ should appear?

75. What are angels, and how are they employed?

76. What one verse refers to the source, flow, and return of rivers?

77. Where is it recorded that a whole army was smitten with blindness?

78. During what famine did women eat their own children?

79. How many Israelites were slain in the battle of Ebenezer, when the Ark of the Lord was won by the Philistines?

80. How many Sirian horsemen fell in battle with David?

81. How many Ephraimites were slain in battle with the Gileadites?

82. How many children of Israel fell victims to a plague in consequence of having joined themselves in idolatry to Baalpeor?

OLD TESTAMENT THINGS.

83. David in vain glory numbered the people, and for a punishment what did he choose, and what was the consequence?

84. How many idolatrous worshippers of the golden calf were slain by order of Moses?

85. How many men and women were killed in the fall of the building that was pulled down by Samson?

86. How many lords of the land were entertained at the feast of Belshazzar?

87. How many Philistines did Samson slay with a jaw bone?

88. How many out of each tribe did Moses send to war against the Midianites?

89. During the siege and famine of Samaria what price was paid for the head of an ass?

90. When and where was meal used as an antidote for poison?

91. To what does the Bible liken the laughter of a fool?

92. Of what was the tabernacle made?

93. How many and what were the coverings of the tabernacle?

94. On what occasion did God employ birds as messengers of mercy?

95. What did the "Holy of holies" in the Temple contain?

96. For what purpose was a great collection taken up in Judah and Jerusalem by order of the king?

97. How was the Ark of the Lord brought from the Philistines when it was returned to Israel?

98. How many comprised the total number of the great draught of fishes?

99. What was the weight of Absalom's annual growth of hair?

100. What was the length of Noah's Ark?

101. How many chariots were kept by Jabin, King of Canaan?

102. How many singers were in the grand jubilee of the Temple?

103. How many stalls were required for the accommodation of Solomon's horses?

104. How many horsemen did Solomon have?

105. How many Egyptian chariots of war in their pursuit of the Israelites were lost in the Red Sea?

106. Quote a passage from which it would appear that in olden time *beacons* were used on the tops of hills as signals or land marks.

107. Where is an unfaithful friend said to be like "a broken tooth and a foot out of joint?"

108. What funeral was suddenly interrupted by an armed band, and with what result?

109. Upon what did the manna fall?

110. It may truly be said that during the forty years journeying through the wilderness the children of Israel were each one a perpetual miracle—how so?

111. Give Bible proof that God observes the acts of children.

112. In what passage of Scripture do we read of wise ladies?

113. Where in prophetic Scripture do we read of parlors?

114. What is the recorded occasion upon which the terror of God was exercised on behalf of his chosen people?

115. Where in the Old Testament is mention made of an iron bedstead being used, and by whom?

116. What two cities are mentioned as having been destroyed with Sodom and Gomorrah?

117. Where has mention been made of land producing a hundred-fold in one year?

118. What was the law among the Jews as to the pledging of raiment?

119. After what great battle was it that the men of Judah were three days in carrying the spoil of their enemies?

120. What was the name given by King Hezekiah to the brazen serpent which Moses had made for the children of Israel in the wilderness?

121. What happened to the Syrians whom the king sent to occupy Samaria?

122. Where in the Bible is the constellation Orion mentioned besides the book of Job?

OLD TESTAMENT THINGS.

123. How were the Ephraimites on one occasion known from the people of the other tribes?

124. What was the present sent to Saul, King of Israel, by Jesse the Bethlemite?

125. What was the sum paid yearly to the King of Israel by Mesta, King of Moab?

126. What prophecy was fulfilled the day after it was uttered?

127 The Jordan was miraculously crossed on three occasions --name them?

128. Mention a tree that was named from the circumstances connected with it?

129. Where is the promise that human life shall be prolonged at the millennium as before the flood?

130. Where is the only instance recorded in Scripture of the marriage of a foreign slave to his master's daughter? Mention it.

131. What two things are said to have happened by chance, one an act of destruction and the other resulting in neglect?

132. The water trickles into the pool of Siloam so softly that it cannot be heard, travellers have remarked. What Scripture does this confirm?

133. What command was given by God to the children of Israel to the make of their garments, and why?

134. Where is the passage found in which the Angels are said to be fellow-servants with mankind?

135. Where is the growth of nettles mentioned as a mark of desolation?

136. What biscuit of modern use is mentioned in the Bible?

137. Give an instance of the avowed foreknowledge of God of events which would come to pass under certain circumstances, but which never did come to pass because these circumstances did not come to pass.

138 Quote a passage from which it appears that the prophets did not always understand the meanings of the visions they saw.

139. Mention a quotation in the New Testament where the

exact place in the Old Testament from which it is taken is given?

140. What sin does the prophet Isaiah say was the cause of the destruction of Moab?

141. What battle lasted seven days, and with what result?

142. What was the origin of the two days of Purim, kept as days of feasting and joy by the Jews?

143. What was to have been the sum of money paid by Haman for the destruction of the Jews.

144. What people are stated to have been most clever in ancient times in cutting down timber?

145. What sin is mentioned as having caused the destruction of Tyre? [Syrian?

146. What present was given to Gehazi by Naaman the

147. How many lepers are mentioned as being outside the gate of Samaria, and who gave warning of the flight of the Syrians?

148. From what two hills were the blessings and cursings pronounced upon the children of Israel; and what tribes took part in each?

149. What two diseases did God especially threaten to bring upon his people for their neglect of his commandments?

150. What was the punishment inflicted by God's command upon a man who had broken the Sabbath?

151. What other inhabitants of Canaan were giants besides the Anakims?

152. What two animals may be eaten for the Passover?

153. What miracle did God work to enable a widow to pay her debts?

154. What country was that in which the king bought all the land from his people and then sent them about as slaves? Quote passage.

155. By what name is the Mount of Olives called in the Book of Kings?

156. Where do we find an account of an army being sent to take one man?

157. Why were not the Jews permitted to sell their land for more than a certain number of years?

158. What was the only condition upon which Nahash, the Ammonite, would make peace with the people of Jobest-Gilead?

159. What great work was undertaken by King Hezekiah in order to provide a more abundant supply of water for the city of Jerusalem?

160. Where, in the Bible, is it stated that the ostrich lays her eggs in the sand to be hatched by the heat thereof?

161. How many of the strangers in the land of Israel were sent to assist the servants of the King of Tyre in cutting down the cedar wood of Lebanon? [power of speech.

162. Give the occasion on which man first exercised the

163. Upon what day in the week were the two greatest acts of divine power that affected man accomplished?

164. What sacred relic divinely appointed, and by which miracles were worked, was destroyed by a good king years subsequently?

165. Moses is made on two occasions an offer which would raise him to honors and destroy the Israelites—name them?

166. God when sending Moses to Pharaoh gave him power to perform miracles—mention them in order?

167. What verse in the Bible gives us David's age?

168. Mention a dinner in which the shoulder was given as a mark of highest respect—why and to whom?

169. What three privileges were attached to the first-born of the family?

170. What is the meaning of Jehovah Shammah?

171. At what part of the dedication service was it that the cloud filled the temple?

172. How did it come to pass that there was the sound of no hammer or tool of iron heard in the building of Solomon's Temple?

173. Give a text from the Old Testament which contains a reason why "we should fear those who kill the body."

174. What does the Scripture say surpasses in greatness the hero who conquers his enemies?

175. Of what are the looking-glasses made that are mentioned in the Scriptures?

176. Where, in the Old Testament, are we told that God gave instruction for the concealment of certain things?

177. Where are we told in one verse not to do a thing and in the next to do it?

178. What was created and destroyed in one night?

179. How was the cedar used in the building of Solomon's temple conveyed from Lebanon to Jerusalem?

180. Where is the only mention made of churning butter in the Scriptures?

181. Where are we told, in the Bible, that there was joy in heaven at the creation of the world?

182. Show that to die childless was regarded by the Jews as a very bitter calamity.

183. What was the origin of the fire with which the Jews offered their burnt offerings? Name two individuals who lost heir lives for using "strange" fire?

184. Where in the Bible is it recorded that fever and ague were inflicted as punishments?

185. What is the Bible remedy for boils, and what king made use of it?

186. Where in the Bible is death by sunstroke recorded?

187. Where is the prophecy recorded that the Jews will one day repent the death of the Messiah?

188. Where do we find the rending of a garment was the prophecy of the downfall of a king?

189. What three remarkable predictions are recorded in the ast chapter of the Old Testament?

190. What chapter of the Bible is remarkable for its beautiful description of natural history?

191. What instrument of healing became an occasion of sin?

192. What petition occurs seven times in one of the Psalm?

193. From the book of Ezekiel give a promise clearly showing that that which is a misfortune to individuals is a benefit to the church.

194. What sentence composed of three words appears no less than 25 times in one book of the Bible, and forms the chief thought in it?

OLD TESTAMENT THINGS.

195. Where is it distinctly predicted that no one shall obtain strength by or in sin?

196. On what occasion did God forbid all funeral pomps and expression?

197. What was the most ancient art of sinful mankind?

198. Where do we read of gods who are less than the man who fashions them?

199. Where do we read that fifty men set out in all directions to seek a corpse?

200. Describe in three words the power of love.

201. Where is the fact recorded of a ransom being paid for 373 persons?

202. Where is it foretold that the Lord would take away as plunder the whole toilet of the women of Jerusalem?

203. Where is sin personified as a wild beast lurking at the door of the human heart?

204. Quote two verses that give the Bible description of the philosopher.

205. Give the words in which the removal of unclean clothes is spoken of as a sign of the forgiveness of sin.

206. Quote the exact words of the oldest letter recorded in the Scriptures.

207. Prove from the Scriptures that it was contrary to the Mosaic Law for a Levite to possess land.

208. Upon what people was consumption threatened as a punishment for sin?

209. When was the rending of a new garment typical of the division of a kingdom?

210. From whom were the Jews forbidden to take garments in pawn?

211. When did a weapon of destruction become a fountain of refreshment?

212. What three mournful events took place in a garden?

213. What prophecy was uttered more than 3000 years ago, and is now being fulfilled?

214. Where can be found copies of two letters written to kings? Who wrote them?

215. What is the most appropriate Psalm to be read during a thunder shower?

216. The first nine words of what Psalm did our Saviour repeat when on the cross?

217. How did God signify his displeasure when the Jews asked for a king?

218. Prove that marking the boundaries of land by stones or monuments is a very ancient custom.

219. When did God prove himself God of the plain as well as God of the mountain?

220. What fruit is recorded in the Bible as growing on a tree without root or branch?

NEW TESTAMENT CURIOSITIES

PERTAINING TO

Things.

[Answers page 63.]

1. How can the Bible be called the word of God when it was written by men?

2. Which of the early Christian churches set the brightest example of liberality?

3. What was the text of our Saviour's first sermon?

4. Prove from the Bible the authorship of the Acts of the Apostles.

5. Prove from the Old Testament that Jesus shares his people's sorrows.

6. What does the Bible tell us to contend earnestly for?

7. What are we told in the Scriptures to covet?

8. In what way does Christ say we may know the truth of his doctrine?

9. What is the unpardonable sin?

10. Where were the first disciples of Christ first called Christians?

11. Prove from the Scripture that God cares for and provides for His children.

12. Prove from Scripture that God protects His children.

13. Prove from Scripture that God hears the cry of His children.

14. Prove from Scripture that God corrects his children in love.

15. For what were the Bereans commended?

16. Where is the Word of God called a sword, and why?

17. Where is the Word of God called a mirror, and why?

18. Where is the Word of God called a well of water, and why?

19. Where is the Word of God called milk, and why?

20. Where will the great feast of the marriage supper of the Lamb be spread?

21. Which of our Lord's miracles were miracles of creation?

22. What New Testament instances have we of miraculous light?

23. Prove from the Bible the necessity of the new birth.

24. How many Old Testament examples have we of God sending sleep on individuals or people?

25. What remarkable event was announced by shepherds?

26. What five things are we commanded in the Bible to hold fast?

27. What was the contents of the Ark of the Covenant?

28. What is the Bible ornament of a Christian woman?

29. What one word in Scripture is said to contain the whole law?

30. Prove from Scripture that it is the duty of a Church to support its ministers.

31. Where is the Word of God compared to a looking-glass?

32. Give a Scripture example of religious convictions being stifled.

33. What governor of Damascus endeavored to take St. Paul and make him a prisoner? [rain?

34. What is mentioned in the Gospel as signs of the coming

35. By whom were the Pharisees and Sadducees called a generation of vipers?

36. What was the value of the books burned at Ephesus by those who dwelt in familiar spirits and used "curious arts?"

37. Where is it mentioned that the earth is God's footstool?

38. Which of Christ's miracles were miracles of creation?

39. Mention a passage in the New Testament where it states that every kind of beast and serpent is capable of being tamed.

40. Where in the New Testament is it stated that a thousand years in God's sight is as one day?

41. Which one of our Lord's miracles was worked by the utterance of one word?

42. Give the text in which our Lord himself distinguishes between His divine and human sonship.

43. An unexampled sorrow betokened by a word used only once in the New Testament, name the passage.

44. Prove that even in the presence of the Lord Jesus, salvation was voluntary?

45. Quote a chapter from Isaiah in which division of the fourfold office of Christ is enumerated.

46. How is it proved that there were more than one hundred and twenty believers at the time of our Lord's ascension?

47. On what occasion were messages brought to this world by the Archangel Gabriel?

48. What three things did the Lord cite as requisite for the bringing forth of good fruit?

49. By what act does a man lose his personal freedom?

50. What is the only revenge permitted by the Christian faith?

51. State three things Scripture says God cannot do

52. In what one verse, do the words of Jesus Christ give a complete plan and draught of the New Testament Ministry?

53. Which of the prophets represents the deliverance by Messiah, and the final victory of God's people over the world as a repetition of Israel's passage through the Red Sea?

54. Where in the New Testament is found a passage in which Divine mercy is called the highest power in the affairs of men?

55. In one word name a precious pearl, with which no possession on earth can bear a comparison.

56. Where do we find a glorious representation of a truly divine ordination to the Christian ministry?

57. In three words give the character of Christian hope.

58. In what respect does the Lord's prayer differ as given by St. Matthew and St. Luke?

59. Among those who sold their land and laid its price at the Apostles' feet was a Levite; give his name and show that it was contrary to the Mosaic law for a Levite to possess land.

60. What one word was employed by Christ to designate that separation from God which sin involves?

61. Give one word used by the Apostle Paul to designate those who are living by faith.

62. Quote three words which denote the whole of the doctrine of Christ, as a commandment to be believed and preached.

63. Prove that the Church of Corinth had not adopted the practice of the Church at Jerusalem with regard to a community of goods and one common purse.

64. On what occasion did God speak in a still small voice?

65. By what four names are Christians called in the Bible?

66. What does the Bible compare to a spider's web?

67. Prove from the Bible that God promises to supply the temporal wants of his people.

68. On what occasion was there such spiritual happiness among the people, that wicked men mocked and said they were full of new wine?

69. Why do you (or Christians) believe the Bible to be the word of God?

CURIOSITIES OF THE BIBLE,

INVOLVING ARITHMETICAL CALCULATIONS IN THEIR SOLUTION.

[Key, Part II., page 67.]

1. A TEACHER being asked how many scholars were in his Sunday-school, replied: "If you multiply the number of Jacob's sons by the number of times which the Israelites compassed Jericho, and add to the product the number of measures of barley which Boaz gave Ruth; divide this by the number of Haman's sons; subtract the number of each kind of clean beasts that went into the ark; multiply by the number of men that went to seek Elijah after he was taken to heaven; subtract from this Joseph's age at the time he stood before Pharaoh; divide by the number of stones David selected to kill Goliath; subtract the number of furlongs that Bethany was distant from Jerusalem; multiply by the number of anchors cast out at the time of Paul's shipwreck; subtract the number of people saved in the ark, and the remainder will be the number of scholars in the school." How many were there? 188.

2. A shepherd being asked the number of sheep in his flock, replied: "If you divide the number of camels which Job had before their capture by the Chaldeans, by the number of men sent to take Jeremiah from the dungeon; add to the quotient the number of lords entertained at the feast of Belshazzar: from this amount subtract the number of righteous persons who could have saved Sodom; multiply by the age when David began to reign; divide by the number in Gideon's band; add the number of Philistines whom Samson slew with a jawbone; subtract the number of Solomon's songs; multiply by the number of days Job's friends tarried without saying a word; subtract the number of fish caught in the draft of the miracle of fishes, and the remainder will be the number of sheep in my flock." How many had he? 575.

3. A clergyman being asked the cost of his church and the height of its spire, replied : "If you divide the talents of gold presented to Solomon in one year, by the temple tax (shekels) after the captivity ; multiply this by the pieces of silver with which our Lord was betrayed ; subtract from this the number of singers in the grand jubilee of the temple ; add to the remainder the number of prophets hid in the cave ; multiply this by the years the children of Israel were in captivity, and the product will be the cost of the church. Divide the cost of the church by the length in cubits of Noah's ark ; from the quotient subtract the number of Rehoboam's children ; to the remainder add the number of persons who suffered shipwreck with St. Paul ; from this number subtract one fourth of the number of fingers and toes which the man of Gath had ; divide the remainder by the number of years it took Solomon to build the temple ; add to this the height of Solomon's temple, and the sum total will be the height of the spire." What was the cost? And what the height? $193.200—148 feet.

NOTE.—The third line should read nine times the temple tax

BIBLE CURIOSITIES

PERTAINING TO

Time.

[Answers page 69.]

1. How long was the infant Moses hid by his mother to escape the death edict of Pharaoh?
2. How many years were the children of Israel oppressed by the Midianites?
3. How long did the Ark of the Lord remain with the Philistines after its capture from Israel?
4. How long did Job live after his great troubles?
5. How many years warning did God give the people of the old world before sending the flood?
6. What was the longest drouth recorded in the Bible?
7. How long was King Herod building his temple?
8. In how many days were the walls of Jerusalem rebuilt?
9. How long was Israel oppressed by the Moabites?
10. How long did the flood cover the earth?
11. Why did the children of Israel wander 40 years in the wilderness?
12. How many Canaanite kings did the children of Israel destroy on taking possession of the promised land?
13. How many days were the spies in searching the promised land?
14. How long did the children of Israel journey in the wilderness before they found water?
15. How long was Solomon building his house?
16. How long was Israel oppressed by the Ammonites?

17. How long was the Ark of the Lord hid, and where?
18. How old was Moses when he demanded of Pharaoh that the children of Israel should go?
19. How old was Eli when he fell from his seat and died?
20. How long were the children of Israel in Egypt?
21. What date in the life of Moses is given in the New Testament but not in the Old?
22. How long was Noah in the Ark.
23. How long did the first plague sent by God upon the Egyptians last?
24. How long did St. Paul live in his own hired house at Rome?
25. How long did David reign over Judah alone in Hebron?
26. How many years did God provide manna for the children of Israel in the wilderness?
27. On what day was the Passover appointed to be kept?
28. How long were the children of Israel in captivity?
29. How long was Saul of Tarsus blind when converted?
30. How many years was Israel governed by judges?
31. How many years did the children of Israel sojourn in Egypt?
32. How old was Joseph when his brethren sold him into slavery?
33. How long was Noah building the Ark?
34. How long time was required to elapse according to the law of Moses, before the Israelites might gather the fruit of a young tree?
35. How long did the Disciples tarry at Jerusalem for the baptism of the Holy Ghost?
36. How long did Job's friend tarry without saying a word when they came to mourn with him?

FAMILIAR QUOTATIONS

OF THE

Bible.

[Key page 67.]

The common use of many passages of Scripture make it desirable that all should know from whence they came, and under what circumstances they were originally written or uttered. A few of the more familiar quotations are annexed as an exercise in "*Searching the Scriptures.*"

1. Where will you find the common phrase—To "make a man an offender for a word?"
2. Where the wise reminder—"The fear of man bringeth a snare?"
3. Where the familiar metaphor—"An arm of flesh?"
4. Where the solemn warning—"Be sure your sin will find you out?"
5. Where the humane injunction—"A righteous man regardeth the life of his beast?"
6. Where is Jehovah described as, "Glorious in holiness, fearful in praise, doing wonders?"
7. Where is it said—"Them that honor Me I will honor; and they that despise me shall be lightly esteemed?"
8. Where is there first found the command to "love and serve the Lord with all the heart and with all the soul?"
9. Where the command to "love the stranger?"
10. Where to "love thy neighbor as thyself?"
11. Showing the debasing effects of an atheistic spirit, "Let us eat and drink for to-morrow we shall die?"
12. Showing the hardening tendency of a long course of sin, "Can the Ethiopian change his skin, or the leopard his spots?'

13. Showing the danger of trifling with conviction and warning, "He that being often reproved hardeneth his neck, shall suddenly be destroyed, and that without remedy."

14. "Nor by might nor by power, but by My Spirit, saith the Lord," showing use of means but dependence only on God?

15. "Thou shalt not follow a multitude to do evil," a most necessary warning, for, alas! how many do "custom and example" lead "to swerve from the truth."

16. "Every imagination of the thoughts of mans heart is only evil continually." A strong statement; but showing the need of Divine grace and discipline (Jer. xvii. 9, 10).

17. "Seekest thou great things for thyself, seek them not."

18. "He that ruleth his spirit is greater than he that taketh a city."

19. "Shall not the Judge of all the earth do right?"

20. "Shall we receive good at the hand of God, and shall we not receive evil?"

21. "Their strength is to sit still. In quietness and in confidence shall be your strength."

22. "How can man be just before God? (since) he cannot answer Him one of a thousand."

23. "And thine ears shall hear a voice behind thee saying, This is the way, walk ye in it."

24. "We are but of yesterday, and know nothing."

25. "The righteous shall hold on his way, and he that hath clean hands shall be stronger and stronger."

26. Where is a king spoken of as "The breath of our nostrils," applied sometimes since in flattery to modern monarchs?

27. Who first employed that powerful simile, now become proverbial, "Like a wild bull in a net?"

28. Christ on two occasions quoted the words, "I will have mercy, and not sacrifice." Where are they to be found in the Old Testament?

29. Who said, "No doubt but ye are the people, and wisdom shall die with you?"

30. Where is to be found the declaration, "Man looketh at the outward appearance, but God looketh at the heart?"

SCRIPTURE METAPHORS

The following questions are to be answered by the mention of words, all of which commence with the letter at the head of each section:— [See Key page 71.]

A.

1. What creature may be regarded as metaphorical of sin in four particulars?
2. What professional office does an apostle make metaphorical of the work of Christ?
3. What instrument is made emblematical of a moral affection? And why?
4. What is made metaphorical of industry, forethought, and individual responsibility?
5. Name something which is made emblematical of frailty, humiliation, and sin. Why?
6. What metaphor is used alike for repentence and resurrection?

B.

7. To whom are young believers metaphorically compared? Give three illustrations, with references.
8. Name a disease which is used metaphorically for sin.
9. What five creatures are tyrants and wicked men compared to?
10. What is treated as metaphorical of great faults in contrast with smaller faults?
11. Name three words which are used as metaphorical of Christ in relation to His church

12. What is made metaphorical of wisdom, prosperity, and consolation?
13. What is used metaphorically in connection with Divine judgment?

C.

14. Find a word which is used metaphorically of immortal life, eternal glory, and heavenly purity.
15. One word represents man's soul, God's favor, and spiritual life. Name it.
16. What word is used metaphorically of protecting, and forgiving?
17. Name a word which is used metaphorically to express death, ruin, strength, enlargement, love, affliction, and sin.
18. What word is used metaphorically for a king, an empire, and the faithful people of God?
19. What word is there that equally represents in metaphor false doctrine and the destruction of the wicked?

D.

20. Name a species of animals to which wicked men are compared. Justify the metaphor in five particulars from Scripture.
21. Name nine words taken from water, which are all used metaphorically.
22. Name a word which is used metaphorically in connection with sorrow, death, secresy, sin, and hell.
23. Name three ways in which the word door is used metaphorically, and justify them.
24. What word is applied metaphorically to Jerusalem and its temple.

E.

25. Give two texts where a word is used metaphorically for reward.
26. What external application is used to indicate spiritual enlightenment?

F.

27. What words are used metaphorically of Christ?
28. What is put metaphorically for the life of man?
29. What occupation is that of Satan compared to?
30. Name a metaphor for dispersing and scattering.
31. Name a word used metaphorically of false prophets and a wicked ruler.

G.

32. Name some things metaphorical of national decay.
33. How are multitudes expressed metaphorically?
34. Name two things which the wicked are compared to
35. What is metaphorical of truth?   And why?

H.

36. What is used metaphorically for the grave, the body, the church, and heaven?
37. Name two things with which God's Word is compared.
38. Name something used metaphorically illustrative of the love of Christ.

I, J, K.

39. What word is used metaphorically to express the Gentiles?
40. What word expresses prayer and the merits of Christ?
41. What is metaphorical of glorified saints?
42. What is thus used for love, reverence, submission, and deceit?
43. What are the saints now compared to, which will be a truer comparison hereafter?

L.

44. What word is used metaphorically in connection with prosperity, eternal life, mortality, and timidity?
45. Name two things to which both Christ and believers are compared.
46. Name something to which Christ, believers, Satan, and wicked men, are all compared.

47. Name a word used metaphorically both of sin and of grace.
48. What is made metaphorical of the word of God, happiness, a good king, true believers, Jesus Christ, and God?
49. Name some ways in which leprosy is metaphorical of sin.
50. Name a word used for temporal calamity and spiritual weakness.

M.

51. Name four things metaphorical of spiritual blessings.
52. What is put for swiftness, Divine truth, and the resurrection?
53. What words are used metaphorically to describe the saints of God?
54. Name something used to express sin and contempt.

N.

55. What is put for death, a time of ignorance, and affliction.
56. What is put for a time of prosperity?
57. What is made metaphorical of safety and security?
58. What word expresses metaphorically the duty of Christian kings and ministers?

O.

59. What is metaphorical of Christ's name, and of brotherly unity?
60. Who are put metaphorically for the church without a comforter?
61. Name something which is made a symbol of vitality.

P.

62. Name something metaphorical of great teachers in the church.
63. What is made metaphorical both of the temple of Jerusalem and the church of God?

SCRIPTURE METAPHORS.

64. Name a word which equally describes sin and the grave.
65. What word is used to express the royal dignity of Christ?
66. What is put for a snare, sorrow and the grave?
67. What is the conversation of the wicked compared to?

Q, R.

68. Name a word which is used metaphorically in connection with love, life, temptation, the Holy Spirit, and Divine wrath.
69. What is put metaphorically for deceitful speech, and for desolating judgment?
70. Name a word used metaphorically for instability, despondency, and disappointing hope.
71. What work is applied metaphorically to ministers and angels?
72. What metaphor denotes the Christian life?

S.

73. Name several metaphorical titles of the Lord's people.
74. Name a metaphor used to describe death.

T, V.

75. Give several metaphorical expressions for wicked men.
76. Name a word used metaphorically of God.
77. What are made metaphorical both of the heavens and of the church?
78. What two words are used metaphorically of the church, including both formalists and true believers?
79. What are wicked men compared to?
80. What is put for human life?

W, Y.

81. What two things is the Holy Ghost compared to?
82. Name two words to denote false teachers in religion.
83. What word metaphorically describes the service of Christ, cruel oppression, and spiritual bondage?

SCRIPTURE ENIGMAS.

ANAGRAMS, ACROSTICS AND PUZZLES.

[Key Page 79.]

SCRIPTURE ENIGMA, No. 1.

Five hundred begins it; five hundred ends it;
  And five in the middle is seen;
The first of all letters, the first of all numbers
  Have taken their stations between;
And if you correctly this medley can spell,
The name of an ancient king then it will tell.

SCRIPTURE ENIGMA, No. 2.

I end as I began,
The weal and woe of man;
Yet do not harshly blame,
I bear my mother's name.

SCRIPTURE ENIGMA, No. 3.

My centre is nothing;
  My first is my last;
And when the long ages
  Are over and past,
Then vengeance divine
  Shall devour me and mine.

SCRIPTURE ENIGMA, No. 4.

Four heads have I, but body none,
And without any legs I run.
'Midst bliss supreme my lot was cast
And joys that could not be surpassed
Yet these delights did I forsake,
And far away my course I take;
Yet, while I wander far or nigh,
Still ever in my bed I lie.

SCRIPTURE ENIGMA, No. 5.

Of nature hard, and yet of purpose soft,
The livelong night it bore its lord aloft;
More vast by far than common mortals know
And fitted well to lay the oppressor low.
Now lowlier still the lord lies in the grave,
While for a trophy conquerors kept the slave.

SCRIPTURE ENIGMA, No. 6.

By changing seasons gently nursed,
From out of a tender bud it burst,
And in a wood it flourished first.

Alas! not long; the forest glade,
Resigns its trust; behind it fade
Its sylvan home and woodland shade.

Death came; but though men called it dead,
A second diverse life it led—
A thing of wonder and of dread.

Then the old life resumed its power,
And, in a dark and anxious hour,
Sweet blooms arose, and fruit and flower.

SCRIPTURE ENIGMA, No. 7.

In the water, in the air, and in the busy brain,
Busy once, but nevermore to hate or love again;
One of five, all like itself, in deadly deed united,
And yet delivering those in whom the Lord of Hosts delighted.

SCRIPTURE ENIGMA, No. 8.

Take from my whole my first away,
Behold it then our direst day,
   Since Time his course began.
Restore again my several part,
My whole brings peace to careworn heart,
   And rest to weary man.

SCRIPTURE ENIGMA, No. 9.

1. A man who made a wretched choice.
2. A man raised up as a deliverer.
3. A woman beautiful and well-favored.
4. A woman called "a mother in Israel."
5. A king of Egypt who besieged Jerusalem.
6. A king of Israel rebuked by a prophet.
7. A queen who made a great feast.
8. A queen who saved her nation.
9. A city famous in the early history of the world.
10. A city in Asia mentioned in the New Testament.
11. A letter which commences no name in the Bible.
12. A letter of the earliest-named place in the Bible.
13. A nation often at war with the Jews.
14. A nation that had wars with Assyria.
15. A place mentioned in Paul's last voyage.
16. A place visited by Paul and Barnabas.
17. A mountain possessed by the Edomites.
18. A mountain where the Lord spake to Israel.

The *initials* give words spoken in a time of great peril.

SCRIPTURE ENIGMA, No. 10.

1. The father of Dathan and Abiram.
2. The beloved physician.
3. The surname of a traitor.
4. The name of a miraculous spring.
5. The mount of cursing.
6. Where a herd of swine perished.
7. A valley where a famous event took place.
8. A city of Phrygia, to which Paul addressed an epistle
9. The place where a Syrian captain was defeated.

The *initials* of the answers will give the name of a sojourner in the land of Moab, and the *finals* that of his native town.

SCRIPTURE ENIGMA, No. 11.

1. An Israelitish leader who conquered the host of Midian.
2. A cunning hunter.
3. A prophet, a native of Elkosh.
4. One whom the Lord refused for his anointed.
5. The wife of Zebedee.
6. The second son of Kohath.
7. The chief ruler of the synagogue at Corinth.

The *initials* and *finals* of the answers will give the names of two books of the Bible.

SCRIPTURE ENIGMA, No. 12.

1. This sacrifice was offered at His birth.
   Who lived, despised and poor, upon the earth.
2. Calling the wise men (for he greatly feared),
   He asked of them what time the star appeared.
3. Warned by an angel, thither Joseph went,
   Ere the dark hours of night were fully spent.
4. He slept, and God, in pity and in love,
   Gave him, in this, a glimpse of heaven above.

SCRIPTURE ENIGMAS.

5. The tribe of one who served God night and day,
   And in the temple lived to watch and pray.
6. Take it upon you, in your Saviour's might;
   In youth 'tis easy, and 'tis rest at night.
7. Men saw its light, at heaven's eastern gate;
   It passed before them, and their joy was great.
8. In haste 'twas eaten, with the staff in hand;
   For Israel's children sought a better land.
9. Her little ones as Christian martyrs slept,
   She knows not, and refusing comfort wept.
10. The prophecy, a virgin shall conceive,
    Will tell the name which she her Son should give.
11. 'Twas here in wisdom and in stature too,
    And grace with God and man, our Saviour grew.
12. The place where Christ bade his disciples stay,
    Whilst he should leave them for a time to pray.

The initials give the whole.

Through God's great mercy, in sin's blackest night,
It came from heaven, to give his people light;
To bid our fears in death's dark shadows cease,
Guiding our feet into the way of peace.

SCRIPTURE ENIGMA, No. 13.

1. A son of Saul, by murderous hands who died
2. A race, Lot's children, thorns in Gilead's side.
3. The father of the ninth apostle named.
4. One as great Moses' father only famed.
5. To Jesus, as the Christ, who Peter brought?
6. Who, Zimri punishing, the kingdom sought?
7. A place where Christ in breaking bread was seen.
8. A sage in Jewish law, Paul had his pupil been.

Of 2, 6, 8, *initials* two you use;
Of third name, four; of fifth name, three; then choose
One of the rest: a title there will be,
Or claim, which in Isaiah we may see
Unto Jehovah thrice, in substance, given:
And twice by Christ assumed, speaking from heaven.

SCRIPTURE ENIGMA, No. 14.

1. Whom did his servants treacherously slay
   As sleeping on his couch at noon he lay?

2. A prince who, with a missionary band,
   Went forth to preach throughout the Holy Land.

3. A town where mighty miracles were wrought,
   Which for its sin was to destruction brought?

4. Before what idol did a Syrian bend
   Lest he his heathen master should offend?

5. Who to withstand the Apostle's preaching sought,
   And on himself a fearful judgment brought?

6. What did once save from death the human race,
   And for a year was their sole dwelling-place?

7. A prophet who was called in early youth,
   And till old age he served the God of truth.

8. A mother who did early teach her boy
   The way that leads to everlasting joy.

9. What king against the tribes of Israel fought
   Because a passage through his land they sought?

10. A word inscribed in Babel's regal hall,
    Her impious king to penitence to call.

11. What king would not take counsel of the wise,
    But did his father's counsellors despise?

12. What makes the gold with purest lustre shine,
    And is an emblem of God's Word Divine?

13. What beauteous creatures dwell in heaven above,
    And visit earth on messages of love?

14. Who did, when Judah's tribe was borne away,
    The ruler of the remnant basely slay?

15. Who brought good news, the apostle's heart to cheer,
    When he was sore oppressed with grief and fear?

16. A blessed emblem of our Saviour dear,
    For those that trust in Him need never fear.

In the *initials* of these words we read
A prayer for that which above all we need.
Without this gift the world would be most drear:
The next be viewed with overwhelming fear.
It casts its beams on every scene of woe,
And throws a radiance on our path below

SCRIPTURE ENIGMA, No. 15.

1. The man whose name is first mentioned in connection with a victory over the Amalekites.
2. A prince of Midian slain by the Ephraimites.
3. The father of Jehu.
4. The captain of Absalom's host.
5 The only weapon used at the siege of Jericho.
6. A prophetess who foretold the evil that should come upon the kingdom of Judah.
7. The country to which the murderers of Sennacherib fled
8. A king who was deprived of his dominion until he would acknowledge that all earthly power was the work of God.

The *initials* and *finals* of the foregoing names (or words) form the names of a father and son: the *initials* give us the son, who was sent to warn David of Absalom's intentions. The *finals*, the father, one of the priests in the reign of David.

SCRIPTURE ENIGMA, No. 16.

1. A servant of God, who followed Him fully.
2. Another servant of God, who feared the Lord greatly.
3. The woman to whom Jesus first appeared after his resurrection.
4. A woman who is said to have been righteous before God
5. The birth place of the father of the faithful.
6. A city where Jesus raised one from the dead.
7. A city in the wilderness, built by King Solomon
8. A place from which gold was brought to King Solomon
9. A prophet who lived in the reign of King Ahaz.
10. A prophet who lived in the reign of King Ahab.

The *initials* form a gracious invitation of the Lord Jesus.

SCRIPTURE ENIGMA, No. 17.

1. One who had better ne'er been born—his second name.
2. He who to David showed his double sin and shame.
3. She who once only good, but evil soon too, knew.
4. Respectful title, given to each more honored Jew.
5. "God's promises in Christ, all, all, are this," 'tis writ.
6. To dwell in Philippi this town did Lydia quit.
7. New name ("a prince of God" it means) by patriarch gained.
8. City of priests, with blood of all its dwellers stained.
9. 'Gainst David's third great sin, God's judgments who declared.
10. A city which, by cunning cheated, Joshua spared
11. In alphabetic Psalm, six Hebrew letter's name.
12. The first of four wise men, whom Solomon passed in fame.
13. A man, who sent his son the asses strayed to find.
14. A lowly son, by God for regal rule designed.

    Of names 3, 12, no letter you refuse;
    Of 6 and 10, the first two only use:

Of others, one. A duty which doth rest,
For faithful Christians, on a promise blest.

SCRIPTURE ENIGMA, No. 18.

1. What office did our Lord fulfil in offering Himself a sacrifice for sin?
2. What expression is used concerning Christ as of the house of David?
3. In what term does St. Paul, in his epistle to the Corinthians, speak of the relation of Christ to the Father.
4. What title of Christ, though given him in contempt by his enemies, was the fulfilment of a prophecy?
5. A name of our Saviour that indicates his wisdom?
6. In what prophetic language is the essential attribute of God ascribed to Christ.
7. A title by which our Lord's human descent is described?
8. Under what designation does prophecy indicate Christ as cleansing from all iniquity?
9. Name the grand office of Christ as our Divine Teacher.
10. What prophetic title of our Saviour shows Him to be both God and Man?
11. One of our Saviour's names taken from the Greek alphabet?
12. How does our Lord show Himself to be the support of that temple built up of his elect?
13. What is it that Christ's people find in Him?

From these *initials* you will find
The love of God to human kind.
He sent his Son from heaven on high,
For us to suffer, bleed, and die.
Oh, happy time, when He shall come
To bring us to our heavenly home—
The war, and strife, and sin shall cease,
And Jesus come to reign in peace.

SCRIPTURE ENIGMA, No. 19.

1. One whom Paul called his own son in the faith.
2. A king who helped Solomon to build the temple.
3. A prophet who was seen hundreds of years after he died
4. The eldest sister of Rachel.
5. The grandfather of King David.
6. The eldest son of Jacob.
7. The youngest son of Jesse.
8. A distinguished teacher at Antioch.
9. A Roman officer who saved Paul's life.
10. A warrior who killed Goliath's brother.
11. A scribe who carried a message to Isaiah.
12. A king's son who killed his father.
13. One of the judges of Israel.
14. One of the best of the kings of Judah.
15. One of the ancestors of our Lord.
16. One of Job's comforters.
17. A great man among the Anakims.
18. A prophet who rebuked King David.
19. A prophetess who judged Israel.
20. The father of the first King of Israel.
22, The steward of Abraham's house.
22. The mother of Timothy.
23. The third Apostle called by Jesus.
24. An orator who accused Paul.
25. A king reproved by John the Baptist
26. A false prophet who withstood Paul.
27. A true prophet in the land of Chaldea

The *initials* express an affectionate wish and devout benediction.

SCRIPTURE ENIGMA, No. 20.

1. "These have the world turned upside down." Where was this said?
2. Paul here, now nearly worshipped, now cast forth as dead

3. The man whose purchased floor became the Temple's site.
4. In art and learning's seat, who hailed the gospel's light?
5. His people to chastise with scorpions, who had will?
6. Who David, weak through age, in battle hoped to kill?
7. Twelve stones were here set up, which they from Jordan drew.
8. The mount where died the chief whose grave ne'er mortal knew.
9. The father of a queen who God's own prophet slew.

Of 1 and 9, *initials* three retain;
Of 3, 5, two; and one of what remain:
A text in Psalms appears, which well may cheer
The heart in every doubt, distress or fear.

SCRIPTURE ENIGMA, No. 21.

1. A servant who gained part of his master's property by slander and deceit.
2. A high priest who tried to hinder a great work of the Lord.
3. A title of honor which our Lord told his disciples to refuse when called by it.
4. One of those classes of people who shall be cast into the lake of fire, which is the second death.
5. The division of Palestine of which, at the beginning of John the Baptist's ministry, Philip, the husband of Herodias was Tetrarch.
6. The soldier who, when with David, took away Saul's spear and cruse of water, while his guards were asleep.
7. The cousin of a prophet who bought a field from him, as a token that the children of Israel should return from their captivity in Babylon.

The *initials* and *finals* give the names of two women, sisters of a famous king of Israel. The first the mother of brave men, in connection with whom her name is often mentioned.

SCRIPTURE ENIGMA, No. 22.

1. A man whose end exemplifies that "the love of money is the root of all evil."
2. A man who "prepared his heart to seek the law of the Lord."
3. The town to which Elkanah belonged.
4. The country which bounded the dominions of Ahasuerus on the east.
5. The king of Elam who took Lot prisoner.
6. One of the prophets who incited the Jews to the building of the second temple.
7 The name which Joshua originally bore.

The *initials* of the above names form the name of a city taken by the Israelites where only one family was spared; the *finals*, of a city built by Omri, which was also his burial-place.

SCRIPTURE ENIGMA, No. 23.

1. A tree with which a famous temple was built.
2. A tree under which idols were buried.
3. A prophet whom a king of Judah slew with the sword.
4. A city in Egypt, prophesied against by three prophets.
5. A tree into which one climbed to see Christ.
6. The place where the spies obtained the bunch of grapes
7. One called "the beloved physician."
8. One whose heart the Lord opened.
9. One from whom our Lord was a descendant.
10. One who caused her son to deceive.

The above *initials* form a name by which our Lord was called in the Old Testament.

SCRIPTURE ENIGMA, No. 24.

1. What prophet did the Saviour's birth-place tell
When He came down as man with men to dwell?

SCRIPTURE ENIGMAS.

2. A term employed in God's most holy Word
   Which doth His truth and faithfulness record?

3. A striking monument of heavenly grace
   Who saw his blessed Saviour face to face?

4. The village where our risen Lord appeared,
   And thus two sorrowing disciples cheered?

5. A holy seer who lived in David's days,
   And sang to God in sweetest songs of praise?

6. To whom did God an holy angel send,
   That He to Peter's message might attend?

7. What bird does on its wings its offspring bear,
   An emblem of our Heavenly Father's care?

8. Who on King David's fortunes did attend,
   And in his trials proved a constant friend?

9. The land from whence arose the world's true light,
   When all around were sunk in deepest night?

10. What prophet's lips were touched with holy fire,
    And spoke great words that still our hope inspire?

11. What beauteous plant did shadow forth our Lord,
    And of His much-loved Church a type afford?

12. A stone the prophet Samuel did raise,
    His God for a deliverance great to praise?

13. Whence did he come who, at his God's command,
    Left home to sojourn in a foreign land?

14. Who in much trouble Zion's walls did raise;
    Then to his God did render songs of praise?

15. The ancestor of one renowned for grace,
    From whom descended the whole Jewish race?

16. A seer who led his people once to show
    Pity and mercy to a fallen foe?

17. What glorious time did shadow forth that day
   When from this earth the curse shall pass away?
18. A prince, who by a pious king was sent,
   That he might lead his people to repent?
19. What mystic word, inscribed on palace wall
   By unknown hand, foretold great Babel's fall?

The *initials* take in order due their place,
And then are read calm words of heavenly grace:
The last best gift that our Redeemer gave
To those loved friends He came from heaven to save:
Oh Lord, give ear unto our earnest prayer,
And grant that we this blessed gift may share.

SCRIPTURE ENIGMA, No. 25.

1. The cousin and wife of one of the patriarchs
2. A king of Bashan who fought against Israel
3. A disobedient wife.
4. A beautiful girl who was the adopted child of her cousin
5. A burden which we are to carry which is light and easy
6. One who is mentioned by St. Paul as a faithful and beloved brother.
7. Paul's helper in Christ.
8. A faithful daughter-in-law.
9. A high priest who helped to rebuild Jerusalem.
10. A captain of the Syrian army in the reign of Benhadad.
11. The eldest brother of a great king of Israel.
12. The heathen god for whom Paul was mistaken.
13 An archer who was the ancestor of a great nation.
14 One who became greater than his elder brother.
15. One who, with his daughters, built the wall of a ruined city.

The *initial* letters of the answers give one of our Lord's commands to those who follow Him.

SCRIPTURE ENIGMA, No. 26.

1. The fifth son of a patriarch's earliest wife.
2. A prophet hither sailing risked his life.

SCRIPTURE ENIGMAS.

3. " An Israelite indeed," as Christ declared.
4. Who, next to Korah named, his ruin shared,
5. Seditious boaster, whom Gamaliel mentions.
6. Here blindness foiled Elisha's foes' intentions.
7 A widow who her home would not resign,
    And say, " Thy God and people shall be mine.
8. The priest, before whom first our Lord they took
9 Loving this present world, who Paul forsook?
10. A word ; but disintangle first the rest,
    And memory, then, this last link will suggest.

Of 1, 2, 6, 7, 8, *initials* two combine
With three or 4 and 5, and one of 3 and 9.
Gracious appeal ! thy highest weal at stake.
Bethink thee well what answer thou wilt make.

SCRIPTURE ENIGMA, No. 27.

1. The only queen that over Judah reigned,
    And her brief reign with cruel murder stained ?
2. Who for herself did carve a tomb on high,
    Then died an exile 'neath a foreign sky?
3. A city where who once its portals gained
    Protection from pursuing foes obtained?
4. Who nobly braved a wicked monarch's ire
    And walked unhurt amid the blazing fire ?
5. A symbol, first of God's forgiving grace,
    That afterward showed the folly of our race ?
6. A shapeless stone which did from heaven fall
    On which for aid the heathen world did call ?
7. An emblem of our Saviour's gentle sway,
    Easy to those who do their God obey ?
8. Who did the brother of Goliath slay,
    And valiantly upheld king David's sway ?
9 A beauteous type of Christ's life-giving power,
    Who doth on earth the richest blessings shower '
10. Who, when a ruler was oppressed with care,
    Assisted him to persevere in prayer ?

11. Whose son taught men to strike the tuneful lyre,
    And did their minds with harmony inspire?
12. Where did the patriarch a pillar raise
    For visions sweet and bright his God to praise?
13. Who made a feast, that former friends might prove
    The blessings of a Saviour's care and love?
14. What mighty empire o'er the earth bore sway
    When here on earth our blessed Lord did stay?
15. Who, when a prophet was by grief oppresst,
    Did come to aid him and procure him rest?
16. The land for Israel's sake supremely blest,
    Type of the Christian's everlasting rest?
17. An altar raised, for Israel's sons to trace
    That they belonged to that much favored race?
18. Who was the grandsire of a mighty seer
    Who taught the Jews to overcome their fear?
19. A beauteous emblem in the temple riven,
    To show that Christ our Lord hath opened heaven?
20. The holy priest who Israel's thousands led,
    And before whom the waves of Jordan fled?

> In these *initials* you will find
> Precept and promise both combined.
> If you, by grace, the first obey,
> You then will find the heavenly way
> That leads you to the realms above,
> Where all is peace, and joy, and love.

SCRIPTURE ENIGMA, No. 28.

1. The man who credence gave on touch of hand.
2. That which is equal to a murderous deed.
3. A fruit much eaten in an Eastern land.
4. Bathsheba's husband, as by Matthew read.
5. What animal on Judah's hills was found?
6. The first five letters of the precious things
   Which in Saul's reign in Israel did abound.

7. The trusting bird that flew with soft white wings
To bring Noah comfort in an olive leaf,
And end at last his time of waiting grief.

Take *firsts* and *finals*, and a text is made,
Which in temptation's hour may prove an aid.

SCRIPTURE ENIGMAS, No. 29.

Afar they watch my whole arise,
Its summit seems to touch the skies;
"When all is done," the crowds exclaim,
" Then shall we make ourselves a name!"

Remove a letter, and behold!
A shepherd issue from his fold,
With blood devoutly draws he nigh,
Himself, alas! how soon to die.

Remove a letter still, and now
Before an idol-god they bow ;
To wood and stone is worship paid,
And men adore what men have made.

Remove a letter yet once more,
We see an altar stained with gore ;
And he who built it named it thus,
To teach a precious truth to us.

SCRIPTURE ENIGMA, No. 30.

1. A word which signifies "peace."
2. A child who was born on the day of a great national calamity.
3. A city which was popularly supposed to produce nothing good.
4. A son of Saul who reigned over Israel for two years.
5. The father of Boaz.
6. An orator who accused St. Paul before Felix.
7. A king of Syria who was anointed by a prophet of Israel

8. David's eldest brother.
9. The queen of Egypt in Solomon's time.
10. The town in which Samuel's house was.
11. The people who erected an altar "to the unknown God".
12. The only leper who was cleansed during the reign of Jehoram, King of Israel.
13. A conqueror whose death was more disastrous to his enemies than his life had been.
14. The country whence Elijah originally came.
15. A Moabitess who married into the tribe of Judah.
16. The Ethiopian eunuch who interceded for Jeremiah.
17. The mountain given to Esau for a possession.
18. The church to whom it was said. "Thou hast a name that thou livest, and art dead."
19. Leah's fifth son.
20. The conqueror of Chushan-rishathaim.
21. A servant whose master granted him leave of absence for twelve years.
22. A runaway slave who was sent back to his master by St. Paul.
23. The age of Moses when he visited his brethren.
24. Absalom's daughter.
25. An Egyptian slave who became the mother of a great nation.
26. The father of Bathsheba.
27. The well near which Isaac dwelt.
28. The tribe to whom it was said, "As thy days, so shall thy strength be."
29. A charge which was given to the disciples and to all Christians.

The *initials* of the above names (or words) give us a definition of sin.

SCRIPTURE ENIGMA, No. 31.

1. Whose army fell beneath an angel's wing?
2. Lo! hence the captive ark they homeward bring.
3. Before this ruler, Paul his case explained.

SCRIPTURE ENIGMAS.

4. A prophet, as deserter, who detained ?
5. Victor in death, heaven opened to his view.
6. Hero tyrant fell by stone a woman threw.
7. An ancient river, famed in Deborah's song,
   That swept the vanquished in its course along.
8. Great city which, by prophet warned, repented.
9. A captured town to Solomon presented.
10. To whom was first earth's future all displayed?
11. A slave escaped, whom Paul a convert made.
12. Chemosh was worshipped on this nation's ground.
13. This governor left Paul unjustly bound.
14. A champion felled by stone a shepherd hurled.
15. Goddess revered by "Asia and the world."

Two of 1, 2, 4, 5, 7, 12 and 14, take
Initials; three of 6; of others one, and make
A text, which sets before the Christian life's chief end,
First of all aims to which his hope should tend.

"Make thou His service thy delight,
Thy wants shall be His care."

SCRIPTURE ENIGMA, No. 32.

1. An emblem of the Lord of life and grace,
   Whose death has wrought salvation for our race?
2. What typifies our Heavenly Father's care
   And shows the love He to his children bare?
3. And in sad contrast, name a type of those
   Who 'gainst God's Word have dared their ears to close.
4. Who first brought sorrow to this world below,
   And was the source of all its sin and woe?
5. A type of Him, of whom it is foretold
   That He shall draw all nations to his fold?
6. A type of Jesus' kind and gentle sway,
   By which He leads us in the heavenly way?
7. To what choice jewel, beautiful and rare,
   Did John the founders of the Church compare?

8. A tree that symbolized the Jews of old,
And in a figure their sad fate foretold?
9. An emblem that our Lord doth typify?
How safe are those who on His aid rely!
10. A symbol brought to show God's wrath did cease,
Which hence became the well-known type of peace!
11. What is of coming day a herald bright,
And typifies the God of love and light?
12. A type of Him who did from heaven descend,
And feeds all those that on His grace depend?
13. A type of that which makes all sorrows light,
And throws a beam across the darkest night?
14. An emblem of a city placed on high
Which dared Almighty power to defy?

    In the *initials* of these types we read
    Not to depend on man in time of need;
    But put our trust in God's Almighty power,
    Who help will give for every trying hour.

SCRIPTURE ENIGMA, No. 33.

1. The prophet who was sent to tell David of the punishment he had incurred by numbering the people.
2. A man who "feared the Lord greatly."
3. The country where the gospel was preached by a man who had once been the terror of the inhabitants.
4. A man who plotted to destroy a whole nation for the offence of one man.
5. The only man who escaped the slaughter of the priests by Saul.
6. The mountain in whose neighborhood Sisera was defeated.
7. The prophet who reproved Asa for trusting to the King of Syria.
8. The name which Jacob gave to the place where the angels of God met him.
9. "A prince and a great man."

10. The king by whose decree the building of the second temple was finished.
11. The wife of Aaron.
12. The man to whom David showed kindness for Jonathan's sake.
13. A man who was spared by a king, and slain by a prophet.
14. The city of the priests.
15. The prophet who was slain by Jehoiakim.
16 Herod's brother.
17 The place where the Israelites fought their first battle after leaving Egypt.
18. The murderer of Gedaliah.
19. The Hebrew name of the place where our Lord was condemned.
20. The father of Lot.
21. The city to which Jehoshaphat attempted to send ships.

The *initials* of the above names (or words) form a statement which shows us that we are "very far gone from original righteousness."

SCRIPTURE ENIGMA, No. 34.

1. He who with Joshua only of the land
   Who quitted Egypt reached the promised land.
2. Name of a street, Saul's blindness here had end.
3. Man plants and tends; God only this can send.
4. A judge who cared not to take either side.
5. A pronoun oft in friendly speech supplied.
6. Who was it, to whom plainly Christ confessed,
   The "Son of Man" was "Son, too, of the Blessed?
7. King of Damascus, when St. Paul thence fled.
8. The city where, in Egypt, Joseph wed.
9. Of Solomon the royal Tyrian friend.
10. Whom Peter smote, his Master to defend.

Initials two of 1, 2, 3, 8, 9,
With four of 4 and 3 of 7 combine;

One of the rest: a counsel thus is made
Of comfort full, yet ill, alas! obeyed.

SCRIPTURE ENIGMA, No. 35.

1. Another name by ancient men
   To land of Edom given.
2. The first four letters of a fruit
   To Nazarites forbidden.
3. What man, for taking a stronghold,
   Obtained his cousin's hand?
4. The place where Lydia purple sold,
   The richest in the land.
5. A Grecian game to which St. Paul
   Compares the Christian's path.
6. A tree of which the Jews burnt much
   On their domestic hearth.
7. A very profitable use, for Scripture,
   Paul did name.
8. The first three letters of a man
   To whom death never came.
9. Name the third mount to whose high top
   King Balak, Balaam led.
10. Give for a parable a name
    In Bible pages read.
11. Reverse the name where gold was found—
    A celebrated place;
12. And give the mighty ancestor
    Of Edom's hardy race.

When you the *firsts* and *finals* find,
 A sentence you may frame,
A promise made by Christ on earth
 Which we in heaven may claim.

SCRIPTURE ENIGMA, No. 36.

Curiously hinged and jointed
  To its fellow hangs my *first*;
To preserve man's life appointed,
  When the ground, through sin, was cursed;
    Yet it never
  Fails to deal destruction round,
    To whatever
  May within its reach be found.

With substantial fabrication
  Is my unseen *second* blest;
Made a wondrous habitation,
  For a still more wondrous guest:
    Framed to cherish
  Force of arm—the warrior's trust;
    Doomed to perish—
  Earth to earth, and dust to dust!

From a feeble creature taken,
  Once my *whole* appeared in sight;
And by strength vindictive shaken,
  Slew a thousand in the fight;
    'Twas selected
  To rebuke the Gentiles' pride;
    Soon rejected,
  Like a weapon cast aside.

SCRIPTURE ENIGMA, No. 37.

(Showing a possession lost for us by the first Adam; regained for us by the second Adam.)

1. The name of one of the first seven deacons.
2. A man who, as a king, offered willingly land and goods to build an altar, and to offer sacrifice to God.
3. A family which earned the approbation and reward from God by their obedience to the command of their ancestor.

4. A maiden given to wife as a reward for capturing a city; and who sought and obtained, of her father, land with springs of water. (N.B.—The account of this is given twice over in the Bible ; give reference to both passages.)

5. The omitted tribe in the account, in the Revelation, of the sealing of the hundred and forty-four thousand.

6. The father of that prophet of the Lord who dared speak unpalatable truth to the wicked king to whom the rest of the prophets had spoken palatable falsehood.

7. A convert called by St. Paul " the first fruits of Achaia,' and whose household that apostle baptized.

8. That prophet whose visions, in the Old Testament, are often much akin to those of St. John the Divine in the New.

The *initials* of the above will give the answer

SCRIPTURE ENIGMA, No. 38.

From the New Testament alone,
    Resolves these questions truly ;
The answers two acrostics make,
    When ranged in order duly.

1. The *brook* that Jesus had to cross,
    The traitor's band to meet?

2. The *symbol* of the prayers of saints,
    Acceptable and sweet?

3. When Mary saw the Master risen,
    Her *cry* of recognition ?

4. The *fourth* of seven—the daily care
    Of widows was their mission ?

5. *He* who, in recklessness profane,
    His birthright blessing sold ?

6. And *he* who vexed his righteous soul
    With Sodom's crimes of old ?

SCRIPTURE ENIGMAS.

7. The *band* wherein a Roman served,
    With right devout behavior?

8. And *he*, at Rome, whom Paul salutes,
    "Our helper" in the Saviour?

9. And lastly, *he*, progenitor
    Of Christ's reputed father,
    Whose name the sixth in upward rank,
    From Joseph's line we gather?

   The *initials* and the *finals* take
     From every term selected,
   Except "the symbol of the prayers,"
     And this must be bisected.

   See the *first Gentile Christian's name*,
     Framed from the signs initial;
   And in the finals upward read,
     Behold *his rank official*.

   May we, like him, by Peter taught,
     Renounce our Gentile pride,
   And by the Spirit from above
     Our hearts be purified!

SCRIPTURE ENIGMA, No. 39.

From the tangled thicket bounding,
    Roars my *first;*
Through the wild his voice, resounding
    Hath dispersed
All the tribes that prowl and prey
    In the night:
From his path they flee away
    With affright.

O'er the path my *second* gliding
    Bites the heels;
In the treacherous wine-cup hiding
    Stings and kills.

But the Christ, creation's Head,
    David's Root,
Shall my *first* and *second* tread
    Under foot!

Look! my *third* has made its dwelling
    Underground ;
And its mimic mountains swelling,
    Rise around :
Image of the carnal mind,
    Child of earth,
'Tis by nature dark and blind
    From its birth.

So my *fourth*, with scanty vision
    Of the light,
Flitting, finds its whole provision
    In the night.
To my *third* and *fourth*, 'tis told,
    Man shall cast
All their gods of sordid gold,
    At the last.

Who the *four* initials borrows,
    Shall display
One, who all our sins and sorrows
    Bore away :
Like this creature—though Divine—
    He became,
And his name, in type and sign,
    Is the same.

SCRIPTURAL ENIGMA, No. 40.

What godly priest on Judah's throne his wife's young nephew placed?

What land unto Urijah gave a shelter, when disgraced?

Who was the youngest son of him who earned a curse, foretold?

What relation was Paul to one who told of plotters bold?
Who mourned when one for Israel's good help from a king received?
What was it last poured out on them for whom our Saviour grieved?
What prophet of the Lord most high did Syrian plots defeat?
What brother in the Lord did Paul for one estranged entreat?
What bishop of an eastern church had learned God's holy truth,
While yet a child, and served the Lord e'en from his early youth?
If you have answered this aright, the *initial* letters prove
Our blessed Saviour's sympathy, his tenderness and love;
And then the *final* letters read, for these will let you know
A place where Christ with tears of love His sympathy did show.

SCRIPTURAL ENIGMA. No. 41.

From the New Testament these questions solve,
And thus these names evolve:

1. Who was it oft-times trembled while he heard
   A Roman prisoner's word?

2. What Jew from Egypt did at Corinth preach
   With strong, persuasive speech?

3. Who, by presentiment of faith possessed,
   His twin-born children bless'd?

4. Who, with a life by earliest faith begun,
   Was call'd the apostle's son?

5. Who, by her daughter's "light fantastic" tread
   Obtained a prophet's head?

6. Whose name stands second in the ascending tree
   Of Jesus's pedigree?

7. What slave was to his injured master sent
   By Paul, a penitent?

8. Who was that Jewess, whose experienced speech
Did a great teacher teach?

9. Who was his mother who, in early youth,
Believed and preached the truth?

10. Who was the first of all the Gentile race
To learn the Saviour's grace?

11. Who—though not first—all Asia led astray,
And turned from Paul away?

12. Who, by one lie, called forth th' apostle's power
And perished the same hour?

13. Who heard the voice of Peter at the gate,
And made the apostle wait?

14. What epithet both marks a traitor's shame,
And clears his namesake's fame?

15. Who for St. Paul his longest letter penned
And kind salute did send?

16. What title, in three vowels, doth express
The Saviour's faithfulness?

Now from each term evolved th' *initial* take,
And an acrostic make.

Three sovereign graces that in Christians dwell,
The several letters spell.

The *first*, without saving power, looks back to see
The Saviour's agony.

The *next*, with steadfast eye, looks upward still
To heavenly Zion's hill.

The *last*, the greatest, labors to be blest
In heaven's eternal rest.

The first completed, and the next made sure
The third shall still endure.

SCRIPTURE ENIGMA, No. 42.

1. The tribe to which Korah belonged?
2. The son of Ruth?
3. That by which the sheep know the shepherd?
4. David's eldest brother?
5. The man whom Philip brought to Christ?
6. The father of Ahab?
7. The birthplace of St. Paul?
8. The man who " boasted himself to be somebody?"
9. The city given by Joshua to Caleb?
10. The prophet who said " I am not better than my fathers""
11. That which Pharaoh's daughter promised to Jochabed?
12. The man who was " blessed because of the Ark of God?"
13. The place where Elkanah lived?
14. That of which Jacob made pottage?
15. The man who was " greatly beloved?"

The *initials* form a precept much needed in this world.

SCRIPTURE ENIGMA, No. 43.

'Tis night—my *first* runs out, another comes,
Another and another, ere the morn
    Wakes up a slumbering world
    And lights the toils of men.

'Tis day—my *second* runs his weary round,
And groans in pain, or travails with his task,
    Or sits enthroned in pride,
    Or in the dungeon pines.

'Tis night again—my *whole* with lofty eye,
Looks out beneath him on a slumbering world.
    The dim horizon scans,
    And kens the coming foe.

Simile.

The Christian's life is like the first ; and he
Should like the second quit himself, be strong,
  Be wise ; and, like the whole,
  Look for his coming Lord.

SCRIPTURE ENIGMA. No. 44.

In the *initials* placed aright,
  Appears that spot of memory sweet,
Where He who dwelt as man on earth
  Loved with his followers to meet.

1. My wicked wiles could not avail
   God's servant to dismay.

2. In bitterness of soul I knelt,
   Before the Lord to pray.

3. Beside a river's bank I stood,
   And viewed a wondrous sight.

4. To me a crown of gold was given,
   And robes of blue and white.

5. In time of danger I concealed
   God's prophets in a cave.

6. In vain to Egypt did I fly,
   My threatened life to save.

7. With saddened heart I left the land
   Where those I loved were laid.

8. In Pekah King of Israel's days,
   I did his land invade.

9. A city I must first besiege,
   Ere I my wife could win.

10. I trembled at my prisoner's words
    Yet would not leave my si...

11. My giant strength became as nought
    Opposed to God's great might.

12. My tribe was chosen by the Lord,
    To serve Him day and night.

13. As musing in the field I walked,
    I saw my bride draw near.

14. I would not, at my lord's command,
    Before his court appear.

15. My harsh reproofs but served to add
    Unto my friend's great woe.

16. I perished on the battle-field,
    But not by sword or foe,
    My own right hand the weapon held,
    Which made my life-blood flow.

SCRIPTURE ENIGMA, No. 45.

The prophet who "loved the wages of unrighteousness."
The native land of Ishmael's wife.
The man who would not part with the inheritance of his fathers.
The tenth part of an ephah.
The city to which Barnabas went to seek Saul.
The number of years that Moses sojourned in Midian.
The saint who, "being dead, yet speaketh."
The medium of communication between Joseph and his brethren.
St. Paul's "own son in the faith."
The father of King Manasseh.
Isaac's brother-in-law.
The prophet visited on his death-bed by King Joash.
The city where Omri was buried.
The Benjamite who cursed David.

These *initials* make a charge of our Saviour to His disciples.

SCRIPTURE ENIGMA, No. 46.

Whose faith and courage saved her people's life ?
  Who won a battle trusting in the Lord ?
Who gained a sharp rebuke for jealous strife ?
  Who perished by a traitor's cruel sword ?
  Who checked his rage to prove a prophet's word ?

The *initial* letters take—they form his name
Who did his foe's unwilling praise proclaim;
Then take the *finals*, and they give the same.

SCRIPTURE ENIGMA. No. 47.

1. A type of our Lord ; one who entered the land of Egypt, and the house of bondage, and there saved his people.

2. One who preferred a present and temporal benefit, to that which was future and eternal, and repented, when too late.

3. The name of a King of Israel ; also of one who, from a persecutor, became an apostle.

4. One who put out a rash hand, unauthorized by God, to steady the ark, which he thought to be in danger, and received not praise, but punishment from God.

5. The name of that church of whose angel (or bishop) was said, " Thou hast a name that thou livest, and art dead."

The *first* letters of these make up the sweetest human name in the world.

>" It makes the wounded spirit whole
> It calms the troubled breast;
>'Tis manna to the hungry soul,
> And to the weary rest.

SCRIPTURE ENIGMA, No. 48

What is Christian worship?—
  You shall quickly know,
When you solve the queries
  Following here below :—

Name the fifth disciple,
  Of Bethsaida he,
Jesus found, and called him,
  Saying, "Follow me!"

How shall we take warning?
  Learning from Lot's wife,
Who, though saved from Sodom
  Turned, and lost her life!

With the traitor's silver,
  When this field was bought,
There the doom he suffered,
  Of the deeds he wrought.

Paul once found at Corinth,
  Lately come from—whence?
Two good souls, when Cæsar
  Drove all Jews from thence.

Early in the morning,
  With the Marys came
One, to look for Jesus;
  Mark recites her name.

Jacob's father's father—
  Tell his worthy name:
In the line of David
  You shall find the same.

First th' *initial* letters,
  Next the *finals* take;
Then, with holy incense
  These sweet offerings make :

> *This* to tell God's mercies,
> *That* to seek his face,
> Through the blood of sprinkling,
> At the throne of grace.

SCRIPTURE ENIGMA, No. 49.

A faithful martyr's honored name,
A prophet-judge's dwelling-place,
A warrior who to David came,
A priest who perished in disgrace,
A prophet's home, a mountain land :

> The *initial* letters spell,
> Reverse their order as they stand,
> A mournful name they tell,
> Which one, oppressed with deepest woes,
> In bitterness of spirit chose.

SCRIPTURE ENIGMA, No. 50.

My *first* is known in every Christian clime,
The fatal instrument of deadly crime.
Abhorred, beloved, accursed, and yet most blest,
A path of trouble to a land of rest.

For the initial letter substitute
The next in alphabetic order found,
And all most valued, held in best repute,
In this vain world most worshipped or renowned,
Weighed with my *first*, so painful, yet so dear
To each true heart, my *second* will appear.

The two first letters of this word remove,
And place instead the initial of her name
Who cheered God's saints with words and deeds of love.
Embraced my *first*, and gloried in the shame.

The word thus formed is used by one most blest,
That great apostle whom she made her guest,
To tell what all the world's wealth, learning, fame,
When he beheld my *first*, to him became.

SCRIPTURE ENIGMA, No. 51.

In many a bosom fondly nursed,
A fiery serpent is my *first* ·
When Jesus came for us to die,
He crushed this deadly enemy.
My *second* is a city's name,
Where Israel's host was put to shame,
Because my *first* still unrevealed,
Was lurking in their camp concealed.
Upon my *whole*, pronounced by heaven,
The knowledge of my *first* was given.
The chosen people gathered round,
And trembled at the dreadful sound.

SCRIPTURE ENIGMA, No. 52.

Earth revolves, and lo! I come,
    Out of darkness springing;
Men and beasts their task resume,
    Birds their carols singing;
Glad my smiling face to see,
Earth wakes up to welcome me.

Earth revolves, and, like again,
    Out of darkness beaming,
Shine I in Night's diadem,
    On the wavelets gleaming;
And my radiance dies away,
  Only in returning day.

Earth revolves, and now 'tis mine,
　　Out of darkness glancing,
To announce the night's decline,
　　And the day's advancing;
And my hopeful brightness, so,
Doth the Saviour's coming show.

SCRIPTURE ENIGMA, No. 53.

From all the names in Scripture,
　　Of just six letters framed,
Find hers who, for her beauty,
　　Was far and justly famed ;
'Tis true her lot was lowly,
　　Yet, though her birth was mean,
She, from a captive maiden,
　　Became a mighty queen.

Transpose the same six letters,
　　And now his name we find,
Whose meditated treason
　　Was timely brought to mind ;
And Providence so ordered,
　　That a great king was taught
To magnify the humble,
　　And bring the proud to nought.

Five of the six exhibit
　　A mount on Dan bestowed,
Where still, though put to tribute,
　　The Amorites abode.

Five show what creatures cover
　　Th' unbrageous forest-lands,
And soon—the prophet tells us—
　　They all shall clap their hands.

SCRIPTURE ENIGMAS.

Five more denote the number
  Of Anak's sons of old
(Not one, nor two, nor many),
  Whose several names are told.

Five changed show what, in vision,
  From heaven to Peter came,
Filled with all living creatures,
  That he might eat the same.

Four of the same selected,
  Describe that other seed
Instead of him—the victim
  Of man's first murderous deed.

Four other letters chosen
  Will Samuel's office show,
What time some urgent matter
  A young man sought to know

Four name that Hebrew letter
  That stands the last but two
The longest psalm, in portions.
  Will prove the answer true.

Four make the sweetest offer
  The weary soul can hear;
Come, and receive it freely,
  Who yoke or burden bear

And four denote the person
  Who with " good comfort " heard
When to the poor blind beggar
  They told the Saviour's word:
And the same voice of comfort
  To every conscience speaks,
When Jesus, by his gospel,
  Each poor blind sinner seeks

SCRIPTURE ENIGMA, No. 54.

Faith shall be swallowed up in sight,
   Hope in fulfilment end,
When on our twilight life the light
   Of heaven shall descend.

A sister-grace to these. more great,
   Shall brighten when they wane;
O let us more and more to this,
   Even in *this* life, attain!

The initials of the following will give the name of this most excellent grace:

1. The grandmother of Timothy.
2. The good servant of a wicked king, who kept one hundred prophets of the Lord from the vengeance of the queen.
3. A queen who resisted her husband's command, and was deposed.
4. A good man, but a bad father.

SCRIPTURE ENIGMA, No. 55.

The father of the first artificer in brass and iron.
The man who said, "I thy servant fear the Lord from my youth."
The wise man's estimate of earthly pleasure.
The place where David slew Goliath.
Rehoboam's successor
The people who stole the oxen of Job.
Herod's chamberlain.
The city where Jehu was anointed king.
The kingdom of Chedorlaomer.
Paul's amanuensis when he wrote the Epistle to the Romans
The mother of Adonijah.
The wife of Mahlon.
The name of the altar that was built by the children of Reuben and Gad.
The younger son of Bilhah.

SCRIPTURE ENIGMA, No. 56.

My *first* enjoins a watchful care,
To see and shun each lurking snare,
With earnest and unceasing prayer.

My *second* speaks a kingdom mine,
Where life and peace and joy divine
In uncorrupted glory shine.

My *third* would contradict my first,
'Tis watchful earnestness reversed,
By careless, prayerless folly nursed.

Faith is my *fourth*, of things not seen
While on the word of truth we lean,
Though clouds and darkness intervene.

These several subjects find in turn,
And as their primal signs you learn,
My *whole* in figure you discern.

This type of Jesus, and His saints
Their living, fruitful union paints,
And patient love that never faints.

SCRIPTURE ENIGMA, No. 57.

THREEFOLD ACROSTIC.

1. R-uin and wrath, and mortal gloom,
2. B-y nature's fall and righteous doom,
3. A-ll drive the sinner to the tomb.

N-one can escape the just reward,
Y-et the long-suffering of the Lord
E-ndures the acts of men abhorred.

D-eath and the grave wide open lie,
D-read and destruction hover nigh,
P-erdition waits, which none can fly.

B-ut lo! the gospel brings to light
U-nlooked-for help in Nature's night.
E-den and life restored to sight.

M-ercy receives the dreadful stroke,
Y-ea, justice doth the doom revoke,
R-emoves the curse, and breaks the yoke.

C-hrist in our flesh the price hath paid,
P-eace through His precious blood is made,
P-ardon and life for man displayed.

T-here, on the shameful cross he bled,
O-ffered to judgment in our stead,
H-umbled, and numbered with the dead!

W-ith hell he fought and won the day,
I-n dying took death's sting away,
A-nd rose triumphant from the fray!

O-to obtain what Christ hath won!
E-njoy the grace on earth begun!
S-o life shall crown what Love hath done.

N-ow may we trust the sure record,
R-eceive what grace and power award,—
E-ternal glory with the Lord!

The *initials* in due order spun,
From every verse selecting one,
Three times acrostically done,
Will show the work of God's dear Son;
His suffering course on earth begun,
And His eternal kingdom won.

SCRIPTURE ENIGMA, No. 58.

The letters in the following words, when re-arranged, form the name of a false god, to whom human sacrifices were offered:—

1. A man noted for wisdom.
2. An unclean beast.

SCRIPTURE ENIGMA, No. 59.

In every clime, through every age,
In history's eventful page.
My *first* will always rise to view,
And wakes our love and hatred too.
My *second* and my *third* will each
Express the self-same part of speech,
And, though two interjections brief,
May paint a world of joy or grief.
My *whole* most surely was my *first*;
But far more brave and firm in faith,
His wife a mighty patriot nursed,
Who nobly died a hero's death.

SCRIPTURE ENIGMA, No. 60.

In *finals* and *initials* may be found
The names of two, for beauty both renowned;
The one, her days 'mid courtly splendors spent,
The other, in a patriarch's lonely tent.

1. Who did in ancient times that city found,
   In Jonah's history afterwards renowned?

2. Who with Agrippa, to the judgment hall,
   Came with great pomp, to hear the case of Paul?

3. Who thought to slay king David in the fight,
   But fell himself before Abishai's might?

4. Whose kindness to a prophet of the Lord,
   Met with a precious unforeseen reward?

5. Who did the Lord his vision bid to write,
   And make it plain that all might read aright?

6. Who did a queen, although his near of kin,
   Deprive of office for her grievous sin?

7. Who viewed his young opponent with disdain,
   Yet by that stripling's hand was quickly slain

SCRIPTURE ENIGMA, No. 61.

The letters constituting the following words, rearranged, will form the name of a murderer who fled from this country:—
1. The father of the inventor of organs and harps.
2. An organ built near Jordan.
3. A man one of whose kindred rebuked a good man

SCRIPTURE ENIGMA, No. 62

The hiding-place of Jonathan and Ahimaaz.
The prophet who was a herdman of Tekoah.
Cain's grandson.
The judge who succeeded Abimelech.
The prophet who foretold the destruction of Edom.
Hezekiah's name for the brazen serpent.
The place where Samson slew the lion.
Nehemiah's father.
Aaron's wife.
The city whence Sennacherib's ambassadors came.
The man of whom St. Paul says, "He was not ashamed of my chain."
The king of Syria who fought with Ahaz.
The tribe omitted when the rest are enumerated in the Book of Revelation.

SCRIPTURE ENIGMA, No. 63.

My *first* is oft prefixed to words,
   And signifies "beneath,"
My *second's* blessing is the Lord's,
   To save from sin and death;
And planted oft on heathen soil,
It well repays the gracious toil.

When patient Job prepared his soul
   To bow beneath the rod,
Without reserve he gave my *whole*
   To meet the will of God.

SCRIPTURE ENIGMA, No. 64

To solve the following questions,
Write numbers one to eleven in rote; then bring
The well-spent names of person, place, or thing,
That answer these suggestions:—

Nos. 1, 4, 5, 2, 8, 9—
Range under these six letters
The name of one found sitting next a throne,
And riding second to the king alone;
His feet once galled with fetters.

Nos. 2, 8, 9, 7, 6—
Make that capacious measure,
Viewed by the prophet as a woman's seat,
Winged with the wind to her secure retreat.
The land of power and pleasure.

Nos. 3, 4, 5, 9, 2, 10—
He last the sceptre wielded,
Ere Israel's throne was humbled to the dust;
A king who vainly did in Egypt trust,
And to Assyria yielded.

Nos. 4, 5, 3, 2, 7—
Through Canaan's utmost borders,
Twelve chieftains journeyed to search out the land
One name appears that did augmented stand
Thenceforth, by Moses' orders.

Nos. 5, 9, 10, 8, 6, 7, 11—
These show that prophet's father,
Who twice received from Israel's mighty seer
His fallen mantle. This will soon appear,
When you these letters gather.

Nos. 6, 2, 11, 3—
Show from what race descended
The man who owned and sold a field and cave,
Where six illustrious strangers found a grave—
By these four letters blended.

Nos. 7, 5, 10, 8, 9—
 'Tis he, with song poetic,
 First of three seers, as ordered by the king ;
 And still his twelve sweet canticles we sing,
 In psalmody prophetic.

Nos. 8, 7, 5, 2., 10, 9, and 8, 6, 7, 5, 2, 10, 9—
 From Babylon returning,
 Lo ! twice recounted the Nethinims' bands ;
 What name, next Uzza, of these fathers' stands
 Its varied form discerning ?

Nos. 9, 4, 5, 7, 6—
 The bounds of Asher tracing,
 From Helkath to the sea-board, I require
 The name next following the strong city Tyre—
 These numbers rightly placing.

Nos. 10, 1, 7, 9—
 From Seir the Horite springing,
 Behold the name of Zibeon's elder son,
 Whose brother's daughter Jacob's brother won—
 These several numbers bringing.

Nos. 11, 4, 10, 3—
 In Kohath's line ascending
 Count back from Samuel, of those sons of song
 Whom David set to lead the choral throng ;
 In Eliel's father ending.

 Behold his name completed,
 Who reigned in Ahab's days on David's throne,
 By whom his righteous father's ways were shown,
 And Judah's foes defeated.

SCRIPTURE ENIGMA, No. 65.

Swift of foot and fearless,
Strong and terrible in fight,
Great of heart and careless
Of the glancing weapons bright ;
Yet a thing forbidden
To be kept or ridden,
By the people of the Lord,
When the tribes of Israel warred.

Mean, debased, and sordid,
Sprung from a corrupted line ;
Yet his name recorded,
Shows an origin divine.
Fragile now, and tender,
Now in power and splendor,
'Tis a paradox involved,
'Tis a riddle unresolved.

By the *first* and *second*
Must the *whole* be brought to light ;
Strong in valor reckoned,
Yet not seldom put to flight :
Hark! the battle rages—
Host with host engages !
Yet the strong, the swift may yield,
And the weak may win the field.

SCRIPTURE ENIGMA, No. 66.

Who prayed for death in dark despair ?
To what did Christ himself compare ?
What queen was fairest of the fair ?

Now either way the *initials* place,
And still the selfsame name they give
Of one who sunk in deep disgrace,
Did yet a glorious home receive.

SCRIPTURE ENIGMA, No. 67.

First name a chief, the bitter foe
  Of Judah's Lord, and Judah's land.
A river next, whose waters flow,
  By old Damascus' heathen strand.
What did the Lord of Hosts o'erthrow,
  In pity to his chosen band?
What word is oft-times used to show
  The wonders of his mighty hand?
Next mark the name first borne in youth,
  By one, who in the cause of truth,
With manly courage risked his life,
  To still the murmuring people's strife.
And, last, his father's name set down,
  Known only by that son's renown;

The *initials* form a monarch's name,
  Who, once a mighty empire swayed;
Yet are his exploits lost to fame,
  And all his glory sunk in shade.
His captain's name the *finals* tell.

SCRIPTURE ENIGMA, No. 68.

The letters in the answers to the following will, if rightly placed, form the name of a learned teacher:—
1. One of the encampments of the Israelites where there were wells of water.
2. A man who conspired against Abimelech, and was thrust out from the city where he had dwelt.

SCRIPTURE ENIGMA, No. 69.

Letters taken from the following give the name of a place where a rich and good man, in the time of Christ, dwelt:—
1. A leading man of the tribe of Naphtali, who was to " stand with " Moses.
2. A son of Ishmael.

SCRIPTURE ENIGMA, No. 70.

Six letters spell the name of one who was early dedicated to God. These six letters are the initials of six proper names which we will describe as follows :—

1. A quiet Prince.
2. An Eastern River.
3. A priest of Baal.
4. A word which sealed the doom of an empire.
5. A mighty man of valor.
6. A Levitical city.

When you have formed these six words, the *initials* of which spell the name of one who was early dedicated to God. The *final* letters of these six words, either up or down, spell his mother's name.

Who was the boy? Who was his mother?

SCRIPTURE ENIGMAS No. 71.

1. Whose mournful death made widows to lament?
2. What woman from her master's house was sent?
3. Who saw bright visions by a river's side?

4. What treach'rous servant to his master lied?
5. What warlike prince upon a rock was slain?
6. Who water sought when God withheld the rain?
7. Who came uninjured from the lion's den?

8. Who once near Lehi slew a thousand men?
9. Whose prayers and tears did a kind answer gain?
10. In what famed valley was a giant slain?
11. Who for his sin most bitterly did weep?
12. Where did his flock the son of Amram keep?
13. Who with a brother was at deadly strife?
14. What woman by her faith did save her life?
15. Who a fierce foe did in a monarch find,
    But in that monarch's son a friend most kind?

Take the initials, and, as noonday clear,
A title of the Saviour will appear.

SCRIPTURE ENIGMA, No. 72.

What woman armies to the battle led?
In troubled times who gave God's prophet bread?
Who told a lie, to please his thirst for gain?
Whose house the holy ark of God received?
Who early of her husband was bereaved?
Who felt a loving father's keenest pain?

> In these *initial* letters find,
> A precept all our deeds to guide,
> That bids us think of others weal,
> And cast all thoughts of self aside.

SCRIPTURE ENIGMA, No. 73.

1. A name, the symbol of mere worldly gain;
   To love it and love God—the attempt is vain.
2. A vale Tobiah sought, with feigned alarm,
   To entrap there Nehemiah to his harm.
3. A plain where building projects of proud aim,
   By heaven confounded, soon was brought to shame.
4. A word of Christ, which ears fast chained unbound.
5. For incense, jewels, gold, a land renowned.

The *initials* of these words read downward and the *finals* upward and you have the names of two brothers.

SCRIPTURE ENIGMA, No. 74.

1. The first Duke on record.
2. The mount on which Aaron died.
3. Aaron's wife.
4. An Apostle whom the Greeks took for their god Jupiter
5. The place where the Israelites murmured for water.
6. The father of Moses.
7. A ruler of the Jews, who secretly sought Jesus that he might be taught by him.
8. A name given to Simon Peter.
9. A prophet in the reign of King Asa.

The *initials* form one of the names of our Lord

SCRIPTURE ENIGMA, No. 75.

1. A foreigner, of royal herdsman, head,
   His tongue to lie, his hand blood swift to shed
2. Who, when his counsel was rejected, died,
   By his own hand, victim of wounded pride.
3. Who ruled, when captive Judah left their land
   The remnant poor and died by treacherous hand.
4. A seer, dissuading Israel (not in vain)
   In bonds their captive brethren to retain.
5. Who, drunken, dared a warrior chief provoke
   His wife averting the avenging stroke.

The word the *initials* form, an idol names,
Made signally to prove Jehovah's claim;
In prostrate shame his glory to display
While through that land reigned trouble and dismay

SCRIPTURE ENIGMA, No. 76.

1. A little plant which grows upon a wall.
2. A tree of Bashan, strong and stout and tall.
3. Those which once sheltered a sad captive race.
4. In room of briars and thorns, this shall have place.
5. In figure, said to flourish, when men fail.
6. 'Mong presents, sent with Joseph to prevail.
7. They camped by Elim's wells, its palms close by.
8. When this puts forth its leaves, lo! summer's nigh
9. 'Tis in the wilderness, from dwelling far.
10. Compared unto thy tens, these, Jacob, are.
11. By God's power flourishing when all is low.
12. A tree not known now by this name to grow.
13. The desert wild shall blossom like to this.
14. All things were perfect in this land of bliss,
15. On either side a river's brink it grew.
16. He shall resemble this, whose life's untrue.
17. Thus often, thou shall tithe thy fields and land.
18. Egyptian corn not smitten by Almighty hand

19. This tree was asked o'er other trees to reign.
20. That which once budded, when man's words were vain.
21 No Nazarite with vow might eat of these.
22 Christ saw Zaccheus, passing 'neath this tree.

> He that hath eyes to see, and heart to love,
> Will quickly guess the *initials* writ above;
> For day by day the earth repeats the same,
> And bids us laud and magnify His name.

SCRIPTURE ENIGMA, No. 77.

1. Who life and pardon for her nation won?
2. The name of noble Samuel's eldest son.
3. Who lost his two sons in a single day?
4. A king who captive led the Jews away.
5. An emperor to whom the world belonged.
6. A king who prayed and had his life prolonged.
7. Assyria's scornful messenger of pride.
8. The seer whose message all his threats defied.
9. Who curst King David as in grief he fled?
10. Who scarce believed Christ risen from the dead?
11. A man who lost, but got again his sight.
12. What Syrian had a dream from God at night?
13. Who brought on all mankind increasing woe?
14. A captain swift of foot as a young roe.
15. A mighty judge betrayed by woman's art.
16. What man did rashly with his birth-right part?
17 A noble monarch, warrior, poet, seer.
18. Who would not let King David taste his cheer?
19. A man who served the Lord in Ahab's court.
20 The place from which the finest gold was brought?
21 A faithful Archite, to King David dear.
22 Who said his wife was not his wife, through fear?
23. From whom did Jesus seven devils cast?
24. The brother Joseph kept and bound so fast.
25. Who quickly for Rebecca water drew?

26. The famous mount where stately cedars grow.
27. Who in his prisoner no evil found ;
And knew him innocent, yet left him bound?

By these *initials* you will plainly see,
To live like Christ, unselfish we must be.

SCRIPTURE ENIGMA, No. 78.

1. What good physician was Paul's loving friend?
2. A place to which, for gold, they used to send?
3. What tree did Jesus with himself compare?
4. The vale whence finest fruits the spies did bear?
5. How oft might man approach the holy place?
6. His house where God's ark rested for a space?
7. Whom did God smite because he touched the ark?
8. Who, old and wise men's counsels would not mark?
9. A holy man of God who never died?
10. Who sought his coming unto Christ to hide
11. An Israelitish king, by Zimri slain.
12. Who over Judah reigned the longest reign?
13. Whom did his son deceive when old and weak?
14. What prophet dumb became, and could not speak?
15. Who owed to woman's wise advice his fall,
His head thrown lifeless from the city wall?

If men obeyed this precept more,
There soon would be an end of war ;
For love would bid contention cease,
And give to all the nations peace.

SCRIPTURE ENIGMA, No. 79.

1. The pious mother of an eminent Christian pastor.
2. A king who records the prophecy taught him by his mother.
3. A stranger and an exile, but a faithful friend.
4. A people who dwelt in the mountains of Canaan.

5. An idol to which the heathen burnt their children in the fire.

6. The father of a bitter enemy of the Jews.

The *initials* and *finals* give the names of two prophets in Israel

SCRIPTURE ENIGMA, No. 80.

1. A woman who guarded the bodies of seven slain men.
2. A queen who was good and beautiful.
3. A Roman emperor who trembled under the reasoning of Paul.
4. A horned and untamable animal never used for sacrifice.
5. A climbing tree of rapid growth, under which the prophet Jonah once sat.
6. The name given to fierce wind mentioned in Acts.

The *initials* give that which Christ promised believers in time of trouble.

SCRIPTURE ENIGMA, No. 81.

1. Word that God alone can claim.
2. A slave who won a dearer name.
3. A holy woman raised to life.
4. A man who took a gleaner wife.
5. A feast of triumph after pain.
6. The robe that martyr myriads gain.
7. The name that "laughter" doth express.
8. A bishop charged to faithfulness.
9. A counsellor and faithful friend.
10. A thing once yours, for ever gone.
11. A name of Christ that means "the end."
12. The light from Aaron's breastplate thrown.

In these *initials* doth there lie,
The full form of the word good-by

SCRIPTURE ENIGMA, No. 82.

1. The first military captain on record.
2. One who interceded with the king for the release of the prophet Jeremiah, when he lay in the dungeon of a prison.
3. The first man who was called a Hebrew.
4. The name given by Jesus to Simon when presented by Andrew.
5. An encampment of the Israelites where were twelve wells of water, and threescore and ten palm-trees.

The *initials* form the legacy Christ left his disciples.

SCRIPTURE ENIGMA, No. 83.

1. The founder of Samaria.
2. A prophet who was imprisoned because his prediction was displeasing to the king.
3. A distinguished soldier, and one in high favor with his king, yet who was afflicted with a horrible disease.
4. A son of Saul who was murdered in his bed.
5. A base time-server, who cursed King David in his adversity, and fawned upon him in prosperity.
6. Naomi's second son.
7. The town to which Paul and Barnabas went when driven from Antioch in Pisidia.
8. A village to which the disciples were going when Jesus joined them after his resurrection.
9. One who, according to the laws of Mosaic economy, separated himself unto the Lord by a vow.
10. The disciple who, not recognizing the risen Saviour, related to him the circumstances of his own death and burial.
11. A prophet whom the Jews expected would reappear upon earth.

The *initials* form one of the incommunicable attributes of the Deity.

SCRIPTURE ENIGMA. No. 84.

1. Sweet home! from whence the feet of Jesus sped,
   With tender sympathy to raise the dead.
2. 'Twas Rezin's mighty king this city chose,
   To give Syria, driving thence her foes.
3. From out these vineyards came a lion wild,
   In angry rage, 'gainst Manoah's favor'd child.
4. Within this city's walls they mourned for shame,
   When evil tidings of Damascus came.
5. An aged patriarch, ere he closed his life,
   Bade his loved son go seek from thence a wife.
6. Oh! woe was thine, for those who dwelt in thee,
   Through Israel's sword, entered captivity.
7. This city of the Jews, in peace he trod,
   Waiting in faith the kingdom of his God.
8. There the disciples saw their risen Lord,
   And worshipped Him, though not with one accord.
9. "Go to this land," he said, "there corn to buy;
   Hasten, my sons, or we shall surely die."

> Nearing Jerusalem, to this place they came.
> (My nine *initial* letters tell its name),
> Where Jesus bade his two disciples speed,
> To loose a colt, and say, the Lord hath need;
> Thine mighty God, is all on land and sea;
> Yet wonderous love! the Lord has need of thee.

SCRIPTURE ENIGMA, No. 85.

1. A teacher of the church of Antioch who ministered to the Lord.
2. A man who is mentioned by one of the apostles as being "subject to like passions as we are."

3. A wicked man who tried to prevent Paul from converting a deputy.
4. A man of Benjamin, whose son was a choice young man and goodly.
5. The time when it is good for a man to bear the yoke.
6. One who was said to be the first fruits of Achaia unto Christ.
7. A man who wrote one of Paul's epistles.
8. A hill where David once hid.
9. One of the boundaries of King Ahasuerus' kingdom.
10. One of three women, who were fairer than any in the land.
11. A son of Amoz, who wrote a book.
12. A woman whose name signified pleasant.
13. A man who received a visit from an angel, while threshing corn.
14. One of the kings of Chaldea of the seed of the Medes.
15. A Moabitess, who married a man of the seed of the Ephrathites.
16. The name of a relation of a leader of the Jews.
17. A prophet to whom the Lord sent a vision concerning Edom.
18. One of the governors of Cæsarea.
19. One of the chief cities of the Philistines.
20. A place where the children of Israel pitched.
21. The wife of Felix.

The *initial* letters of the answers to the above questions give a Scripture exhortation of the highest importance.

SCRIPTURE ENIGMA, No. 86.

An element sometimes used as a symbol of the Holy Ghost.
The place to which he belonged who, together with Nicodemus, buried Christ.
A disciple whom Peter raised from the dead.
The father of Achan.
A river by the banks of which Daniel saw a vision

An inspired herdman.

A prophetess who endeavored to intimidate Nehemiah when engaged in rebuilding the well of Jerusalem.

One who stirred up a revolt against Paul at Ephesus.

One who, for his godly zeal, had conferred upon him and his posterity an everlasting priesthood.

A king of Syria who drove the Jews from Elath.

A place of which it was proverbially said, in old time, "They shall surely ask counsel, and so end the matter."

That which is good for a man to bear in his youth.

The *initials* of the above words form a solemn admonition given by our Saviour.

SCRIPTURE ENIGMA, No. 87.

1. The son of Phineas.
2. A city in central Palestine
3. A name borne by one of the children of Anak.
4. One of the sons of Ashur.
5 An herb named by our Lord.
6. The builder of Jericho.

The *initials* and *finals* give the names of two great prophets.

SCRIPTURE ENIGMA, No. 88.

1. A doubter.
2. A proud courtier.
3. A scribe.
4. A king who remembered his mother's teachings.
5. The first judge of Israel.
6. A foolish young man.
7. A heathen king who acknowledged the power of the true God.
8. A king's son who was murdered in his bed.
9. One who tried craft to hinder a good work.
10. One who wished to entertain an angel.
11. A burden, which, when Christ's, is easy and light.
12. A selfish nephew.

SCRIPTURE ENIGMAS.

13. The assassin of one of Nebuchadnezzar's governors.
14. One who suffered for avarice and untruthfulness.
15. A man whose wife was more famous than himself.
16. A king of Assyria, at the time Pekah king of Israel.

The *initials* give a saying of the Psalmist expressing faith and joy.

SCRIPTURE ENIGMA, No. 89.

One who, when the evil deeds he subsequently committed were foretold by the prophet, was horrified at the recital.

One whose covetousness was punished with death.

One "who through faith subdued kingdoms."

A man who, when a woman threw a stone upon his head, begged his armor-bearer to slay him, that he might escape the reproach of being killed by a woman.

The city of waters.

The *initials* of the preceding words form the name of the first person on record to whom an angel appeared.

SCRIPTURE ENIGMA, No. 90.

1. To what doth God compare His holy Word?
2. What did a refuge to our race afford?
3. From whence was Paul compelled in haste to fly?
4. A city famed for cloth of choicest dye.
5. The haven where we all desire to go,
   Reserved for those who serve their Lord below.

If these *initials* side by side you place,
You find what strengthens every Christian grace;
What doth this world of pomp and sin o'ercome,
And give us power to reach our heavenly home.

SCRIPTURE ENIGMA, No. 91.

1. That to which the trial of faith is compared.
2. That by which the Lord confirmed his promise to Abraham.

3. The wages of sin.

4. He who, according to Solomon, "shall suffer hunger."

5. An emblem to which our Saviour likens the righteous

6. The mystic form in which the Saviour was seen by John in the Apocalyptic vision.

7. An animal with which Israel is unfavorably contrasted; for even the dumb beast knoweth its owner.

8. That which at the crucifixion was torn asunder, as a sign that the Mosaic economy was superseded.

9. The bird to which David compared Saul and Jonathan in his lamentations for their death.

The *initials* form a statement which fills the heart of him who realizes it with adoration and joy.

SCRIPTURE ENIGMA, No. 92.

1. The name of one connected with another—
   The eldest born of a great patriarch's brother.

2. In peace and purity her life was past,
   Till entered sin, and sorrow came at last.

3. His daughters an inheritance was given,
   Because a son had been denied by Heaven.

4. The mother of a minister of truth,
   Who knew the sacred Scriptures from his youth.

5. They failed him in the day of his distress,
   When sickness came, and none stood by to bless.

6. Faithful and true where'er the king might be.
   A stranger in a foreign land was he.

7. The thing his mother valued most he took,
   And straightway burnt, by Kidron's peaceful brook.

8. This man is known under two separate names;
   He glorified his Maker in the flames.

My *final* letters of a sovereign tell
Who lost his eyesight when Jerusalem fell;
And my *initials* form another name,
To whom, in prayer, a gracious answer came.
Both bent in patience 'neath the chastening rod
So must our wills before the will of God.

SCRIPTURE ENIGMA, No. 94.

The physician beloved by St. Paul.
The name which signifies "a prince of God."
The tree used as a figure of Christ and His people.
The place where there was twelve wells and seventy palm-trees.
The Church that ministered to St. Paul when he was in Thessalonica.
"A ready scribe in the law of Moses."
The prophet whose words were quoted by St. James, in his address to the apostles and elders at Jerusalem.
The province in which St. Paul was born.
The son of Josiah whose name was changed to Jehoiakim.
The captain of Saul's host.
The mother of Solomon.
The tribe that left the kingdom of Israel for that of Judah.
That time when it is good for a man to bear the yoke.

The *initial* letters of these names compose a precept which I obeyed, would cause "wars to cease."

SCRIPTURE ENIGMA, No 95.

1. On Lebanon, the trees of God,
    The stately cedars, grew;
  What strength supplied them as they stood,
    And made their beauties new?

  What sends the Lord of Nature forth
    In morsels from the frozen north

3. Where did the blessed Saviour rest,
   When to God's holy law
   He gave the meaning, ever blest,
   But never knew before.

4. What word will give the sacred three
   Their unity and Trinity?

5. When torn with anguish and distress,
   God's ready help we crave,
   What simple word may best express
   He is at hand to save,
   And will attend the humble prayer,
   And soothe the mourner's weary care?

The *initial* letters of these words combine,
   A great apostle's name will rise to view,
And if the *finals* we proceed to find,
   We then shall gain his chosen surname, too.

SCRIPTURE ENIGMA, No. 96.

That which Saul called David, when dissuading him from encountering Goliath.
The father of Bathsheba.
The city to which Demas went when he forsook St. Paul.
The place where Zimri "slew his master."
The father of Milcah.
The native land of Ebedmelech.
The woman who was "justified by works."
The mother of David's sixth son.
The materials of which Jabin's chariots were made.
The ruler who was beaten before Gallio's judgment-seat
The father of the man to whom Jehu displayed his zeal.
The rival of Tibni.
The child whose grandmother was his nurse,
The first word written on the wall of Belshazzar's palace.

The *initials* of these words make a sentence in one of the parables which suggests that the day of grace is not yet past.

SCRIPTURE ENIGMA, No. 97.

1. The witness-stone that kinsman raised
   On Gilead's mount on solemn day.
2. Whence came the spoilers whom the sword
   Of God and Gideon swept away?
3. A hill where outlaws spared a king,
   And foes were quickly turned to friends.
4. A warrior, whom, with change of name,
   His chieftain on employment sends.
5. Once nigh to perish; of twelve sons
   The father, and of mighty race.
6. A city whence invaders driven,
   In mourning seek Jehovah's grace.
7. Where o'er the pain the idol reared
   Its height, and martyrs God revered.
8. Unrighteous judge, degenerate child;
   Brief was the rule his sin defiled.

   Th' *initials* and the *finals* show
   A loyal friend, a traitorous foe;
   Over a royal head they strive,
   And one departeth not alive;
   The latter justly death o'ertakes,
   The former gratitude forsakes.

SCRIPTURE ENIGMA, No. 98.

1. A captain and a murderer,
   With sword he smote and perished so.
2. Foolish, while seeking to be wise,
   Tempted and tempting, wrought she woe.
3. Eye hath not seen, ear hath not heard,
   What else, but this we know "remaineth"

4. God's priest, with too compliant art,
    A king's idolatry sustaineth.

5. Prince of the sons of Simeon
    In their appointed place.

6. Title of "the Jews' enemy,"
    That marked his God cursed race.

7. A city "quiet, and secure,"
    Till swift in ruin buried.

8. A Jewess of true Christian faith,
    To Grecian husband married.

9. Where the angels of God a wanderer met,
    Like a guardian camp around him set.

Th' *initials* and the *finals* show
    Two cities great and small;
    The first a kingdom's capital,
Rich with all beauty, bright with history's glow;
The second honored more, in power less,
Little, yet not the least, royal in humbleness.

SCRIPTURE ENIGMA, No. 99.

1. The first country visited by St. Paul after his conversion
2. Saul's eldest daughter.
3. A judge of Israel during eight years.
4. A town of Crete, by which St. Paul passed.
5. The possession of the children of Lot.

The *initials* and the *finals* give the names of two captains alike in birth and service, alike in their end.

SCRIPTURE ENIGMA, No. 100.

The city where Amaziah was slain.
The country which was a general resort in time of famine.
The rival of Omri.
The word which signifies "Thou art weighed in the balances and art found wanting."

The man who is emphatically called "the Jews' enemy."
The prophet who foretold the death of Ahab and Jezebel.
The mother whose love for her children, when they were dead, is without earthly parallel.
Sennacherib's successor.
The man whom God appointed to utter destruction.
The king of Moab whom Israel served eighteen years.
The tribe which was set apart to bear the ark of the covenant.
The prophet who foretold the discomfiture of Sennacherib.
The mountain where Saul was slain.
The father of the prophet Jehu.
The king of Assyria who distressed Ahaz.

The *initial* letters of these names form a command which illustrates in the most sublime manner the power of God.

SCRIPTURE ENIGMA, No. 101.

The man who brought David before Saul with Goliath's head in his hand.
The disciple whose surname was Thaddeus.
The city where St. Paul was when the inhabitants attempted to worship him.
The King of Heshbon.
The man who said, "I will not eat till I have told mine errand"
The first born son of Seth.
The place where the spies were sent.
Absalom's daughter.
The woman who "lent her child to the Lord."
The prophet who was told to anoint Hazael king.
The band to which Cornelius belonged.
"The city of waters."
The country to which Jehoshaphat attempted to send ships for gold.

The place where Jonathan found honey.
The city where the angel appeared to the Virgin Mary.

The *initial* letters of these words show the universal selfishness of human nature.

SCRIPTURE ENIGMA, No. 102.

That which is the Christian's reproach and yet his glory.

That which is a burden to be carried, and yet as wings to bear him along.

That which upon his forehead, is either the badge of Christ's soldier, or the brand of the deserter-may be discovered by the last letters of the following words:

1. One who digged again the wells of his father, which the enemy had stopped.
2. The mountain in which Esau dwelt.
3. A King of Egypt whose name consists of two letters.
4. The head of a household baptized by St. Paul.
5. The name of the Apostle who took the place of the traitor Judas.

SCRIPTURE ENIGMA, No. 103.

1. First name a woman whose heroic faith
   Saved all his kindred from impending death.
2. A proposition next proceed to find,
   Two words of gracious invitation joined.
3. Who judged God's people three-and-twenty years?
4. Who Abraham's brother's first born son appears?

   The *final* letters form the name of one
   Who was that first heroic woman's son.
   The *initials* give his name (his willing bride)
   Who was to her near kinsman first allied.
   Both bride and mother came of heathen race.
   Yet both were honored with special grace.

From them not kings alone may trace their birth,
But one far greater than the kings of earth.
When God vouchsafed to take our mortal frame,
Him as their child may both these woman claim.

SCRIPTURE ENIGMA, No. 104.

Into what "parts" was Jesus led,
What time he had four thousand fed?

And what was Paul, by birth, that he
Should be from bonds and scourges free?

What epithet was once applied
To him who Israel's host defied.

To Dura's plain the grandees go,
Their seventh high rank and title show.

Through what was Christ, Pilate led,
"Denied" and "killed" as Peter said?

Who is that king who gave the word,
That he had from his mother heard?

Jezreel and Lo-ruhamah—tell
Their young brother's name as well.

What "King of Kings" of mighty fame
To Ezra wrote? Take half his name.

With care and diligence combined,
An answer to each question find.

Write down each name of subject next,
And prove it from the sacred text.

The first and final letters scanned,
Behold! two names conjunctive stand.

One was a Jewess, one her lord,
Who heard a Roman prisoner's word.

He said, though trembling, "Go thy way;
I'll hear thee more another day."

Like him, alas! too many hear,
But their obedient faith defer.

SCRIPTURE ENIGMA, No. 105.

When Ruth had gleaned the field all day,
She threshed and bore my first away
To where the good Naomi dwelt,
And eased the care the master felt.

When Barek fought and Sisera fled,
My second came into his head;
By Jael forcibly suggested,
And Deborah's song the deed attested.

When Paul was in Damascus kept,
My third conveyed him while they slept,
That so he might escape their hand,
And safely reach his fatherland.

Divide in halves these terms rehearsed,
And of their sections take the first;
Then with due care combine the same,
And you shall find a good man's name.

With Paul at Lystra see him now—
They hail him Jupiter! and bow;
But soon they drive, with changed opinion,
The apostles forth from their dominion.

SCRIPTURE ENIGMA, No. 106.

Go to the land of Uz; that tried one see;
Ask for his second daughter—lo! 'tis she.

Go to that mighty man, the third of three;
Ask for the Hararite—behold! 'tis he.

> Go to Shusham, a proud man's sons there be;
> Ask for the second, and behold! 'tis he.
>
> Go to your tent; the childless patriarch see;
> Ask for his steward, and behold! 'tis he.
>
> Go to Jerusalem; David's children see;
> Ask for Bathshua's eldest—lo! 'tis he.
>
> Go down where Moses and his people be;
> Ask for the son of Raguel—lo! 'tis he.

The *initials* down, the *finals* upward trace,
And lo! the scene of Israel's dire disgrace.

> God said, "Go up, possess the land!"
> But they drew back from his command.

There they rebelled. Through unbelief they fell.
If we their said example shun, 'tis well;

> We too are called a rest to win,
> But only faith shall enter in.

SCRIPTURE ENIGMA, No. 107.

The father of Shimei.
The man who took Kirjath-Sepher.
The wife who delivered her husband into the hands of his enemies.
A servant in the house of John surnamed Mark.
The only one of our great religious festivals that is mentioned in the Bible.
The name of the palace of Artaxerxes.
The place to which Paul and Barnabas came when they were expelled from Antioch in Pisidia.
The wilderness between Elim and Sinai.
The birth place of St. Paul.
The man who in the most ungodly age of the world prophesied of the coming of the Lord with all his Saints.
An impostor who collected 400 followers, but was eventually slain.

The place which was built seven years before Zoan.

The place "whose merchants" were princes and "whose traffickers" were "the honorable of the earth."

The king of Judah who broke the brazen serpent in pieces

The tribe to which Joshua belonged.

The man to whom Michal was given when Saul took her from David.

A mother who taught her son deceit.

The governor of Ahab's house.

The king of Judah who was struck with leprosy

A mother in Israel.

The *initials* of these names or words form a statement, showing us God's estimation of a sin the world thinks lightly of.

SCRIPTURE ENIGMA, No. 108.

Three prophets' names suggest,
Whose minor rank their words attest,
With brevity expressed.

The first his vision told
Of Nineveh, renowned of old,
To wrath and vengeance sold.

With long foretokened gloom,
The second published Esau's doom,
Whom Joseph should consume.

In Jotham's days the third,
To Salem brought Jehovah's word,
And all Samaria heard.

Divide each several name,
And the first syllables proclaim,
A widowed matron's fame.

From Bethlehem's fertile plain,
She did a pilgrim's toil sustain,
Then flourished there again.

SCRIPTURE ENIGMA, No. 109.

A people who wept through unbelief in God's power to deliver
A place where came destroying fire:
Another name for prophet.
The name of one to whom a certain leader said, "Thou mayest be to us instead of eyes."
A handsome but rebellious young man.
One who heard the gospel by a river-side.
An Evangelist who travelled with the Apostle St. Paul.
A place where lived one who forgot all care when listening to words of Jesus.
A valley around which Paul and his army gathered for battle
What is better than rubies?
The name of one who saw wonderful visions by a river-side.
A son of Jacob and Leah.
The father of Noah.
Who journeyed far, carrying gifts to an infant?
The youth who nearly perished when cast out into the wilderness.
A mountain of Palestine.
Another mountain where God gave the Law to Moses.
The city of a woman who sold "purple."
One of the sons of Eli.
An ancient river whose name means "good and abounding
A woman who tended sheep.
A patriarch who was deceived by his own son.
One afflicted through life for deceit and lying.
A king who watched a sun-dial with great anxiety.
A city over which Hiram once reigned.
A man of Bethlehem, Judah, who went to sojourn in Moab in times of famine.
A prophet who proclaimed the doom of Edom.
A sacred emblem worn by Aaron.
A word of gladness in the song of the redeemed.

The *initials* of these words give a truth known to those who place their trust in Christian righteousness

SCRIPTURE ENIGMA, No. 110.

Name the awful mystery worn
By the priest on holy morn.

Who delighted in the Lord
When she proved how true his word?

Whose whole family was blest
When he took the ark in rest?

By what river dreamed the seer
Scenes of many a distant year?

On what sea though lacking rest,
Jesus walked, God manifest?

Where the deadly angel stayed?
Who a mighty man betrayed?

Whom did Peter doom to death?
Name the son of righteous Seth?

Seek the town his cousin built?
Who the blood of thousands spilt?

Who through Peter lived once more?
With the poor she lived before?

Name the land of Reuel's well!
And the vale where Giant fell?

A truth lies here that we must prove
Like the poor outcast—may it be in love

SCRIPTURE ENIGMA, No. 111

The people to whom Joseph was sold.
Jesse's second son.
The mother of Asa.
The place where the wise woman lived who interceded with David for Absalom.
The prophet whose writings contain these words, " The just shall live by his faith."

SCRIPTURE ENIGMAS.

The counsellor who forsook David for Absalom.
The city where Lydia lived.
One of Saul's sons "who reigned for two dire years over Israel."
The place to which Abiathar was banished by Solomon.
The prophet whose words the Angel Gabriel quoted in his interview with Zacharias.

The *initials* of the above words give the Divine name as declared in the words from heaven.

SCRIPTURE ENIGMA, No. 112.

Where first did David seek his promised crown?
Who won his wife by capturing a town?
Where fled a man before his brother's threat?
Who in a desert land three monarchs met?
Who seeking Canaan died upon the way?
Who killed his master that in sickness lay?
Name where an exiled king in sorrow trod,
Whose son in cunning service wrought from God?
What prince was slain at noon upon his bed?
Say at whose threshing floor a priest fell dead.
Where first did Israel eat of Canaan's corn?
What son to Boaz was in gladness born?
Who sought to turn Paul's teaching into scorn?

Learn with the Psalmist, from whose words we borrow
To serve the Lord and trust him for the morrow.

SCRIPTURE ENIGMA, No. 113.

An Edomite who was an adversary to Solomon.
The birthplace of Apollos.
The city which St. Paul said he "must see."
The plain where the golden image was set up.
The valley where David slew Goliath.
Jeroboam's successor.

The prophet that was honored by being left out of Adonijah's counsels.

The prophet who forbade the children of Israel to make slaves of their brethren.

St. Paul's secretary when he wrote to the Romans.

A word which is typical of dominion.

The sixth son of Jesse.

The man whom David killed with the sword of the children of Ammon.

The place where Amalek first fought with Israel.

Manasseh's mother.

The word which signifies "be opened."

The woman given to Joseph to wife.

The woman commended in the New Testament, both for faith and works.

The Ephesian in whose school St. Paul disputed.

The people who carried off Job's oxen and asses.

Now take the *initials*, and you have my whole.

SCRIPTURE ENIGMA, No. 114.

1. What prophet, sent by God's own voice,
   Forced on a king a dreadful choice?

2. The place by Jacob Bethel named—
   For evil afterwards so famed.

3. A righteous man who feared the Lord,
   And saved his prophets from the sword.

4. A king of Syria, Judah's bane,
   And by Tiglath-Pileser slain.

5. How oft did Jephthah's friends bemoan,
   The vow that made his daughter lone?

6. A place where Jephthah's dwelt,
   And Pharaoh's powerful sway was felt.

7. A house that God profusely blest,
   Because his ark in it did rest.

SCRIPTURE ENIGMAS

8. What city did King Asa found,
   When he razed Ramah to the ground?

9. A house by Paul beloved, whose head,
   As far as we can tell, was dead.

10. A nurse who after death was laid,
    Beneath a mighty oak-tree's shade.

    In these *initials* you may find
    What's due to God from all mankind.

The *initials* of the above names (or words) form a caution given to the Jewish nation by David and repeated by St. Paul.

SCRIPTURE ENIGMA, No. 115.

An Easter Acrostic.

The first of men who made and tasted **wine**.
He foretold the fall of Edom's line.
That which is due to none but God alone.
A judge, of whom but little now is known.

The place o'er which an ancient priest was **king**.
A town that oft Jesu's words did ring.
A prophet at the time of the return.
People from whom God told the Jews to learn.

A Gittite chieftain of King David's host.
Assyria's king, so fond of foolish boast.
An Ammonite who greatly vexed the **Jews**.
The place where Joshua Amalek subdues.

A son of Saul most treacherously slain.
A Seer who prayed for thunderings and **rain**.
The "stone of help" that Samuel once set **up**.
The man who handed Artaxerxes' cup.

A man who trembled at the words he heard.
The place where Samuel dwelt and was interred.

King Elah's chief who reigned a wicked reign.
A priest of Baal in his temple slain.

An orator who once accused Paul.
An envious man who compassed his own fall.
A man who rescue from a prophet sought.
A place from which the prophet he was brought.
An altar which at Shalem Jacob made.
A man who stole and dearly for it paid.
He who tries hard in sin to snare the soul.

SCRIPTURE ENIGMA, No. 116.

"An eloquent man, and mighty in the Scriptures."
A woman of Athens who believed St. Paul's preaching.
The god of the Philistines.
The governor of the west of the Euphrates.
The man whose threshing-floor was the site of the Temple
A manufacture imported by Solomon from Europe.
The prophet who foretold the destruction of Edom.
Job's native land.
One of the wells that Isaac's servants dug in Zeror.
The successor of Felix.
A "fellow soldier" of St. Paul.
A giant slain by Abishai.
The name of the tenth month.
The mother of Adonijah.
A type of the house of Israel.
The land that was made desolate as a punishment for rejoicing at the desolation of Israel.
The father of Hobab.
A king of Hamoth who sent presents to David.
A king of Judah in whose reign there was an earthquake.
The descendants of Esau.

The *initials* of the above names (or words) form a receipt which shows us that "faith without work is dead."

SCRIPTURE ENIGMA, No. 117.

1. Who through faith had sight restored?
2. Who through scorn lost sight deplored?
3. Seek from whence an angel went.
   Warning Israel to repent.
4. Where did sudden waters play?
5. Where did waters heaped, delay?
6. Where was once an image raised,
   Which a mighty nation praised.
7. Who to Gerar went for food?
8. Who a sinning king withstood?
9. Who, when bribed, refused his aid.
10. Who the temple vessels made?
11. What Moabite ruled Israel?
12. Where did Paul a cripple heal?
13. Who in camp received a crown?
14. Name Elkanah's native town.
15. Where did one, a Syrian king,
    Vainly send a seer to bring?

    Find the *initials* and they will recall
    The lessons of the mercies given to all.

SCRIPTURE ENIGMA, No. 118.

1. Where in the Temple, with sad delay,
   Did the Lord's glory in departing stay?
2. Whose wicked scheme against a captive race,
   Procured his death of terrible disgrace?
3. Name from what prophet Paul essayed to prove,
   That God would call the Gentiles in his love?
4. Who through his wife, by Matthew is embraced
   Among the names by which Christ's birth is traced
5. Who would have killed the Baptist in her spite?
6. Who wished to slay a sleeping king by night?
7. Who through his land the pilgrim host forbade?
8. Then say what Micah with ephod made?

9. What power did Peter say came not of man
10. What warlike king the Temple did profane?
11. Whose merchants were called princes by the seer?
In burning words they were too proud to fear.
12. What place remembered with a ghastly name,
Is linked for ever with a deed of shame?
13. From whence did Machir much provisions bring
To cheer the heart of his desponding king?
14. Upon what mountain did an altar rise,
To burn a large and varied sacrifice?

The *initials* and *finals* discovered will prove a fond recognition of measureless love.

SCRIPTURE ENIGMA, No. 119.

The man who was full of the "spirit of wisdom."
The city which worshipped Baalzebub.
One of the five kings of Midian who was slain in consequence of the idolatry of Baal-peor.
A country famed for its wisdom.
The man to whom David showed kindness for Jonathan's sake.
The ruler of the half tribe of Manasseh in the reign of David.
The emblem of industry.
The place where Israel defeated Arad the Canaanite.

The *initials* of the above names (or words) give the name of a prophet who was also a priest; the *finals* the name of the city where he dwelt.

SCRIPTURE ENIGMA, No. 120.

1. One who received the blessed gift of sight
   From Him who came to be the world's true light.

2. What priest of God with all his sons were slain
   The favor of a tyrant king to gain?

3. What people did their fathers' law obey,
   From ancient times until the prophet's day?
4. To what great city was a prophet sent,
   Whose people with contrite grief repent?
5. Whence came that mighty host, by angels slain,
   To prove that God o'er all the earth doth reign?
6. What beauteous sign was placed the earth above,
   Emblem of God's sure truth and love?
7. To what lone land did holy Paul retreat,
   To make himself by his high office meet?
8. What monarch o'er a mighty realm had sway,
   And bore the tribes of Israel far away?

If the initials side by side you place,
You'll find the name of one renowned for grace.
His name, the comfort that he brought, will show,
To those that were in trouble and in woe.
He gladly gave up all that he possessed,
To aid the church of Christ, when sore distressed.
He was among the first of those who bore
The gospel light to many a heathen shore.
Oh! may we imitate his works of love,
And share with him in glorious joys above.

SCRIPTURE ENIGMA, No. 121.

Rebekah's nurse.
A river of Damascus.
The priest of Baal in the reign of Athaliah.
A friend of St. Paul who was a tentmaker.
The father of Boaz.
The messenger who was despatched to David with tidings of Absalom's death.
An Israelite who lost his life on a day of great national rejoicing.
The name which means "princess."

The *initials* of the above words form the name of the city in whose outskirts occured the most wonderful consecration on record; the *finals* give the Jewish name of Shachach.

SCRIPTURE ENIGMA, No. 122.

1. A holy woman famed for works of love.
2. The saint who was first called to heaven above.
3. Who led a king his fearful love to see?
4. Who from his childhood home was forced to flee?
5. From whence with mighty signs was Israel brought?
6. What king was by his mother's wisdom taught?

> In the *initials* you may trace,
> A noble youth, who, by God's grace,
> Was not ashamed his faith to own,
> Before a heathen tyrant's throne.

SCRIPTURE ENIGMA, No. 123.

1. The most liberal contributor to the treasury of God.
2. Jesse's second son.
3. The place where God appeared to Samuel.
4. Queen Esther's other name.
5. The people who burned Ziklag with fire.
6. The sister of Tubal Cain.
7. The first city in which St. Paul preached Christ.
8. The king of whom Ahab said " he is my brother."
9. The city where Tyrannus lived.
10. The place where Nabal sheared his sheep.
11. St. Paul's hostess at Philippi.
12. Hagar's native land.
13. The prince who raised a monument to his own memory
14. The idol in whose temple Sennacherib was slain.

The *initial* letters of these words show the remedy prescribed to a great captain who was suffering under a malady that only God could cure.

SCRIPTURE ENIGMA, No. 124.

1. The great apostle of the Gentile race?
2. The first man who in heaven found a place?
3. A youthful Christian in God's law well read?
5. The Lord's peculiar people by him led?
5. One who his birthright for a trifle sold?
6. An Israelite, indeed—one of Christ's fold?
7. The promised land with milk and honey blest?
8. A younger son by God beloved best?

The *initial* letters take and you will find,
One virtue of the lowly Christian mind.

SCRIPTURE ENIGMA, No. 125.

1. A wanderer guilty of his brother's blood?
2. The father of the seer who saw the flood?
3. 4. Cain's mother next, and then her husband take,
5. Then one who mourned in heart for Zion's sake,
6. A king whose sinning caused his early fall,
7. And one who toiled with the Apostle Paul.
8. Who wrote the long epistle unto Rome?
9. What hill did hunted David make his home?
10. What prophet pleaded for the captive race?
11. What priest made altars for his monarch base?
12. Who vainly sought to know an angel's name?
13. What altar knew no sacrificial flame?
14. Who left a prisoner bound to please the Jews?
15. What king did the council of the wise refuse?
16. What city, famed, to Joseph gave a wife?
17. What king, defeated, took a prince's life?
18. Who smiled contemptuous at an angel's word?
19. Whose bitter rage was calmed with flocks and herds?
20. What pagan prince was God's anointed named?
21. Whose family for temperance was famed?
22. What well did Isaac yield to those who strove?
23. Who would his faith by actual vision prove?

CURIOSITIES OF THE BIBLE

24. From whom did Paul to Cæsar's court appeal?
25. What soldier did the thing accursed steal?
26. Who sinned in fearing lest the ark should fall?
27. What man did Jesus from the grave recall?
28. Who vainly did the Apostle Paul accuse?
29. What seer a king's entreaty did refuse?

    Range these *initials*, and in all thy need,
    Remember still this searching prayer to plead.

SCRIPTURE ENIGMA, No. 126.

1. The name of David's second son disclosed,
   A name a prophet afterward did bear.
2. Where was the son of Zedekiah killed?
3. Whose son was in the temple long concealed?
4. Where did a woman once two men bestow?
5. A priestly city Doeg filled with woe?
6. Name from what giant David once was saved,
7. And one whom none but he before had braved.
8. What seer did Asa into prison cast?
   Who told of wars throughout his life to last?
9. Where did a judge's son though conquering meet
   The death that did his shameful life befit?
10. Who grieved, though could not leave her widowed home?
11. Where did the legion-hunted maniac roam?
12. Who to a trembling monarch sold his land,
    While both beheld an angel near them stand?
13. Whence did a prophet lead a blinded band?

    Learn the injunction which these *initials* give
    And in their strict observance seek to live.

SCRIPTURE ENIGMA, No. 127.

1. He, loving rest, a double burden fears.
2. God's chief delight when He creation rears.
3. Him, in his blind old age, his son deceived.
4. They charge of God's most Holy things received.

SCRIPTURE ENIGMAS.

5. The place where weapon small great carnage makes
6. He, branded for his sin, God's presence fled.
7. Who hid and fed the prophets in a cave?
8. He who his blessing unto Abraham gave.
9. God's priest, yet his house could not command.
10. Whose counsel did his father's friend withstand?
11. A city overthrown for wicked deeds.
12 Once and again great tidings speeds!
13. The glory gone, the ark the Gentiles prize.
14. Where, Moses sees the goodly land and dies?

The *initials* manifest his promise dear,
Who ever lives our waiting hearts to cheer.

SCRIPTURE ENIGMA, No. 128.

1. A town where Peter performed a miracle, and afterwards saw a vision, the object of which was to teach him that he must preach the gospel to the Gentiles as well as to the Jews.
2. Naomi's husband.
3. David's fifth son.
4. A king who served God during the early part of his reign, which was consequently prosperous, but who, becoming self-confident, fell into error and was severely punished.
5. An Amanuensis to St. Paul, and one whose house was said to have been the first fruits of Achaia.
6. One of the names of Christ.
7. David's eldest brother.
8. The birthplace of Rachel.
9. The father of Abraham.

The *initials* of the above names give an incident in the life of
  Christ which marks more impressively, perhaps, than any
  other, his perfect humanity.

SCRIPTURE ENIGMA, No. 129.

1. The king to whom a prophet said "Set thine house in order, for thou shalt die, and not live."
2. A priest whose city name consisted of two letters.

3. One of the two cities which the Hebrews built for Pharoah.
4. Noah's godly ancestors.
5. A city which formed part of the first kingdom on record

The *initials* give the mount on which was the rock typical of Christ.

SCRIPTURE ENIGMA, No. 130.

1. The name of one of whom it was said "as thy days, so shall thy strength be."
2. Moses' eldest son.
3. A man of the tribe of Dan, who was one of the twelve spies sent out by Moses to see and report on the land of Canaan.
4. One who prophesied of Christ in the words "There shall come a star out of Jacob, and a spectre shall arise out of Israel."
5. The birthplace of Haran, Lot's father.
6. A King of Egypt who made war upon Judah, in the reign of Rehoboam.

The *initials* of the above names give one of the New Testament prophets.

SCRIPTURE ENIGMA, No. 131.

1. From whence did Israel precious metal bring?
2. Of what sweet tree did ancient prophets sing?
3. A holy seer who wondrous visions saw.
4. Whose children did obey their father's law?
5. What wicked man did take his brother's life?
6. Who took a city to obtain a wife?
7. Seven of this name are found in holy writ.
8. The land which Israel once in haste did quit.
9. Who uttered forth a deep and bitter cry?
10. Whose son was sent the promised land to spy?

11. What aged saint with deepest grief opprest,
    Saw not that all was ordered for the best?
12. Who when on earth, his sufferings meekly bore,
13. Then, led by angels, up to heaven did soar?
14. Who with a stone did once a conqueror slay?
15. Who sent his daughters from their home away?
16. What merchant city once was rich and great,
    But through it's sins was brought to low estate?
17. The mount from whence the blessing did proceed.
18. Who succored prophets in their greatest need?
19. The bird that sat on Babel's ruined towers.
20. A youth who served his God with all his powers.
    In the *initials* of these names combined,
    A heavenly receipt you will clearly find;
    Which if we humbly from our hearts obey,
    Will make us victors in the heavenly way.

SCRIPTURE ENIGMA, No. 132.

1. The name which Jacob gave to Luz, in memory of the Lord's appearing to him when he fled from Esau.
2. The wife of Moses.
3. A woman noted for her affection to her mother-in-law.
4. A man remarkable for his swiftness of foot,

The *initials* give the name of a priest and ready scribe.

SCRIPTURE ENIGMA, No. 133.

1. "Woe unto thee!" 'twas thus the Saviour spake,
   And named two cities; we the first one take.

2. Here the disciples Jesus' love rehears'd,
   Here it was men called them Christian first.

3. A church which had not yet the faith denied.
   But sheltered those who to serve Satan tried.

4. Tell whilst Apollos was to Corinth brought,
   In what great city Paul the Apostle taught.

5. To what famed place did Paul a prisoner come
   And dwelt two years in his own hired house.
6. Here men were pardoned when they turned to God.
   And this displeased a prophet of the Lord.
7. A place where heathen superstition trod,
   Where was an altar to the unknown God.
8. His land who could alike in good or ill,
   In health or sickness, " bless his Maker " still
9. Four hundred shekels was the price he paid,
   And in this cave the patriarchs wife was laid.

    The city's name in these *initials* given
    Was once exalted ; as it seemed to heaven :
    But from its blest estate through sin it fell,
    And grace despised brought it down to hell.

SCRIPTURE ENIGMA, No. 134.

1. Three of the seven churches, deserts now,
   By man forsaken and by God laid low.
2. The ruler whom our Saviour taught by night,
   Because he feared to come when day was bright.
3. The man who ministered to Paul in need.
4. A youth who proved a man of God indeed.
5. Easy to bear if by our Saviour given.
6. The mount whence Christ ascended unto heaven.
7. That which in every christian home should reign.
8. The blessed name our Saviour died to gain.
9. The wife whose prayer a child from heaven brought
10. The Judge who watched her lips with evil thought.
11. A singer of sweet songs in David's time.
12. A place where refuge might be found for crime.
13. A lake enclosed by scenery sublime.
14. A pool where healing gifts were said to dwell.
15. A man who from an upper window fell.
16. An ancient town for commerce greatly famed.

17. The last who king of Syria was named.
18. A man who saved one hundred holy lives.
19. Then he who foremost in the battle strives.
20. Because his wife was deemed divinely fair.
21. The place which sheltered Jonathan's lame heir.
22 A queen who saved her race from death and shame
23. A King who from our Saviour's parents came.

    The *initial* letters of each name will show,
    Dear words of comfort breathed by Christ below.

SCRIPTURE ENIGMA, No. 135.

Oh listen! listen to those pleading tones :
Two sorrowing mothers mourn their little ones
Yet let us check the sympathetic sigh,
Their errand glorious, and their mission high ;
Unerring wisdom marks the way they take,
And joy and praise in thousand hearts awake.
They die ; but at their death a nation lives,
And peace and plenty the great Giver gives.

SCRIPTURE ENIGMA, No. 136

    Not within and not without ;
      Yet it could content
    One who sought to know about
      News to sinners sent.

    Ah, beware! The place is not
      A proper seat for all.
    Few are safe in such a spot ;
      One, alas ! did fall.

SCRIPTURE ENIGMA, No. 137.

Oh skilful the workers, oh mournful the day,
When within its recesses they hid him away,
So gracious, so noble, the pride of the State,
Their friend and their patron, the good and the great.

Oh wondrous the moment when forth from the land
They bore it, fulfilling the solemn command;
Still truly remembering the vows of the past,
And keeping the long-cherished promise at last.

Oh great the rejoicing when, after long years,
Its treasure unfolded still changeless appears;
Unfolded awhile, then for ever concealed
Till the day when the secrets of all are revealed.

SCRIPTURE ENIGMA, No. 138.

It is a word I love to hear,
   Though not of English birth :
A gentle word that fitly falls
   From hapless sons of earth—
From patient souls that seek and love
The help which cometh from above.

No plainer words, no simpler words,
   To baby lips belong ;
For turn this way, or turn it that.
   You cannot turn it wrong ;
And yet the holiest lips were heard
To utter first this simple word ;

Two letters make this simple word ;
   But oh ! how much they mean ;
They touch our earth, they soar to heaven
   They span the gulf between ;
And when its mission here is o'er,
This word shall reach the further shore.

SCRIPTURE ENIGMA, No. 139.

1. "A son and shield," is God the Lord, the sons of Korah chanted,
And they record his two great gifts, to all the upright granted ·
What these shall be you soon may see by noting this suggestion:—
First to obtain an answer plain to every following question:

I.

1. What Christian virtue stands the sixth in one of Peter's letters?
2. And who are they that scarcely saved one till to mercy debtors?
3. And how are hope and faith described in Christ securely resting?
4. And how does John describe the same God's faithfulness attesting?
5. And what God's sovereign purpose is that full determination?
That make the greater serve the less and bring the Saint salvation?
The *initials* show—in one short row, for all the answers quoted—
The eternal source and steadfast course of man's redemption noted.

II.

1. Then what is godliness combined with thankful moderation ?
2. And what surpasses hope and faith in absolute duration?
3. What name of Jesus tells the end of earth's completed story?
4. Tell the reward of troubled Saints when Christ appears in glory?
5. And what are all the promises to each believer spoken
6. When Christ himself is made of these the earnest and the token?

The *initials* quote and these denote the Saints' full joy and blessings ;
When Christ appears, their toils and tears in endless life redressing.

SCRIPTURE ENIGMA, No. 140.

The man from whose instruction St. Luke wrote.
The place where Miriam was smitten with leprosy.
The word that signifies, "be opened."
A mighty hunter before the Lord.
The man that went out to meditate at Eventide.
Moses' eldest son.
The third river of the Garden of Eden.
The city where St. Paul left his cloak.
The place where Nathanael came.
The man who helped Ahab to seek pasture for his cattle.
Hezekiah's successor.
The place near Salem where John baptized.
The fellow-laborer to whom St. Paul said, " Let no man despise thy youth."
The father of Lot.
The *initials* suggest a solemn warning.

SCRIPTURE ENIGMA No. 141.

1. What Priest his son-in-law did keep,
   To watch and tend his fleecy sheep ?
2. Who for a relatives resort,
   Prepared the temple's sacred court?
3. What servant did a King endow,
   With riches his esteem to show ?
4. First named of two who prophesied,
   While Joshua to prevent them tried?
5. What name a water-fount received
   When an angel human grief revealed?
6. Who gladdened with a child a wife,
   And raised that child, when dead, to life ?

SCRIPTURE ENIGMAS

7. Who had a son who God did save,
   While many found a watery grave?

   Once in Samaria's lovely land,
   In peace and quietude they trod
   And dwelt a holy prophet band,
   The servants of the living God.
   But soon the Queen resolved in hate,
   Nor headed all their deep distress,
   These prophets to exterminate,
   Unmindful of their faithfulness.
   But ere the wicked earthborn plan
   Its author satisfaction gave,
   The Lord designed a godly man
   His persecuted ones should save.

   The King's chief governor kindly led,
   And hid them in a hollow rock,
   And there with bread and water fed
   The Lord's preserved and faithful flock.
   In *initials* you may read
   The queens unhallowed name;
   The *finals* show the men whose deed
   Will live in long recorded fame.

SCRIPTURE ENIGMA, No. 142.

1. Whose house gave refuge to a sacred thing,
   While Israel mourned and never murmured for a king?

2. There with the poor, the leprous, and the vile,
   Was found our Lord's last earthly domicile.

3. This they broke up, to let the sick man through,
   And try what he, the sinners friend could do.

4. Seven Persian princes—this the third—had place
   Next to the monarch, and beheld his face.

5. Daughter of Israel, weep! thy Priests are slain
   He and his brother love the ark in vain!

6. Say, on what mount did all mankind combine
   In solemn sacrifice and songs divine?

7. There on that hill-top, see the patriarch stand ;
   The victim bound by his obedient hand.

First the *initials* then the finals quote,
And therein two acrostics will denote
Who found imputed righteouness, and how
Then go and follow his example now.

SCRIPTURE ENIGMA, No. 143.

1. From Paul they parted, ere their work was done;
   But mark the cause of strife was MARY'S SON.

2. Yes, but persuasion had the bait so gilded,
   That, just for once she looked admired and yielded

3. Of Judah's tribe Ahumai's *brother* see,
   But once inscribed in Shabals pedigree.

4. Some of *her* house conveyed to Paul sad tidings,
   Of the Corinthian's schisms and party tidings.

5. *Thy* daughter love him whom his servants slew
   But quickly was the treasure punished too.

6. What single sign is that, both ways the same
   What ofttimes stand for God's most glorious name

The initials down, the finals up,
    Reveal a Name
    Of wondrous fame,
Of one who hold the Priestly cup
And breaks the bread and pours the wine

And gives the benison divine
And lo! a royal diadem
    Encircles now
    His lofty brow
With glory from the God of Shem

SCRIPTURE ENIGMA, No. 144.

The city in the siege of which Uriah the Hittite was killed?
The place where Baal-zebub was worshipped?
The metropolis of Ahab?
The city built by Solomon in the wilderness?
The Father of twelve princes?
The invader from whom Saul delivered Jabesh Gilead?
The place to which Jonah thought to flee?
The rebuilder of Jericho?
The man who rescued Jeremiah from the dungeon?
The author of the last chapter of Proverbs?
The mountain ascended by David when he fled from Absalom?
The mother of Armoni and Mephibosheth?
The birth place of Abraham's steward?

The initials will give a receipt of Consolation.

SCRIPTURE ENIGMA, No. 145.

1. 'Tis the loving friend of David who prepared,
   Stone and timber for the temple ready squared.

2. 'Tis the brother of a Priest, whose hasty touch,
   Cost him his life, and grieved King David much.

3. 'Tis the King of Eglon hiding in a cave,
   Where he quickly found his ruin and his grave.

4. 'Tis his threshing floor that once became the scene,
   Of such mourning as in Canaan had not been.

5. 'Tis she that with the Mary's stood amazed,
   When into the empty sepulchre they gazed.

6. 'Tis Eliakim's grandson in the line
   Of a King whose last descendants were divine.

7. 'Tis the fifth of those great chamberlains that stood,
   To fulfil what e'er the Persian King thought good.

8. 'Tis the chamberlain who did the maidens bring,
   In their order, to the presence of the king.

When you these correctly frame,
The *initials* spell her name,
Whose rare beauty won her fame,
Which her station could not claim.
What though Persia's royal dame
Was in anger put to shame;
And in virtue of the same,
She a mighty queen became.

And her cousin's name as well,
Who did near the palace dwell,
Then the *final* letters spell
And the royal records tell,
How he did the treason quell ;
And the changes that befell
When his adversary fell,
Who with pride and wrath did swell.

SCRIPTURE ENIGMA, No. 146.

1. Four giant chiefs whom David's warriors slew
   Dwelt in one city bring its name to view.

2. Last of eight officers in David's court,
   One the chief ruler stood—his name report.

3. Second of twelve who furnished a kings table,
   Tell me his fathers name if thou art able.

4. When three old sages failed to answer one,
   This youth adventured, and the task was done

5. An oak, a wine press, and an angels visit,
   An altar, and a grave—behold! where is it?

6. Think of a Levite chief consumed by fire
   'f his next Brother' half require.

The *initials* downward, make his well known name.
Whose steadfast faith and dauntless courage claim
To be by all remembered evermore:
His sword Israel put mighty foes to shame,
His victories still Jehovah's power proclaim,
Who still defend his people as of yore;
The *finals*, upwards, meant the humble fame
Of one the faithful servant of the same—
Who did, with him, the hostile camp explore.

SCRIPTURE ENIGMA, No. 147.

My first descends
From Heaven, and tends
To make the gems of nature grow;
My second bends
And swiftly sends
Destruction to a distant foe;
My *whole* attends
Where wrath impends
God's covenant of peace to show;
And beauty blends,
And witness lends
Of God's good-will to all below.

SCRIPTURE ENIGMA, No. 148.

My *first* is luscious, sweet, and round,
And pleasant to the taste is found;
My *second* in the forest grows,
And bears an acorn or a rose:
My *whole* may in a vineyard stand,
And well repay the planter's hand,
Or else seem flourishing and fair,
And yet stand profitless and bare,
And only mock the masters care

So once when Jesus sought my first,
Sought vainly—he my second cursed ;
And so my whole, with swift decay,
Stood withered on that solemn day,
That all might fear that passed that way.

SCRIPTURE ENIGMA, No. 149.

1 My name a glowing gem of price ;
2 A " nothing " groved by man's device !
3 What may not pass a needles eye ;
4 And what we call the slowy sky ;
5 What all thing have when gone and part.
6 And a rich odorous ointment last.
   The *initial* letters joined will tell.
   What men so often love too well,
   Yet lead down multitudes to hell.

SCRIPTURE ENIGMA, No. 150.

1. A place where the ark of God rested.
2. The Babylonian name of one of the months of the year,
3 A king one of whose governors wished to apprehend Paul, but failed to do so.

The *initials* both in order and *reversed* form the name of one who obeyed God, and caused others to do right. The *third* letters, with orders *reversed*, the name of one who disobeyed God and caused others to do wrong.

SCRIPTURE ENIGMA, No. 151.

1. Think of a precious sense in men ?
2. Its duplex organs think of them ?
3. What most befits the weary think ?
4. And into what the wicked sink ?

5. Think what will melt with fervent heat?
6. What pierced the Saviour's hands and feet?
7. What were his fellow sufferers tell?
   And mark the initial letters well.
   These show who told the earliest lie,
   And made our tempted parents die.

SCRIPTURE ENIGMA, No. 152.

First find these places all in Canaan's border,
Among their names are letters in due order,
(In line will serve, in column would be better.)
Then take from every name a single letter ;
Select the letters *nearest to the middle*
And you shall find a key to solve my riddle.

    Wonders of power and pity
  Were oft within her busy streets displayed ;
1. And yet we hear the Saviour's voice upbraid
    This unrepenting city.

    There twice the battle raged
  Against the living God and Israel ;
2. And there two champion Giants fell,
    Whom David's chiefs engaged.

    Though obscure and lowly,—
  The least of cities—yet must One have birth,
3. Within her walls the ruler of the earth,
    The faithful and the holy !

    'Twas the Priests gave aid
  To David, fleeing from the face of Saul,
4. Who in his anger sought to slay them all,
    In their kind deed betrayed.

    The wail of woe and sadness !
  Rings through her gates and echoes o'er the plains !
5. But lo ! the lost ones shall return again
    And change her grief to gladness!

On Arnon's brink arose
This ancient city; but the mighty hand
6. Of Israel's leader seized on Canaan's land,
And dispossessed their foes.

'Twas there they kept the wedding,
When Sampson's Bride the riddle did disclose,
7 But to bestow the prize he stopped his foes,
Their blood in vengeance shedding.

SCRIPTURE ENIGMA, No. 153.

1. A city noted for wonderful preservation of life.
2. One whom God's spirit made to prophesy, and whom, a young man afterwards a pious ruler wished to be prevented from prophesying.
3. A mighty king who lost his kingdom for a time but was afterwards restored to it.
4. A king's mother who was carried captive.
5. A father whose three children were all famous amongst the children of Israel.
6. A city against which Christ promised woe for its impenitence.
6. A chamberlain of a king ruling from India to Ethiopia.
8. A hiding place of David.
9. A city where a Christian sought and found Paul.
10. A child of promise.
11. One of the idols worshipped by the children of Israel.

The *initials* form the name of a king that was slain ; the *finals* that of one of his sons, who assisted in slaying him.

SCRIPTURE ENIGMA, No. 154.

1. The son of Zuph, an Ephrathite in the fourth generation;
The ancestor of one who gave two kings to Israel's nation.

2. The King of Zabath went to war with chariots and with horses;
But David smote and spoiled him and scattered all his forces.

3. The aged priest of Israel grieved by his son's backslidings,
Fell down at last and perished, overwhelmed with evil tidings.

4. There, when God sent his Angels, to tell them of their failing;
All Israel wept and called it the place of tears and wailings.

5. The last of five great Princes who in Midian's country reigned,
Whom Moses smote, and Reuben their fruitful land obtained.

6. The Ezrahite prophetic, who sang Jehovah's mercies,
To David and his kingdom, in joyful, mournful verses.

7. The father of the officer who David made recorder,
Then David judged the people to Canaan's farthest border.

8. The Horonite that envied the cities renovation,
What time King Artaxerxes gave the Jews their restoration.

9. The place where they complained for Egypt's pleasures yearning,
But Israel's God was angry, and punished them with burning.

10. The second son of Jacob's heirs, from his chief place rejected,
Then to his birthright portion a younger was elected.

11. The city that was captured, and for their dwelling claimed it,
Who sprang from Bilhah's elder son, and after him they named it.

12. The lofty place in Canaan where Israel's bounds extended,
   From the salt sea and onward its sunny side ascended.

13. The king who heard when David subdued a hostile nation,
   And sent his son to bless him, with gifts and salutation

14. The keeper of the household, beneath his royal master,
   Then Judah's land was saved by Assyria's great disaster.

If the *first* and *final* letters from all these names be quoted,
You will find in two acrostics two wondrous things denoted.
The one was worn by Aaron four rows of jewels showing,
The other shone around it, with heavenly lustre glowing,
Oft as the priest was standing in service mediatorial,
The one he wore, the other bore his peoples bright memorial ;
This well adorned his person upon his robes of glory,
That told in signs mysterious some glad or gracious story,
Some message from Jehovah, their God and King and Saviour,
To teach them his good precepts, and their behaviour,
And our High Priest in heaven, his robes of glory wearing
From richer gems reflected, a bright radiance bearing,
Still lives to make memorial of all for whom he suffered,
And bears their names upon him for whom his blood was offered,
And those that trust his mercy nought from his love shall sever,
He will guide them with his counsel, and lift them up for ever.

SCRIPTURE ENIGMAS.

SCRIPTURE ENIGMA No. 155.

1. Who like the lion seeketh to devour
   The godly man in an unguarded hour?
2. Whose occupation did the apostle share,
   When forced to labor for his daily fare?
3. In what did Ruth her present take away,
   Which to her mother she did straight convey?
4. To what great sin was Israel's nation prone,
   Which robbed their God of what was his alone?
5. Who was by faith enabled to despise
   The lion's yawning jaws and glaring eyes?

Take the above initials, and you'll find
The name of one most favored of mankind;
One from a number chosen by the Lord
To rule a nation by his sacred word.
Sweet were the sounds that issued from his songs
In praise of him to whom all praise belongs.
He, choosing in his youth the better part,
Was styled by God one after his own heart.

SCRIPTURE ENIGMA No. 156.

1. Who challenged Israel's hosts to single fight?
2. What prophets hid in caves as dark as night?
3. What poet sounded forth his Maker's praise?
4. Who was expelled from his home in early days?
5. What king neglected and despised God's word?
6. What woman's heart " was opened by the Lord?"
7. What conquering king the towers of Shemer raised?
8. Who would not come to hear her beauty praised?
9. And who to heaven on fiery wheels was borne,
   His mantle falling on his friend forlorn?

Take the initials, and in them you'll find
Wise words of counsel, for the young designed.

CURIOSITIES OF THE BIBLE.

SCRIPTURE ENIGMA No. 157.

1. Whither did Jonah vainly seek from God to flee?
2. Who once three angels entertained beneath a tree?
3. A noted brook that flowed beside Jerusalem?
4. A "ready scribe" who wrote the book that bears his name?
5. A judge who hoped to gain a bribe for Paul's release?
6. Who made a molten calf rebellious tribes to please?
7. A man that grossly mocked and cast stones at his king?
8. Whom did Paul ask his parchments, books, and cloak to bring?
9. Who unto Solomon for God's house workmen sent?
10. And where was it for precious gold his servants went?
11. Whom, four days dead, out of the grave did Jesus call?
12. Who loved this evil world, and hence deserted Paul?
13. On whose behalf did Paul an earnest letter write?
14. To whom was he conveyed a prisoner by night?
15. Whom did his godly father on an altar bind?
16. And for whose vineyard was it that a king repined?
17. A word th' Ephraimites could not pronounce aright?
18. Where Paul, from Troas travelling, tarried for a night?
19. Where was the birthplace of the prophet Samuel?
20. Who touched God's ark, and instantly a victim fell?
21. Who cherished angry thoughts, and then his brother killed?
22. And into whose young mind were holy truths instilled?
23. A king's son on his bed once barbarously slain?
24. Who proved a friend to Paul, ashamed not of his chain?
25. A man that timidly, with deeply felt concern,
  Came unto Christ by night, the way of truth to learn?

In the first letters of each name combined,
A gracious attribute of God you find.

SCRIPTURE ENIGMA No 158.

1. Whose son was raised by Christ's almighty power?
2. What friend of God proved faithless for one hour?
3. Whose youthful life was saved for future fame?
4. Who cast a lustre on a mother's name?

5 On whose behalf did Paul the apostle plead?
6. O'er fall'n Jerusalem whose heart did bleed?

7 Whose life was saved that many might rejoice?
8. Who for the ruined temple raised his voice?
9. Who did with Baal's prophets long contend?

10. To whom did Abram prove the firmest friend?
11. Who feared to tell the king the prophet's word?
12. Where dwelt the judge so faithful to the Lord?
13. And who, though oft by Satan's wiles deceived,
    A man of God's own heart the name received?

The initial letters form a Scripture exhortation.

SCRIPTURE ENIGMA No. 159.

1. In whom did Jesus say there was no guile?
2. What king did hinder Israel for awhile?
3. Who sought by letter Ezra's work to stay?
4. Whose fame for wisdom sounded far away?
5. Who called his wives to hear his doleful tale?
6. What friend of Paul in trouble did not fail?
7. What was the faithful Abram's father's name?
8 Who trembled at the Saviour's growing fame?
9. Before whose bar did Paul most nobly plead?
10. What warlike man for David's crime did bleed?
11. What book shows forth the prophet's grief and pain!
12. And by whose hands was Gedaliah slain?
13. Whose vineyard did the wicked Ahab claim?

14. And what blind man did Jesus not disdain?
15. Where dwelt a patriarch of early date?
16. Who owed to woman's hand his direful fate?
17. What name proclaims the Saviour's ever near?
18. What Ammonite made Israel's heart to fear?
19. What faithful servant sought help from the Lord?
20. Who, firm in faith, feared neither fire nor sword?
21. Who, taking the infant Jesus in his arms,
    Bade Mary's heart prepare for great alarms?

These initials show, when read aright,
A precept wise and true,
To do with all thy power and might
Whate'er thou find'st to do.

SCRIPTURE ENIGMA No. 160.

1. What gates did Samson bear with ease away?
2. Whose debt did Paul take on himself to pay?
3. What god before the ark fell flatly down?
4. Whose father died beneath God's angry frown?
5. Whose servant bore an open letter forth?
6. What Syrian's flocks were bless'd for Jacob's worth?
7. Who by his brav'ry won his cousin's hand?
8. Who boldly disobeyed her lord's command?
9. What country nourished Israel's chosen race,
   Till friendly kings to cruel ones gave place?

Take now the letter that begins each name:
A very precious text you'll find the same.

SCRIPTURE ENIGMA No. 161.

1. What ruler of the Jews did Paul baptize?
2. Who saw a man of God to glory rise?
3. Who fell'd a bough to fire a city tow'r?
4. Who with great skill could speak of tree and flow'r?
5. What Hebrew bore a gift to Moab's king?

6. From whence did Solomon much treasure bring?
7. Whose threshing-floor stood on the temple's site?
8. Whose men did swear their king should no more fight?
9. Who forty years' repose for Israel gained?

10. What Moabitish king o'er them then reigned?
11. What queen in royal house a feast did make?
12. Who from a husband fond a wife did take?
13. Whose worldly choice became to him a snare,
    And says with warning voice to us, Beware?

You'll solve my rhyme, whate'er may be your age,
If well you search the Bible's sacred page;
Name after name must its initial give,
And if you heed the text your soul shall live.

SCRIPTURE ENIGMA, No. 162.

1. Who in a chariot preach'd with telling power?
2. Who met her future lord at eve's calm hour?
3. Who first was stoned with stones, then burn'd with fire?
4. What kind of pigeon did the law require?

5. From whence was cast a sinful queen to die?
6. Who had twelve sons, with towns and castles high?
7. Whence came one to plead with Israel's king?
8. A prophet's mother who with joy did sing?
9. Who built a town upon a hill he bought?
10. To whom was husbandry with pleasure fraught?
11. Where was a burning quench'd by earnest prayer?

12. Who drove three giants forth with courage rare?
13. A cunning hunter, to his father dear?
14. Who hired an army ere he fought with Seir?
15. What king, when wounded, ended his own life?
16. For whom did Eliezer seek a wife?
17. Who had a guileless heart, that priceless boon?
18. Where stood the sun, while also stayed the moon?

Your Bibles search (an act the Papist blames !)
These questions all must answer'd be by names.
The letter first of each place in a line .
To obey the words may God your heart incline!

SCRIPTURE ENIGMA, No. 163.

1. What Jew became a convert of our Lord,
   And with the seventy went to preach the word ?
2. What name was given to Phinehas' infant son,
   Significant of Israel's glory gone?
3. Where David was compelled with foes to live,
   What city to him did king Achish give ?
4. Who was a chosen vessel of the Lord,
   To guide his church and spread his name abroad ?
5. Who was the victim spared by Saul's command,
   Who fell at length by Samuel's feeble hand ?
6. What favored minion had a gallows made,
   And fell into the snare himself had laid ?

The above initials will name a place
Whose story-pleases every child of grace,
Since to a covenant God we there commend
The present and the future of our friend.

SCRIPTURE ENIGMA, No. 164.

1. On what high mountain were seven altars made ?
2. Who was for her son's safety much afraid ?
3. From what town were th' apostles forced to flee ?
4. Whom did our Saviour 'neath the fig tree see ?
5. Who to a king did tidings sad convey ?
6. And who did once Goliath's brother slay ?
7 Whose valor was rewarded with a wife ?
8. Who trembled when Paul preached a future life ?
9. What king to Abram did his wife restore ?
10. Who was a ready scribe in Moses' law ?

SCRIPTURE ENIGMAS.

12. A king of Judah in his chariot slain ?
12. A town where Jesus did some time remain ?
13. Who walked with God, and knew not death or pain ?

Take these initials; and a name they form
Of Him who, speaking, hushed the angry storm,
And where he walked, in gentleness and might,
A peaceful radiance shed, the Lord of light.
Oh may his reign within our hearts begin,
And his abounding grace prevail against our sin!

SCRIPTURE ENIGMA, No. 165.

1. The word whereby the test was once applied,
   Where nations met beside the swelling tide ?
2. The portion of the day first named on earth ?
3. The power that gave created things their birth ?
4. The dried-up stem that blossomed like the rose ?
5. The number of the saints whose hands disclose
   The Saviour's mark ?   The prophet's earnest call
6. To take the water offered unto all ?
7. The twice-repeated words by God once spoken,
8. To save the house that all his laws had broken ?
9. What Christ is to his church ?   The frame wherein
10. Time's cycles move ?   In what should we begin
11. To worship God ?   The word each one is bound
    To speak, inviting others by the sound
12. To drink the living waters ?   Christ's command—
    What we should be who seek the better land ?
13. In what did the Creator fashion man,
    Last of his works, yet chief in all the plan ?
14. The last bequest the Saviour gave to those
    Who heard his voice in blessing when he rose ?
15. That which the lilies do not, and yet they
    A glory greater than a king display ?
16. By what was judgment asked before the Lord,
    When Joshua first assumed the leader's sword ?

17. What Christ declared the people went to see
Who waited on his herald's ministry?
18. How the rich man shall sadly go away?
19. What we shall be who love the Lord's great day?

In one great precept the initials weave:
Obey, and you shall Christ himself perceive;
He spake the words, and all who seek his face
Shall find him in them, full of truth and grace.

SCRIPTURE ENIGMA, No. 166.

1. The king whom Abram slew to save Lot's life?
2. The king whose son took Jezebel to wife?
3. The king whose pride by God was brought down low?
4. The king who, fearful, to a witch did go?
5. The king's son who was murdered on his bed?
6. The king who mourned in song his foe when dead?
7. The king who to Jehoiachin was kind?
8. The king who would not aged counsellors mind?
9. The king whose warlike help king Ahaz prayed?
10. The king who begged that God would grant him aid?
11. The king who cruelly died by Ehud's blade?
12. The king whose mother words of wisdom taught?
13. The king's court which the gentle Esther sought?
14. The king-built city where the king was slain?
15. The king's consoler sent to ease his pain?
16. The king whose brothers twain their father slew?
17. The king who, more than any, heavenly wisdom knew?

Combine the initials of these royal names;
They give a text which man's poor splendor shames.
In summer glory God the earth arrays,
And crowns with beauty the succeeding days
Go, walk the fields and breathe the fragrant air
And mark the perfect wisdom everywhere:
What palace is there like the vaulted sky?

What king's attire can with these flowerets vie?
Oh thou, who clothest thus the verdant field,
To us the needed blessing daily yield.

SCRIPTURE ENIGMA, No. 167.

1. Who sheltered David in an hour of need?
2. Who died 'mid household grief and public gloom?
3. Who stained the young earth with a cruel deed?
4. Whose words averted Judah's coming doom?
5. Who through an erring monarch's treachery died?
6. Whose faltering conscience saved his brother's life?
7. Who did the toils of Nehemiah deride?
8. Who bore a gift and a destroying knife?
9. What infant's birth made glad a widow's heart?
10. Who for untimely forwardness was slain?
11. Who rashly with a God-sent gift did part?
    Yet by his death a victory did gain?

In the initial letters see,
  A precept that 'twere well to heed,
For it imparts the cheering charm,
  Which in its turn each heart doth need.

SCRIPTURE ENIGMA. No. 168

The *initials* tell of one who
  For Christ his life laid down;
The *finals* of another,
  That later won that crown.
They died his faithful martyrs
  Their warfare ended well;
And 'mid the "noble army"
  With him in triumph dwell.

1. A city where a widow
   Received a reverend guest.
2. On earth the Christian's portion,

For this is not his rest.
3. A land of slave and tyrant,
   God's freedmen stay not there.
4. Here, from a loathsome dungeon,
   Hymns freight the midnight **air**
5. This seek in every danger
   Of God, and not of man.
6. A priest and a reformer,
   Who marched in freedom's van
7. He once approached the Master
   In darkness and in gloom ;
   Again, a bolder mourner,
   Enriched that Master's tomb.

SCRIPTURE ENIGMA, No. 169.

These *initials* and *finals* two cousins declare
   Who wandered with Israel many a year:
The latter was chosen the priesthood to share,
   The former the sanctuary's vessels to bear.

1. An Eastern province often named,
2. A rocky mount for curses famed.
3. A city with an empire wide.
4. A city on a mountain side.
5. A nephew of a patriarch.
6. A spy sent Canaan's land to mark.
7. A homeless prince's generous host; true to his king
   Whose throne was lost.

SCRIPTURE (CHRISTMAS) ENIGMA, No. 170.

Comes again the festive season ;
   Peals again the gladsome bell ;
Sounds again the wondrous story ;
   God with us is come to dwell :
Praise to Bethlehem's Babe we bring·
   Child of earth is heaven's King'

SCRIPTURE ENIGMAS.

Listen to the joyful tidings :
" Unto us a Child is born ,
" Unto us a Son is given : "
Hail this happy Christmas morn !
Prophecy fulfilled we see,
Man enshrines the Deity.

1. Who foretold his humble birth,—
Crowned him " Prince of peace " on earth ?

2. Who supplied his wants—reproved,
Even as she served and loved ?

3. Who sat listening at his feet—
Attitude for woman meet ?

4. Who within the temple knew
Mary's babe as Christ the true ?

5. Who embalmed his Lord when dead,
Ere in Joseph's tomb he laid ?

6. Where dwelt he whose promised son
Typified th' anointed One ?

7. Where were they who mourned their Lord
Gladdened by himself restored ?

8. Who awoke and left his tomb,
Bid by Jesus rise and come ?

The initials of their names will make
His name of whom the prophet spake ;
A name to human hearts how dear,
For lo ! it brings the Godhead near.
Thrice welcome day, when Christ was born .
Be GOD WITH US this sacred morn !

SCRIPTURE ENIGMA, No. 171.

FOR THE NEW YEAR.

1 Who, by the preaching of Paul knew the Lord, and with gladness his servants received ?

2. Who, taught of Christ, his apostle sought out, and in time of sore trouble relieved?
3. Who, in the service of Master above, learned his duty to master below?
4. Who against God and his high priest rebelled, and met death in confusion and woe?
5. Who in the years yet to come saw his Lord, as the child unto us that is born?
6. Who came in secret to Jesus by night, nor could meet the Jews' hatred and scorn?
7. Who for the truth's sake in Christ was beloved by apostle most dear to the Lord?
8. Who in the pride of his heart forsook God, and was smitten a leper abhorred?
9. Who in his doubt went to Jesus, and found that from Nazareth came Israel's king?
10. Who, as a brother beloved in the Lord, did from Paul news to Ephesus bring?
11. Who in the fear of the Lord hid his saints from the wrath of an impious queen?
12. Who, when the mob to take Jesus drew near, in their front a lost traitor was seen?
13. Who by the aid of his God restored health to a leper reproving his pride?
14. Who bearing witness to Jesus was stoned, and forgiving his enemies died?
15. Whence came the patriarch, faithful when tried, and the pattern of all who believe?
16. Whom did our Saviour forewarn of the sin, over which he should bitterly grieve?

Join the initials of each of these names, and a motto they give for the year:
Heeding the which in our journey through life ever safe is our pathway and clear.

SCRIPTURE ANAGRAM, No. 1.

Six letters in one name appear,
As in the sequel will be clear!

And numbered thus in order due,
May be discovered by this clue :—
You find in six, five, one, two, three,
One hung on his own gallows-tree.

Three, four, five, six, his name compose,
From whom man's second lineage flows.

In six, two, one, his son you find,
The least beloved of all his kind.
In one, two, three, you clearly trace,
The name of our degenerate race.

From one, two, four, and three, you ken,
Of Judah's twos the first of ten.
Three, two, five, one, of Judah's tribes
The least of Caleb's sons describe.

Two old Egyptian cities see,—
This in three, four, and that four, three.
With all the six, describe at length,
The Father of the man of strength.

SCRIPTURE ANAGRAM, No. 2.

My fourteen letters will a name unfold,
In vision imagined by a head of gold.
You must not guess the characters to tell,
But in the sacred pages search and spell.
First find the following names, the *initials* take,
And these combined the monarch's title make.

1. Find numbers one, seven, eight, thirteen and three
   And one who died for sacrilege you see.

2. Find ten, twelve, fourteen, seven,—a scribe is found
Who raised a fallen city from the ground.

3. Three, thirteen, fourteen, four, five, six, denote,
A scribe who twice the prophets warning wrote.

4. Four, twelve, eleven, seven, and six, and such
His name who died for one unlawful touch.

5. Five, sixteen, fourteen, four, and three, will bring,
A wondrous creature with an outspread wing.

6. Find six, ten, three, two, fourteen, you shall view
A man whose wife the weary Sisera slew.

7. Find seven, three, nine, ten, fourteen, and recall
The great war captain of the house of Saul.

8. Eight, four, fourteen, and seven,—its plain extends
Where nations to a golden image bend.

9. One, ten, seven, six, reveal, the utmost bound,
The eastern limit of Zebulun's ground.

10. Ten, eight, two, nine,—behold a garden fair!
And lo! a matchless couple dwelling there.

11. Eleven, two, fourteen, ten, and eight,—appears,
Israel's last journey in the forty years.

12. Twelve, thirteen, three, four, eight,—you apprehend
The son of Nathan, and a wise king's friend.

13. Find thirteen, twelve, eleven, seven, six, and tell
The utmost border where the Avims dwell.

14. Fourteen, two, four,—behold the patriarch's name,
The son of Peleg, in the line of Shem.

SCRIPTURE ANAGRAMS, NO. 3.

I am a word of fourteen letters.
My 9, 10, 14, will give the name of Saul's uncle.
10, 11, 14, 13, A godly scribe.
3, 2, 11, 10, 14, A city of refuge.
4, 11, The dwelling-place of a patriarch.
5, 7, 9, 13, A town of Galilee.
6, 4, 14, A friend of Moses.
7, 3, 13, 9, 7, A river of Damascus.
8, 7, 9, A tribe of Israel.
1, 4, 9, A father of a general.
2, 6, 4, 8, A judge of Israel.
11, 10, 2, 3, A prince slain at a wine press.
11, 10, 3, 7, 6, A king of Midian.
13, 3, 1, 2, 14, A warrior.
14, 10, 4, 3, 2, 1, A son of Jacob.

The first letters of each of these names united will give the name of a proud imperious king.

SCRIPTURE ANAGRAM, NO. 4.

I am a word of nine letters.
My 1, 6, 2, 7, will give the name of one mentioned in the Bible as "Blessed above women."
My 2, 7, 6, 9, The eldest son of Shem.
My 3, 6, 9, One of the sons of Hezron.
My 4, 3, The birthplace of Abraham.
My 5, 6, 9, 4, 8, 7, The last judge of Israel.
My 6, 3, The chief town of Moab.
My 7, 2, 9, 4, 8, 7, A king whose instructions are in the last chapter of the book of Proverbs.
My 8, 5, 6, 4, The father of the Edomites.
My 9, 6, 3, 5, A hill on which St. Paul preached to the people of Athens.
My whole is a city of ancient fame.

BIBLE PICTURES.

From the Book of Ruth.

1. A hostile land a Gentile name describes,
   Apart from Israel's tribes.
2. Four strangers there, by famine forced to roam,
   Found refuge and a home.
3. Of Judah's lineage, and of good renown,
   They left their native town.
4. One of the four was to his burial borne,
   And one was left to mourn.
5. Two Gentile damsels gave their heart and hand,
   To join that little band.
6. Three widowed mourners now our tears engage,
   Alike—but not in age.
7. Two went their husband's heritage to find,
   But one was left behind.
8. And one, though urged to stay, with fixed intent,
   To that far country went.
9. When earth again th' abundant harvest yields,
   She goes to glean the fields.
10. Led by God's providence, she turns her hand
    To glean a kinsman's land.
11. The lowly stranger there her kinsman spied,
    And she became his bride.
12. The once lone widow, with maternal joy,
    Embraced a darling boy.
13. And from her darling, crowned with manly grace,
    Sprang a right royal race

BIBLE CHARACTERS.

BIBLE CHARACTERS, No. 1. [Key

A noted teacher of Jewish law, whose reasoning had great weight with the council at Jerusalem.

The initials of the following prove the name:—

1. The portion of Palestine which was the birthplace of many of the apostles.
2. An aged widow remarkable for a life of fasting and prayer.
3. A disciple of Cyprus, with whom Paul lodged during his last visit to Jerusalem.
4. The name of one whose sudden death brought great fear on all the church.
5. The only companion of St. Paul during his last imprisonment at Rome.
6. The city in Asia Minor from whence the Jews came who stoned Paul.
7. The village where our Saviour spent the first evening after his resurrection.
8. A city where the apostle Peter ministered to the saints.

BIBLE CHARACTERS, No. 2.

An Eastern king, whose lying awake at night had important consequences.

The initials of the following prove the name:—

1. A woman whose discretion and courteous behavior led to great exaltation.
2. The place where an eminent high priest died.
3. The cousin of Saul, who was captain of his host.
4. A violent opposer of the rebuilding of the temple.
5. One whose ill-timed zeal provoked the anger of the Lord.
6. A servant, the first named in Scripture.
7. A city of refuge.
8. A monosyllabic name, the early home of an Old Testament character.
9. An Old Testament name of Christ.

BIBLE CHARACTERS, No. 3.

The meeting-place of four hundred discontented Israelites.

The initials of the following prove the name :—

1. One " who through faith quenched the violence of fire."
2. The feeding-place of Israel's flock, and in later times the scene of a miracle.
3. The name of a king of Judah who was punished for his presumption.
4. The uncle of Esau.
5. The old name of Bethel.
6. The name of one who, through covetousness, "troubled Israel."
7. A Danite, the father of a famous Judge in Israel.

BIBLE CHARACTERS, No. 4.

A flourishing church of Asia Minor.

The initials of the following prove the name :—

1. A Christian householder.
2. A kinsman of St. Paul.
3. One of the divisions of the Holy Land mentioned in the New Testament.
4. A place where St. Paul was in peril from his own countrymen.
5. An eloquent man, and one mighty in the Scriptures.
6. A city from which St. Paul narrowly escaped with his life.
7. The first fruits of Achaia.
8. One of the apostles.
9. A succorer of St. Paul.
10. A political sect among the Jews.
11. A division of the Roman army.
12. A New Testament prophet.

BIBLE CHARACTERS, No. 5.

A man who left his native city when famine arose.

The Initials of the following prove the name:—

One of the brothers of the king of Israel, famous for his commanding stature.
2. The original name of the city of Dan.
3. The district in Palestine likened to an ass bowing down between two burdens.
4. The burial-place of a patriarchal family.
5. An Ethiopian who delivered a prophet from danger.
6. The mountain which the Hebrew lawgiver prayed to see.
7. The seaport where a royal fleet was wrecked.
8. A king prophesied of by name.
9. The rebuilder of Jericho.

BIBLE CHARACTERS, No. 6.

The talented politician who proved a traitor to his king and country.

The Initials of the following prove the name:—

1. The only member of a royal family in Israel who was to be mourned for and buried.
2. A prophetess whose teaching proved a temporary check to idolatry in Judah.
3. One of whom it was prophesied, "He shall dwell in the presence of his brethren."
4. The burial-place of the great military leader of the children of Israel.
5. The minister of an Eastern king whose ambition resulted in his ruin.
6. The husbandman with the kingly heart.
7. The watery grave of a multitude.
8. The birthplace of Absalom.
9. A memorial of deliverance in battle.
10. The father of the second founder of the human race.

BIBLE CHARACTERS, No. 7.

The godly governor of an idolatrous household.

The initials of the following prove the name:—

1. One who chose idolatry and home rather than suffer affliction with the people of God.
2. A city of Judah, for many years the abode of the Ark of the Lord.
3. The inspired herdsman of Tekoa.
4. A faithful servant of God, in whom was fulfilled the promise, " Them that honor me I will honor."
5. A giant, out of whose hands king David was delivered by one of his chief captains.
6. A wife promised and given as the reward of valor.
7. The builder of a city which lay under the curse of God.

BIBLE CHARACTERS. No. 8.

Whose eagerness to secure a blessing for her son brought sorrow instead of joy?

The initials of the following prove the name:—

1. Whose rejection of faithful counsellors led to a national rebellion?
2. To whom was the charge of the tabernacle committed during the wilderness journey?
3. The ambitious prophet who perished among the enemies of the Lord.
4. The prophet who was a witness for God before multitudes, yet fled for his life at the threat of a woman.
5. What city did David deliver from the Philistines, but its inhabitants would not protect David from the anger of Saul?
6. At what place was Israel's army first defeated after entering Canaan?
7. Whose navy was celebrated in old times, and brought great riches to Jerusalem?

BIBLE CHARACTERS, No. 9.

The loyal and attached subject of a fugitive king.

The initials of the following prove the name :—

1. The meeting-place of a king and patriarch.
2. The favorite child—a leader of revolt.
3. A people whose obedience was a subject of Divine commendation.
4. The person whose daughters were the first female inheritors of land in Palestine.
5. One of the grandsons of Eli.
6. The city where a king of Judah met with a violent death.
7. What tribe was prohibited from having any possessions in the land of Israel?
8. The prince and great warrior killed in revenge.
9. The faith of a son proved by the faith of a father.

BIBLE CHARACTERS, No. 10.

What king set aside God's laws, and established laws of his own, to gain the affections of his people?

The initials of the following prove the name :—

1. The father of a king beloved of God
2. One of the river boundaries of the Promised Land.
3. The dwelling-place of one who served God and judged Israel all his life.
4. A deliverer and judge of Israel's people.
5. The mother of Israel's mightiest monarch.
6. The king of one of the nations destroyed by God's command when Israel entered Canaan.
7. One who took a principal part in bringing the ark of God out of the Philistine's land.
8. A Jew who rose to great honors in a foreign court.

BIBLE CHARACTERS, No. 11.

Whose covetous and deceitful conduct brought immediate and lasting punishment on himself and family?

The initials of the following prove the name :—

1. Where was the first memorial raised to tell of Israel s entrance into Canaan?
2. The meeting-place of a king and a wicked woman.
3. One of the supporters of Moses during the battle with Amalek.
4. Who alone escaped from the massacre of the priests of Nob?
5. Where was want changed to sufficiency in time of national distress?
6. The eastern boundary of the Persian empire.

BIBLE CHARACTERS, No. 12.

A Gentile soldier who was fruitful in good works.

The initials of the following prove the name :—

1. Who gave largely of his substance to be counted a Roman citizen?
2. One who sought out and aided an imprisoned apostle.
3. From what city were all Jews expelled by law in the first century?
4. Where was a widow's heart turned from mourning to rejoicing?
5. A tempestuous wind, to which St. Paul was exposed in one of his voyages.
6. A Christian church noted for its lukewarmness and self-righteous spirit.
7. In what country bordering on the Adriatic Sea did St. Paul preach the gospel?
8. One who assisted St. Paul in his missionary work.
9. Whose history is given us in the words, "She ministered to Christ of her substance?"

BIBLE CHARACTERS, No. 13.

A great man, who used his newly acquired power to help a su brother.

The initials of the following will supply the name:—

1. What were some of the lowest of the Jews?
2. A garment used to promote a parent's comfort.
3. A sleepless occupant of a comfortable bed.
4. One of the offerings in the temple.
5. One of the plagues.
6. A country which sheltered both the type and the anti type.
7. An herb of note among the Pharisees.
8. An object of regret.
9. A servant who betrayed a fugitive to his master.
10. A form of speech adopted by Job.
11. The innocent cause of a father's despair.
12. A man who, without being a king, may possess a crown.

BIBLE CHARACTERS, No. 14.

The initials form the name of a young man whose life was in danger, but who was saved in answer to prayer. The finals form the name of his father.

1. One of David's chief rulers
2. The youngest son of the builder of a noted city.
3. One whose sons sold part of their land.
4. The assumed name of a child of sorrow.
5. A farmer who offered some of his property to the service of God.
6. The country of an anxious inquirer after truth.
7. The character of one of the early churches.

No. 15. What Scripture characters most strikingly illustrate the power of maternal influence for good or for evil?

No. 16. What Scripture characters show the danger and evil of self-trust?

No. 17. What Scripture characters exhibit the sin and punishment of irreverently treating holy persons and things?

No. 18. Who were those on whose devotion God put distinguished honor?

No. 19. What Scripture characters exhibit the power of faith?

No. 20. What Scripture characters illustrate the blessedness of early devotedness to the service of God?

Concert Exercise.

THE LORD'S PRAYER—BIBLE PROOFS.

"Our Father"..................................Isa. lxiii. 16.
1. By right of creation.......................Mal. ii. 10.
2. By bountiful providence....................Ps. cxlv. 16.
3. By gracious adoption.......................Eph. i. 5.
"Which art in heaven"........................1 Kings viii. 43.
4. The throne of Thy glory...................Isa. lxiii. 15.
5. The portion of Thy children...............1 Pet. i. 4
"Hallowed be Thy name."
6. By the thoughts of our hearts.............Ps. lxxxvi. 11.
7. By the words of our lips..................Ps. li. 15.
8. By the works of our hands.................1 Cor. x. 31.
"Thy kingdom come".........................Ps. cx. 2.
9. Of providence, to defend us...............Ps. xvii. 8.
10. Of grace, to sanctify us..................1 Thess. v. 23.
11. Of glory, to crown us.....................Col. iii. 4.
"Thy will be done on earth, as it is in heaven"......Acts xxi. 14.
12. Toward us, without resistance.............2 Sam. iii. 18.
13. By us, without compulsion.................Ps. cxix. 36.
14. Universally, without exception............Luke i. 6.
15. Eternally, without declension.............Ps. cxix. 93.
"Give us this day our daily bread."
16. Of necessity, for our bodies..............Prov. xxx. 8.
17. Of eternal life, for our souls............John vi. 34.
"And forgive us our trespasses"............Ps. xxv. 11.
18. Against Thy commands......................1 John iii. 4.
19. Against the grace of Thy gospel...........1 Tim. i. 16.
"As we forgive them that trespass against"...Matt. vi. 15.
20. By defaming our character.................Matt. v. 11.
21. By embezzling our property................Heb. x. 34.
22. By abusing our persons....................Acts. vii. 60.
"And lead us not into temptation, but deliver us from evil."
23. Of overwhelming affliction................Ps. cxxx. 1.

24. Of worldly enticements.................1 John ii. 15.
25. Of Satan's devices......................1 Tim. iii. 7.
26. Of sinful affections....................Rom. i. 26.
"For thine is the kingdom, and the power, and the glory, for ever."
27. Thy kingdom governs all................Ps. ciii. 19.
28. Thy power subdues all..................2 Chron. xx. 6.
29. Thy glory is above all..:..............Ps. cxlviii. 13.
"Amen."....................................Eph. i. 11.
30. As it is in Thy purposes................Isa. xiv. 27.
31. So it is in Thy promises................2 Cor. i. 20.
32. So be it in our prayers.................Rev. xxii. 20.
33. So shall it be to Thy praise............Rev. xix. 4.

Concert Exercise.

NINE ATTRIBUTES OF GOD,

As taught in the 145th Psalm. Each person should read or recite in concert the appropriate passage, followed by explanations and illustrations by the leader.

1. Omnipresence.......(v. 18), The Lord is nigh unto all, etc. [present everywhere].
2. Omniscience.........(v. 15), The eyes of all, etc. [knowing all things].
3. Omnipotence.......(v. 10, having all power), All Thy works shall praise Thee.
4. Eternity........(v. 13) endureth throughout all generations [living always].
5. Benevolence.........(v. 9), The Lord is good to all [perfect goodness and kindness].
6. Holiness.....(v. 17), Holy in all His works [perfect holiness].
7. Mercy.........(v. 9), Tender mercies are over all His works [perfect mercy].
8. Justice......(v. 17), Righteous in all His ways [always just].
9. Truth......(v. 18), Nigh to all that call upon Him in truth.

Concert Exercise.

THE LIFE AND TIMES OF ST. PAUL.

What do the Scriptures tell us of his *childhood, education*, and early religious *belief?* .....1. Acts xxii. 3; 2. Acts xxvi. 4, 5; 3. Phil. iii. 5.
What of his persecuting zeal? .....4. Acts xxii. 20; 5. Acts viii. 3; 6. Acts ix. 12; 7. Acts xxii. 4, 5; 8. Acts xxvi. 9, 10, 11.
What of his conversion to Christianity? ....9. Acts ix. 3-9. (If desired, two other accounts.)
What of his baptism? ....10. Acts xxii. 12-16.
What of his promptness and zeal in preaching Christ?..11. Acts ix. 20-22; 12. Acts xvii. 1-3; 13. Acts xxviii. 23.
What of his commission to preach the gospel?....14. Gal. i. 1; 15. Gal. i. 11, 12.
What of his doctrine, addresses, and epistles?......16. 1 Cor. i. 23, 24; 17. 1 Cor. xv. 3, 4; 18. Rom. iii. 23, 24.
What of his address to the Athenians?........19. Acts xix. 31.
What of the miracles he wrought?....20. Acts xvi. 16-18; 21. Acts xiv. 8-10.
What of his miracles not recorded?.......22. Acts xix. 11, 12.
What of the treatment he received from his countrymen?....23. Acts ix. 23, 24; 24. Acts xxiii. 12-15.
What of his own narrations of perils and sufferings?......25. 2 Cor. xi. 24-28.
What of the success that attended his labors?..26. Acts ix. 31; 27. Acts xiv. 1, 3; 28. Acts xvii. 4; 29. Acts xviii. 8; 30. Acts xix. 20.
What of his miraculous deliverance from prison?......31. Acts xvi. 25-30.
What of the viper that fastened on his hand?...32. Acts xxviii. 3-5.
What of the closing record found in the Acts of Apostles?..33. Acts xxviii. 16, 30, 31.
—*S. S. Times.*

THE YOUNG BIBLE READER.

As you look upon the board, you see a very important *charge*, that was given by an *aged* servant of God, to a *youthful* disciple: "Give attendance to reading." Paul gave the charge, and Timothy received it. He wished Timothy to take his copy of the Old Testament Scriptures, and read *very* carefully and constantly. He urged him to *attend* to it. Mark the fact that this was not a *new* book to Timothy. He had *often* read it before, and understood it very well. Turn to 2 Tim. iii. 15, and you will see the proof: "*From a child* thou hast *known* the holy scriptures." But though he had *known* the book so well, and for so long a time, Paul did not excuse him from reading it. Many now excuse themselves from this duty, because the Bible is an old familiar book. They throw it aside for something *new.* What a mistake! Remember the *charge* to this young Bible reader. You may read papers, periodicals, and books on art, science, and literature, but do not neglect *the* book. "Give *attendance* to reading."

You also see the figure of a hand, having several words written upon it. On the palm is the word "Read," and on the fingers and thumb you see other words in the form of questions. Let us take these questions in their order, and see what answers can be obtained. The first is, " *Why* " should we read ? *When ? What ? Where ? How ?* (Give answers, with Bible proof of each.) William King, the poet, was a great reader. It is said that when he was yet quite young " he had read over and made remarks upon considerably more than twenty thousand books and manuscripts."—*Buck*. He gave *attendance* to reading.

The Marquis of Lorne, now Governor-General of Canada, is a Bible reader, and recently published a metrical version of the Psalms of David.

You also see a book in the picture, and a statement written upon its pages. It is very positive and emphatic. " The Bible is the Book of Books." That is *true*. Think of its *Author*. "All scripture is given *by inspiration of God*." 2 Tim. iii. 16. Think of its *teachings*. They make men " wise unto salvation." 2 Tim. iii. 15. Think of its *duration*. Not " one jot or tittle shall pass till all be fulfilled." Matt. v. 18. What book can compare with it ? " When John Jay, at the age of eighty-two years, was urged to tell his children on what foundation he rested his hopes, and from what source he drew his consolation, his brief reply was, ' They have the book.' "—*Foster*.

Children, *you* also have the book. *Read it.*

If we do not see the golden thread through all the Bible marking out Christ, we read the Scripture without the key.— *Cecil.*

HOW TO SEARCH THE SCRIPTURES.

S-eriously......................Acts xvii. 11; 2 Tim. ii. 15.
E-arnestly ....Josh. i. 8; Ps. cxix. 12.
A-nxiously.....................John xx. 31; Ps. cxix. 9.
R-egularly.....................Acts xvii. 11; Ps. i. 2.
C-arefully................Luke xxiv. 27 ; 2 Tim. iii. 16, 17.
H-umbly........................Luke xxiv. 45; Jas. i. 22.

LIGHT ON OUR PATHWAY. Ps. cxix: 105.

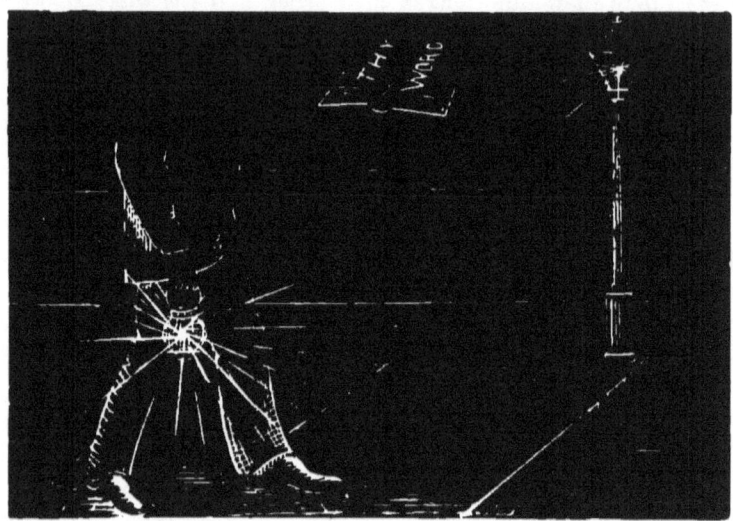

Here we have a picture which, at first sight, may not seem to be very interesting, and yet it is one of the most instructive that can be produced. Look at it for a moment, and see what it represents. You see, in part at least, the figure of a man, and he seems to be walking. You also see the outlines of a street, and at the corner you observe a lamp-post. In the man's hand you see a burning lamp, while the street-lamp also sends out its rays of light upon the darkness, thus enabling the man to see his way. Near the top of the picture you also see a book, which represents the Bible, the word of God. How beautifully the picture illustrates the Psalmist's declaration, "Thy word is a lamp unto my feet, and a light unto my path."

This man is carrying the light because he *needs it*. If the sun were shining, or the moon or stars, he might not need it. But it is *night*, and *so dark* that he must have the light. So we *need* the light of God's word. "It is not in man that walketh to direct his steps." Jer. x. 23. The way is dark, and he cannot tell where to go. He *wanders*, *stumbles*, and *falls*. But when he turns to God's word he finds "a lamp unto his feet, and a light unto his path." I have read of a traveller on the mountains who was for a time enveloped in a heavy mist, and could scarcely see his way from one rocky spur to another. Suddenly the mist rolled away, and to his surprise he found himself standing on the verge of a fearful precipice. The misty cloud was swept away just in time to show him his danger. So, when God's word becomes a "lamp to our feet," it shows us the perils of the way, and we walk in safety. "The entrance of thy words giveth light. Ps. cxix. 130. Let us remember that we are to *keep* this light with us wherever we go. A lamp will do us no good on a dark night if we leave it at home. What is this man, in the picture, doing with his light? You say, "Carrying it with him." Yes. And you are to take the word of God with you. Do you ask how? Carry it on the tablet of your *memory*. Keep it there. Do as the little boy did, who had to give up his Bible to the priest. The priest burned up the book, but the little boy said, "Thank God, you cannot burn up the twenty-eight chapters of Matthew that I have got in my head." He carried the light with him. We are *pilgrims*. Our *way* is *dark*. Let us take the light with us, and we shall walk in comfort, confidence, and safety.

WHY WE SHOULD TAKE GOD FOR OUR GUIDE.
1. Because as travellers we need a guide............Jer. iii. 4.
2. Because He knows the road...................Heb. iv. 15.
3. Because He has Himself encountered its dangers..Heb. ii. 10.
4. Because He goes with the traveller all the way. .Ps. xxiii. 4.
5. Because He cheers and supports when weary..Ps. xxxvii. 23.
6. Because as travellers we must follow our guide..1 Peter ii. 21.

WHAT IS HEAVEN ACCORDING TO THE BIBLE.
1. Our Father's house.......John xiv. 2; Isa. lxiii. 15; 1 Kings viii. 30; Matt. xxiii. 9, Matt. vi. 9; Matt. vii. 11.
2. The home of Jesus......John iii. 13; John vi. 38; John xx. 17; Acts iii. 21; Heb. ix. 24; 1 Thess. i 10.
3. The future abode of believers....John xiv. 2, 3; 2 Cor. v. 1; Heb. xi. 10.
[G. A.]

THE SPIDER'S WEB.

We have here the picture of a spider's web. The spider is a repulsive insect, and few, indeed, admire him. I have read of a man who had a "pet spider," and, when a tune was whistled, the little creature would instantly come out of its hole to listen. Few, however, would like such a "pet." We may dislike the spider, but we cannot fail to admire his work. See the delicate fibres, and the perfect form of this web. What ingenuity and skill it shows! But let us look a little more closely at the spider's work, and see if it has a lesson for us. See, first of all, how *orderly* and *systematic* it is. The lines running from the centre to the outer edge seem to be of equal length, and the distance between them seems to be equal also. Then, there are cords that cross the long threads, and these, too, are arranged with perfect order and system. Here is a lesson for us. We are not to work in a *hap-hazard* way. We are to have *order* in our plans and pursuits. We are to have "a place for everything, and everything in its place." "To everything there is a season." Eccl. iii. 1. The time to serve God is now. "Seek ye *first* the kingdom of God." That is the *order* we are to obobserve.

See, again, how this work of the spider becomes an agency of *torture* and *destruction*. The chief mission of the spider seems to be to *ensnare* and *capture* other insects. Many a thoughtless fly comes buzzing along, and is hopelessly entangled in the web. It tries in *vain* to escape. It dies a slow, lingering death. How full of meaning are the words you see on the board: "Lying in wait to *destroy*." Many things in this life become a *snare* to us; they *deceive* us and lead to *ruin*. The wineglass may seem tempting, but it carries *death* in its sparkling contents. "He that is deceived thereby is not wise." Prov. xx. 1. The saloon may be gilded, and the hall of revelry may be attractive; but beware of them, for, like the spider's web, they may become agencies of *destruction*. The prophet tells us that the "wicked may weave the spider's web." Isa. lix. 6.

What do you see written above the web? "Keep me from the snare." That is a prayer. Let us adopt it. This is a prayer for those who want to *keep out* of the snare. "Keep me *from* the snare." Some people run right into snares, and then wonder *why* they are caught. It is good to *get out* of the snare, but a thousand times better to *keep out*. "Watch and pray that ye *enter not* into temptation." Matt. xxvi. 41.

WHAT WE ARE BY NATURE.

1. Evil in our thoughts continually................Gen. vi. 5.
2. Unclean..Job xiv. 4.
3. Shapen in iniquity.............................Ps. li. 5.
4. Unclean and as filthy rags.....................Isa. lxiv. 6.
5. Deceitful and desperately wicked...............Jere. xii. 9.
6. All under sin..................................Rom. iii. 9–23.
7. The children of wrath..........................Eph. ii. 3.
8. Aliens from the commonwealth of Israel.........Eph. ii. 12.
9. Alienated from the life of God.................Eph. iv. 18.
10. Dead in trespasses and sin....................Col. ii. 13.

THE DOOR OPEN OR SHUT.

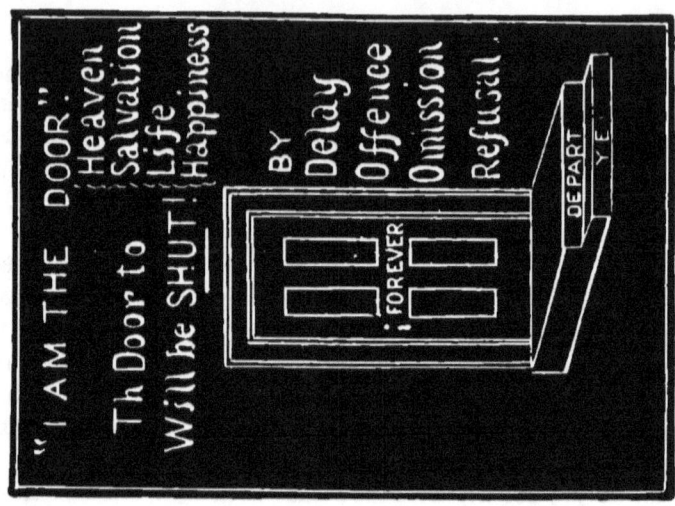

THE CLOSED DOOR.

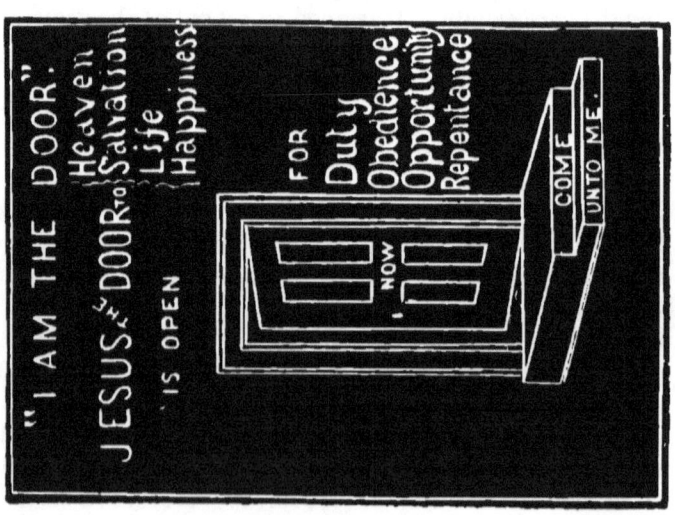

THE OPEN DOOR.

The term door literally means *entrance*, and denotes the way into a building. Jesus uses the term in a metaphorical sense, and applies it to Himself. "I am the door." John x. 9. He is the only way of entrance into spiritual life, into the church, and into heaven. Hence, his language is, "I am the way." John xiv. 6. How clearly did the ancient Fathers teach this truth, when they said, "Christ, from the foundation of the world, has been the Father's *way* to earth and the sinner's way to God."

That open door has a very *gracious* meaning. It means that Jesus is *now* ready to receive us. He is saying to us all, "Come unto me." Matt. xi. 28. An open door invites us to enter, and so Jesus *waits* to receive us as we come to Him. Listen to His cheering words: "Him that cometh to me, I will in no wise cast out." John vi. 37. Enter the door *now*, while you are young. Many as young as you have done so. Polycarp entered when he was only *four years old*. At the age of ninety he said, "Eighty and six years have I served Him." Lady Huntington entered it when she was only *nine years old*. Bishop Hedding sought Christ at the age of *four* years. Alfred Cookman entered the door when he was *ten years old*. How true the promise: "Those that seek me early shall find me." Prov. viii. 17. Remember the door is open *now*. But the door that is shut has a very *sad and solemn meaning*. It means that Jesus, at the last, refuses to receive those who have refused Him. Can you pass through a doorway when it is *closed against* you? No. You turn away, and say the "door is shut." The foolish virgins found the "door was shut." Matt. xxv. 10. How terrible it will be for the soul to be *homeless* forever, and *unsheltered* amid the storms of eternity. If *this* door is shut against us, *no other* will open to receive us. *Wait*, and the door may be shut. Then you will *vainly* cry, "Lord, Lord, open unto us." Luke xiii. 25. "Too late, too late, ye cannot enter now."—*Tennyson*. A blacksmith, when he pulled his iron out of the fire, used to call out to his son, "Quick! quick! Now or never."—*Foster*. "Remember *now* thy Creator in the days of thy youth." Eccl. xii. 1. It may be now or never with us.

THE VINE AND ITS BRANCHES.

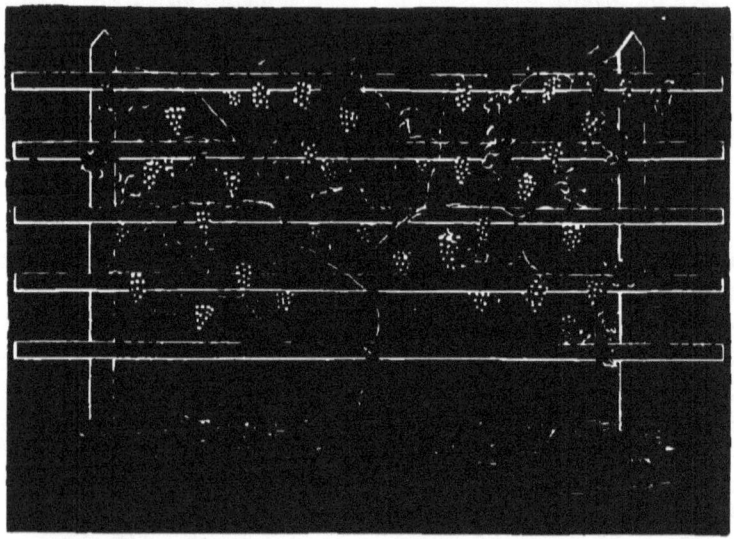

We have here a picture of a well-known vine. Let us see if we can learn a few lessons from it.

And, first of all, it does not claim to be anything but a *vine*—a grape-vine.

Look at it, and it *appears like one;* touch or test it in any form you please, and it always shows itself in its true character. It never tries to put on the appearance of some beautiful plant, nor look like some tall, stately oak. We, too, should always show ourselves to be *as* and *what* we are. *Bad* men often try to make others believe that they are *good*. They are ashamed to be known to others just as they are known to themselves. They claim to be what they are not. The vine, in this respect, *rebukes* them, for it *is* always just what it *seems* to be. Let all our boys and girls be *true*, and avoid deception of every kind. Henry Clay once said, "I would rather be *right* than to be President."

The vine also shows us the necessity of having some *suitable support.* Does this vine stand *alone,* or seem to hold itself in an upright position by its own strength? There is a trellis or frame to which it clings, and this frame gives it *support.*

Children, can we stand *alone* in life? Certainly not. We need each other's help. "Bear ye one another's burdens." Gal. vi. 2. We need Christ's help still more. He has said, "Without me, ye can do nothing." John xv. 5. Take away the trellis, and what would happen to the vine? Fall? Yes, it would fall to the ground. Many are in the dust to-day, because they have forsaken God, their only strength and support. "God is our refuge and *strength,* a very present *help* in trouble."

The vine also teaches us a lesson on *fruitfulness.* Some vines have perfect branches, heavy foliage, and pretty blossoms, but *no* fruit. The vine here represented is full of rich clusters. How fruitful it appears! Shall our lives be *barren?* If *vines* bear fruits, shall *souls* be unfruitful? Jesus once found a tree bearing upon its branches "*nothing but leaves.*" Mark xi. 13. What a disappointment? Nothing but leaves. Trees and vines all covered with rustling leaves and fragrant blossoms, may be very beautiful indeed, but to be *useful* they must bear *fruit.*

"In Eastern poetry they tell of a wondrous tree on which grew golden apples and silver bells, and every time the breeze went by and shook the fragrant branches, a shower of these golden apples fell, and the living bells chimed and tinkled forth their airy ravishment."—*Biblical Museum.*

Children, so live that the fruit of your lives may be more sweet, wholesome, and valuable than all the "golden apples and silver bells" that fancy ever painted.

GOD'S BEST GIFTS.

1. Joy in believing..................................Ps. xxv. 9.
2. Rest............................Matt. xi. 28; Jer. vi. 16.
3. Peace.........John xiv. 27; Isa. xxvi. 3, 4; Job xxii. 21.
4. Eternal life....................John x. 28; John iii. 36.
5. The Holy Spirit.....John xiv. 16; Ps. li. 12; Titus iii. 5; 2 Cor. iii. 17; 1 Thess. i. 6.

SIN AND SALVATION.

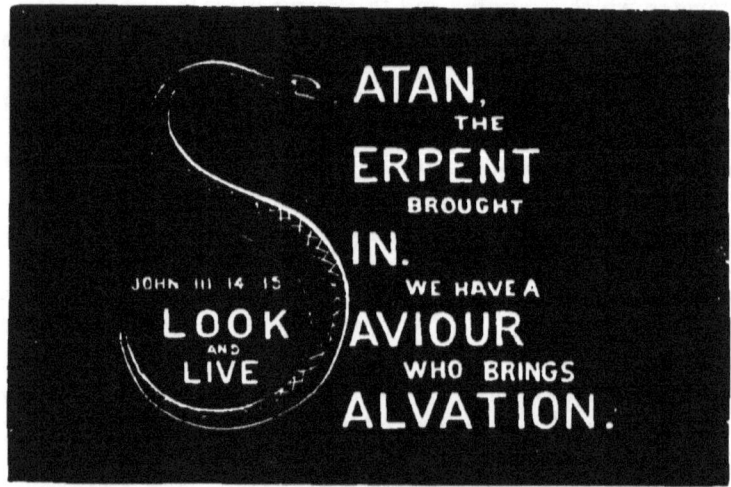

We have here the figure of a serpent. In Gen. iii. 1, we have the first scriptural mention of the serpent. The serpent represents Satan, and led Eve to disobey God in paradise. Said she, "The serpent beguiled me, and I did eat." Gen. iii. 13. How true, then, the words written upon the board: "Satan the Serpent brought Sin."

We are to remember that *sin* is a great *evil*. It is *here*—all around us and *within* us. What is the Bible definition of sin? "Sin is the *transgression* of the law." 1 John iii. 4.

If we break the law *voluntarily* and *knowingly*, then we are guilty of sinning. Have we not done *this* in some way and at some time? Yes. "For *all* have sinned." Rom. iii. 23. True, we may not have broken the *whole* law, but we are *no less sinners*, even though we have transgressed only a *small* portion of it.

"Whosoever shall keep the *whole law*, and yet offend in *one point*, he is *guilty of all*." Jas. ii. 10.

Where is the person who has not transgressed "one point," at least, of God's law?

"We sprang from the men whose guilty fall,
Corrupts his race and taints us *all*."

This picture presents another great fact, and that is *salvation*. Salvation denotes *deliverance* from dangers or from enemies.

Turn now to the picture and read, "We have a *Saviour* who brings *salvation*." Satan brings sin, but the Saviour brings salvation. We have the *one;* shall we not have the *other?*

We brought with us into this world a *sinful nature, without our consent,* but we can have salvation only by choice. "*Choose* you this day whom you will serve." Josh. xxiv. 15.

Salvation never will be *thrust* upon us. Jesus is the "Saviour of all men, *specially of those that believe.*" 1 Tim. iv. 10. Remember, then, though we have a Saviour, He will not save us, unless we "*believe* on Him."

We have Sunday schools, churches, Bibles, and Christian example, yet, if we do not love the Saviour, we shall be lost. "The saddest road to hell is that which runs under the pulpit, past the Bible, and through the midst of warnings and invitations."—*Ryle.*

Rev. John Newton, in his last moments, said that he remembered two things:

1st. That he was a great sinner.
2d. That Jesus Christ was a great Saviour.

"How shall *we* escape, if we neglect *so great* salvation." Heb. ii. 3.

WHAT THE BIBLE SAYS OF THE FOOL.

1. His belief.................Ps. xiv. 1. There is no God.
2. His walk...................Eccl. ii. 14—is in darkness.
3. His standing before God....Eccl. v. 4. No pleasure in him.
4. His heart.............Eccl. vii. 4—is in the house of mirth.
5. His food.....Eccl. x. 12. His life will swallow up himself.
6. His house............Matt. vii. 26—is built on the sand.
7. His end.........................Luke xii. 20. Death.

THE BOW IN THE CLOUD.

(Draw the rainbow with pieces of colored crayons, held sidewise, and write the words heavily with white crayon. A beautiful effect may be produced if skilfully drawn.)

"And the bow shall be in the cloud; and I will look upon it, that I may remember the everlasting covenant between God and every living creature of all flesh that is upon the face of the earth." Gen. ix. 16.

State the facts of the flood, and so onward, until this covenant of God. Dwell on the shape and colors of the bow. These may be remembered by the initial word, "*Vib gy or-y*," and these letters placed in the several spaces.

The bow is the *token* of God's promise. Explain the word "token" by instancing gifts of parents, teachers, etc. Explain covenant or *agreement*. The first covenant made by God with man. *God's* covenant, wherein the Lord agrees never again to destroy the world with a flood. Man is asked for no agreement in return. The Lord says, v. 13, "*My* bow." Token of God's *forbearance*. God *forbears* what He might justly do: drown the world again and again. His *condescension* is brought visibly to our minds when we see His bow in the clouds. He *condescends* to bind Himself by covenant promise, and to give us a token of it.

Thus He displays His grace, that source of all His blessings. 1 Cor. xv. 10.

These lessons are taught by His bow over *the world* (which write, as in diagram, under the bow). And the rainbow, this token of God's forbearance, condescension, and grace, surrounds *His throne* forever in heaven. Read Rev. iv. 3, and have the children repeat it in concert, as also the text which is the theme of the lesson.—From *Teacher and Class.*

WHAT CHRISTIANS HAVE.

Faith in God..................................Mark xi. 22.
Everlasting life...............................John iii. 36.
Light of life..................................John viii. 12.
My joy fulfilled in themselves.................John xvii. 13.
Hope toward God...............................Acts xxiv. 15.
A conscience void of offence..................Acts xxiv. 16.
Peace with God................................Rom. v. 1.
Access by faith...............................Rom. v. 2.
Fruit unto holiness...........................Rom. vi. 22.
First fruits of the Spirit....................Rom. viii. 23.
A building of God not made with hands.........2 Cor. v. 1.
These promises................................2 Cor. vii. 1.
All sufficiency in all things.................2 Cor. ix. 8.

COME TO JESUS FOR WHAT?

Pardon..........Eph. i. 5–7.	Peace..........John xiv. 27.
Comfort.........Isa. lxi. 2–3.	Joy..........John xv. 10, 11.
Health......Matt. viii. 16, 17.	Rest............Matt. xi. 28.
Strength.........Phil. iv. 13.	Happiness...Prov. xiii. 17, 18.
Holiness.......John xv. 4. 5.	Eternal life.......John vi. 47.

LIGHT FROM THE BIBLE.

In this picture you see a lamp, a torch, a rock, a ship, and a book. All these objects are *suggestive*. Lamps and torches are used to light up *dark places*. If we go down into deep mines, or caves, or into some dens of the city, what do we find? Darkness. Yes. The sunlight never enters these places, and so we must take the lamp or torch along to light up the way. Go down into the Mammoth Cave of Kentucky, and you must flash your torch upon the darkness if you would see.

There is darkness in the *spiritual* as well as in the natural world. Hence, Paul said of wicked men, "Their foolish heart was *darkened*." Rom. i. 21. He also affirms that the Gentiles had "the understanding *darkened*." Eph. iv. 18. Now, what do we need in this *darkness* of the soul? Light. Yes. Where shall we find it? In the Bible. Men who *follow* the Bible never go *astray*. It *banishes* their darkness. Hear what Peter says about it: "We have also a more sure word of prophecy; whereunto ye do well that ye take heed, *as unto a light* that shineth in a dark place." 2 Pet. i. 19.

This is the book we love to study Sabbath after Sabbath, and no other book can guide us to heaven. What would we do without it? "Rob us of our Bible, and our sky has lost its sun, and in the best of other books we have naught but the glimmer of twinkling stars."—*Guthrie.*

In the picture you also see a vessel and in the distance a rock. The vessel seems to be dashing right on toward the rock. But there is a chart on board, and this gives *timely* warning, and the vessel is saved. There are *rocks* in the current of your lives, children. Name some of them. Pride, Revenge, Falsehood, Disobedience, etc. Take the Bible for your chart. After one of the old Reformers had finished a controversy with an enemy of the truth, a friend begged to see the notes he had used in the discussion, and was surprised to find written there, many times in succession, the words, "More light, Lord—more light, more light!" Make this your prayer. "More light, more light!"

THE BIBLE MIRROR.

1. It is a wonderful mirror....................Ps. cxix. 129.
2. It shows us our own image..................Jas. i. 23-25.
3. It shows us what is wrong.....Luke vii. 40-47, Ps. cxix. 9.
4. It reveals a glorious light........John i. 14 ; 1 John i. 1, 2.
5. It reflects a light on those who look into it..Ex. xxxiv. 29, 30.
6. It should be used daily...........................Ps. i. 2.

HOW MAY WE GET TO HEAVEN?

1. Through our God, He will save us..........Isa. xxv. 8, 9.
2. By serving the Lord with all our heart..1 Sam. xii. 23, 24.
3. By following after righteousness.............Prov. xv. 9.
4. By doing the will of our Father............Matt. vii. 21.
5. Through Christ, the door.....................John x. 9.
6. Through Christ, the way, the truth, and the life.John xiv. 4.
7. By access through Christ and the Spirit to the Father.
   Eph. ii, 18.
8. Through Christ bearing our sins..........Heb. ix. 27, 28.
9. By the blood of Jesus.... ....Heb. x. 19.
10. Through the open door..................... .Rev. iii. 8.

THE GREAT SHIP AND THE LITTLE HELM.

Turn to James, iii. 4, and you will read as follows: "Behold also the ships, which though they be so great, and are driven of fierce winds, yet are they turned about with a very small helm, withersoever the governor listeth." Now, look at the picture, and you will see the "*helm*" of which St. James speaks. Observe the fact that it is very *small* compared to the great size of the ship. The masts are tall and the body of the vessel seems large, but the "helm" is "*very small.*"

What power it exerts upon that huge ship! Here we learn the importance of *little* things. We read that the " Conies are but a *feeble folk*," Prov. xxx. 26; and we also read of the "*little* foxes that spoil the vines." Song ii. 15. The "tongue is a *little* member and boasteth great things." Jas. iii. 5. These expressions show the importance of *little* things. A clever Dutchman amused himself one day by cutting some letters of the alphabet on the bark of a tree. It was a very small thing, but out of that little thing came the art of printing. Little things often produce great results. "Who hath despised the day of small things?" Zech. iv. 10. But observe that while this helm is so very small, it *controls* the movements of the vessel. To this fact St. James here calls special attention. He reminds us that these "*great*" ships are "*turned about*" by the helm. "Turned about." They are *guided* and *kept* in their *proper* course by the helm. The vessel would *drift* along with the wind and tide if left to itself, but the pilot's hand is on the helm and that guides the ship to its destination. We are all out on the stormy ocean of life. We shall *drift* with the tide of evil influences and drift into ruin, unless we are *guided* in our movements. Let God be our *Guide*, and the promise is, "He shall *direct* thy paths." Prov. iii. 6. Said David, "Thou shalt *guide* me with thy counsel." Ps. lxxiii. 24. The ship never refuses to "*mind*" the helm. So let us *follow* our Divine Guide, and we shall reach the eternal harbor.

Then we will sing:

> "Drop the anchor, furl the sail,
> We are safe within the vale."

SIX COMMANDS OF CHRIST.

1. Turn from death .... Mark i. 14, 15.
2. Look for life .... John i. 29.
3. Come for rest .... Matt. xi. 28.
4. Abide for fruitfulness .... John xv. 4.
5. Obey for friendship .... John xv. 14.
6. Watch in readiness for His coming .... Mark xiii. 35-37.

INDISPENSABLE THINGS.

1. Without shedding of blood is no remission ...... Heb. ix. 22.
2. Without faith it is impossible to please God ..... Heb. xi. 6.
3. Without holiness no man shall see the Lord .... Heb. xii. 14.
4. Without works faith is dead .... Jas. ii. 26.
5. Without love I am nothing .... 1. Cor. xiii. 1, 3.
6. Without chastisement ye are not sons .... Heb. xii. 8.
7. Without me (Jesus) ye can do nothing .... John xv. 5.

FIGS OR THISTLES—WHICH?

You see here a cluster of *grapes* and a branch of the *thorn-bush*. Then, in the words written upon the board, you see a reference to *figs* and *thistles*. The question relates to these *four* objects. We find it in Matt. vii. 16. Two of these objects, grapes and figs, are *useful;* the other two, thorns and thistles, are *worthless*. If we should ask, "*Which* do you prefer?" you would quickly answer, and not one of you would choose the *thorn* nor *thistle*. You would "gather" the grapes and figs. Let it be your aim always to choose the *good* in the moral world rather than the *evil*. Let the thistles, which *irritate* and *annoy*, and the thorns which *pierce* and *pain* be rejected. God offers you pleasant, palatable, healthful things in abundance. Take these, and let the *bad* and *barren* things alone. Be like Mary. "Mary hath chosen that *good* part." Luke x. 42.

But this question of the Saviour implies that fruit will **always** *harmonize* in its *essence* with the *nature* of the plant or tree that produces it. This is the chief point of the question. A certain tree or a plant has a *capacity* to produce a certain kind of fruit. It *cannot* bear anything else. A thorn cannot bear **grapes, nor** a thistle figs. The idea is that a *bad* life cannot produce *good* results.

Hence, said Jesus, "Neither can a *corrupt* tree bring forth *good* fruit." Matt. vii. 18.

"We cannot have *right* virtues without *right* conditions."— *Beecher*.

"A good man out of the good treasure of the heart, bringeth forth good things." Matt. xii. 35.

Let us strive to *be* good, and *do* good. How *little* good have we done! "A very *small page* will serve for the number of our good works when *vast volumes* will not contain our evil deeds." —*Bishop Wilson*. Let us be more fruitful in the gospel vineyard. The Egyptian fig-tree is said to bear fruit *seven times* every year. In Spain, it is said, there is nothing barren or not in some way useful. So may it be in *this* Sunday-school.

EXAMPLES OF PRAYER IN DANGER, AND BY WHOM.

1. Jacob, from his brother..................Gen. xxxii. 9–12.
2. Joshua, for deliverance of his people..........Jos. vii. 5–9.
3. Gideon, for deliverance of his people......Judges vi. 13–16.
4. Elisha, for deliverance from an army........2 Kings vi. 17.
5. Jehoahaz, for deliverance of his people......2 Kings xiii. 4.
6. Hezekiah, for deliverance of his people...2 Chron. xxxii. 20.
7. Josiah, for mercy........................2 Kings xxii. 13.
8. Asa, for deliverance of his people.........2 Chron. xiv. 11.
9. Jehoshaphat, for deliverance of his people...2 Chron. xx. 4.
10. David, in fear......Ps. xxxii. 6, 7; Ps. lvi. 3; Ps. cxvi. 3–6.
11. Disciples in the storm...................Mark iv. 37, etc.
12. Peter in prison.........................Acts. xii. 5–17.
13. Paul and Silas in prison.................Acts xvi. 25–34.
14. Paul on his voyage.................... Acts xxvii. 22, etc.

THE UPLIFTED SAVIOUR.

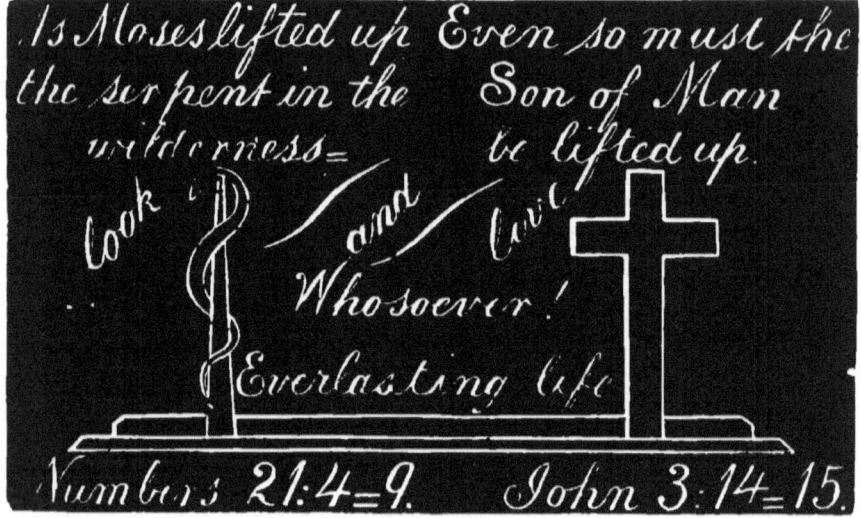

This picture recalls a very interesting event in the history of the Israelites. They were *journeying* through the wilderness. They suffered many painful *hardships*. Their trials overtaxed their patience, and at last they began to *murmur* and *complain* most bitterly. As a *punishment*, God sent serpents into their camp, and the murmuring people were bitten by them. "And the Lord sent fiery serpents among the people, and they bit the people; and much people of Israel died." Num. xxi. 6. God is never *at a loss* for means to punish the wicked. He can make the *winds* and the *waves* do His will. Here fiery serpents become the ministers of his wrath. Observe they did not enter the camp and bite simply *because* it was their nature to do so, for the "Lord *sent* fiery serpents among the people." Let us take care how we *provoke* Him. Moses was directed to "make a serpent of brass and set it up upon a pole," and the bitten ones looked upon it and were healed. They did not have to *go to it*, but only *look* upon it, and they lived. How *simple*, how easy the method of their cure. Now, this uplifted serpent reminds us of the uplifted Saviour. Read the words of Jesus: "As Moses lifted up the serpent in the wilderness, even so must the son of man be lifted up." John iii. 14, 15.

This refers to His crucifixion:

He *was* "taken, and by wicked hands crucified and slain." Acts ii. 23. He was "lifted up" upon the cross, and He *suffered for sins*, the just for the unjust, that He might bring us to God. 1 Pet. iii. 18. We *need a remedy* for sin as much as the Israelites needed one for the poisonous bite of the serpent. They found theirs in the uplifted serpent; we find ours in the uplifted Christ. They *looked* and lived. Are *you* "looking unto Jesus"? Heb. xii. 2. Hear the command of God: "Look unto me, and be ye saved." Isa. xlv. 22. This you *all* can do. How *simple* it is. "Here is one little word of four letter, and two of them are alike! *Look*."—*Spurgeon*. Let us *look, believe,* and *live*.

WHAT CHRIST IS TO US.

The door....................John x. 9. Enter and be saved.
The Way....................John xiv. 6. Walk ye in Him.
The Light of the World....John viii. 12. Walk in the Light.
The Bread of Life..........John vi. 35. Eat and be satisfied.
The Smitten Rock....1 Cor. x. 4. Drink of the living streams.
Our Saviour....................2 Tim. i, 10. Receive Him.
Our Peace....................Eph. ii. 14. Rest in Him.
Our Shepherd..................John x. 11. Hear His voice.
Our Example..................John xiii. 15. Follow Him.
Our High Priest..............Heb. vii. 26. Look up to Him.
Our Lord....................John xiii. 13. Obey Him.
The King of kings.....Rev. xix. 16. Wait for His appearing.

THE CHRISTIAN'S DEDICATION.

I take God the Father to be my God.............1 Thess. i. 9.
I take God the Son to be my Saviour.............Acts v. 31.
I take God the Holy Ghost to be my Sanctifier.....1 Peter i. 2.
I take the Word of God to be my rule........2 Tim. iii. 16, 17.
I take the people of God to be my people.......Ruth i. 16, 17.
I likewise dedicate my whole self to the Lord...Rom. xiv. 7, 8.
And I do this deliberately—Josh. xxiv. 15. Sincerely—2 Cor. i. 12. Freely—Psalm cx. 3. And forever—Rom. viii. 35-39.

248   CURIOSITIES OF THE BIBLE.

SIGNALS OF DANGER.

In this picture you see a portion of a railroad track, and just at the curve you see a locomotive. You also see a line of telegraph-wires, and, located near them, is an electric battery, which is put in motion when the train passes, and thus gives notice of its coming. A person walking on the track or waiting at the station hears the alarm-bell ring and knows that the train is *near*. It is to him a signal of *danger*.

Our *pathway* in life is beset with many *dangers*, and there are *alarm-signals* out on every side. Dangers on the railroad are often met with at the *curves*. Persons walking there do not see the train, and it dashes upon them and destroys them. There is danger *at the curve*, and they must watch the signal. So there are curves or *turning-points* in every life. Be careful *how* you approach them—*how* you go around them. As you go out of childhood into youth, you pass a *curve* on life's pathway. As you go from youth into manhood you pass another. These are turning-points in your history. And just at these points life may become a *bane* or a *blessing*. Some round the curve with no thought of what they are to do as they pass it. Go around the curve with a *purpose*. Resolve to make all your *after-life* better than it was before. Some are in a feverish hurry to get around the curve. They want to press on to honor, pleasure, and wealth with *undue haste*. And here is their danger. They are *too eager*, too venturesome. Sometimes scholars decide to *leave* the school. Then they reach a *turning-point* in their history. There is danger before them. They are too hasty and inconsiderate. They may go astray, and never return to the right way. Let us look out for danger at these turning-points in life.

Signals of danger will be *useless* if we do not heed them. Let the whistle blow or the alarm-bell ring; but if the man on the track *does not heed it*, he will be destroyed. Let the mariner *ignore* the lighthouse, and his vessel will run upon the rocks, and all may be lost.

A bell was once so arranged that in a storm it would ring loudly, and thus warn mariners of their danger. Some pirates muffled the bell so that it would not ring out its alarm, hoping that, in its silence, some unfortunate vessel might be driven upon the rocks and become their prey. Strange to say, they themselves were the first to suffer. They had *silenced* the warning-bell, and all perished. Let us *never* muffle the bell of conscience. Let us *heed* the warnings of truth.

THE GOSPEL RAILROAD.

The graded road..................Isa. xl. 3-5; Isa. lxii. 10.
The track, Jesus.........................John xiv. 6.
The engine, Charity......................1 Cor. xiii. 13.
The engineer, The Holy Spirit..........John xiv. 26; xv. 26.
The headlight, The Word of God..............Ps. cxix. 105.
The red lights, danger signals................Matt vii. 13, 14.
The car, our Saviour.........................John x. 9.
The conductor, our Heavenly Father........Ps. xxxiii. 18-20.
The travellers, Believers....................Rev. vii. 9, 10.
The destination Heaven..1 Peter i. 3, 4; Heb. xiii. 14; 2 Cor. v. 1.

GAINING AND LOSING.

There you see a pair of scales. One side hangs down, as though it were heavily loaded, and the other rises upward, as though it had only a light burden to bear. On one side we see a representation of the World, and the other is supposed to be borne down by something more solid and valuable than the world itself —even a *soul*. A *soul* on one side, the *world* on the other. What a difference! Bear this in mind, and you will see the force of the question. "What shall it profit a man if he shall gain the whole world and lose his own soul!" Mark viii. 36. Your soul is greatly superior to the world, and should not be exchanged for it.

A little blind girl once asked, "What is soul?" Her instructor answered, "That which thinks, feels, hopes, loves." How little, how meagre, how trivial are all the pleasures, riches, honors, and glories of the world. "One soul *outweighs* them all." You have only one soul, and if you lose that, all is gone forever and ever. We sometimes lose *one* friend, but we have others left. Sometimes one portion of property will be taken away, but some other portion remains. Lose the soul, and all is gone. You cannot recall it, you cannot replace it. "He that is unjust, *let him be unjust still.*" Rev. xxii. 11. Your soul cost an immense price, and is valuable beyond all computation. "Ye are bought with a price." 1 Cor. vi. 20. That "price" is the blood of the Son of God. "We have redemption *through his blood.*" Eph. i. 7. Estimated by its cost, how valuable the soul is! What profit will it be for a man to lose his precious soul, and have nothing in exchange, but a *vain, worthless, decaying* world. That soul will live on forever and ever. Yea, it will live, "when the riches, powers, and pleasures of the world have passed away like a snow-wreath beneath a vernal shower."— *Rowland Hill.*

Gain as much of the world as you can *consistently*, but at the same time resolve to save your soul. A collegian, distinguished for his mathematical attainments, was fond of challenging his fellow-students to a trial of skill in solving difficult problems. One day a class-mate came into his study, and, laying a folded paper before him, said, "There is a problem I wish you would help me to solve," and immediately left the room.

The paper was eagerly unfolded, and there, instead of a question in mathematics, were traced the lines, "What shall it profit a man if he gain the whole world and lose his own soul; or what shall a man give in exchange for his soul?"

With a gesture of impatience he tore the paper to atoms and turned again to his books. But in vain he tried to shake off the impressions of the solemn words he had read. The Holy Spirit pressed home his conviction of guilt and danger, so that he could find no peace till he found it in believing in Jesus. He subsequently became a minister of the Gospel he had once despised, and his first sermon was from the words, so blessed to his own soul, "What shall it profit a man if he gain the whole world and lose his own soul?"

The apostles were very full, because very empty; full of the spirit of God, because empty of the spirit of the world.—*St. Augustine.*

THE CHRISTIAN'S DEFENCE—2 KINGS VI. 8-18.

Our lesson finds the man of God sore beset. Enemies are all around him, and there is no apparent escape. Yet how perfect is his security and safety. The one on his side is infinitely more than all his enemies. *If God be for us*, we have One who is more than all they that be against us.

Notice his perfect trust. While his servant is stricken with fear, his heart is calm. The plot of his wicked enemies seemed complete, but it had one fatal defect—God was not for them.

The true servant of God is surrounded by enemies—sin and temptation surround him. They are our foes, but we have a heavenly Defender. If God be for us, we shall surely *overcome*. To have God for us, we must be clearly and decidedly for God; we must be on the Lord's side.

There is no surrender in the fight with sin and Satan—no parleying or making terms with Satan. We are to *"fight the good fight."* We are to resist the devil, if we would have him flee from us. If we had only our own strength to depend upon there would be but little hope of *victory ;* but the weapons of our defence are heavenly. The shield of *Faith* is a sure defence. Trust in God never disappoints.

We are not only to fight, but to *conquer the evil one.* God will not only keep us through faith in Him, but he gives us a precious and priceless weapon of defence—" *the sword of the Spirit.*"

How necessary an acquaintance with its use—a knowledge of its power. The word of God should be " hid in our hearts" that we may delight in it and feel its power in our lives.

God is not only our Defender, but our *Reward.* Faithful here, victory will be sure, and the reward of His presence forever.

[Diagram by J. G. Phipps, Indianapolis.]

GOD IS ABLE.

Able to save.................................Jas. iv. 12.
" " " from the furnace heat............Dan. iii. 13–18.
" " " " the lion's mouth............Dan. vi. 18–24.
" " " " all uncleanness............Ezek. xxxvi. 29.
" " " " our sins......................Matt. i. 21.
" " " " death........ ....Heb. v. 7.
" " " to the uttermost....................Heb. vii. 25.
Able to succor the tempted......................Heb. ii. 18
" make us stand.. ....Rom. xiv. 4.
" build us up...........................Acts xx. 32.
" keep us from evil.....................2 Thes. iii. 3.
" keep us from falling................. ....Jude xxiv.
" keep that which we commit to Him......2 Tim. i. 12.
" perform His promises...................Rom. iv. 21
" do more than we ask...................Eph. iii. 20.
" make all grace abound.................2 Cor. ix. 8.
" subdue all things to Himself............Phil. iii. 21.
" raise us from the dead..................Heb. xi. 19.
" present us faultless.................... .Jude xxiv,

THE TWO LADDERS.

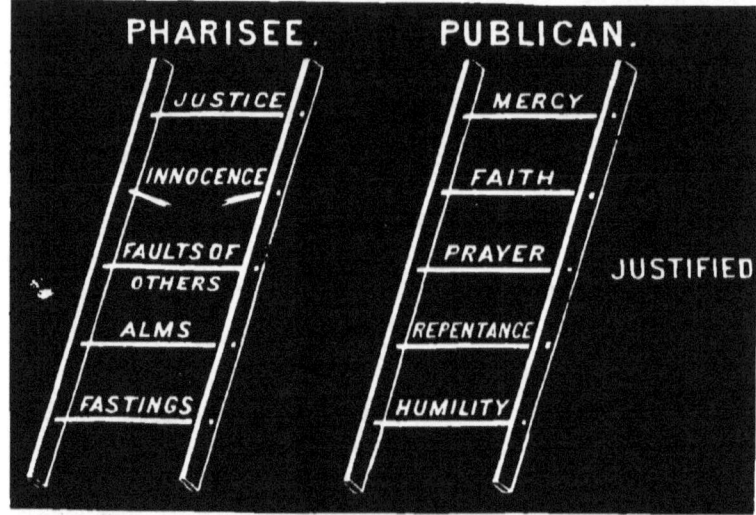

These two ladders are intended to represent the moral character and life of the Pharisee and the Publican. These characters differ very widely from each other, and the ladders drawn upon the board, with their peculiar inscriptions, make the difference between them all the more apparent. The parable is given by the Saviour in Luke xviii. 10-14. In the ladder which the Pharisee is represented as climbing, you see five rounds, bearing significant names, and these indicate the various *stages* or *steps* by which he hopes to reach heaven. The first round is *fasting*. See how he magnifies it. He is careful to mention that he fasts *twice* in the week. Will that make a man *good*, or *save* him? No. He might fast twice as often and yet be lost. Fasting is a Christian duty, but we cannot be saved by it. The second round is *alms*. That means gifts to the poor and needy. And this man was liberal, for he gave one-tenth of all he had. It is right to give to the destitute. Jesus said, "Ye have the poor always with you." Matt. xxvi. 11. We are to remember that "He that hath pity upon the poor, lendeth unto the Lord,"

Prov. xix. 17. "A *miser* is a monster that no one can love."— Dr. Thomas.

The next round is described as the *faults* of *others*. He names a list of faults. How natural it is for us to see the sins of *other* people. It would be better to see *our own*, and forsake them. "If the best man's faults were written on his forehead, it would make him pull his hat over his eyes."—*Gaelic Proverb*.

The next round is a *broken* one. It is marked *innocence*. All the other rounds seemed strong enough to hold the Pharisee, but when he reached that round it gave way. He was far from being an innocent man. Every human scheme breaks down at this point. "*All* have sinned and come short of the glory of God. Rom. iii. 23.

The next round is *justice*. Of course he could not reach that, for the round below was broken, and his upward course was arrested. All this suggests one of the most striking utterances of the Saviour, "He that climbeth up some other way, the same is a thief and a robber." John x. 1.

Now look at the other ladder, which represents the course pursued by the Publican. You see the same number of rounds, and each one has a proper title. Name them. You see no *broken* rounds in this ladder. Each one is solid and strong. The Pharisee failed, but the Publican did not. Will *you* follow the Publican? He went down to his house justified. Be humble and prayerful, and ever trust in God. "The devil told St. Marcarius, "I can surpass thee in watching, fasting, and many other things; but humility conquers and disarms me."—*Foster*.

THE PATH TO ETERNAL LIFE.

1. Is a straight path.............Prov. iv. 25-27; Heb. xii. 13.
2. Is a narrow path......................Matt. vii. 13, 14.
3. Is an upward path...............Prov. xv. 24; Isa. xl. 31.
4. Is an old path...............................Jer. vi. 16.
5. Is a pleasant path..........................Prov. iii. 17.
6. Is a light path.............................Prov. iv. 18.
7. Which leads to a glorious city.................Ps. cvii. 7.

THE YOKE OF CHRIST—Matt. xi. 30.

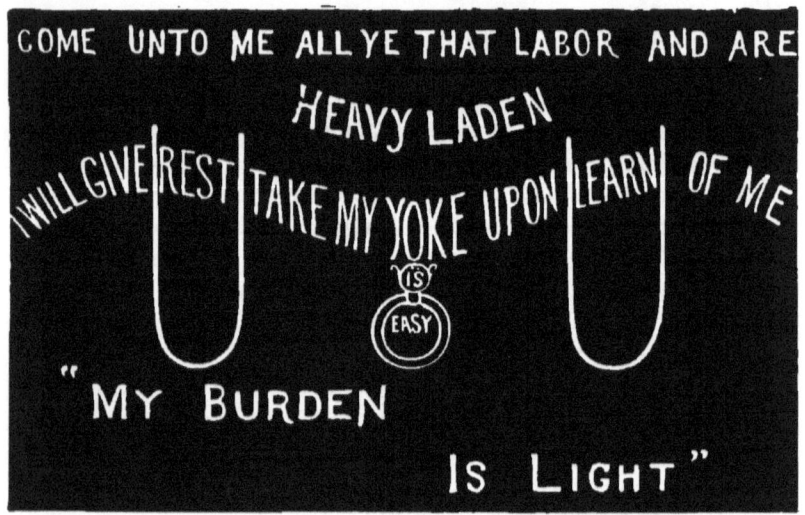

Having drawn the text upon the blackboard or slate, as explained above, call special attention to the fact that the yoke is intended for *use*.

It never is regarded merely as an *ornament*, but is designed for *service*. It may be very strong, and quite perfect in every respect; but unless it is *used* it will be almost worthless.

The yoke of Christ's teaching and example will be serviceable to us if we *use it*. He says to us: "*Take* my yoke upon you."

Did a yoke ever place itself upon the neck of the oxen?

No, it had to be put there by somebody. So, when you wear the yoke of Christ, it must be taken upon you. Remember, children, the Saviour asks you to *take it;* He does not try to *force it* upon you. Yokes sometimes seem heavy, because of the burdens that are attached to them.. But Christ tells us that His yoke is *easy*, and His *burden* is *light*. Animals that bear the yoke have no rest until the yoke is removed. But the Christian has rest, even while he bears the yoke of Christ. Will you try it, children?

Mr. Moody tells us that "the service of Christ is the *only true liberty.*" The best time to bear the yoke is in *youth.*

It is a yoke of *restraint.* Learn *self-control* now. It is a yoke of *service.* Learn to render *service* now. It is a yoke of sacrifice. Learn to practise *self-denial* now.

The prophet tells us that "it is good for a man that he bear the yoke in his youth." Lam. iii. 27.

"Remember now thy Creator in the days of thy youth."

"COMES" OF THE OLD TESTAMENT.

Come into the Ark	Gen. vii. 1.
Come thou with us	Numbers x. 29.
Come, let us reason together	Isa. i. 18.
Come, return	Isa. xxi. 12.
Come, my people, enter into thy chambers	Isa. xxvi. 20.
Come ye to the waters	Isa. lv. 1.
Come unto me	Isa. lv. 3.

"COMES" OF THE NEW TESTAMENT,

Come unto me all ye that labor	Matt. xi. 28.
Come, ye blessed	Matt. xxv. 34
Come apart and rest	Mark. vi. 31.
Come down	Luke xix. 5
Come and see	John i. 39.
Come unto me and drink	John vii. 37.
Come forth	John xi. 43.
Come and dine	John xxi. 12.
I will come again	John xiv. 3.
Come over and help us	Acts xvi. 9.
Come out and be ye separate	2 Cor. vi. 17.
Come boldly unto the throne of grace	Heb. iv. 16.
Come out of her, my people	Rev. xviii. 4.
Come, the Spirit and the Bride say	Rev. xxii. 17.

THE CHRISTIAN'S CROWN.

We have here an object, at once beautiful and immensely valuable. It is a crown—the crown of life. In Rev. ii. 10, we read, "Be thou faithful unto death, and I will give thee a crown of life. Crowns are worn by earthly sovereigns to denote their royal character, official dignity, and dominion. On state occasions, crowns, sparkling with courtly splendor, deck the brows of princes, kings, and queens. The Christian has the promise of a crown. He is now a king in his *minority*. "There is *laid up for me* a crown of righteousness," is his triumphant utterance. 2 Tim. iv. 8. It is *waiting* for him in the "crown-chamber" above.

This crown will *never fade away*. The laurel wreath that rests upon the victor's brow withers, and he soon casts it aside as worthless. The brightest diadem of earth soon loses its lustre. But this crown always remains untarnished. "Ye shall receive a crown of glory that *fadeth not away*." 1 Pet. v. 4. Try to win this crown. The worldling's crown is "corruptible," the Christian's "incorruptible." 1 Cor. ix. 25. This crown is invested with *great value*.

Many things in this world are prized because they are *rare* and *costly*. "The Queen of England wears a crown of gold, filled with diamonds and precious stones, worth $20,000,000."

One of the Queen's crown jewels alone is valued at $1,500,-000. But here is a crown surpassing the value of all the crowns of earth combined. It *outshines* them, *outweighs* them, *outlasts* them.

Remember that the crown is to *follow* the cross. One has said, "After the cross cometh the crown." *Bear* the cross, if you would *wear* the crown. "Forty brave soldiers of the Thundering Legion were called to adjure Christ or die. One of them said, 'Let us forty ask God to send us to our crowns together.'"—*Foster*. They laid down forty crosses and took up forty crowns. A dying saint caught a glimpse of the crown-chamber, and shouted, "Crowns! crowns! crowns of glory shall adorn this head of mine ere long." Ask the question earnestly, "Shall the crown be mine?" "*Hold fast*, that which thou hast, that no man take thy crown." Rev. iii. 11.

"The crown that worldlings covet,
Is not the crown for me;
Its beauty fades as quickly
As sunshine on the sea."

"So run that ye may obtain." 1 Cor. ix. 24.

GOD'S WAY AND OURS CONTRASTED.

Pleasantness and peace..Prov. iii. 17.	Folly............Ps. xlix. 13.
Strength.........Prov. x. 29.	Wasting and destruction...Isa. lix. 7
Good and upright..Ps. xxv. 8.	Upside down.....Ps. cxlvi. 9.
Restful..........Jere. vi. 16.	Hard or weary...Prov. xiii. 15.
Righteousness and life...Prov. xii. 28.	Death..........Prov. xiv. 12.

THE FULL SURRENDER.

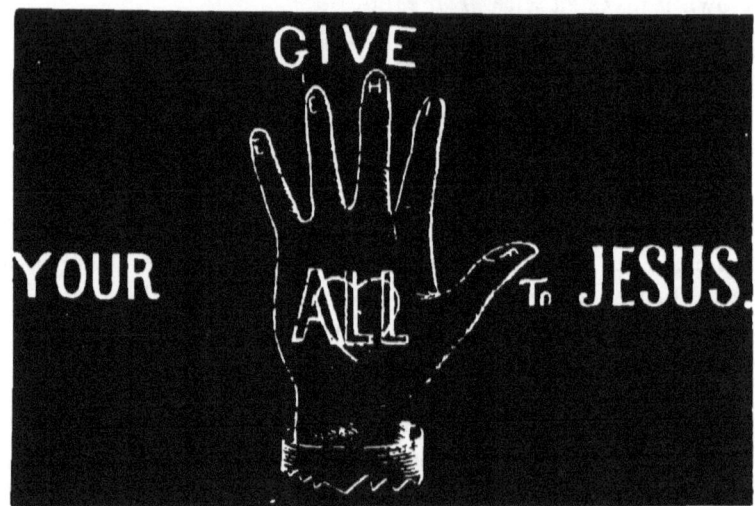

We have here the picture of a *hand*. It is *open*, thus showing that nothing is kept within its grasp, nor even concealed from sight. Some persons boast that they never "*Show their hands*" in what they do. They love to appear *shrewd* and *sly*. But Jesus wants boys and girls to *show* their hands in His service.

This open hand and the motto, and also the letters you see written upon the fingers, are intended to show that *all* we have should be given to the Saviour. It is said that, on the occasion of a missionary collection, a young man was so anxious to serve the Saviour that he wrote upon a card the single word "Myself," and dropped it into the basket. What a grand sentiment! *Myself for Jesus.* Nothing kept back—*all* given to Christ.

Children, open your hearts and give *all* the sympathy and love that throbs in them to the Saviour. Hear His voice, saying to you each : "Son, give me thy heart." Give it to Him *entirely*. Do not think that He will be pleased with just a little place in your heart, for He wants it *all*, and will have no rival. "**The Roman soldiery** chose Valentinian to be their emperor; afterwards they consulted how they might join a partner with him in the throne. On hearing this, the emperor replied, that, although it had been in their power to give him the empire, it was no longer in their power to give him a colleague."—*Biblical Museum.*

He wanted the *whole* empire under his rule. So Jesus wants the *whole empire* of the soul.

Children, go with *open* hands to Jesus, and *keep nothing back.* Can you tell me who tried to "keep back part of the price," and received a terrible punishment for the crime? Yes, Ananias and Sapphira. How dreadful their doom! Keep back nothing that the Lord claims. Let your *brains think* for Christ. Let your *hearts* beat with His love; let your *eyes* be fixed upon Him; let your *hands* bear His cross; let your *feet* walk in the "straight and narrow way." *All* your hearts for Jesus, *now* and *always.*

TEMPERANCE.

Bible proofs that strong drink leads to—

Shame........	Example of	Noah...............	Gen. ix. 21.
Confusion.....	"	" Lot................	Gen. xix. 33.
Folly	"	" Ahasuerus........	Esther i. 10, 11.
Defeat........	"	" Benhadad......	1 Kings xx. 16-20.
Poverty.......	Warnings of Solomon..........		Prov. xxiii. 21.
Trouble.......	" " "		......Prov. xxiii. 29, 30.
Sacrilege......	Example of Belshazzar...........		Dan. v. 1-5.
Eternal rejection of God......................			1 Cor. vi. 10.

They that tarry long at the wine Have Babbling, Redness of Eyes, Wounds, Sorrow, Woe.—Prov. xxiii. 29.

Wine is a mocker, strong drink is raging, and whosoever is deceived thereby is not wise.—Prov. xx. 1.

Drink waters out of thine own cistern and running waters out of thine own well.— Prov. v. 15,

Look not thou upon the wine when it is red. —Prov. xxiii. 31. "Touch not, taste not, handle not."

THE CROSS OF CHRIST.

The cross here represented is surmounted with a crown, and there are written upon it four letters of the alphabet. These letters are intended to denote knowledge, belief, love, and obedience. You also see two arrows pointing towards a central letter X, and this letter is used to denote the word Christ. These letters suggest that we are to know, believe, love, and obey Christ. The arrow pointing towards the central letter indicates that Christ is the *centre of attraction.* "Jesus only." Matt. xvii. 8. At the foot of the cross you read: "God forbid that I should glory, save in the cross." Gal. vi. 14.

The *literal* cross was a gibbet made of two pieces of wood, crossing each other. The vilest criminals were put to death upon the cross. Hence it became a badge of shame. But Paul accepted it as though it were the highest badge of honor, and gloried in it.

We glory in the cross, because it is the symbol of Christianity. We see the zealous Jew bearing a *yoke* as the symbol of his faith, a heavy, burdensome yoke of rites and ceremonies; but the Christian finds his symbol of faith in the cross. "By the cross, then, we mean that which embodies the great doctrines of the Gospel, and presents them in all their clearness and force to the mind. Here the whole Deity is known. No wonder Paul glories in it. We glory in the cross, because it is an *independent* moral force. There is only *one* cross, and it stands *alone*. It does its own work and will win its way to universal triumph. "I would say to the insidious skeptic: Sir, Christianity asks no permission to live from either you or me—she draws her life from a higher source."—*Bishop Clark.*

Constantine looks up into the beautiful heavens at noon, and beholds, written upon a cross of wondrous beauty, the words, "In this sign conquer." Christianity will conquer by the cross —the cross alone. "There is none other name given under heaven among men, whereby we must be saved." Acts iv. 12. Take the cross and glory in it. "The old crusaders used to wear a cross upon their shoulders. This was their badge of service."—*Foster.* Jesus says, "If any man will come after me, let him deny himself, and *take up his cross*, and follow me." Matt. xvi. 24. Take the cross and let it *elevate* the soul. A heathen ruler, who had heard the story of the cross, was dying. He said to his attendants, "Make a cross, and lay me upon it." They did so, and as he lay there dying, he laid hold on the blood of Christ, and said, "It lifts me up; it lifts me; it lifts me; it lifts me."—*Bible Museum.* So may it lift us all into light and life.

John Newton, in commenting upon Paul's statement to the Corinthians concerning himself (1 Cor. xv. 10), says: "I am not what I *ought* to be; I am not what I *wish* to be; I am not what I *hope* to be. Yet though I am not what I ought to be, nor what I wish to be, nor what I hope to be, *I am not what I once was,* and 'by the grace of God I am what I am.'" How much of truth, thought, and experience in these few words!

THE TWO PATHS. Prov. iv. 10–19

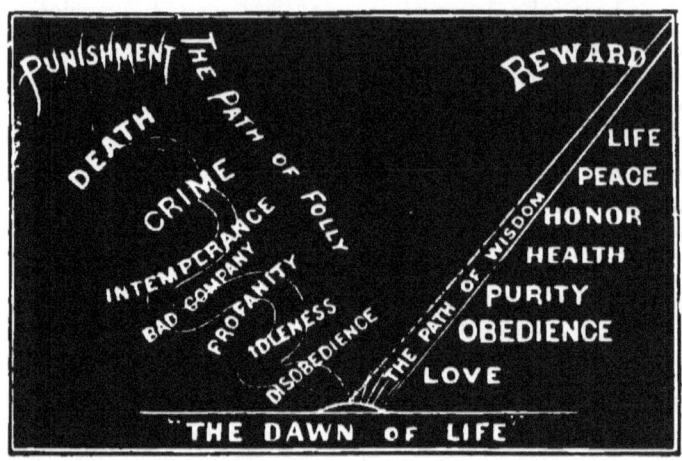

Commencing with the dawn of our lives, the beginning of our knowledge of right and wrong, we choose our own path in which we walk in this life. Two paths before each of us. The sin in our hearts will lead us in the path of *disobedience*, which through all its wanderings will lead at last to death and punishment.

Trace the steps in this "way of the wicked," writing them upon the board as in the diagram, enlarging and illustrating. The very first step in the " path of the just " is *love*.

Trace the progressive steps, and refer to the passages of Scripture indicating them. The end of the two ways. Practical and personal enforcement of the lesson: in which path am *I?*

Give familiar illustration of losing the way and taking the *wrong path*. In order to reach our home we must get in the right way. Our heavenly home. But one right way—the " path of wisdom." Not to love God and keep His law is wicked and foolish. The path of wisdom leads to heaven. The path of folly takes us farther and farther from God. Need of getting into the right path, in youth.—*J. B. Phipps*.

Concert Exercise.

WANTED FOR THE LORD'S SERVICE.

1. Men like Daniel, who dare to do right.....Dan. vi. 10-16.
2. Men like Shadrach, ready to suffer.Ex. xx. 4, 5; Dan. iii. 4-7.
3. Men in authority, with Nehemiah's faith....Neh. xiii. 4-9.
4. Men like Isaiah, full of eloquence and fervor..Isa. lv. 1-13.
5. Men of courage like Joshua...Num. xiv. 6-9; Josh. vi. 16.
6. Men like Elijah, bold to proclaim the truth..1 Kings xvii. 1.
7. Men like Paul, taught of the Spirit..........1 Cor. xii. 3.
8. Men like Timothy, zealous for the Lord. ..2 Cor. xvi. 10.
9. Men like the Bereans, gifted with wisdom..Acts xvii.10, 12.
10. Young men, like Jabez, who fear God.....1 Chron. iv. 10.
11. Young women, like gracious Ruth.........Ruth i. 16, 17.
12. Matrons, like the pious Shunamite......2 Kings iv. 8, 13.
13. Fathers, like Abraham............Gen. xxii.; Prov. x. 21.
14. Brethren, like Aaron and Hur ....Ex. xvii. 9-12.
15. Sisters, who, like Mary, sit at Jesus' feet....Luke x. 38, 39.
16. Heads of families, like Caleb.....Acts x. 2; Num. xiv. 24.
17. Wives, models in their lives............Prov. xxxi. 10-31.
18. Mothers, like Hannah, consecrating their children...1 Sam. i. 10.
19. Maidens, taught of God..2 Kings v. 1-4, 15; Prov. xv. 23.
20. Servants of Christ, like Barnabas. Acts xi. 22-26; Acts ix. 27.

SOWING AND REAPING—Gal. vi. 7.

SEED.	HARVEST
Idleness	Poverty.
Unkindness	Unkindness.
Tippling	Drunkard's grave.
Profanity	God's curse.
Sinful life	Wretched death.
Rejection of Jesus	Eternal death.

What are you sowing?

M. T. B.

THE FAMILY IN THE ARK.

We have here a picture of the ark. How long was Noah occupied in building it? One hundred and twenty years. How large was it? "If you should put it into one story and one floor, it would have been about sixteen feet high, two hundred and forty feet wide, and one thousand five hundred feet long."—*Moody*. God told Noah how large it must be. Gen. vi. 15. When God said to Noah, "Come thou and all thy house into the ark," the whole family marched in, and were safe while the deluge swept over the earth. That family consisted of eight persons—Noah and his wife, his three sons and their wives.

You see the word Christ written upon the ark in the picture. That shows that Jesus is the *soul's ark*. In him we find safety, happiness, and life eternal. God wanted the *whole* family of Noah saved. So to-day Jesus wants to get our families into the ark of salvation. How blessed it is for a whole family to be saved. How sad Noah would have felt, had any of his household been left out of the ark. It is a great joy to have *some* of the family in the ark, but we want them *all* saved. Some of you have parents in the ark, and they want you to join them. Some one has said, "Noah went in *first* and his children *followed* him." Follow your friends into the ark.

How *possible* it is for a whole family to be saved. There was room in the ark for Noah's family, and there is room in the loving heart of Jesus for us all. He takes the children of the family to His heart, and tells us that "Of *such* is the kingdom of heaven." Matt. xix. 14.

He also waits to welcome the older members of the home-circle. *All* may come. "Whosoever will, let him take the water of life freely." Rev. xxii. 17.

As the ark carried Noah to a happy destination, so will Christ, the spiritual ark, convey us home to heaven at last. Some are there *now*. They await us. A dying child, after exhorting her friends to meet her in heaven, said, "I'll be watching for you." Be anxious to get into the ark, every one of you. A little girl stood on the deck of a sinking vessel, and, when the life-boat came near, she sprang into the sea, crying, "Save me next! save me next." *Hasten* to the ark. Cry out, save *me*—save me *now*.

THE SIX ONE THINGS.

Sinner—One thing thou lackest............Matt. xix. 20, 21.
Blind man—One thing I know..................John ix. 25.
Mary—Hath the one thing needful...............Luke x. 42.
Christ—One is your Master........ ....Matt. xxiii. 10.
Paul—One thing I do...................... ....Phil. iii. 13.
Joshua—Not one thing has failed.............Josh. xxiii. 14.

D. L. MOODY.

WHAT THE CHRISTIAN SOLDIER MUST DO.

1. Must fight......................................Tim. vi. 12.
2. Must obey his commander......Luke vii. 8; Acts xxvii. 23.
3. Must be armed for war....Eph. vi. 11-18; Ps. xviii. 34, 35.
4. Must never desert, but be ready to die in the service.
Heb. xii. 4; 2 Tim. iv. 6, 7.
5. Must not engage in other service...2 Tim. ii. 4; Matt. vi. 24.
6. *Result*—victory and reward. Rom. viii. 36; 2 Tim. iv. 8; iii. 3.

LOVE NOT THE WORLD.

The picture of the world, here given, is designed to illustrate the meaning of the passage of Scripture written on the board, found in 1 John ii. 15. "If any man love the world, the love of the Father is not in him." This does not mean that we are not to love the *material* world: for its hills and plains, and mountains, and its rippling brooks and rolling oceans, its plants and trees and flowers, all are very beautiful, and challenge our love.

But we are not to love the *bad* spirit, nor follow the unchristian practice of the world. Paul speaks of it as "this present *evil* world." Gal. i. 4. Again, in Romans xii. 2, he admonishes his brethren against being "*conformed to this world.*" In the picture we have a reference to some of the things we are not to love. Its teachings, honors, etc. The man who loves these cannot have the love of the Father in him. There is not room enough for God and the world in any one heart. One or the other must be crowded out. "Ye cannot serve God and Mammon." Matt. vi. 24. Dr. Franklin once gave an apple to a very little child. The child could scarcely hold it in his hand; he then gave another, which occupied the other hand. Then choosing another, remarkable for its size and beauty, he presented that also. The child, after many ineffectual attempts to hold the three, dropped the last on the floor, and burst into tears. "See there," said Franklin, "there is a little man with more happiness than he can enjoy." If the world *fills* our hearts and hands, there will be *no room* for the Master. Let us be wise and give our love to the Father. Demas was charged with the crime of forsaking Paul, and the reason assigned was that he "*loved* this present world." 2 Tim. iv. 10. How many have given up their hope of heaven for the pleasures and follies of a sinful world. How disappointed they will be, when they find how insufficient and unsatisfactory the world is to the soul. It will allure you to its embrace, and promise you much pleasure; but remember that the "pleasures of sin" are but "for a season." Heb. xi. 25. "In St. Mark's Church, Venice, will be found the tomb of Duke Sebastian Foscarinus. Upon it are inscribed these words: 'Hear, O ye Venetians! and I will tell you which is the best thing in the world; it is to contemn and despise riches.'"—*Foster.*

WHAT IT IS TO BE A CHRISTIAN.

In faith, a believer in Christ..................Mark xvi. 16.
In knowledge, a disciple......................John viii. 31.
In character, a saint.........................Rom. i. 7
In influence, a light.........................Matt. v. 14
In conflict, a soldier........................2 Tim. ii. 3.
In communion, a friend........................John xv. 15.
In progress, a pilgrim........................Heb. xi. 13.
In relationship, a child......................Rom. viii. 16.
In expectation, an heir.......................Rom. viii. 17.

STEPS IN SIN. 2 Kings v. 20-27

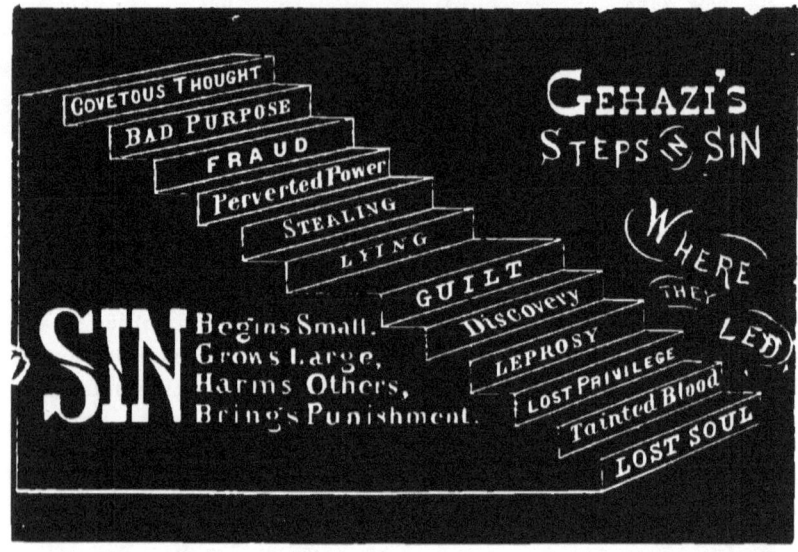

Draw a picture of steps, twelve in number, with the upper and lower pairs divided. The six upper steps are *Gehazi's steps in sin;* the six lower, the results to which they lead. He *took* the first six voluntarily, the other six necessarily.

Place in order the six sins of Gehazi; begin with the *Covetous Thought*, ending with *Lying*.

"Perverted Power" refers to the fact that he misused the spiritual gifts of Elisha for his own personal gain.

When a sinner begins, he knows not where he shall end. Having taken these steps, he was compelled to receive six consequences. Guilt, Discovery, etc. "Lost Privileges;" but for this sin he might have been Elisha's successor in the prophetic office.

"Tainted Blood;" the leprosy extending to his seed after him.

On the margin (or other side of the board) write the four lessons as taught by this event, as per diagram.—*Rev. J. L. Hurlburt.*

Concert Exercise.

THE BLOOD OF CHRIST.

Atones for the soul	Lev. xvii. 11.
Brings us into the covenant of grace	Matt. xxvi. 28.
Cleanses us from all sin	1 John i. 7.
Delivers God's people from judgment	Ex. xii. 13
Everlasting in its value	Heb. xiii. 20.
Furnishes the only ground of peace with God	Col. i. 20.
Gives us access into His presence	Heb. x. 19–21.
Has already obtained for us redemption	Eph. i. 7.
Imparts eternal life	John vi. 54.
Justifies us in the sight of God	Rom. v. 9.
Keeps us in the holy of holies	Heb. ix. 22–26.
Links us to God's electing purpose	1 Peter i. 2.
Makes us nigh to Him	Eph. ii. 13.
Never needs to be offered again	Heb. ix. 12.
Overcomes the power of Satan	Rev. xii. 11.
Purchases us	Acts xx. 28
Quenches the righteous wrath of God	Rom. iii. 25.
Redeems us from our state of ruin	1 Peter i. 18, 19.
Speaks to God and to us of salvation	Heb. xii. 24.
Tunes the voices of the saints in holy song	Rev. v. 9.
Unites us in Christian communion	1 Cor. x. 16.
Victorious over tribulation	Rev. vii. 14.
Washes us from every stain	Rev. i. 6.
X-ian's hope, is the	1 Tim. i. 1.
Yields the price that bought the church	Acts xx. 28.
Zealous of good works, makes us	Titus ii. 14.

THE PRECIOUS PROMISES.

I will *help* thee	Isa. xli. 10.
I will *hold* thee	Isa. xlii. 6.
I will *hear* thee	Isa. lxv. 24.
I will *heal* thee	Isa. lvii. 17.

THE DOOR OF THE HEART—Rev. III. 20.

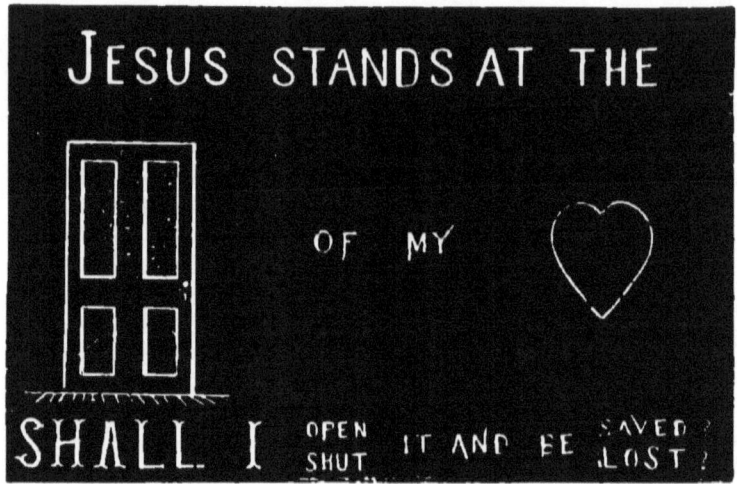

Jesus speaks of the soul as though it were a *house* into which He would like to enter, and abide as a *guest*. He calls it "The Door." His language is, "Behold, I stand at the door and knock." Your *heart* is the door. Did you ever think that the Saviour stands there *waiting* for you to open the door, so that He may come in and abide there? When some friend comes and knocks at the door of your house, you or some one quickly hastens to open the door, and let that friend come in. You do not keep your friend standing and waiting very long, if you can help it, but you throw open the door just as soon as possible. How do you treat the Saviour who comes and asks you to let Him come in?

How would your friends feel if they knew you were listening to their knocking, and yet would not let them come in? They would be *grieved*, and very likely would go away in great sorrow and anger. But do you not fear that the Saviour will become weary, and turn away and leave you all alone in your sins and sorrows? Sometimes you may not desire to have a person enter your house; but surely you would not feel like refusing to admit such a guest as the Saviour. It will make but little difference to you, sometimes, whether you open the door or not, when *some* persons are knocking, for you will be just as happy without their presence; but not so in this case.

It will make a great difference whether you open the door or keep it closed against the Saviour.

Open it, and He will come in, and help you and comfort you, and save you at last in His heavenly kingdom.

When the Prince of Wales came to this country, what a welcome he received; there wasn't anything too good for him. When the Prince of Russia came to this country, I saw him as he was escorted up Broadway, and cheer upon cheer went up all the way.—*Moody.*

But Jesus is the Prince of Life Eternal. Give Him a glad welcome.

WHAT WE DO BY FAITH.

We live....................................Gal. ii. 20.
We stand..................................2 Cor. i. 24.
We walk...................................2 Cor. v. 7.
We fight..................................1 Tim. vi. 12.
We overcome...............................1 John v. 4.
We die....................................Rom. vi. 11.
We sit with Him...........................Rev. iii. 21.

NEW THINGS OF THE BIBLE.

New birth (conversion)....................John iii. 3.
New nature (Christian life)..........2 Cor. v. 17; 2 Peter i. 4.
New heart (affections changed)............Ezekiel xi. 19.
New friends (Christians).......John xv. 15; Heb. xii. 22-24.
New name (Sons of God).1 John iii. 1; Rev. ii. 17; Rev. iii. 12.
New food (Heavenly Manna)......John vi. 48-51; Rev. ii. 17.
New tongue (To tell the story)........Mark xvi. 17; Acts ii. 4.
New song (Redemption).....................Rev. v. 9.
New home (Mansions above).................Rev. xxi. 1-4.
All things new (in Christ)..........2 Cor. v. 17; Rev. xxi. 5.

GOD'S PROMISE IN THE RAINBOW.

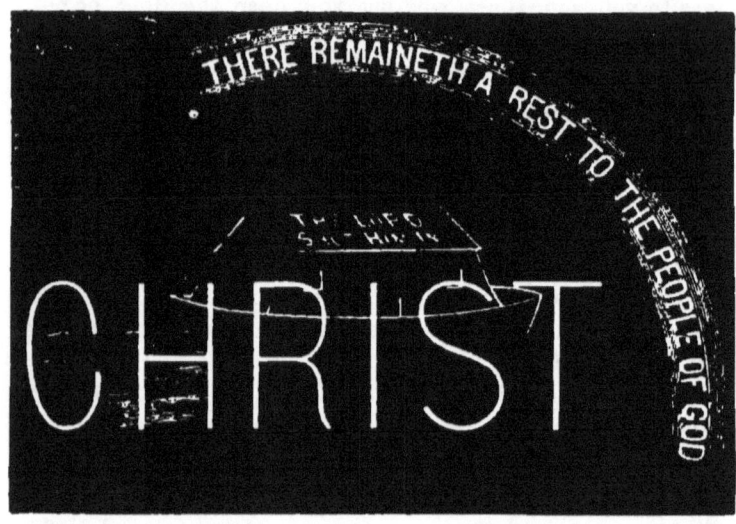

When Noah left the ark, God gave him a promise not to destroy the race again with a flood. As a "token" of this covenant, He "set His bow in the cloud." Gen. ix. 13. Every time Noah saw the beautiful bow spanning the heavens he knew that God was keeping the promise, and he felt happy and secure. The bow was *silent*, and yet it *seemed to say*, " God is faithful to His promise."

Let us turn our attention to some features of the rainbow.

And, first, the rainbow is always associated with a storm. We do not see it when the noon-day sun is shining, but we must wait till the clouds gather and the rain-drops fall. Then the bow appears and delights our eyes. So in the storms of life, we see the beauty of God's promise shining through the gloom. The bow of His promise spans many a dark cloud of sorrow.

Again, the rainbow appears *very often*.

We suppose Noah saw it a great many times. Even some of our younger children have seen it quite often. God is never at a loss for a rainbow. He can make one at any time, and it would seem as though He had already made a great many. So many rainbows are so many *renewals* of His promise. And He has *many* promises for us all in the Bible. Some one has it that there are more than *thirty thousand* distinct promises in the Word of God. Think of it—thirty thousand *bows of promise* in the Bible. Take this one, children, as *your own:* "Those that seek me *early* shall find me." Prov. viii. 17.

The rainbow has all its *original beauty* unimpaired. It is just as brilliant to-day as when it first spanned the heavens. It has not changed its form, nor lost any of its bright colors. It is still God's token, *unchanged* and unchangeable. Some one has termed it "an *old* thing, invested with a *new* meaning." So His promises are *firm* and *true*. "All the promises of God in him are *yea*, and in him *Amen*." 2 Cor. i. 20. "An old man once told me that he had marked at all the promises of God the letters 'P. T.'—which stood for 'Proved and Tried.' None of the promises of God ever will or can fail."—*Moody.*

Well may it be said, "The Lord is not slack concerning his promise." 2 Pet. iii. 9. What promise is written upon the bow in the picture? Will *you* try to obtain that rest?

THE APOSTLES' CREED.

I believe in God the Father .... Jer. xxxii. 17.
In Jesus the Son of God .... 1 John iv. 9.
In His human birth .... Rom. i. 3.
In His sufferings under Pilate .... John xix. 1.
In His crucifixion .... Luke xxiii. 33.
In His death .... John xix. 30.
In His burial .... Matt. xxvii. 59, 60.
In His resurrection .... Matt. xxviii. 5, 6.
In His ascension .... Mark xvi. 19.

W. F. C.

THE ASCENDING LORD.

From Heaven	He	came............John iii. 13; 1 Cor. xv. 47.
Of	"	" spake...........................Matt. v. 12.
To	"	" pointed.........Matt. iv. 17; John xvii. 24.
To	"	" ascended............Heb. x. 12; Acts ii. 33.
To	"	" invites us.......Matt. vi. 19–21; Rev. iii. 21.
In	"	" intercedes for us...Rom. viii. 34; Heb. vii. 25.
In	"	" prepares a place for us..........John xiv. 2
From	"	" will come again....................Lesson.

 How to witness for JESUS. **W**AIT for **HIM.** **W**ORK **W**ALK with

READY WHEN HE COMES!

Seed Thought: "Lamps trimmed and burning."

Some will be { Sorry.......................... Rev. i. 7.
{ Glad.....................1 Thess. ii. 19.

How Will I Be?

The teacher's unconscious influence, like "bread cast upon the waters to return after many days," is beautifully set forth in the above exercise, as put upon the blackboard by Richard P. Clark, teacher of the Young Ladies' Bible Class, Puritan Church, Brooklyn, N. Y. The lesson for the day—Easter Sunday—was, the Resurrection, outlined as above, with comments full of tenderness and pathos, contrasting the glories and miseries of that eventful day, with the direct appeal, Is your lamp trimmed and burning? The truths of the lesson left their convicting and converting influence upon at least one member of the class, who was taken sick during the week and died in the glorious triumphs of a risen Saviour. Before her death she sent word to her teacher thanking him for the faithful presentation of that lesson, and assuring him that it, through him, had been instrumental in bringing peace and comfort to her heart, and that her lamp was trimmed and burning.

Mr. Clark was then sick: that Easter Sunday was his last appearance before the class, his last diagram upon the blackboard, the last lesson he taught. He died with the blessed satisfaction of knowing that his Sabbath-school efforts had not been in vain, and passed to his reward.

"*He that reapeth receiveth wages, and gathereth fruit unto life eternal, that both he that soweth and he that reapeth may rejoice together.*" John iv. 36.

May this lesson, so eminently suggestive, prove an incentive to Sunday-school workers everywhere.

WHAT JESUS SAYS.

"Behold I stand at the door and knock. If any man hear my voice and open the door, I will come in to him and sup with him and he with ME. Rev. iii. 20; John xiv. 20."

This is a representation of what Christ is actually doing at the door of every human heart. We cannot doubt it, for He Himself declares it to be a fact. Besides this we all feel at times that His hand does gently touch our hearts. How *near* He comes. "*At the door.*" How *patient* He is. We have refused to open the door, and yet He lingers and waits. How *earnest* He is. He does not stand in *silence*, but "*knocks,*" pleads, begs for admission. He comes to our hearts. Open *now*. Receive this heavenly guest, and the "feast shall be everlasting love."

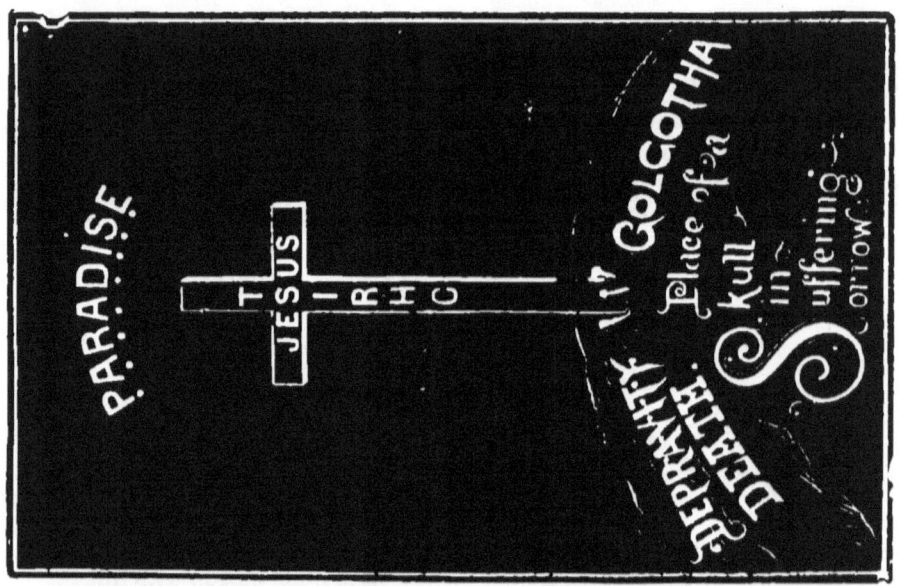

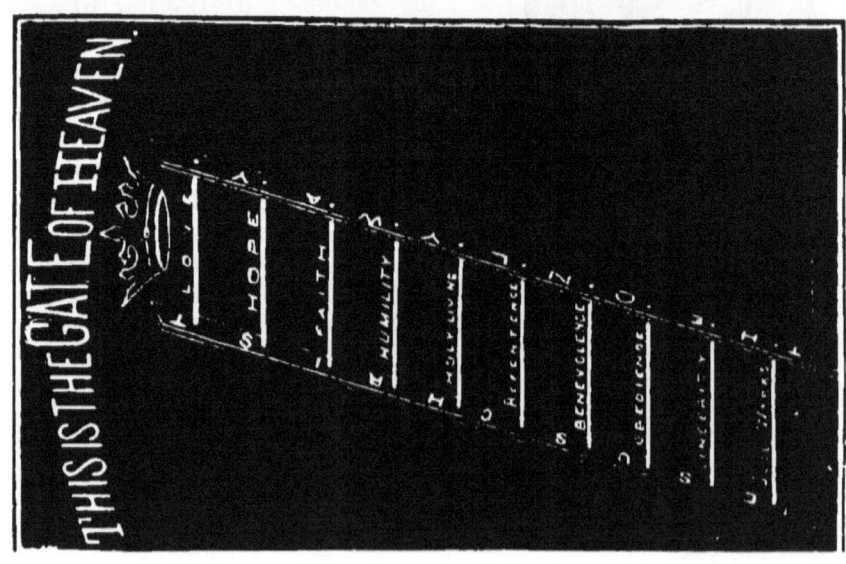

TRIUMPHS OF THE CROSS.

The cross upon which the crucified Redeemer suffered and died was placed on Golgotha, or Calvary, the place of a skull, so named from the sufferings and tortures of the wretched malefactors who were there crucified.

The gospel, with its plan of salvation, is based on human depravity. When this lost and ruined state is fully recognized in us and understood by us, then we can rightly appreciate the gospel message that comes to us through the cross, ever pointing heavenward to the Paradise of Saints; even to the throne of God.

Between earth and Paradise, Jesus Christ, the Saviour of the world, hung in agonies unutterable, and by His death He triumphed over *sin*, *suffering*, *sorrow*, and even *death*.

JACOB'S LADDER. GEN. XXVIII. 10–23.

"This is none other but the house of God; this is the gate of heaven." Thus said Jacob as he awoke from his dream on the stony pillow at Luz (afterward called Bethel). The gate of heaven is nearer to each of us than we think. It is good to remember that God is always near; and this thought should be our guard against yielding to temptation and sin. Our loneliness and times of trial are often the occasions when God manifests Himself nearer and dearer to us, and gives us clearer and more precious views of His purposes concerning us. Jacob's pillow became a pillow of remembrance—a memorial; his lonely resting-place upon the plain, a Bethel—a House of God. Do we set up pillars of remembrance of His mercies to us? Jacob's ladder is emblematic of the way of salvation, which is like a ladder "set up on earth," its top reaching to heaven. Our *good works, sincerity, and acts* are like rounds or steps by which we hope to reach the heavenly home; these alone will not save us. Our only hope is through *Christ*. The rounds of a ladder are useless without sides. Let the sides represent Christ. If our desires, intentions, and acts are sanctified by resting in and through Christ, then we have that hope which is as an anchor to the soul, sure and steadfast. Without Christ all will be useless.

THE WORLD FOR JESUS.

More than eighteen hundred years ago, Jesus said to His Apostles: "Go ye into all the world and preach the gospel to every creature." He thus taught that His gospel is to be the heritage of the *whole* world. It is a gospel for the *entire* race, and is to be proclaimed everywhere. The picture shows the *effect* of the

gospel where it has been preached. It has carried *light* to the people, and will yet banish darkness from the pagan world. It is to spread from clime to clime in its conquering sweep, until

"Jesus shall reign where'er the sun
Does his successive journeys run."

The day will *surely* come when the "earth shall be *filled* with the knowledge of God as the waters cover the great deep."

The field is *vast*, the work is *great*, and the difficulties *formidable*, but victory is assured. "Ask of me and I shall give thee the heathen for thine inheritance, and the uttermost parts of the earth for thy possession." Ps. ii. 8.

"The Duke of Wellington once met a young clergyman, who, being aware of his former residence in the East, and of his familiarity with the ignorance and obstinacy of the Hindoos in support of their false religion, proposed the following question: "Does not your grace think it almost useless and extravagant to preach the gospel to the Hindoos?" The Duke immediately replied: "Look, sir, to your marching orders. 'Preach the gospel to every creature.'"—*Foster.* [tory.

Obedience to these "*marching orders*" will lead to final vic-
But this conquest will be achieved only by the prayers, sacrifices, and toil of God's people. The old and the young are to join in the work. Some may become missionaries. Some may be called to *teach* and others to *preach* the word. Some may obtain *wealth*, and that is to be consecrated to God. "The church must fling down her gold at the feet of Jesus."—*Dr. Eddy.* "God loveth a cheerful giver." The missionary cause waits for the gifts of the people. There is room here for all *workers.* There is a demand for *all* talents. Be ready to take your place when the call comes. If God asks your best *personal* service, give it. If He asks your time, talent, or wealth, lay it *all* upon the altar in the Master's name. He is saying to you, "*Go.*" Go then, in *some* way, and *minister* to the *spiritual wants* of the world. H. H. B.

HE LEADETH US.

To living fountains of water......................Rev. vii. 17.
Beside still waters.............................Ps. xxiii. 2.
In green pastures..............................Ps. xxiii. 2.
Through the depths............................Ps. cvi. 9.
Safely..Ps. lxxviii. 53.
Through the wilderness........................Ps. cxxxvi. 16.
Through the deep..............................Isa. lxiii. 13.
In the right way.................Gen. xxiv. 48 ; Ps. cvii. 7.
In a plain path................................Ps. xxvii. 11.
To the rock that is higher......................Ps. lxi. 2.
Being in the way, the Lord led me... ....Gen. xxiv. 27.

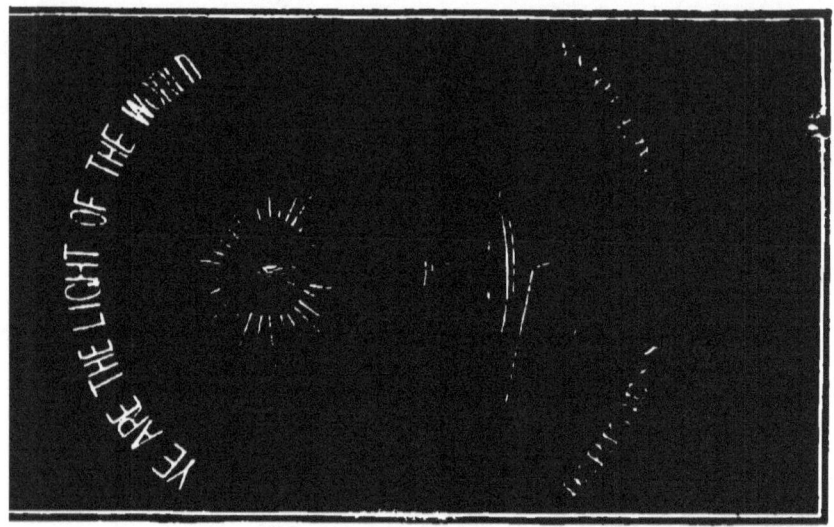

CHRISTIANS THE LIGHT OF THE WORLD.

Christ teaches us that he is represented in the moral world by His people, who are to let their "light *shine* before men." Matt. v. 16. This is *your* privilege, even though you are so young. The light often shines through young hearts just as clearly as it does from aged saints. You are to banish darkness from your homes and from the social circles in which you move. Keep the light shining in *your own* heart. Keep it shining on the pathway of *others*.

> "Let the lower lights be burning!
> Send a gleam across the wave!
> Some poor fainting, struggling seamen
> You may rescue, you may save."
>
> P. P. BLISS.

THE CROSS.

The chief idea conveyed by this illustration is that the Christian reaches heaven by the way of the cross. The word *Christ* stands out very prominently on this ladder, indicating that Christ is the source of its strength; while above it we have a glimpse of the sun, showing that it leads to a fair and sunny land. On the rounds of this ladder we see the words of Peter written in his 2d Epistle, 1st chapter, 5th and 6th verses. The order, however, seems to be reversed. Peter says: "Add to your faith, virtue," etc., and the most natural thought would be that "faith" should be at the *lower* round, and all the other virtues above it; and then *ascending* the ladder, we might "*add*" all other essential graces. But we see the wisdom of this order when we remember that the grandest exhibitions of *charity* are found in the lower realm of human life. He who is at the top of the ladder needs no charity for the angels nor the saints in light, but he does need it for those who are *below* him. Exercise charity. Let faith lift you up to Christ, and then you will have His spirit, and you will be true to yourselves and true to others.

CHRIST OUR GUIDING STAR.

Christ, the hope of the world, may be symbolized by a star, leading men to a better life, and pointing them heavenward. The magis and shepherds found Christ through the light and guidance of the star of Bethlehem. Christ is revealed in all the Scriptures, both Old and New Testament, as the Saviour for *All*, and *Forever*. The Bible has been, and is, such a star to-day, and by its light all men may be led to Christ which taketh away the sin of the world.

In 2 Pet. i. 19 reference is made to *the Word* as a light shining in a dark place, and to Christ as a *day Star*.

The points of the star, the lights and shadows composing it, all point to or centre in Christ.

In the diagram the various portions of the Bible that make up the grand luminary are indicated as follows: P. for Pentateuch; H. for Historical Books of the O. T.; Po. for Poetic Books; L. Pr. for five Longer Prophets; S. Pr. for Shorter Prophets; G. for Gospel; A. for Acts; E. for Epistles, and R. for Revelation. The whole Bible shining as one star, with the pre-eminent purpose of bringing all men to a saving knowledge of the truth as it is in Jesus; and to illustrate the universal reign of Christ and His salvation for the whole human family, we represent upon the outer points of the star the far-off nations or races of the world. C. for Caucasian, or white; A. for American or Indian; E. for Ethiopian or Negro; Ma. for Malay; Mo. for Mongolian. All of which, through the enlightening and converting influence of the gospel, are to be brought to know Christ as the Lord of lords and King of kings.

> "Jesus shall reign where'er the sun
> Does his successive journeys run;
> His kingdom stretch from shore to shore
> Till moons shall wax and wane no more."

"COMES" OF CHRIST.

1. Come unto me............................Matt. xi. 28.
2. Come, ye blessed.........................Matt. xxv. 34.
3. Come apart and rest......................Mark vi. 31.
4. Come down...............................Luke xix. 5.
5. Come forth..............................John xi. 43.
6. Come and dine...........................John xxi. 12.
7. Come and see............................John i. 39.
8. I will come again.......................John xiv. 3.

LESSONS FROM THE LION.

The lion is the king of the forest, and from this proud, noble monarch of the animal kingdom we may learn some useful lessons.

The lion is *destructive* when enraged. A single stroke of his paw lays the strongest man in the dust. Satan, in this respect, is a being in the moral world that is compared to the lion. He "goeth about as a roaring lion, seeking whom he may *devour*."

Beware of this lion of the *soul*, for he is *more* cruel than the lion of the forest.

The lion is *bold*. His eye never quails, his form never trembles with *fear*. The "righteous" are said to be as "*bold* as a lion." Will *you* also be "bold" in *opposing* the wrong, and in *defending* the right? *Cowards* are detestable. Be lion-like in *courage*. Learn to say *no* when necessary. "When sinners entice thee, consent thou not." Be *strong* and *bold*.

"The wicked flee when no man pursueth; but **the righteous are bold as a lion.**" Prov. xxviii. 1.

SEARCHING THE SCRIPTURES.

We are to do this for various reasons. It would be sufficient to say that Jesus has commanded us to do so. "Search ye the scriptures, for in them ye think ye have eternal life." John v. 39. No book has been searched as the Bible has, from its origin to the present time. Foes have searched it with *evil* designs, but it *bears* their severest criticisms. Friends have searched it with sincere motives, and have found in it a *response* to all their *longings* and *hopes*.

How it *rewards* all who search it. It offers *light* for their darkness, and *truth* for error. It kindles *hope* in the soul, *comforts* it in sorrow, and reveals the way of *salvation*. Its teachings thrill the soul with *joy*, and lead to the precious boon of *peace*, here and hereafter. *Search* it, young and old. It is able to make us "wise unto salvation."

"All scripture is given by inspiration of God, and is profitable for doctrine, for reproof, for correction, for instruction in righteousness:

"That the man of God may be perfect, thoroughly furnished unto all good works." 2 Tim. iii. 16, 17.

288   CURIOSITIES OF THE BIBLE.

THE WINE CUP.

Behold the *ingredients* of the cup!

See the serpent coiled within the glass, waiting to fix his poisonous fangs upon the unsuspecting victim, and thrust the deadly poison through both body and soul. The glass may *seem* harmless, but it is *surcharged* with the elements of *destruction*. It may glow and sparkle, but the *hiss* of the serpent is in it. "At the last it biteth *like* a serpent." Prov. xxiii. 32. No wonder the Bible comes to us saying: "Look not thou upon the wine." Prov. xxiii. 31; xx. 1.

Children, beware of wine, and beware of *beer* as well. It is a very popular drink in America as well as in Europe, but it is a *dangerous*, *ruinous* beverage. Some say it is *nutritious*. How *false*. Liebig shows that "one must drink twenty-three barrels of it to get as much nutriment as there is in a five-pound loaf of bread." Try the *bread*, and shun the *beer*. Let this be our motto, "Touch not, taste not, handle not."

WHAT A PRAYER MEETING SHOULD BE.

1. Regular and punctual attendance....Heb. x. 25; Ps. lxxxiv. 1, 4; Acts ii. 1, 6.
2. Bring others...........Num. x. 29; Ps. xlii. 4; Dan. xii. 3.
3. Come praying..................John xii. 21; John xv. 5.
4. Continue in prayer..Phil. iv. 6; Gen. xxxii. 26; Eph. vi. 18.
5. Avoid criticism..Ps. cxxxiii. 1; Rom. xii. 10; John xvii. 23.
6. Participate promptly and heartily...Col. iii. 16; Heb. iv. 16.
7. Let all exercises be brief..........Eccles. v. 2; Matt. vi. 7.
8. Keep in mind that we speak and sing before God.....2 Cor. xii. 19; 1 Sam. xvi. 7.
9. Christian testimony.....Ps. xl. 10; Ps. li. 15; Ps. lxiii. 3–5; Mal. iii. 16, 17; Heb. iii. 13; James v. 16.—W. F. C.

CHARACTERISTICS OF GOD'S PEOPLE.

Ye are a P-raying.............................Eph. vi. 18.
E-arnest...............................Jude iii.
C-onsecrated.........................1 Cor. i. 8.
U-nited.............................Eph. iv. 13.
L-oving............................Rom. xiii. 8.
I-mmortal............... ....Ps. xxxvii. 29.
A-ctive... ....2 Peter i. 5.
R-ighteous....... ..People........ ....Isa. lx. 21.
Ye are a chosen generation; a royal priesthood; a holy nation; a peculiar PEOPLE................1 Pet. ii. 9.—J. B. A.

THE TWO MASTERS.

The work of
The D-eceives, Rev. xii. 9......But J-ustifies, Rom. iii. 26.
    E-ntices, 2 Tim. ii. 26.....   E-levates, Matt. xxv. 23.
    V-itiates, 2 Cor. iv. 4......   S-anctifies, 1 Cor. vi. 11.
    I-nfatuates, John xiii. 2...   U-nites to God, Eph. ii. 14.
    L-eads to hell, Matt. xxv.   S aves, John iii. 17.
      41; 1 John iii. 8.......   S. W. M.

HOW SHALL I APPROACH THE MERCY-SEAT—
Heb. iv. 16.

B-elieving God.................................Matt. xxi. 22.
O-beying God...............................Heb. v. 9.
L-oving God..Gal. v. 6.
D-epending on God..............................Jas. i. 17.
L-ooking to God................................Heb. xii. 2.
Y-ielding to God..............................Rom. vi. 13.

J. B. A.

WHAT SHALL I DO WITH JESUS?

Prove Him.......................................Mal. iii. 10.
Prize Him.......................................Eph. i. 21.
Praise Him...Ps. c.
Preach Him....................................2 Cor. iv. 5.
Pray to Him....................................John xiv. 14.

J. B. A.

HOW SHALL I FIND JESUS?

If I S-incerely..................................Phil. i. 10.
   E-arnestly....................................Heb. ii. 1.
   A-ttentively..............................Luke xix. 48.
   R-epeatedly...............................Phil. vi. 18.
   C-arefully.................................1 Peter iv. 7.
   H-onestly.................................1 Tim. ii. 1–3.

    Seek **HIM** while He may be found.
   Call upon **HIM** while He is near..........Isa. iv. 6.

TO WHOM SHALL WE GO FOR SAFETY?

Flee to C-aptain of our salvation..................Heb ii. 10.
    H-orn of salvation.......................Ps. xviii. 2.
    R-oot of Jesse.............................Isa. ii. 10
    I-mmanuel................................Isa. vii. 14.
    S-hepherd of Israel......................Ps. lxxx. i.
    T-rue God..............................1 John v. 20.

W. F. C.

PRAYER MEETING OUTLINES.

SEVEN CONFESSIONS OF THE BIBLE.

"*I have sinned*"—By whom and the motive of each.
1. Pharaoh, from slavish fear.............Ex. ix. 27; x. 16.
2. Balaam, for a reward.....................Num. xxii. 34.
3. Achan, being detected of God.............Joshua vii. 20.
4. Saul, from cowardice....................1 Sam. xv. 24.
5. David, being reproved...................2 Sam. xii. 13.
6. Judas, from despair.....................Matt. xxvii. 4.
7. Prodigal Son, from an honest heart......Luke xv. 18, 21.

GOD'S PROVIDENCE.

Mysterious.......................Psalm x. 5; Job xi. 7–9.
Seems sometimes not to regard the right.......Ps. lxxiii. 2–16,
But really upholds the right..Ps. lxxiii. 17–20; Eccl. viii. 12, 13.
Brings good out of evil...Gen. l. 20; Ex. xiv. 4; Deut. xxiii. 5.
Directs events...........Ezra v. 5; Prov. xvi. 9; Prov. xxi. 1.

THE ATONING SAVIOUR.

CHRIST DIED FOR THE

U-NWORTHY, Acts xiii. 46.
N-EEDY, Matt. ix. 12.
G-UILTY, Rom. iii. 19.
O-LD, Ps. xxxvii. 25.
D-RUNKARD, 1 Cor. vi. 10.
L-OST, Luke xix. 10.
Y-OUNG, Eccl. xii. 1.

C. N. P.

ALL THINGS THROUGH CHRIST.

WE KNOW THAT **ALL**

T-RIALS, 2 Cor. iv. 17.
H-ATRED OF FOES, Gen. xl. 5.
I-NFIRMITIES, Acts iii. 11.
N-ECESSITIES, Ps. xxxvii. 25.
G-RIEFS, Heb. xii. 11.
S-UFFERINGS, 2 Cor. xi. 23–28.

WORK

Together for them that love G-O-D ood to Rom. viii. 28.

J. B. A.

SEVEN THINGS TO HOLD FAST.

1. That which is good..........................1. Thess. v. 1.
2. The faithful word............................Titus i. 9.
3. The form of sound words....................2 Tim. i. 13.
4. The confidence and rejoicing of the hope..........Heb. iii. 6.
5. The profession of our faith....................Heb. x. 23.
6. That we have, that no man take our crown......Rev. iii. 11.
7. The unfaithful, hold fast and repent............Rev. iii. 3.

THE SEVEN "MUSTS."

1. What MUST I do to be saved?................Acts xvi. 30.
2. Ye MUST be born again........................John iii. 7.
3. No other name under heaven, whereby we MUST be saved.
   Acts iv. 12.
4. So MUST the Son of man be lifted up.........John iii. 14.
5. As thou hast said so MUST we do..............Ezra x. 12.
6. Zacchæus, To-day I MUST abide at thy house....Luke xix. 5.
7. For we MUST all appear before the judgment seat of Christ.
   2 Cor. v. 10.

THINGS TO WHICH WE SHOULD TAKE HEED.

That no man deceive us....Mark xiii. 33-37; 1 Cor. i. 7; Titus ii. 13; Heb. ix. 28.
What we hear.........Mark iv. 24; Prov. vi. 27; Isa. viii. 20; Jer. xxii. 29; John xvi. 13.
How we hear........1 Sam. iii. 9, 10; Ps. cxix. 11; Heb. ii. 1.
To ourselves..........Luke xxi. 34; Phil. ii. 3; Mark vii. 21, 23; 1 Cor. x. 12; 1 Tim. iv. 16.
How we build....1 Cor. iii. 10, 11; 1 Cor. x. 31; Matt. vii. 24.
Lest there be in any of us an evil heart of unbelief....Heb. iii. 12; Rom. xi. 20; 1 Pet. i. 8.
To the sure word of prophecy.......2 Pet. i. 19; 2 Tim. iv. 4; Heb. x. 37; Rev. xxii. 20.
That we endure to the end.......Heb. iv. 1; Rev. ii. 26; Rev. iii. 21; 2 Tim. ii. 3.

PART II.—KEY.

ANSWERS
To
BIBLE CURIOSITIES
PERTAINING TO
First Things.

1. Light.... ....Gen. i. 3.
2. The coming of Christ ....Gen. iii. 15.
3. Cain. The city of Enoch.........Gen. iv. 17.
4. Moses............................Num. i. 1.
5. Moses. ....Ex. xviii. 13
6. Abram.....................Gen. xii. 1, 6.
7. Abel..........................Gen. iv. 4.
8. Cain..........................Gen. iv. 9.
9. Water turned into blood..........Exodus vii. 20.
10. When the morning stars sang together ...Job xxxviii. 7
11. Aaron.....................Exodus xxviii. 1.
12. The woman Eve......Gen. iii. 1; Tim. ii. 14.
13. Adam.........................Gen. ii. 15.
14. Rebekah.................Gen. xxiv. 64, 65.
15. Tubal-Cain...................Gen. iv. 22.
16. Adam.........................Gen. iii. 24.
17. Ear-rings, bracelets, jewels, &c.....Gen. xxiv. 22, 30, 53.
18. The words "Holiness to the Lord" upon Aaron's mitre..............Ex. xxviii. 36; Ex. xxxix. 30
19. Moses...........................Ex. xxiv. 4

20. Abraham....................... Gen. xxiii. 3, 4, 16, 18
21. Nimrod......................... Gen. x. 8, 9.
22. Noah. The ark................ Gen. vi. 14, 22
23. Cain........................... Gen. iv. 14.
24. Stephen........................ Acts vii. 58.
25. Pharaoh........................ Gen. xli. 42
26. Abraham........................ Gen. xxii 3
27. Ishmael........................ Gen. xvi. 11.
28 Hagar in the wilderness........ Gen. xxi. 16.
29. Moses (?)...................... Ex. xxxii. 19.
30. Abel........................... Gen. iv. 8
31. Adam........................... Gen. v. 5
32. Song of Moses.................. Ex. xv
33. Jacob.......................... Gen. xxxii. 9
34. Rachel......................... Gen. xxxi. 19
35. Jewelry........................ Ex. xxxii. 2
36. Rachel......................... Gen. xxix. 9
37. The son of Zarephath's daughter...... 1 Kings xvii. 21
38. Jacob at the grave of Rachel........... Gen. xxxv. 20
39. Maaseiah....................... Ezra x. 18
40. Ararat......................... Gen. viii. 4
41. Be fruitful and multiply, &c... Gen. i. 28
42. The Eunuch of Ethiopia......... Acts viii. 27, 38
43 Abram.......................... Gen. xiv. 13.
44. Solomon's navy................. 1 Kings ix. 26.
45. When the men of Judah crossed the Jordan at Gilgal
    to King David.................. 2 Sam. xix. 18.
46. By God. After the creation.... Gen. ii. 2, 3.
47. At Antioch by Paul and Barnabas........ Acts xiv. 26.
48. Abraham purchased a burying place for Sarah at
    Machpelah...................... Gen. xxiii. 3.
49. See............................ Job xix. 23, 24.
50. By Abraham in the purchase of land.... Gen. xxiii. 16.
51. Repent......................... Matt. iv. 17.
52. On giving names to the animal creation.... Gen. ii. 19.
53. The defeat of the armies of Israel by the tribe of Benjamin .... Judges xx. 26.

54. St. Peter. By the selection of a particular passage and the explanation thereof................Acts ii. 14.
55. Daniel, appointed by King Darius over a province of Chaldea.............................Dan. vi. 2.
56. To Noah and his family after the flood......Gen. ix. 3.
57. When Deborah judged Israel............Judges iv. 4.
58. The tribe of Judah...................... Num. x. 14.
59. Water turned to wine....................John ii. 1.
60. The men of Sodom.................... Gen. xiii. 13.
61. Abraham.....................Gen. xxi. 24; xxiv. 3.
62. The house of the rolls, or books, the king's library,
Ezra vi. 1.
63. The Lord shall reign for ever and ever.....Ex. xv. 18.
64. God save the king.................... 1 Sam. x. 24.
65. See...............................Psalms cix. 10.
66. Swords into plowshares, &c., and learn war no more,
Isa. ii. 4.
67. Joshua in dividing the land............ Josh. xviii. 8.
68. See........................Acts xviii. 17; xv. 23.
69. B.C. 607 years. By children of Rachab..Jer. xxxv. 1, 11.
70. In the wilderness, by Anah............Gen. xxxvi. 24

ANSWERS

TO

OLD TESTAMENT CURIOSITIES

PERTAINING TO

Persons.

---

1. Abraham..................................Gen. xv. 5.
   Zedekiah for deliverance................Jer. xxxviii. 3.
2. Five.   Pharoah to be relieved of the plagues...Ex. viii. 8
   Israel to be relieved of serpents...........Num. xxi. 7.
   Jeroboam when his hand withered......1 Kings xiii. 6.
   Simeon's prayer........................Acts viii. 24.
3. Maachah........................ ......1 Kings xv. 13.
4. Cyrus......................Isa. xliv. 28; Ezra i. 1.
5. Because of their cruelty to the Shechemites.Gen. xlix. 7.
6. Abimelech............................Judges ix. 45.
7. Jethro...............................Exodus iii. 1.
8. Elisha and Elijah.................... 1 Kings xix. 19.
9. John the Baptist......................Malachi iv. 5, 6.
10. During the siege of Samaria............2 Kings vi. 29.
11. Jehoshabeath.   Joash................2 Chron. xxii. 11.
12. Cave of Adullam....... ....1 Sam. xiii. 6.
13. Jachin and Boaz........................1 Kings vii. 21.
14. Makkedah..............................Josh. x. 26.
15. Elisha................................1 Kings xix. 19
16. Ahab..... .... 1 Kings xxii. 39

17. A iathar.............................1 Sam. xxii. 20.
18. Eliphaz................................Job iv. 15.
19. Nebuchadezzar...........................Jer. lii. 4.
20. Zedekiah..............................Jer. lii. 8
21. Hoshea............................2 Kings xvii. 6.
22. Mount Tabor......................2 Kings xxii. 29
23. Saul..............................1 Sam. xxii. 18
24. Athaliah ....2 Chron. xxii. 10.
25. After the captivity.....................Neh. viii. 17.
26. Zedekiah.............................. Jer. lii. 11.
27. On Mount Carmel by King Ahab.....1 Kings xviii. 20
28. Deborah............................Judges iv. 4, 5.
29. Ehud............................... Judges iii. 15.
30. Abimelech..........................Judges ix. 5.
31. Men of Shechem ....Judges ix. 24.
32. Abimelech..........................Judges ix. 53.
33. Hezekiah...........................2 Kings xx. 6.
34. Balaam.......................... Numbers xxiii. 10.
35. Vopshi, Num. xiii. 14 ; Vashni, 1 Chron. vi. 28 ; Vashti, Esther i. 9.
36. Abimelech at Mount Zalmon............Judges ix. 48.
37. Joash............................2 Chron. xxiii. 11.
38. Ahaz............................2 Chron. xxviii. 24.
39. Zophar, Bildad and Eliphaz by Job.......Job xiii. 26.
40. Aaron ....Numbers xvi. 48.
41. Uzziah...........................2 Chron. xxvi. 20.
42. Adoni-bezek...........................Judges i. 6, 7.
43 Jehu the blood of Jezabel.............1 Kings xxi. 23
44 Abimelech at Thebez..................Judges ix. 54.
45. Esther...
46. Jehoshaphat, King of Judah ......2 Chron. xvii. 7, 11.
47. Moses to Hobab........................ Num. x. 29
48. Saul and Jonathan.................   ...2 Sam. i. 23
49. Shamgar.... ....Judges iii. 31.
50. Pharaoh's daughter....................Exodus ii. 10
51. Bera..............................Gen. xiv. 2
52. Birsha ....Gen. xiv. 2

53. He held his peace........................Lev. x. 3
54. Jonah.................................Jonah i. 3
55. In the valley of Moab................Deut. xxxiv. 6
56. Seers.................................1 Sam. ix. 9.
57. One thousand and five................ 1 Kings iv. 32.
58. Song of the well................ Numbers xxi. 17, 18.
59. Benhadad, King of Assyria........ 2 Kings viii. 7, 15
60. Jair..................................1 Chron. ii. 22
61. Tiglathpileser, first King of Assyria....2 Kings xv. 29
62. Ahasuerus............................Esther viii. 10.
63. Abraham..............................Gen. xii. 2.
64. Saul, by falling on his sword.............2 Sam. i. 6.
65. Workmen on the temple..............2 Kings xxii. 7.
66. Jonathan and Ahismaz .... .2 Sam. xvii. 17.
67. Jonathan ....2 Sam. i. 25.
68. Saul and Jonathan......................2 Sam. i. 23.
69. Hadadezer, captured by David..........2 Sam. viii. 4.
70. King of Salem.......................Gen. xiv. 18, 21.
71. Jehu.................................2 Kings x. 15.
72. Jeroboam. Arm withered .... 1 Kings xiii. 4.
73. Zipporah.... ....Exodus ii. 21.
74. Korah...............................Num. xvi. 31.
75. Agur................................ Proverbs xxx. 8.
76. Job.................................Job xiii. 15.
77. Bildad the Shuhite (Shoe-height)..........Job ii. 11.
78. Josh. x. 14; Judges vi. 2; 1 Sam. xiii. 6; 1 Sam. xxii. 1.
79. Love them as themselves ....Lev. xix. 33, 34
8). Gibeonites, by order of Joshua ....Josh. ix. 23.
81. Hewers of wood and drawers of water......Josh. ix. 27
82. Amalekites........................ ..Ex. xvii. 8, 13.
83. Obediah............................ ..1 Kings xviii. 4.
84 Jacob's.............................Gen. 1. 9.
85. Jeremiah........................ Jeremiah xix. 9.
86. Pashur, because he smote the prophet Jeremiah.Jer. xx. 4.
87. Jeremiah............................Jer. xx. 4.
88. To repair the house of the Lord..2 Chron. xxiv. 4, 11.
89. Rebekah..............

90. Achan.................................Joshua vii. 21
91. Abraham............................Deut. xxxiv. 7.
92. Abigail and David...................1 Sam. xxv. 42
93. Job......................................Job iii. 17.
94. David, 1 Sam. xxi. 13 ; Abraham, Gen. xii. 13 ; xx. 1,12.
95. Michal the daughter of Saul..........2 Sam. vi. 20, 23
96. The Lord gave, &c...................Job i. 21 ; ii. 10
97. Elisheba.............................Exodus vi. 23.
98. "It is the Lord, let him do what seemeth good,"
 1 Sam. iii. 18.
99. Ezekiel to Chebar......................Ezekiel i. 1.
100. Samuel...............................1 Sam. ix. 25.
101. Amos, herdsman of Tekoa..........Amos i. 1 ; vii. 14.
102. Son of Isaiah........................Jer. xxxviii. 6.
103. Aaron, the golden calf..............Ex. xxxii. 4, 20 ;
104. The children of Israel under Ahaz captured Judah,
 2 Chron. xxviii. 8.
105. Obed.............................2 Chron. xxviii. 9.
106. David..............................2 Sam. xxiv. 1.
107. Elisha, the Shunamite widow and her two sons,
 2 Kings iv. 1
108. Solomon............................1 Kings x. 22
109. The prophet Ezekiel at the death of his wife,
 Ezekiel xxiv 16
110. Gad, 2 Sam. xxiv. 11-19 Nathan 2 Sam. xii.; 1 Chron. xxi.
111. Ahaz.............................2 Chron. xxviii. 3.
112. David. Three days pestilence. Because he numbered
 the people.....................2 Sam. xxiv. 13.
113. He that ruleth his spirit................Prov. xvi. 32.
114. David their father................ ..2 Sam. i. 17, 27.
115. Maher-shalal-hash-baz.................Isa. viii. 1, 4.
116. Jeremiah..............................Isa. viii. 1, 4
117. David................................2 Sam. xxiv. 14.
118. Ezekiel........................Ezekiel ii. 9 ; iii. 2.
119. { Miriam, Ex. xv. 20; Deborah..........Judges iv. 4.
 Huldah, 2 Kings xxii. 14 ; Anna ....Luke ii. 36.
 Philip's daughters. . ...Acts xxi. 9

OLD TESTAMENT PERSONS

120. Josiah .... 2 Kings xxiii
121. David and Jonathan .... 1 Sam. xviii. 1.
122. He was first to smite the Jebusites ..... 1 Chron. xi. 6.
123. Asa .... 2 Chron. xiv. 11.
124. Moses, Num. xi. 15 ; Elijah .... 1 Kings xix. 4.
    Jonah .... Jonah iv. 3 ; v. 8.
125. From Heaven .... Lev. ix. 24.
126. Moses, Ex. ii. 10 ; Hadassah .... Esther ii. 7
127. Ahab .... 1 Kings xxi. 25
128. Sons of Joseph .... 1 Chron. v. 1, 2
129. Abijah .... 1 Kings xiv. 13.
130. Sidonians .... 1 Kings v. 6.
131. Deborah .... Gen. xxxv. 8.
132. Elijah's .... 1 Kings ; xviii. 41.
133. Nehemiah .... Neh. vi. 10, 13.
134. Nazarites .... Num. vi. 1.
135. David .... 1 Sam. xvi. 11; xvii. 15.
136. That he might die the death of the righteous,
    Num. xxiii. 10.
137. Hoshea .... 2 Kings xv. 30.
138. See .... Exodus xxv. 40.
139. Solomon .... 2 Chron. vii. 12.
140. Sacred Singers .... 1 Chron. ix 33.
141 Midianites .... Judges viii. 26.
142 Korah, Dathan, Abiram .... Num xxvi. 10.
143 "They which are of faith" and "if ye be Christ's,"
    Gal. iii. 7, 29.
144. Children of Rachab .... Jer. xxxv. 1, 10
145. Gideon with his band of three hundred,
    Judges vii. 4, 5
146. Midianite army .... Judges vii. 12.
147. Uzziah .... 2 Chron. xxvi. 19
148. Shaphat .... 1 Kings xix. 19
149. Gideon .... Judges viii. 24
150. Joshua .... Joshua viii. 30
151. Ahaz .... 2 Chron. xxviii. 24
152. Joshua .... Joshua x. 11

CURIOSITIES OF THE BIBLE.

153. Gideon and Phurah..............Judges vii. 7, 10.
154. The city of Timnath-serah..........Joshua xix. 50
155. Zachariah............................Zach. viii. 5.
156. Cain..................................Gen. iv. 17
157. Uzza..........................1 Chron. xiii. 9, 13.
158. Adoni-zedek, Hoham, Piram, Japhia and Debir,
    Josh. x. 3.
159. Obed-edom. Three months........1 Chron. xiii. 13.
160. Jonathan's house. The prophet Jeremiah,
    Jer. xxxvii. 15.
161. Irijah, the captain of the ward........Jer. xxxvii. 13.
162. The Jews.................... ....Neh. v. 3.
163. Nehemiah........................Neh. v. 14, 18.
164. Abel..................................Gen. iv. 8.
165. Adam ....Gen. v. 5
166. Nebuzaradan....................2 Kings xxv. 8, 9.
167. Hezekiah............................2 Kings xx. 1.
168. Three thousand....................1 Kings iv. 32.
169. Moses........................Exodus xxxiv. 33.
170. Shammua, from the Tribe of Reuben.
    Shaphat,   "   "   "   Simeon.
    Caleb,   "   "   "   Judah.
    Igal,   "   "   "   Issachar.
    Oshea, afterwards called Joshua, tribe of Ephraim.
    Palti,   "   "   "   Benjamin.
    Gaddiel,   "   "   "   Zebulun.
    Gaddi,   "   "   "   Manasseh.
    Ammiel   "   "   "   Dan.
    Sethur,   "   "   "   Asher.
    Nahbi,   "   "   "   Naphthali.
    Geuel,   "   "   "   Gad.
    Numbers xiii. 4, 16
171 By his own sword, because defeated... 1 Chron. x. 4.
172. Naaman..............................2 Kings v. 1.
173. David. He slew Goliath.........1 Sam. xvii. 12, 24.
174. Daniel..........................Dan. v. 7, 16, 29
175. Moses, upheld by Aaron and Hur.....Ex. xvii. 9, 13

176. Manoah........................Judges xiii. 20.
177. Solomon his son...................1 Kings v. 1
178. Manoah..........................Judge xiii. 21
179. Samson's father...................Judges xiii. 21.
180. Elijah in the cave on Mount Horeb. 1 Kings xix. 8, 9.
181. Four.   Jesus'......................Luke i. 28
         John the Baptist's.............. Luke i. 13.
         Isaac's......................Gen. xviii. 10.
         Samson's....................Judges xiii. 3
182. Lot............................Genesis xix. 15
183. Joshua............................ Joshua v.13.
184. Two.   Gabriel............Dan. ix. 21; Luke i. 28.
         Michael................Rev. xii. 7; Jude ix
185. Thirty-one......................Joshua xii. 1, 24.
186. Abishai.........................2 Sam. xxiii. 18.
187. Adino..........................2 Sam. xxiii. 8.
188. Benaiah........................1 Chron. xi. 23.
189. Jacob............................Gen. xxxii. 9.
190. Maaseiah..........................Ezra. x. 18.
191. The Angel that appeared to Abraham....Gen. xix. 2.
192. Daniel...........................Dan. ix. 21.
193. Jeroboam........................1 Kings xi. 29
194. Samson........................Judges xiii. 5.
195. Four.   Sennacherib's army..2 Kings xix. 35; 2 Chron.
                  xxxii. 21; Isa. xxxvii. 36.
         First born in Egypt ....Ex. xii. 29
         Israelites............ { 2 Sam. xxiv. 16, 17
                                 1 Chron. xxi. 14, 15
         Herod..................... Acts xii. 23
196. Elijah..........................1 Kings xix. 4, 8.
197. Joab............................1 Chron. xi. 6
198. Benaiah........................1 Chron. xi. 23.
199. Gather all nations and sever the wicked from the
     just......................... Matt. xiii. 41, 49.
200. Abraham..................Gen. xviii. 2, 4 ; xix. 2.
201. { Samson........................Judges xiv. 5
     { David.........................1 Sam. xvii. 34
     { Benaiah....................... 2 Sam xxiii. 20

202. Moses................... Ex. iii. 5; Joshua v. 13, 15
203. The first to smite the Jebusites........1 Chron. xi. 6.
204. Jethro.. .... Exodus xviii. 5.
205. Anak the Canaanite, during 40 years' wanderings.
Num. xiii. 33
206. Put to death by a plague.................Num. xiv. 37.
207. Ahijah...................... ....1 Kings xi. 31
208. Moses and Lazarus....... ......Jude 9 ; Luke xvii. 22.
209. Jeremiah............................. Jer. xiii. 4.
210. Amos............................... Amos vii. 14
211. Shishak, King of Egypt...........1 Kings xiv. 25, 26.
212. Hannah............................1 Sam. ii. 19.
213. Abraham...............................Gen. xv. 1.
214. Nebuchadnezzar, King of Babylon. 2 Kings xxv. 1, 11.
215. Daniel... .... Daniel vi. 10.
216. He that ruleth his spirit.............. Prov. xvi. 32.
217. Nebuchadnezzar........................Dan. iv. 37.
218. Nebuchadnezzar........................Dan. iv. 33.
219. Builders of wall of Jerusalem..........Neh. iv. 16, 18
220. Hezekiah to messengers of Merodach Baladan,Isa.xxxix.
221. Cyrus..................................Ezra i. 7.
222. Hananiah from Jeremiah..........Jer. xxviii. 10, 11.
223. Joshua................................Josh. viii. 2.
224. King of Ai................. ....Josh. viii. 23, 29
225. Oshea................................Num. xiii. 16.
226. Jeroboam, King of Israel.............1 Kings xii. 28
227. Nebuchadnezzar........................Dan. iv. 30.
228. Spies sent into Jericho.............. ....Joshua ii.
229. Vision of the Cherubim..............Ezekiel i. 1, 28.
230. Solomon.....⁎...............1 Kings ii. 2 Chron. v. 7.
231. By the coming of Christ.Malachi iii. 1. Luke ii. 27. 46.
232. Isaac............................... Gen. xxiv. 63.
233. Nebuchadnezzar....................... Dan. iv. 33.
234. Nebuchadnezzar.......................2 Kings xxv. 7.
235. Joseph by Pharaoh................... Gen. xxxix. 5.
236. Jeremiah...................... ....Jer. xxvii. 2
237. David......................... ......1 Chron. xxix. 1, 5

238. Zerubbabel fifty-two years after the destruction of the first temple..........................Ezra v. 2.
239. Haggai ....Haggai ii. 6, 9.
240. Ezekiel ....Ezek. xxxvii.
241. Elijah's . ...1 Kings xvii. 1; xviii, 42
242. The men of Jabesh-gilead........1 Sam. xxxi. 11-13.
243. Samuel............................1 Sam. xv. 22.
244. Jeroboam, King of Israel..............1 Kings xiii. 1.
245. Nebachadnezzar......................Dan. iv. 24, 36.
246. Solomon..........................1 King ix· 18.
247. Isaiah..............2 Kings xx. 7; Isa. xxxviii. 21.
248. Daniel, Shadrach, Meshach, and Abednego Dan. i. 6, 16
249. See...........................Deut. xxiii. 3, 4
250. Elisha.............................1 Kings xix. 20
251. Job.............................Job xlii. 11.
252. Ezra.............................Ezra ix. 3, 12.
253. Rebekah and Isaac....................Gen. xxiv. 59.
254. The prophet Jonah against Nineveh.......Jonah iii. 4.
255. The prophet Nahum's....................Nahum iii.
256. Joshua in Jordan as a memoral of God's deliverance Jos. iv. 9.
257. By Jacob and his brethren when he covenanted with Laban..............................Gen. xxxi. 46.
258. He commanded Daniel to be clothed in scarlet and that a gold chain be put about his neck for interpreting his dream.......... ....Dan. v. 7.
259. Darius the Median.....................Dan. v. 31
260. Barak with prophetess Deborah.........Judges iv 8
261. Miriam..............................Ex. xv. 20.
262 Shadrach ; Meshach; and Abednego.....Dan. iii. 30
263 Belshazzar, grandson of Nebuchadnezzar...Dan. v. 18.
264 Daniel appointed by Darius King of the Chaldeans. Dan. vi. 2
265. Nehemiah...........................Neh. ii. 5, 18.
266. Simeon.........................Luke ii. 25, 27
267. Because they served idols and forsook the commandments of their God............2 Kings xvii. 7, 2:

268. Manassah....................2 Chron. xxxiii. 11. 13
269. Six cubits and a span (11 feet 8 in.)....1 Sam. xvii. 4
270. A man of Gath...... ....2 Sam. xxi. 20
271. Ezekiel—Noah, Daniel and Job.........Ezekiel xiv. 14
272. Seventy souls. Jacob and his family....Gen. xlvi. 27.
273. Six hundred thousand... ....Ex. xii. 37
274. Doeg by command of Saul............1 Sam. xxii. 18.
275. Jonathan..................1 Sam. xiv. 24, 27, 43, 45
276. Josiah.........................2 Chron. xxxiv. 18.
277. Shebna.........................Isaiah xxii. 15, 18.
278. Absalom........................2 Sam. xviii. 18.
279. Ahab and Zedekiah..................Jer. xxix. 22.
280. Son of Zaraphath's widow by Elijah..1 Kings xvii. 22.
     Shunamite's son by Elisha.............2 Kings iv. 30
     The man in the Sepulchre by Elisha..2.Kings xiii. 21.
281. King Asa........................2 Chron. xiv. 9.
282. Ahab............................1 Kings xxi. 29.
283. Ahab............................1 Kings xxii. 30.
284. Azubah..........................1 Kings xxii. 42.
285. Ezra................................Ezra vii. 6.
286. Ahab............................1 Kings xxi. 25.
287. Jeremiah.............................Jer xx. 2
288. Because of his cruelty to the prophet Jeremiah..Jer. xx.3.
289. Evil-merodach.........................Jer. lii. 31.
290. Nehemiah.........................Neh. i. and ii.
291. Adonijah........1 Kings i. 50; Joab. 1 Kings ii. 28.
292. Elisha................ ....2 Kings iii. 15.
293. King Solomon......................1 Kings x. 27.
294. Ahab...........................1 Kings xxii. 38.
295. Samuel, 1 Sam. i. 1, 4 ; Abijah. 1 Kings xiv. 1, 13.
     Obadiah, 1 Kings xviii. 12; Josiah, 2 Kings xxii. 1, 2;
     Solomon, David, Shadrach, Meshach and Abednego,
     Dan. i. 6, 17 ; Timothy.............2 Tim. iii. 15.
296. Lahmi, slain by Elhanan, son of Jair..2 Sam. xxi. 19.
     1 Chron. xx. 5...........................
297. The Moabite in the sepulchre of Elisha 2 Kings xiii. 20
298. Levites, the Lord was their inheritance..Deut. xviii 1, 5.

OLD TESTAMENT PERSONS.

299. King Joash by Elisha...........2 Kings xiii. 14, 18
300. Obadiah.............. ....1 Kings xviii. 4
301. Pharaoh to Jacob. 130 years...........Gen. xlvii. 8
302. Micah ....Judges xvii. 10
303. Naaman, by the little captive maid.... ...2 Kings v
304. Daniel's prayer for the restoration of Jerusalem,
Dan. ix. 20
The prayer of the Church for Peter in prison,
Acts xii. 5
305. The sons of Jonadab................Jer. xxxv. 8, 10
306. Micah stole eleven hundred sheckels...Judges xvii. 2
307. "Out of the eater came forth meat and out of the strong came forth sweetness".........Judges xiv. 14
308. Jacob............................. Gen. xxxii. 24.
309. The seventy sons of Ahab by Jehu......2 Kings x. 7
310. Og, King of Bashan....................Deut. iii. 11
311. The Philistines, and were dug out by Isaac,
Gen. xxvi. 15
312. The Shunamite....................2 Kings viii. 1, 6.
313. By Jonah in the whale's belly, in the Mediteranean Sea.................................Jonah ii. 1.
314. Job ....Job xxx. 23.
315. Absalom....................... 2 Sam. xviii. 9, 18.
316. Rehoboam......................1 Kings xii. 8, 19.
317. Pul.......... ....1 Chron. v. 26.
318. Josiah, 1 Kings xiii. 2; Christ....... ... Isa. ix. 6.
319. Asshur........................... Gen. x. 11
320. Reubenites, Gadites and the half tribe Manassa,
1 Chron. v. 26.
321. Joseph................................ Gen. l. 17.
322. Eber, being 464 years old, surviving Abraham about four years...........................Gen. xi. 17.
323. Miriam and Deborah prophesied, and those of the tribe of Levi sang in the temple,
Exodus xv. 2, 20; Judges iv. 4
324. Sarah the mother of the faithful, aged 127 years,
Gen. xxiii. 1

325. Joash ....2 Kings xiii. 14
326. Eleazar ....2 Sam. xxiii. 8.
327. King Uzziah is called Azariah, 2 Chron.; 2 Kings xv.; Jehoichin is quoted Coniah, 2 Kings xxiv. 8 ; Jer. xxii. 24 ; Jehoahaza, is called Shallum, 2 Kings xxiii. 31 ; 1 Chron. iii. 15.
328. Dan shall judge thee. Samson was the son of Manoah, which was of the tribe of Dan ....Gen. xlix. 16.
329. Dan is omitted from the list in Rev. vii.; Simeon from that in ....Deut. xxxiii.
330. See....Ex. xii. 23.; 2 Kings xix. 35.; 1 Chron. xxi. 16.
331. Because a band of men who had come with the Arabians had slain all the eldest sons.......2 Chron. xxii. 1.
332. By covering the spies with stalks of flax, and afterwards by letting them down through a window with a cord.............................Josh. ii. 6, 15.
333. Elias. "And Elijah said, If I be a man of God, then let fire come down from heaven and consume thee and thy fifty," and there came down fire from heaven and consumed him and his fifty...2 Kings i. 10, 12.
334. To illustrate God's dealings with those of the house of Judah who had gone into captivity, and with those who were left behind in Jerusalem..Jer. xxiv. 1, 3.
335. That the daughters should marry to some one in their own tribe....................... Num. xxxvi. 6.
336. To show where Nebuchadnezzar would set up his throne in his conquest with Egypt, which the prophet then foretold........................... Jer. xliii. 9.
337. A hundred talents of silver..........2 Chron. xxv. 6.
338. Omri........................... 1 Kings xvi. 23.
339. When Ebed-melech, the Ethiopian, drew up Jeremiah out of a dungeon........ ..... Jer. xxxviii. 11, 12
340. Jehoiachin...................... 2 Chron. xxxvi. 9.
341. The son of Shelomith, of the tribe of Dan,
Lev. xxiv. 10, 11
342. As a token against the rebels, and as a proof that Aaron had been especially chosen by God... Num. xvii. 8.

OLD TESTAMENT PERSONS

343. Under the oak of Jabesh, by the men of Jabesh-gilead
   1 Chron. x. 11, 12
344. Ahab, 1 Kings xxii. 34 ; Josiah... 2 Chron. xxxv. 22
345. David.................................... Psalms i. 4.
346. Uncle............................. 1 Chron. ii. 16
347. By putting an image in the bed, with a pillow of goat's hair for his bolster............... 1 Sam. xix. 13
348. Jehoiachin..................... 2 Chron. xxxvi. 9.
349. Joel (or Vashui) and Abiah............ 1 Sam. viii. 2
350. Rise up, Lord, and let thine enemies be scattered, and let them that hate thee flee before thee. " Return, O Lord, to the many thousands of Israel."
   Num. x. 35.
351. Uzziah........................ 2 Chron. xxvi. 19
352. The daughters of Shallum, the son of Halohesh.
   Neh. iii. 12
353. Jonathan, his uncle.............. 1 Chron. xxvii. 32.
354. Deborah........................... Gen. xxxv. 8
355. Nebucar-adan.................... Jer. xxxix. 11, 14.
356. By means of his Prophet Elisha, he multiplied the widow's oil..................... 2 Kings iv. 4, 7.
357. Forty-two thousand, three hundred and three score.
   Ezra ii. 64
358. Oman and his four sons............ 1 Chron. xxi. 15
359. Huldah, the prophetess
   2 Kings xxii. 14; 2 Chron. xxxiv. 22.
360. See ye how this son of a murderer has sent to take away mine head................ 2 Kings vi. 32.
361. The mighty men who came to David at Ziklag.
   1 Chron. xii. 1, 2
362. They were destroyed by fire from the Lord, because they offered strange fire................ Lev. x. 1.
363. See.   .... Exodus iv. 6
364. The body of Saul.................... 1 Sam. xxxi. 10
365. Of seven hundred of the tribe of Benjamin.
   Judges xx. 16.
366. Benaiah   Chron. xi. 22

CURIOSITIES OF THE BIBLE.

367. Joash.................................2 Kings xiii. 14.
368. Issachar............................1 Chron. xii. 32.
369. Ebed-melech....................Jer. xxxix. 16.
370. Ishmael.............................Jer. xli. 1.
371. Jeremiah..........................Jer. xliii. 10,
372. Elam.................................Jer. xlix. 36
373. They put out his eyes......Jer. lii. 8.
374. Joshua..............................Num. xi. 28.
375. Zebulun............................1 Chron. xii. 33.
376. Ornan...............................1 Chron. xxi. 20.
377. Adopted daughter............Esth. ii. 7.
378. Samuel.............................1 Sam. ix. 13.
379. Uzziah..............................2 Chron. xxvi. 10.
380. Benaiah............................1 Chron. xi. 22.
381. Moses...............................Exod. iv. 24.
382. Michal..............................2 Sam. iii. 14.
383. Potipher at the priest of On his grandsons were Joseph's sons, Ephraim and Manessah........Gen. xli. 45.
384. Jehoiada..........................2 Chron. xxiv. 22.
385. Solomon..........................1 Chron. xxii. 9.
386. Gedaliah..........................Jer. lx. 14.
387. Issacher...........................1 Chron. xii. 32.
388. ......Exod. xii. 23; 2 Sam. xxiv. 16; Kings xix. 35.
389. David..............................1 Sam. xx. 3.
390. Baruch............................Jer. xlv. 5.
391. Thirty.............................Jer. xxxviii. 10.
392. See..................................2 Chron. xxx. 10.
393. Uzziah............................2 Chron. xxvi. 19.
394. Nahash...........................1 Sam. xi 2.
395. Elijah.............................2 Kings i. 9, 18.
396. Ishmael, Isaac, Solomon, Josiah, Cyrus, John and Jesus
397. The high priest..............Lev. xxi. 14.
398. Abiram and Segub.....Josh. vi. 26; 1 Kings xvi. 34
399. David, Ps. lxxxv. 2, 3; Hezekiah, Isa. xxxviii. 17
400. See..................................1 Chron. iv. 23.
401. Ahithophel and Hushai..........1 Chron. xxvii. 33.
402. Rehoboam......................2 Chron. xi. 21.

OLD TESTAMENT PERSONS.

403. See................Acts i. 16 ; 2 Sam. xxiii. 1, 2.
404. The tribe of Issachar..............1 Sam. xxiii. 12.
405. Ezekiel...........................Ezek. xlvii. 12
406. See..............................Isa. xxvi. 19.
407. Ezra the scribe.....................Neh. viii. 4.
408. Moses and Caleb......Deut. xxxiv. 7; Josh. xiv. 11.
409. Araunah........................2 Sam. xxiv. 23
410. Amaziah........................2 Kings xiv. 19
411. Uzziah.........................2 Chron. xxvi. 10.
412. All the people sat in the street,...........Ezra x. 9.
413. Joash to Elisha ....2 Kings xiii. 14.
    Elisha to Elijah..................2 Kings ii. 12.
414. Joseph, aged 110 years ....Gen. l. 26.
415. The old man of Ephraim..............Jud. xix. 29.
416. When Anaziah said to Amos " Go fly thee away into the land of Judah, and there eat bread and prophesy,' Amos answered and said, " I was no prophet, neither was I a prophet's son "..........Amos vii. 12, 14.
417. Uzziah was struck with a leprosy for trespassing on the priest's office. 2. Chron. xxvi. Isa. xxiii. 43, 44.
418. Moabites............................Isa. xv. 2.
419. Gen. xii. 3 ; Gen. xvii 8 ; Gen. xvii. 16.
420. See.........................Deut. xviii. 15, 19.
421. Because he asked for a Shunamite's wife.
                                1 Kings ii. 13, 25.
422. Isaac...............................Gen. xxii. 6.
423. For the *free will* offering a blemished animal might be offered...........................Lev. xxii. 23.
424. Abraham.................Gen. xxii 18 ; xxi. 12.
    Isaac........Gen. xxvi. 4 ; Jacob Gen. xxviii. 14
425. King David to Joab.................2 Sam. xi. 15
426. The son of the widow of Zarepath. 1 Kings xvii. 17, 23.
    The Shunamite's son...........2 Kings iv. 18, 37.
    The man buried in Elisha's grave. .2 King xiii. 21.
427. Because God said "Ye shall henceforth return no more that way".......................Deut. xvii. 16.
428. Doeg the Edomite......... ....1 Sam. xxii. 19

429. The King of the Ammonites...........2 Sam. xii. 30
430. Hiel, the Bethelite, fulfilling the prophecy of Joshua,
                        Josh. vi. 26.1 King xvi. 34.
431. See...............................2 Kings vi. 32
432. Saul and his Armor bearer ....1 Sam. xxxi. 4
     Ahithophel.......................2 Sam. xvii. 23
     Samson Judges.......... ....xvi. 35
     Zimri, 1 Kings xvi. 18; Judas......Matt. xxvii. 5
433. Forty-eight.......................Josh.xxi. 11.
434. Jehoiakim......................Jer. xxii. 18, 19.
435. Ishmael..... .... Gen. xvii. 20.
436. By Nathan he was called Jedediah....2 Sam. xii. 25.
     By his mother he was called Lemuel. Prov. xxxi.
437. The wicked judges................... Ps. lviii. 4
438. Pashur, a governor of Judah.............Jer. xx. 4.
439. Ahaz............................... Isa. vii. 14.
440. Moses and Elijah.......Ex. xxiv. 18; 1 Kings xix. 8.
441. Seven sons of Saul...................2 Sam. xxi. 9.
442. Hezekiah, Because the children of Israel did burn in-
     cense to it......................2 Kings xviii. 4.
443. Nadab and Abihu....................Lev. x. 1, 2.
444. "Thou shall not put any in thy vessel," Deut. xxiii. 24
445. Jubal.................................Gen. iv. 21.
446. The Amalekite in hope of winning David's favor, de-
     clared falsely that he had slain Saul, 2 Sam. i. 15.
447. Ahasuerus........................Esther v. 3, 6
     Herod.........................Mark vi. 22, 23
448. Abner slain by Joab in Hebron.......2 Sam. iii. 27
449. Moses and Jeremiah the furnace of iron,
                      Deut. iv. 20; Jer. xi. 4
450. Jeroboam......................1 Kings xiv. 11
     Baasha........................1 Kings xvi. 4.
     Ahab.........................1 Kings xxii. 38
451. Death by fire.....................Lev. x. 1, 3.
452. Ishmael.........................Gen. xvii. 20.
453. The battle of the four Kings..............Gen. xiv
454. Smothered by Hazael................2 Kings viii. 8

OLD TESTAMENT PERSONS.

455. Because they put their trust in horses and chariots,
Isa xxxi. 1
456. Baasha. 1 Kings xvi. 17; Jehoshaphat,
2 Chron. xix. 2
457. Eldad and Medad....................Num. xi. 16.
458. Potipher, Gen. xxxix. 5; Laban........Gen. xxx. 27
459. Mesha................................2 Kings iii. 4.
460. Ahijah the Shilinite..................1 Kings xi. 29.
461. Jonathan and Ahimaaz..............2 Sam. xvii. 20
462. Twice.................................1 Kings ix. 2.
463. See....................................Deut. vii. 8
464. See....................................Job xvi. 11.
465. Ezeikel..............................Ezek. xxiv. 15.
466. Balaam, Num. xxii; Caiaphas..........John xi. 49.
467. By Balaam...........................Num. xxxi. 15.
468. At the dedication of the Temple....1 Kings viii. 46;
2 Chron. vi. 36.
469. That of Ephraim....................2 Sam. xvii. 17.
470. Adah and Zillah, the wives of Lamech, and his daughter Naamah.........................Gen. iv. 19.
471. The Wench, &c.....................2 Sam. xvii. 17
472. Balaam....2 Pet. ii. 15; Num. xxxi. 8; Achan, Josh. vii. 20; Ahab, 1 Kings xxi.; Ananias and Sapphira, Acts v.; Judas, Matt. xxvi. 15; Acts i. 18.
473. See.................................2 Kings xxi. 18.
474. (1) Isa viii. 20; (2) John v. 39; Acts xv. 11; (3) Thess. ii. 13; Heb. iv. 12.
475. The children of Israel did burn incense to it, "therefore, Hezekiah broke it in pieces"..2 Kings xviii. 4.
476. In the wilderness of Pharan...........Num. xii. 16.
477. David, for numbering the people, made choice of a three day's pestilence .... 2 Sam. xxiv. 13.
478. Shimei...............................1 Kings ii. 36.
479. Jezebel used Ahab's name............1 Kings xxi. 8.
480. Ezekiel in his vision.................Ezek. viii. 3
481. David.................................1 Sam. xxi. 12
482. Samson to Delilah...................Judges xvi. 6

483. Noah, Daniel and Job.................Ezek. xiv 14
484. "Yet now there is hope," &c............Ezra. x. 2
485. The God of Abraham, the God of Isaac, and the God of Jacob, Ex. iii. 6, 15, 16; Christ said, God is not the God of the dead, but of the living. Matt xxii. 32.
486. Speaking of their father; he died in his own sin...........................Num. xxvii. 2
487. The mother of Sisera..................Judges v. 28.
488. Ahijah. King Jeroboam's wife.......1 Kings xiv. 4.
490. Jonah was sent to the heathen city of Nineveh,
Jonah. i
491. Zachariah being stoned to death...Matt. xxiii. 35, 37
492. Hagar and Ishmael.................Gen. xxi. 14, 17.
493. The birth of Samson to the wife of Manoah..Judges xiii.
494. David............................2 Sam. xviii. 3.
495. Adonibezek.......................... Judges i. 6
496. Joab of King David's army........1 Chron. xxvii. 34.
497. Ahasuerus. The good service of Mordecai,
Esther vi. 1, 3.
498. Nehemiah sent by Sanballat..............Neh. vi. 5.
499. Elisha............................2 Kings vii. 1.
500. Agag, King of the Amalekites, by Samuel,
1 Sam. xv. 33.
501. See............Zechariah xii. 11 ; 2 Kings xxiii. 29 ;
2 Chron. xxxv. 24, 25.
502. See...................................Job. iv. 9.
503. Abraham's expedition against the kings of the East..............................Gen. xiv.
504. Melchizedek, King of Salem, blessed Abraham as priest of "the most high God "...Gen. xiv. 18, 19.
505. Amos.............................Amos v. 25.
506. After Moses slew the Egyptian
Ex. ii. 11, 15 ; Acts vii. 24, 29
507. For the Israelites the way through the Red Sea was a way of life, for the Egyptians it was a way of death..................................Ex. xiv.
508. Ishmael.   ....Gen. xxi. 17

OLD TESTAMENT PERSONS.

509. The prophet Isaiah...................... Isa. vi
510 Joel..................................Joel i. 20
511 One of the children of the prophets, by Jehu the king,
   2 Kings ix. 1, 11
512 He fell down through a lattice in his upper chamber,
   2 Kings i 2
513. Moabites. Because Ahaziah worshipped Baal,
   1 Kings xxii. 51, 53; 2 Kings i. :
514. Elijah's, in which "dogs should lick his blood"
   1 Kings xxi. 19, 22, 24
515. Bigthan and Teresh. They were hanged on a tree
   Esther ii. 21
516. Athaliah, 2 Kings xi. 1; Esther.........Esther ii. 17
517. Jehoram (Elijah's prophecy).........2 Chron. xxi. 19.
518. Jehoshaphat, King of Judah. Encouraged by the
   Prophet Jahaziel................2 Chron. xx. 1£.
519. Zechariah stoned to death because he reproved Joash
   King of Judah................2 Chron. xxiv. 21.
520. Jehu, by one of the children of the prophets,
   2 Kings xi. 2.
521. The tribes of Reuben, Gad and Mannasseh were the
   first to suffer, as from their position on the East of
   the Jordan they were exposed, while their country,
   being rich in pasture-land, would be very attractive
   to neighboring nations..........2 Kings x. 32, 33.
522. Athaliah..........................2 Chron. xxiv. 7
523. Jehoram........................2 Chron. xxi 20

524. Dukes............................Gen. xxxvi. 15
525. Gehazi, servant of Elisha.............2 Kings v. 27
526. Jemima. Kezia, Kerenhappuck, daughters of Job,
   Job xlii. 14.
527 Jonah when he refused to go as missionary to Nineveh.... .... Jonah first and second chaps.
528 Saul.................... ....1 Sam. xiv. 52.

529. Samuel..............................1 Sam. xii. 2.
530. Ahab appropriated Naboths...........1 Kings xxi. 7.
531. Jehosaphat........................1 Kings xxii. 30.
532. David by Shimei....................2 Sam. xvi. 5.
533. Abraham............................Gen. xviii. 27.
534. Sarah, 127, Gen. xxiii. 1; Anna, 84,......Luke ii. 36.
535. Samuel..............................1 Sam. vii. 15.
536. His son Eleazer, and Moses.............Num. xx. 28.
537. When God ordered Samuel to go to Bethlehem and anoint David as King. ... .1 Sam xvi. 2.
538. Moses took the blood of a ram which had been offered up and put it on the tip of their right ears and upon the thumbs of their right hands and upon the great toes of their right feet .. ...Lev. viii. 23, 24.
539. Because he was first successful in the attack upon the Jebusites........................;......1 Chron. xi. 6.
540. Because he had told King Artaxerxes that God would keep them from danger and therefore he was ashamed to ask the king for help..............Ezra viii. 22.
541. Isaiah to Hezekiah ....2 Kings xx. 7.
542. Asa..............................2 Chron. xvi. 12.
543. Zedekiah.........................2 Kings xxv. 7
544. Eleazar............................Num. xx. 26.
545. Ammonites........................2 Sam xii. 31.
546. Jacob..............................Gen. xxviii. 17.
547. Bildad, Eliphaz and Zophar..............Job. ii. 11.
548. Ebenezer. By Samuel after the victory of Israel over the Philistines....................1 Sam. vii. 12
549 The law of inheritance. Moses. Daughters of Zelophehad............................Num. xxvii. 1,11
550 The two kings of the Amorites ....Joshua xxiv. 12

ANSWERS TO
NEW TESTAMENT CURIOSITIES
PERTAINING TO
Persons.

---

1. Felix, Acts xxiii. 24 ; Festus. Acts xxiv. 27.
   Fortunatus..........................1 Cor. xvi. 17
2. Lydia at Thyatira......................Acts xvi. 14.
3. Phebe.................................Romans xvi. 27.
4. Felix before Paul......................Acts xxiv. 25.
5. Forty men to kill St. Paul.............Acts xxiii. 21.
6. Tertullus.............................Acts xxiv. 1.
7. Tertullus.............................Acts xxiv. 5.
8. St. Paul..............................Acts xxi. 34, 40.
9. His address at Jerusalem...............Acts xxii.
10. Quartus..............................Rom. xvi. 23.
11. Him that overcometh..................Rev. ii. 17.
12. St. Paul.............................Acts xx. 7.
13. Peter................................John xiii. 37.
14. James................................Acts xii. 2.
15. At the stoning of Stephen.............Acts vii. 58.
16. Peter. Malchus......................John xviii. 10.
17. See....................John i. 45; John xii. 20-22.
18. Tarsus...............................Acts xxii. 3
19. Pharisee.............................Acts xxvi 5

20. The angel to the Laodiceans.. ....Rev. iii. 16
21. He knew no sin................. ....2 Cor. v. 21.
22. Go, teach all nations, baptizing them, &c, Matt. xxviii. 19
23. Apollos.............................Acts xviii. 24.
24. The apostle John....................John xxi. 25.
25. If ye have love one to another..........John xiii. 35.
26. I exceedingly fear and quake........ . .Heb. xii. 21
27. When rebuked for healing on the Sabbath, Mark iii. 5; and for blessing little children......Mark x. 14.
28. See ....John xxi. 18, 19.
29. I am with you always...............Matt. xxviii. 20.
30. Eutychus.............................Acts xx. 9.
31. St. Paul.............................Acts xxiv. 5.
32. The eunuch.........................Acts viii. 26-39.
33. Agabus.............................Acts xxi. 10-11.
34. Anna the prophetess....................Luke ii. 36.
35. Jesus....................John i. 9; viii. 12; xii. 46.
36. Persecuting the disciples.........Acts ix. 18; xxii. 5-6.
37. Lord what wilt thou have me to do.......Acts ix. 6-11.
38. Ananias............................Acts ix. 9-18.
39. Corinthians........................ ...1 Cor. ix. 2.
40. The Jews.............................Rom. x. 2.
41. John x. 20; Paul, Acts xxvi. 24.
42. Gamaliel..................... ....Acts v. 34; xxii. 3.
43. 1930 years......................Bible Chronology.
44. He first appeared to her.................Mark xvi. 9.
45. Cleopas and Luke, two of his disciples....Luke xxiv. 15.
46. To the eleven Apostles..................Mark xvi. 14.
47. By our Saviour to the Apostles, "as they sat at meat" after his resurrection and just previous to his ascension?.........................Mark xvi. 14-15.
48. ONE VOICE IN BEHALF OF JESUS.—Amid all the Scribes. and Pharisees and devout Jews; among all the disciples who were at Jerusalem at the passover; in all that excited multitude which seemed hungry for the blood of the captive Christ, there was one voice that was publicly lifted up in behalf of that

" Just man." Only one! The Apostles were affrighted. Bold Peter acted the coward and the craven. The Marys and Marthas felt themselves forlorn and impotent to help. But one woman, the wife of the heathen governor, Pontius Pilate, boldly petitioned for the life of the innocent. This noble act was deemed worthy of a record in the Gospel. It should be ever remembered to the honor of womanhood,
Matt. xxvii. 19.

49. Nicodemus....................................John iii. 2.
50. Simon a Cyrenian........................Mark xv. 21.
51. Father forgive them for they know not what they do............................Luke xxiii. 34.
To-day thou shalt be with me in paradise, Luke xxiii. 43
Woman behold thy Son.................John xix. 26.
Behold thy mother......................John xix. 27.
Eloi, Eloi, lama sabachthani............Mark xv. 34.
I thirst..................................John xix. 28.
It is finished...........................John xix. 30.
Father into thy hands I commend my spirit,
Luke xxiii. 46.
52. Art thou the King of the Jews?.........Luke xxiii. 3.
53. Peter, James and John................. ..Gal. ii. 9.
54. Our Saviour............................ John v. 39.
55. John...
56. Simon the leper ....Matt. xxvi. 6.
57. Paul........ ....Acts xvii. 28.
58. Peter...................................Acts xii. 8.
59. When healing the cripple at Lystra.......Acts xiv. 8.
60. Mercurius, by the heathen at Lystria, when he healed the cripple........................Acts xiv. 12.
61. Jupiter............................... Acts xiv. 12.
62. Dionysius.... .. .. Acts xvii. 34.
63. Demas .... 2 Tim. iv. 10.
64. St. Paul to the Philippians...............Phil. ii. 10.
65. Gaius...........Rom. xvi. 23; John, 3rd Epistle, v. 6

66. Those that have washed their robes and made them white in the blood of the Lamb....Rev. vii. 13, 17.
67. A professed Christian and yet a malicious person 3 John 9.
68. Agabus.................................Acts xi. 28.
69. Paul....................................Acts xxiii. 2.
70. Jesus Christ........................... John xix. 23
71. New Jerusalem.......................Rev. xxi. 14
72. Paul at Damascus........... Acts ix. 25; 2 Cor. xi. 32.
73. Tentmaking............................Acts xviii. 3.
74. Damaris...............................Acts xvii. 34.
75. Ananias and Sapphria...............Acts v. 1, 10.
76. Peter. That they might be healed........ Acts v. 15.
77. Paul ....Acts xxviii. 3. 6.
78. Stephen's .... Acts vi. 15.
79. { Jairus' daughter........................Matt. ix. 25.
    { Widow's son of Nain..................Luke vii. 15.
    { Lazarus................................John xi. 44.
80. { Tabitha by Peter......................Acts ix. 40.
    { Eutychus by Paul.....................Acts xx. 10.
81. The saints which slept................Matt. xxvii. 52.
82. Two whole years..................... Acts xxviii. 30.
83. St. Paul's ....Acts xxiii. 12.
84. Matthias................................Acts i. 23.
85. By the sword, by order of Herod.............Acts xii. 2.
86. The Queen of Sheba..... 1 Kings x. 1; 2 Chron. ix. 1.
87. Diotrephes..........................3 John ix. 10.
88. Stephens..............................Acts vii. 60.
89. See..................... Matt. iv. 11; Luke xxii. 43.
90. St. Luke................................Luke x. 1
91. St. Paul................................ Rom. x. 19.
92. Ephesus..............................Acts xxi. 29.
93. Herod Agrippa.......................... Acts xii. 2
94. The law of Moses, the prophets, and the Psalms,
Luke xxiv. 44.
95. See...................John iii. 1; vii. 50; xix. 39.
96. Barnabas........................... Acts iv. 34, 37.
97. At the beginning of his ministry,
John ii. 14, 16 and near its close Matt xxi. 12, 13.

NEW TESTAMENT PERSONS.

98. The raising of Jairus' daughter, Matt ix. 23; Mark v. 38.
99. See....... Matt. viii. 29; Mark iii. 11; Luke iv. 34, 41.
100. Before Annas, John xviii. 13; Caiaphas, Matt. xxvi. 57
The council....................... Luke xxiii. 3.
101. St. Paul. By the people when he healed the impotent man............................... Acts xiv. 12.
102. Peter..................................1 Peter ii. 25.
103. Philemon............................... Phil. xxii.
104. See..................................... Acts xv. 36.
105. Twice. St. Paul........... Gal. vi. 9; 2 Thess. iii. 13.
106. See.................................... John xvii. 3
107. .... Gen. xl. 20; Matt. xiv. 6.
108. Jesus answered and said "If I had spoken evil, bear witness of the evil, but if well, why smitest thou me?"..........................John xviii. 23.
109. The Apostle Peter..................... 2 Peter ii. 5.
110. Drusilla, the Jewess................... Acts xxiv. 24.
111. Because he believed not the angel who told him of the birth of his son.......................Luke i. 20
112. Agabus.................................Acts xi. 28.
113. The preaching of Christ crucified .... 1 Cor. i. 23.
114. Herod............................... Luke xiii. 35.
115. The salutation of Paul with mine own hand which is the token in every epistle ....2 Thess. iii. 17.
116. Wherefore we would have come unto you, even I, Paul, once and again, but Satan hindered us,
1 Thess. ii. 18.
117. When he took upon himself the vow of a Nazarite and went into the temple to fulfil the same according to the Lord....... Num. vi. 2, 21; Acts xxi. 23, 27.
118. Epaphroditus, whom St. Paul sent as a messenger from Rome to the Philippians............ Phil. ii. 25, 9,
119. St. Paul. Whensoever I take my journey into Spain. I will come by you into Spain .....Rom. xv. 24, 28.
120. Zenis.................................Titus iii. 13
121. Publius............................. Acts xxviii. 7

122. When Peter wished to know what would happen to St. John..........................John xxi. 21, 23.
123. The Epistle to the Galatians ....Gal. vi. 11.
124. Lucius, Jason and Sosipater.............Rom. xvi. 21.
125. That in the upper room, waiting with the apostles the out-pouring of the Holy Ghost......... Acts i. 14.
126. Because the disciples were the witnesses of his resurrection, and the full reception of this fact was necessary for the faith of future ages ....Acts i. 2.
127. The gift of the Comforter and his own personal return.
John xii. 16, 19, 22, 28.
128. Menander..............................Cor. xv. 33.
Epimendes............................. Titus i. 12.
129. See.................................. John xvii. 15.
130. .... Acts vii. 45; xiii. 6; Col. iv. 11
131. (1.) St. Paul........................ ....Phil. iii. 8.
(1.) The rich fool ....Luke xii. 18.
(1.) Balaam..........................Num. xxiii. 10.
132. The seven sons of Sceva................Acts xix. 14.
133. Agabus. ....Acts xxi. 14.
134. Mephibos th, the son of Jonathan, the son of Saul,
2 Sam. iv. 4.
135. Trophimus. ....Acts xx. 4.
136. How is it th e sought me ? Wist ye not that I must be about n father's business, and it is finished,
John xix. 30; Luke ii. 49.
137 Of Simeon, Pet and Andrew his brother..Mark i. 17.
138. St. Peter...... ....1 Peter ii. 25.
139. To Philemon... .... Phil. xxii.
140. See........... .... Matt. xxi. 16.
141. Diotrephes ....3 John 9, 10.
142. Archelaus........ .... Matt. ii. 22.
143. See.............. ....John v. 7.
144. The Sadducees say th is no resurrection, neither anger nor spirit, but the Pharisees confirm both,
Acts xxiii. 8
145. Body............ .. .. Heb. x. 5

Soul. .... John xii. 27.
Spirit.................................. John xiii. 21
146. Thirteen times as seated, but only once as standing,
Acts vii. 56.
147. His body unconfined by the laws of nature, he appeared, the doors being shut, and vanished from the sight of the two disciples of Emmaus, Luke xxiv. 31; John xv. 19; finally unrestrained by the laws of gravitation, rose materially into a cloud that received him out of their sight .... Acts i. 9.
148. " A dark place "........................ 2 Peter i. 19.
149. " Whatsoever He saith unto you, do it...... John ii. 5.
150. " Darkness." The darkness comprehended it not,
John i. 5.
151. See....................................... John i. 15.
152. See........................ 2 John x ; Titus iii. 10.
153. Nathaniel. " Behold an Israelite, indeed, &c."
John i. 47.
154. "Passed from death unto life."
1 John iii. 14 ; John v. 24.
155. When Satan is cast out and overcome..... Rev. xii. 12.
156. John the Baptist: "I am the voice of one crying in the wilderness"...........................John i. 23.
157. Stephen.............................Acts vii. 55. 56.
158. "Which is, and which was, and which is to come, the Almighty.................... Rev. i. 8.
159. Spoken to the angel of the church in Sardis,
Rev. iii. 1.
160 The two malefactors crucified with our Lord,
Luke xxiii. 32-43.
161 Claudius................................Acts xviii. 2.
162. Epaphroditus........................ Phil. iv. 18,24.
163. Julius................................Acts xxvii. 1.
164. Paul to the Jews...................... Acts xviii. 6.
165. See .. .. John v. 24.
166. At the grave of Lazarus................ John xi. 33.
Over Jerusalem.................... ..Luke xix. 41

In Gethsemane...............Heb. v. 7
167. See......................James ii. 19.
168. Crispus, Gaius, & Stephanas..........1 Cor. i. 14, 16
169. See........................Luke i. 47.
170. Salome, the mother of Zebedee's children. Matt. xx. 20.
171. Peter on the day of Pentecost..............Acts ii. 41.
172. Pergamos : " Where Satan's seat is," or where Satan
dwelleth........ .... Rev ii. 13.
173. Paul and his companions before the shipwreck,
Acts xxvii. 37.
174. "That for which I give thanks "..........1 Cor. x. 30
175. On His way to Cavalry. " Weep for yourselves, &c."
Luke xxiii.

ANSWERS

TO

OLD TESTAMENT CURIOSITIES

PERTAINING TO

Places and Localities.

1. Zoar..................................Genesis xix. 23
2. By Adam in the Garden of Eden............Gen. iii. 8.
3. Nineveh................................Jonah iii. 4.
4. Jerusalem.............................2 King xxi. 13.
5. Jericho.............................2 Chron xxviii. 15.
6. Bethlehem........................Gen. xxxv. 19, 20.
7. Babylon...............Isa. xiii. 19, 20; Jer. xxv. 12.
8. From the river of Egypt to the Euphrates...Gen. xv. 18.
9. See................................2 Sam. vii. 24.
10. See................................2 Sam. xix. 18.
11. Solomon's navy at Ezion-geber on the
    Red Sea........................1 Kings ix. 26.
12. Gibeon............................Josh. ix. 3, 15.
13. In Jerusalem in the reign of Solomon.....2 Chron. i. 15
14. Babylon..................................Isa. xiii. 19
15. Nob................................1 Sam. xxi. 1, 6.
16. Mount Ebal..........................Deut. xxvii. 13
17. Damascus. See Bible Dictionary...........Gen. xiv. 15
18. Mount Tabor......................2 Kings xxiii. 29
19. Mount Carmel by King Ahab........1 Kings xviii. 20
20. Makkedah............................Josh. x. 16

21. Sisera and Barek......................Judges iv. 15
22. See................ ..Isa. xiii.1, 22 ; xiv. 22; Jer. l.
23. Shall stand before kings and not before mean men,
Prov. xxii. 29
24. A lion... ....1 Kings xiii. 24.
25. The turtle dove and pigeon. ....Lev. v. 7.
26. See............Lev. v. 5; Prov. xxviii. 13; 1 John i. 9
27 See.............Prov. iii. 12; Heb. xii. 6; Rev. iii. 19.
28 See..Gen.vii. 1; xix. 12; xxx 27; xxxix. 5; Acts. xxvii. 23.
29. Stork, turtle, crane, and swallow..........Jer. viii. 7.
30. Righteousness....Prov. xiv. 34; Ps. xxxiii. 12; cxliv. 15.
31. A dove................. .... Gen. viii. 12.
32. Genesis..............................xv. 18; xvii 8.
33. Gibeon, Chephirah, Buroth, and Kerjath jearim,
Josh. ix. 17
34. Ai............. ....Josh viii. 5, 25.
35. Mount Moriah in Jerusalem............2 Chron. iii. 1
36. Nimrod....................... ......Gen. x. 8, 12.
37. The name given by Laban to the monument erected by Jacob, signifying, "The Lord watch between me and thee, when we are absent one from another,"
Gen. xxxi. 49.
38. If ten righteous persons could be found...Gen xviii. 20.
39. Six. Kedesh, Shechem, Hebron, Bezor, Ramoth-Gilead, and Golon.................. ....Josh. xx. 7.
40. Fifty................................Num. viii. 25.
41. The stone which Joshua set up as a memorial and witness of a covenant with the tribes of Shechem,
Josh xxiv. 27.
42 Nineveh..................... ....Nahum iii. 10.
43. At Jehovah-jireh....:. ....Gen. xxii. 14.
44. Solomon's temple was built on Mount Moriah where Abraham built the altar for Isaac....2 Chron. iii. 1.
45. See ....2 Chron. xxv. 12.
46 The territory that Caleb passed over when he spied the land ....Deut. i. 36.
47 Shechem....................... ... .Jud iy 45

OLD TESTAMENT PLACES AND LOCALITIES. 43

48. See..Jud. vi. 21.
49. See..Jud. x. 4.
50. Mount of Corruption................2 Kings xxiii. 13. See origin in same verse.
51. Eagles indicated Romans..Deut. xxviii.49; Matt. xxiv. 28.
52. Forty-eight............................Josh. xxi. 41.
53. By Heile, the Bethelite, fulfilling the prophecy of Joshua.............Josh. vi. 26; 1 Kings xvi. 34
54. Because he took the city from the Jebusites.2 Sam. v. 7.
55. King Omri, Hill of Samaria...........1 Kings xvi. 24.
56. Mount Gerizim.....................Deut. xxvii. 12
57. Mount Ebol........................Deut. xxvii. 13.
58. Mount Gilboa...........................2 Sam. i. 6.
59. Thirty-one............................Judges xii. 24.
60. Jerusalem..............................Jer. lii. 4, 6
61. See...................Gen. xxviii. 19; Hosea iv. 15.
62. The fall of Jericho.....................Joshua vi.
63. "Bethel shall come to naught"..........Amos v. 5

ANSWERS
TO
NEW TESTAMENT CURIOSITIES
PERTAINING TO
Places and Localities.

1. The mourning made for Jacob by his son Joseph. Gen. l. 11
2. Gadarenes; compare Matt. viii. 28; Mark v. 1
3. Mount Olivet.. ....Acts i. 12.
4. Cana in Galilee........................John i. 47.
5. At Antioch in Picidia..................Acts xiii. 14.
6. Betheny........Matt. xxvi. 6; Mark xiv. 3; John xii. 1.
7. Mount of Olives............Luke xxi. 37 ; John viii. 1.
8. Melita.................................Acts xxvii. 41.
9. Antioch. ....Acts xiv. 26.
10. Lystrea..............................Acts xiv. 19.
11. Paphos in Cyprus......................Acts xiii. 6.
12. Gath-hepher........................2 Kings xiv. 25.
13. Capernaum............................Matt. xi. 23
14. At Thessalonica, of the disciples........Acts. xvii. 1, 6
15. Roman................................Luke ii. 1
16. Nazareth ....John i. 46
17. Athens................................Acts xvii. 22

ANSWERS
TO
OLD TESTAMENT CURIOSITIES
PERTAINING TO
Things.

1. A cherubim and a flaming sword............Gen. iii. 24.
2. The Serpent...............................Gen. iii. 14.
3. Gopher wood..............................Gen. vi. 14.
4. That water had abated from the face of the earth,
   Gen. viii. 8.
5. Balm, honey, spices, myrrh, nuts and almonds,
   Gen. xliii. 11.
6. Shittim wood.............................Ex. xxv. 10.
7. Fear God and keep his commandments......Eccl. xii. 13.
8. A brother offended......................Prov. xviii. 19.
9. Cold water to a thirsty soul............Prov. xxv. 25.
10. Pen of iron and point of diamond........Jer. xvii 1.
11. On palm leaves, bark of trees and papyrus,
    Isa. xxx. 8 ; Luke i. 63.
12. The glory is departed. By Phinehas' wife to her son whom she named Ichabod...........1 Sam. iv. 21.
13. See book of Esther.
14. 1st. A lion killed the disobedient prophet.
    1 Kings xiii. 24

2d, A lion killed the man that disobeyed the prophet
1 King xx. 35, 36
3d, Lions killed Daniel's enemies........Daniel vi. 24
4th, Bears killed Elisha's mockers ....2 King ii. 24.
15. 150 Shekels (at 33c) about $80 ....2 Chron. i. 17.
16. Seven years..........................1 Kings vi 38
17. His mantle.... ....2 Kings ii. 13
18. Fire came from heaven and consumed the sacrifice
Glory of the Lord filled the house
1 Kings viii. 11; 2 Chron. vii. 1.
19 Two. 1st, Elijah....1 Kings xviii. 42; James v. 17, 18.
1st, Samuel...............1 Sam. xii. 16, 18.
20. By Elijah or Elias..1 Kings xvii. 1; James. v. 17, 18.
21. Pillar of cloud by day; pillar of fire by night,
Ex. xiii. 21.
22. Jewels of gold and silver and raiment....Gen. xxiv. 53.
23. The confusion of tongues..............Gen. xi. 6, 9.
24. Men of Succoth to Gideons army......Judges viii. 4, 6.
25. Assyrian army......................2 Kings vii. 39.
26. Suits of apparel, rings, &c.............Isa iii. 18, 23.
27. A coat of many colors from Jacob to Joseph,
Gen. xxxvii. 3.
28. A linen girdle. On the bank of the Euphrates,
Jer. xiii. 4.
29. The Hebrews of the Egyptians............Ex. xii. 35.
30. Trees used for meat. They are man's life.
Deut. xx. 19, 20.
31. Death of the first born.................Exodus xi. 5
32. See....................Prov. i. 10; i. 15; iv. 14, 15.
33. Three thousand.........................Job i. 3
34. All things.........................1 Cor. iii. 21, 23.
35. Jacob..........Gen. l. 8. Joseph.........Gen. l. 26.
36. The nation of Israel......Exodus xxxi. 13; Lev. 22, 9.
The first born......................Num. viii. 17
Aaron and his family..................Ex. xxix. 44.
The tribe of Levi........Num. viii. 14; Ex. xviii. 25.
The tabernacle... . ...Ex. xxix. 43.

OLD TESTAMENT THINGS. 53

    The temple........................ ..2 Chron. vii. 16.
37. Bulls....Ps. xxii. 12. Trees....Isa, ii. 13. Fatlings
    Ezek. xxxix. 18.
38. One third of a shekel..... ....Neh. x. 32.
39. It descended from heaven, ...Lev. ix. 24.
40. The plague of darkness.... ....Ex. x. 22, 23.
41. Songs of Solomon....................Chap. ii. 11, 13.
42. See.........Ps. xxxiii 16; Isa. xxx. 1, 7 ; Jer. xvii. 5, 6.
43. See.......................Luke viii. 24 ; Jonah i. 5.
44. See........Isa. xxxiv. 16 ; xli. 17, 18; Matt. vi. 26, 31.
45. See.......................................Isa. xviii. 2.
46. By the navies of Hiram and Tarshish.....1 King x. 22.
47. Six hundred and sixty-six talents valued at $56,900 each, or a total of $37,895,400,......1 King x. 14.
48. Hewers of wood and drawers of water....Joshua ix. 22.
49. By Elisha when he caused iron to swim...2 King vi. 6
50. Balaams ass—....................Num. xxii. 28, 30.
51. Sennacherib, King of Assyria........2 Kings xix. 36
52. The prophet Ezekiel...............Ezek. xxxvii. 15.
53. The fiftieth year.......................Lev. xxv. 9.
54. Cursed...............................Josh. vi. 26.
55. See.....................Luke v. 21 ; Isa. xliii. 25.
56. In the case of Zacheus.................Luke xix. 2.
57. By sea on floats.......................1 Kings v. 9.
58. See.............................Psa. xxix. 3, 10.
59. { When Joshua commanded it to stand still,
                            Josh. x. 12, 13
    When Hezekiah prayed that it should be turned back ten degrees as a sign.............2 Kings xx. 11.
60. Paul..Rom. v. 3. James..Jas. i. 2. Peter..Pet. iv. 12
    2 Cor. xii. 9, 10.
61. Josh. vii. 16 ; 1 Sam. x. 20 ; xiv. 41; John xix. 23;
    Acts i. 26.
62. Moses deliverance of Israel....Ex. iii. 11 ; Josh. vi. 20. Judges vii. 7, 22 ; 1 Sam. xvii. 4; 2 Chron. xiv. 13. 12 ; xvi. 8.
63. Fear God and keep his commandments... Eccl. xii. 13

64. The golden rule........................James ii. 8
65. In the days of the prophet Samuel......1 Sam. xii. 18
66. A good name............................Eccl. vii. 1
67. The blessing of the Lord.................Prov. x. 22
68. Ruling one's spirit.....................Prov. xvi. 32.
69. The tables of stone....................2 Chron. v. 10
70 Seven.   At the creation.................Gen. ii. 2.
    In the wilderness on the giving of manna...Ex. xvi. 25.
    In the fourth commandment...............Ex. xx. 10
    In the Sabbath of the seven years........Lev. xxv. 4.
    In the jubilee seven times seven years.....Lev. xxv. 9
    The Sabbath of the land in the 70 years captivity,
                                        2 Chron. xxxvi. 21
    The prophetic Sabbath of the world........Heb. iv. 9
                                                Ps. xcv. 11
71. Death.............................Lev. xxiv. 16.
72. Yes. See...............Isa. lv. 7; Ezek. xviii. 21, 22.
73. Two or three......................Deut. xix. 15.
74. Two................Gen. xlix. 10 ; Dan. ix. 24, 37
75. See...................................Heb. i. 14.
76. See...................................Eccles i. 7.
77. The Syrian army at Dothan............2 Kings vi. 18.
78. At the siege of Samaria...............2 Kings vi. 27.
79. Thirty thousand......................1. Sam. iv. 6.
80. Forty thousand.......................2 Sam. x. 18.
81 Forty-two thousand....................Judges xii. 6.
82. Twenty-four thousand................Num. xxv. 9.
83. A three day's pestilence. 70,000 die   Sam. xxiv, 15.
) Chron. xxi. 14.
84. Three thousand................... Ex. xxxii. 28
85. Three thousand ....Judges xvi. 27
86. One thousand.....................Dan. v. 1.
87. One thousand.....................Judges xv. 15.
88. One thousand......................Num. xxxi 4.
89. Eighty pieces of silver ($45).......... 2 Kings vi. 25.
90. By Elisha in restoring the poisoned pottage at Gilgal
                                         2 Kings iv. 41

OLD TESTAMENT THINGS.

91. Crackling of thorns under a pot..........Eccles. vii. 6.
92. Boards of shittim wood overlaid with gold
                                    Exodus xxvi. 15, 30.
93. Four. 1st, twined linen; 2d, goats' hair; 3d rams' skins; 4th, skin of an unknown (badger) animal
                                    Exodus xxvi. 1, 14
94. The ravens that fed Elijah............1 Kings xvii. 3, 6.
95. Ark of the covenant. Exod. xl. 20, 21. Inside of the ark was the "testimony," or the two tables of stone, on which were engraved "ten commandments." 1 Kings viii. 9. Before the ark was laid a pot containing an omer (five one-tenths pints) of manna. Exod. xvi. 32, 34. Aaron's rod that budded. Num. xvii. 10. By the side of the ark was a copy of the book of the law. Deut. xxxi. 26. Paul says the pot of manna and Aaron's rod were inside the ark.
                                    Heb. ix. 4.
96. To repair the temple.................2 Chron. xxiv. 9.
97. Drawn on a new cart by two cows........1 Sam. vi. 7.
98. One hundred and fifty-three..................John xxi. 11.
99. Two hundred shekels weight (6 pounds)..2 Sam. xiv. 26.
100. Three hundred cubits (547 ft.) ....Gen. vi. 15.
101. Nine hundred chariots of iron...........Judges iv. 3.
102. Four thousand.....................1 Chron. xxiii. 5.
103. Four thousand ....2 Chron. ix. 25
104. Twelve thousand ....1 Kings iv. 26
105. Six hundred...........................Ex. xiv. 7
106. Till ye be left as a beacon upon the top of a mountain.
                                    Isaiah xxx. 17
107. See.... ....Prov. xxv. 19
108. See.................. ....2 Kings xiii. 20, 21.
109. The dew ....Num. xi ?
110. Their clothes waxed not old ....Deut. viii. 4.
111 King Jehoiachin was only eight years old and was said to have done evil in the sight of the Lord
                                    2 Chron. **xxxvi.** 9
112. See................................ . ....Jud. v. 29

113. See..............................Judges iii. 20
114. See.................................Gen. xxxv. 5.
115. By Og, King of Bashan.................Deut. iii. 11.
116. Admah and Zeboim...............Deut. xxix. 23.
117. Then Isaac sowed in that land (Gerar) and received in the same year an hundredfold....Gen. xxvi. 12
118. That all raiment of the poor should be returned at sunset, and that a widow's raiment was never to be taken in pledge at all..............Deut. xxiv. 10.
119. After the battle against the Moabites and Ammonites...........................2 Chron. xx. 25.
120. Nehushtan........................2 Kings xviii. 4.
121. One hundred thousand were slain......1 Kings xx. 20.
122. See...................................Amos v. 8
123. By not being able to pronounce the "h" in the word "Shibboleth"....................Judg. xii. 6.
124. And Jesse took an ass laden with bread and a bottle of wine and a kid, and sent them by David his son unto Saul........................1 Sam. xvi. 20.
125. Mesha King of Moab, was a sheepmaster and rendered unto the King of Israel an hundred thousand lambs and an hundred thousand rams, with the wool
2 Kings iii. 4.
126. Exod. xii. 23 ; 2 Kings xix. 35.
127. 1. At the deliveration of the Israelites from Egypt
Josh. iii. 14.
2. By Elijah......................2 Kings ii. 8.
3. By Elisha.....................2 Kings ii. 14.
128. The oak under which Deborah was buried was called Allon-bachuth, or the oak of weeping..Gen. xxxv. 8.
129. See................................Isa. lxv. 20.
130. Sheshan had a servant, an Egyptian, whose name was Jarhan, and Shesan gave his daughter, Jarhan to wife.......................1 Chron. ii. 34, 35.
131. A certain man drew a bow at a venture and smote the King of Israel between the joints of the harness
2 Chron. xviii. 33

OLD TESTAMENT THINGS

By chance there came down a priest that way and passed on the other side..............Luke x. 31.
132. See ....Isa. viii. 6.
133. "Speak unto the children of Israel, and bid them that they make them fringe in the borders of their garments, and that they put upon the fringe of the border a riband of blue, that ye may look upon and remember all the commandments of the Lord and do them"............................Num. xv. 38.
134 See...................................Rev. xxii. 9.
135. See..................................Isa. xxxiv. 13.
136. Cracknels..........................1 Kings xiv. 3
137. David at Keilah....................1 Sam. xxiii. 11.
138. And I heard but understood not..........Dan. xii. 8
139. See.. ....Acts xiii. 33
140. Pride................................Isa. xvi. 6.
141. Syrians against Israel; 100,000 Syrians slain
                                        1 Kings xx. 29.
142. The attempt made by Haman to destroy all the Jews in the kingdom of Ahasuerus.........Esther ix. 20.
143. Ten thousand talents of silver..........Esther iii. 9.
144. The Sidomites......................1 Kings v. 6.
145. Because the Prince of Tyre had set himself up as God and lifted up his heart in pride.... Ezek. xxviii. 2.
146. Two talents of silver and two changes of garments
                                        2 Kings v. 23.
147. Four.................................2 Kings vii. 3.
148. The blessing from mount Gerizim, upon which stood the elders of the tribe of Simeon, Levi, Judah, Issachar, Joseph, and Benjamin; the cursing from mount Ebal, upon which stood the elders of Reuben, Gad, Asher, Zebulun, Dan, and Naphtali
                                        Deut xxvii. 12, 13
149. Consumption and burning ague.......Lev. xxvi. 16.
150. Stoned to death.....................Num. xv. 36.
151. The Emims..........................Deut. ii. 11.
152. A lamb or a kid...... ....Exod. xii. 5.

153. By means of His prophet Elisha He multiplied the widow's oil..................2 Kings iv. 4, 7.
154. And Joseph bought all the land of Egypt for Pharoah; for the Egyptians sold every man his field because the famine prevailed over them: so the land became Pharaoh's........................Gen. xlvii. 20.
155. Mount of Corruption..............2 Kings xxiii. 13
156. See..............................2 Kings vi. 13.
157. Because the land was God's and they were only strangers and sojourners there................Lev. xxv. 23.
158. That he might thrust out all their right eyes and lay it for reproach upon all Israel............1 Sam. xi. 2.
159. He stopped the upper water source of Gihon and brought it straight down to the west side of the city of David
2 Chron. xxxii. 30.
160. See............................Job xxxix. 13, 14.
161. One hundred and fifty-three thousand and six hundred..........................2 Chron. ii. 17
162. On the occasion of giving names to the animal creation..............................Gen. ii. 19.
163. On the sixth day, Friday, man, and subsequently redeemed................Gen. i. 31; Luke xxiii. 54.
164. The brazen serpent that Moses had made was broken in pieces by Hezekiah............2 Kings xviii. 4.
165. See................Exod. xxxii. 10; Num. xiv. 12.
166. See..............................Exod. iv. 21.
167. David was thirty years old when he began to reign, and he reigned forty years ....2 Sam. v. 4.
168. Samuel ordered that portion for Saul, which was a mark of highest respect, the shoulder being the priests' portion....1 Sam. ix. 24; Lev. vii. 32; Num. vi. 20
169. Birthright, priesthood, and blessing......Deut xxi. 15
170. A prophetic name of Jerusalem......Ezek. xlviii. 35.
171. When the voice of united praise was heard
2 Chron. v. 13.
172. Because every stone was chiselled, every beam sawn

OLD TESTAMENT THINGS.

every hole drilled, and every bolt fitted before being brought to the city .... 1. King vi. 7.
173. See. .... Isa viii. 13
174. He that ruleth his spirit .... Prov. xvi. 32
175. Polished brass .... Exod. xxxviii. 8
176. Take great stones in thy hand and hide them in the clay in the brick kiln .... Jer. xliii. 9
177. See .... Prov. xxvi. 4, 5
178. Jonah's gourd .... Jonah iv. 10.
179. On floats by sea to Joppa .... 2 Chron. ii. 16.
180. See. .... Prov. xxx. 33
181. See. .... Job xxxviii. 7.
182. .... Jeremiah vi. 26; Amos viii. 10; Zech. xii. 10.
183. It decended from heaven .... Lev. ix. 24. Nadab and Abihu .... Lev. x. 1, 2.
184. See. .... Lev. xxvi. 16.
185. Figs. Prescribed by the Prophet Isaiah for King Hezekiah .... Isa. xxxviii. 21.
186. See .... 2 Kings iv. 18, 20.
187. See .... Zech. xii. 10.
188. Samuel prophecying concerning Saul. 1 Sam. xv-26, 28.
189. The coming of John the Baptist in the spirit and power of Elijah, Malachi iv. 5. The manifestation of Christ, under the emblem of the Son of Righteousness, Malachi iv. 2. The destruction of Jerusalem. under the emblem of a burning oven consuming everything cast into it .... Malachi iv. 1
190. See .... Job xxviii chapter
191. The brazen serpent .... 2 Kings xviii. 4.
192. "Teach me thy statutes" .... Ps. cxix.
193. See .... Ezekiel xx. 36
194. "All is vanity" .... Ecclesiastes.
195. See .... Ezekiel vii. 13.
196. At the death of the Prophet Ezekiel's wife
Ezekiel xxiv. 15, 18
197 Sewing fig leaves .... Gen. iii. 7

198. See.................Deut. iv. 28 and other passages
199. When the prophetic disciples searched for the body of Elijah............................2 Kings ii. 16.
200. "Strong as death".........Solomon's Song viii. 6.
201. See...........................Num. iii. 43, 49.
202. See............................Isaiah iii. 18, 23
203. If thou dost not well, sin lieth at the door...Gen. iv. 7
204. See..................................Prov. i. 5, 6
205. See................................. Zech. iii. 4.
206. "Set ye Uriah in the fore front of the hottest battle, and retire ye from him that he may be smitten and die.............................2 Sam. xi. 15.
207. See..........................Numbers xviii. 20.
208. Those that did not keep the commandments........
................................Lev. xxvi. 16
209. When the Prophet Ahijah tore King Jeroboam's cloak in twelve pieces...............1 Kings xi. 29, 31.
210. The widow.......................Deut. xxiv. 17.
211. The jaw bone used by Samson......Judges xv. 15, 19.
212. The fall of the first, the agony and the burial of the second Adam, Genesis iii. 3, 7; John xviii. 1, 2; Luke xxii. 44; John xix. 41, 42 ; 1 Corinthians xv. 45.
213. See............................Deut. xxviii. 37.
214. Rehum and Shimshai to Artaxerxes.......Ezra iv. 9. Tatnai and others to Darius..............Ezra v. 6.
215. See..... ....Psalm xviii.
216. My God, my God, why hast thou forsaken me
Psalm. xxii. 1.
217. By thunder and rain.................1 Sam. xii. 17.
218 Some remove the land marks...........Job xxiv. 2
219. In the battle of Israel with Syria, 100,000 of the latter were slain....................1 Kings xx. 28, 29
220 Almond ....Num. xvii. 8

ANSWERS
TO
NEW TESTAMENT CURIOSITIES
PERTAINING TO
Things.

1. All Scripture is given by inspiration of God .... 2 Tim. iii. 16.
   Holy men of God spake as they were moved by the Holy Ghost............................ 2 Peter i. 21.
2. Macedonia............ 2 Cor. viii. 1, 5; Phil. iv. 15, 18.
3. Repent................................. Matt. iv. 17.
4. See.................................... Acts xi. 12.
5. See........................... Isa. xliii. 9 ; Zec. ii. 3.
6. The faith of the saints...................... Jude 3.
7. The best gifts........................ 1 Cor. xii. 31.
8. "If any man do His will"................ John vii. 17.
9. Sin against the Holy Ghost............. Matt. xii. 31
10. At Antioch........................... Acts xi. 26.
11. See. .... Matt. vi. 22 ; Rom. viii. 17.
12. See .... Matt. x. 29.
13. See .... Matt. vi. 6 ; Luke xi. 11.
14. See..................... Heb. xii. 5 ; Prov. iii. 11
15. Searching the Scriptures................ Acts xvii. 11.
16. See.................................. Heb. iv. 12.
17. See.............................. 2 Cor. iii. 18

18. See.................. ....John iv. 14 ; Isaiah xii. 3
19. See..........1 Peter ii. 2 ; 1 Cor. iii. 2; Heb. v. 12, 13
20. Heaven................................Rev. xix. 9.
21. Feeding the multitude............Mark vi. 35; viii. 5.
22. The angel announcing the birth of Christ...Luke ii. 9.
St. Paul's conversion.......... ....Acts ix. 3.
Peter's deliverance from prison...............Acts xii. 7.
23. See .. ..John iii. 6 ; Titus iii. 5.
24. Adam..Gen. ii. 21 ; Abraham..Gen. xv. 12 ; Saul and
   his army......................1 Sam. xxvi. 12.
25. Birth of Christ........................Luke ii. 8.
26. That which is good....................1 Thes. v. 21.
  The form of sound words...............2 Tim. i. 13.
  Our confidence..........................Heb. iii. 14.
  Our profession..........................Heb. iv. 14.
  That which ye have already..............Rev. ii. 25.
27. The golden pot, Aaron's rod, and tables of the covenant
            Heb. ix. 4.
28. A meek and quiet spirit............ .1 Peter iii. 4.
29. Love................................Rom. xiii. 10.
30. See.......................1 Cor. ix. 14; Gal. vi. 6.
31. See...James i. 23.
32. Felix.......................................Acts xxiv. 25.
33. Aretas...................................2 Cor. xi. 32
34. A red and lowering sky in the morning....Matt. xvi. 2.

35. St. John the Baptist................. ...Matt. xvi. 21
36. Fifty thousand pieces of silver...........Acts xix. 19.
37. See ....Matt. v. 34.
38. The turning water into wine............John ii. 7, 10.
  The feeding of the multitudes on two occasions.
       Matt. xiv. 15, 21 ; xv. 34, 38.
39. See.......................................James iii. 7
40. See.....................................2 Peter iii. 8.
41. The deaf man by the word, Ephphatha....Mark vii. 34
42. See..John v. 19
43. And being in agony....... ....Luke xxii. 44

44. He never compelled His followers to obey His invitation to become His disciples .... John vi. 67.
45. The Lord is our Judge, the Lord is our Lawgiver, the Lord is our King: He will save us.... Isa. xxxiii. 22.
46 He was seen of five hundred brethren at once
1 Cor. xv. 6
47 To Daniel in his visions................. Dan. viii. 15
To Zacharias............................ Luke i. 19.
And to Mary, mother of Jesus........ .... Luke i. 28.
48. Earnestness, determination, and patience.. Luke viii. 15.
49. Whosoever committeth sin is the servant(slave) of sin.
John viii. 34.
50. Retaliation by forgiveness.............. Rom. xii. 20.
51. He cannot sin nor repent, or deny himself.. 2 Tim. ii. 13.
52. See...... .... Acts xxvi. 18.
53. Isaiah................................. Isa. xi. 15, 16.
54. See................................... Rom. ix. 16.
55. Wisdom............ Job xxviii. 18 ; Matt. xiii. 45, 46.
56. That I may " make (or ordain) thee a minister."
Acts xxvi. 16, 18.
57. " Maketh not ashamed "................... Rom. v. 5.
58. And forgive us our sins................... Luke xi. 4.
And forgive us our debts................ Matt. vi. 12.
59. Barnabas................. Acts iv. 34 ; Num. xviii. 20.
60. Death.................................. John v. 24.
61 Light................................... Eph. v. 8.
62. The holy commandment................. 2 Peter xi. 21.
63 See.............. .... 1 Cor. xvi. 2
64 On the day of Penticost............... ..... Acts ii. 2
65. Saints, believers, disciples, and brethren....
66. The hypocrite's hope.................. .... Job viii. 13.
67. See........... Isa. xxxiii. 16 ; xli. 17 ; Matt. vi. 26, 31.
68. On the day of Penticost........ .... Acts ii. 13
69. FROM EVIDENCES WITHIN ITSELF—" All Scripture is given by inspiration of God." 2 Tim. iii. 16. " For the prophecy came not in old time by the will of man

but holy men of God spoke as they were moved by the Holy Ghost." 2 Peter i. 21.

From Traditionary Evidence—It *claims* to be, and *establishes* the claim beyond all reasonable dispute.

The Jews preserved it as such; the Church has held it as such; and its *own teachings*, and especially its *predictions*, so clearly *fulfilled*, prove it to be the word of God.

From Presumptive Evidence—It being admitted that there is a Creator, then creation implies *government*—and government implies *law*—*man* created a moral agent, it is presumed his Creator would give him a revelation, or some law or rule of action.

From Positive Evidence—*External*—The antiquity of the Scriptures, as proven by the persons, who were the immediate instruments of these revelations, being contemporaneous with the events of which they wrote, also the concurring dates of the books containing the doctrines. The testimony of ancient authors, (Strabo, Justin, Pliny, Tacitus, Josephus, &c.). The uncorrupted preservation of the books of Scripture, as proven by the Septuagint and Josephus the Jewish historian. The credibility of the testimony of the sacred writers; they were in circumstances to know the truth and had no interest in making a good story; their interest lay in another direction.

From miracles, as those of Moses in the passage of the Red Sea, &c., and those of Christ, the greatest of which was His resurrection. From prophecies and their fulfillment, such as the prediction to Adam of the serpent and the seed of the woman; the apostacies, punishments and restoration of the Jewish nation, and upwards of 100 distinct predictions concerning the birth, life, sufferings, death and resurrection of Christ. The unity that pervades the different books of the

NEW TESTAMENT THINGS.

Bible, though written by different men of different ages and in different languages.

Internal—The character and attributes of God. The divine government. The moral and beneficial tendency of the Scriptures. The style and manner of the sacred writers. The influence of the Holy Spirit. The gospel plan of salvation. The faithful promises of God as exemplified in the life and character of believers.

FROM COLLATERAL EVIDENCE—The marvellous diffusion of Christianity, especially during the first three centuries of the Christian era, when it became the established religion of the Roman Empire. The actual effect produced upon mankind.

FROM CORROBORATIVE EVIDENCE—Modern discoveries among the ruins of ancient Nineveh and other cities of Bible antiquity.

KEY TO "CURIOSITIES"

Involving arithmetical calculations in their solution:

No. 1. 12(Genesis xxxv-22) × 7(Joshua vi-4)+6(Ruth iii-15)÷10(Esther ix-10)−2(Genesis vii-9) × 50(II Kings ii-16)−30(Genesis xli-46)÷5(I Samuel xvii-40)−15(John xi-18) × 4(Acts xxvii-29)−8(Genesis viii-18)——188 scholars.

No. 2. 3000(Job i-3)÷30(Jerem. xxxviii-10)+1000 (Dan'l v-1-)−10(Genesis xviii-32) × 30(II Samuel v-4)÷300(Judges vii-8)+1000(Judges xv-15)−1005 (I Kings iv-32) × 7(Job ii-13)−153(John xxi-11)—— 575 sheep.

No. 3. 666(I Kings x-14)÷3(Neh. x-32) × 30(Matt. xxvi-15)−4000(I Chron xxiii-5)+100(I Kings xviii -4) × 70(Jerem. xxv-12)——cost 193,200+300(Genesis vi-15)−88(II Chron xi-21)+276(Acts xxvii-37) −6(II Samuel xxi-20)÷7(I Kings vi-38)+30(I Kings vi-2)——148 ft. high.

KEY TO BIBLE PICTURES

FROM THE BOOK OF RUTH.

1. Moab.
2. Elimelech and his family.
3. Bethlehem.
4. Elimelech—Naomi.
5. Orpah and Ruth.
6. Naomi, Orpah, and Ruth.
7. Naomi and Ruth—Orpah
8. Ruth.
9. Ruth.
10. Fields of Boaz.
11. Boaz and Ruth
12. Obed.
13. David and Christ

KEY TO FAMILIAR QUOTATIONS.

1. Isaiah xxix. 21.
2. Proverbs xxix. 25.
3. 1. Chronicles xxxii. 8.
4. Jeremiah xvii. 5.
5. Proverbs xii. 10.
6. Exodus xv. 11.
7. 1 Sam. ii. 30.
8. Deut. x. 12; xi. 1.
9. Deut. x. 19.
10. Lev. xix. 18, 34.
11. Isaiah xxii. 12, 13.
12. Jeremiah xiii. 23.
13. Proverbs xxix. 1.
14. Zechariah iv. 6, 10.
15. Exodus xxii. 2.
16. Genesis vi. 5; viii. 21.
17. Jer. xiv. 5; 1 Tim. vi. 5—10
18. Prov xvi. 32; Eccles. vii 8, 9.
19. Gen. xviii. 25; Deut. xxxii. 4.
20. Job ii. 10; Jer. x. 24.
21. Isa. xxx. 2, 7, 15, 16.
22. Job ix. 2, 3; Psa. xi. 12 cxliii. 2.
23. Isa. xxx. 21; Prov. iii. 5, 6
24. Job viii. 9; John xiii. 7
25. Job xvii. 9; Psa. i. 3.
26. Lam. iv. 20.
27. Isa. ii. 20.
28. Hosea vi. 6.
29. Job xii. 2.
30. 1 Sam xvi. 7

ANSWERS
TO
BIBLE CURIOSITIES
PERTAINING TO
Time.

---

1. Three months.................................Ex. ii. 2.
2. Seven years.............. ....Judges vi. 1.
3. Seven months............................1 Sam. vi. 1.
4. One hundred and forty years.............Job xlii. 16.
5. One hundred and twenty years.............Gen. vi. 3.
6. Three years and six months in the days of Elias.
   Luke iv. 25.
7. Forty-six years........................John ii. 20.
8. Fifty-two.............................Neh. vi. 15
9. Eighteen years........................Judges iii. 14
10. One hundred and fifty days.............Gen. vii. 24.
11. Because they believed evil reports and cowardly refused
    to enter the promised land ....Num. xiv. 34
12. Thirty-one........................ Joshua xii. 1, 24.
13. Forty................................Num. xiii. 25
14. Three days...........................Ex. xv. 22.
15. Thirteen years.......................1 Kings vii. 1.
16. Eighteen years.....................Judges x. 8.
17. Three months in the house of Obed-edom..2 Sam. vi. 11.
18. Eighty years ....Ex. vii. 7.
19. Ninety-eight...   ....1 Sam. iv. 15

20. Two hundred and fifteen years ....
21. His time in the land of Midian...........Acts vii. 30
22. One hundred and fifty days ....Gen. vii
23. Seven days............................Ex. vii. 25
24. Two whole years ....Acts xxviii. 30
25. Seven years and six months..............2 Sam. ii. 11.
26. Forty......................Ex. xvi. 35; Josh. v. 12.
27. The fourteenth day........................Ex. xii. 6.
28. Seventy years..........................Jer. xxv. 11.
29. Three days...............................Acts ix. 9
30. Four hundred and fifty.................Acts xiii. 20
31. Four hundred and thirty.................Ex. xii. 40.
32. Seventeen years......................Gen. xxxvii. 2.
33. About one hundred years.....Gen. vi. 3 ; 1 Pet. iii. 20.
34. Five years.... ....Lev. xix. 25.
35. Ten days..................................
36. Seven days and nights .... Job ii. 13.

KEY TO SCRIPTURE METAPHORS.

A.

1. ADDER. Because (1st) it is often *deaf,* Ps. lviii. 4. (2nd) It is *poisonous,* Ps. cxi. 3. (3rd) It *stings,* Prov. xxiii. 32 Note.—It stings our conscience, Rom. ii. 15; and it stings to death, Jas. i. 15; 1 Cor. xv. 56. (4th) It is to be *trodden under foot,* Ps. xci. 13. Hence Gen. iii. 15; Rom. xvi. 20.
2. ADVOCATE. 1 John ii. 1; because he is a mediator between the judge and the prisoner, 1 Tim. i. 5.
3. ANCHOR. This is made an emblem of hope, because (1st) *It fastens itself on something out of sight,* Heb. vi. 19; and (2nd) *It stays the ship in the storm,* Ps. xlii. 5; Rom. viii. 24.
4. ANTS. Used metaphorically of *industry,* in Prov. vi. 6; of *forethought,* in Prov. xxx. 25; and of *individual responsibility,* in Prov. vi. 7, 8.
5. ASHES. Metaphorical of *frailty* in Gen. xviii. 27; because worthless, and the remains of something better: of *humiliation* in Esther iv. 1; Isa. lxi. 3: of *sin* in Isa. xliv. 20, because unsatisfying, and miserable to the taste.
6. AWAKING. Used of *repentance* in Rom. xiii. 11; Eph. v 14; and of *resurrection* in Job. xiv. 12; John xi. 11 Dan. xii. 2.

B.

7. BABES. 1 Pet. ii. 2. (1st) They are *free from pride and malice,* Mark x. 14, 15. (2nd) They *partake of the nature of their father,* John iii. 6. (3rd) *They grow as they advance in years,* 2 Pet. iii. 18.
8. BLINDNESS. 2 Cor. iv. 4; Eph. iv. 18.
9. BULLS, in Ps. xxii. 12, 13; Isa. xxxiv. 7. BEARS. in

Prov. xxviii. 15; BOARS, in Ps. lxxx. 13; BEES, in Ps. cxviii. 12; BIRDS, in Rev. xviii. 2.

10. BEAM, in contrast with *Mote*, Matt. vii. 3, 4.
11. BRIDEGROOM. Matt. xxv. 5, 6. BISHOP. 1 Pet. ii. 25. BREAD. John vi. 48.
12 BROOKS. Used metaphorically of *wisdom* in Prov. xviii. 4; of *prosperity* in Job xx. 17; of *consolation* in Ps. xlii. 1, cx. 7.
13. BALANCES Dan. v. 27.

C.

14. CROWN. Used for *immortal life* in Jas. i. 12; Rev. ii. 10. for *eternal glory* in 1 Pet. v. 4: and for *heavenly purity* in 2 Tim. iv. 8.
15. CANDLE. Signifies the *soul of man* in Prov. xx. 27: the *favor of God* in Job xxix. 3: and *spiritual gifts* in Matt. v. 15.
16. COVER. (*verb*). Used for *protecting* in Ps. xci. 4; and for *pardoning* in Ps. xxxii. 1.
17 CORD. Is associated with *death* in Eccles. xii. 6; *ruin* in Jer. x. 20; *strength* in Eccles. iv. 12; *enlargement* in Isa. liv. 2; *love* in Hos. xi. 4; *affliction* in Job. xxx. 11, and xxxvi. 8; *sin* in Prov. v. 32, and Isa. v. 18.
18. CEDAR. It denotes a *king*, 2 Kings xiv. 9; an *empire*, Ezek. xxxi. 3; the *faithful people of God*, Ps. xcii. 12.
19 CHAFF. Used of *false doctrine*, Jer. xxiii. 28; and of the *destruction of the wicked* in Ps. i. 4; Isa. v. 24.

D.

20. DOGS Ps. xx ii. 16; Matt. xv. 26. This metaphor possesses its forces from the contempt in which dogs are held in Eastern towns:—(1) Dogs *snarl and gnash with their teeth*. So the wicked, Ps. xxxvii. 12. (2) Dogs have to be *shut out of doors*. So the wicked from heaven, Rev. xxii. 15. (3) Dogs are *greedy* and *dissatisfied*. So are the wicked, Isa. lvi. 11. (4) Dogs are *foolish*, Prov. xxvi. 11 (5) Dogs are *to be avoided*, Phil. iii. 2.

21. Dew. Ps. cx. 3; Hos. vi 4. Distil Deut. xxxii. 2 Draw. Isa. xii. 3. Drown. 1. Tim. vi. 9. Drop. Ps. lxv. 11; Ezek. xx. 46; Prov. xix. 13. Drink. Job xv 16. Drought. Isa. lviii. 11. Ditch. Job. ix. 31. Deep Ps. xlii. 7: or Depths. Mic. vii. 19.
22. Darkness. Used for *sorrow* in Joel ii. 2; for *death* in Job x. 21, 22; for *secrecy* in Matt. x. 27; for *sin* in John i. 5; for *hell* in Matt. viii. 12; 2 Pet. ii. 4.
23. The word Door is used (1) of *Christ*, in John x. 9, because he is the only way into heaven for sinners; (2nd) of *faith*, in Acts xiv. 27, because faith opened salvation to the Gentiles; 3rd) of *opportunity for preaching*, in 1 Cor. xvi. 9, Col. iv. 3, because, by the utterance of the mouth, preaching enters into the heart; (4th) of the *heart* in Rev. iii. 20, as giving entrance to truth; (5th) of the *lips*, as sending forth the voice, Ps. cxli. 3; (6th) of *heaven*, Matt. xxv. 10; (7th) of *sloth*, Prov. xxvi. 14.
24. Den. Applied to Jerusalem in Jer. ix. 11; and to the Temple in Matt. xxi. 13.

E.

25. End. Prov. xxiii. 18, and 1 Pet. i. 9.
26. Eye-salve. Rev. iii. 18.

F.

27. Foundation. Isa. xxviii. 16; 1 Cor. iii. 11. Fountain. Zech. xiii. 1. Forerunner. Heb. vi. 20. Firstfruits. 1 Cor. xv. 20.
28. Flower. Job. xiv. 2.
29. Fowler. Prov. vi. 5.
30. Fan. Jer. xv. 7, and Matt. iii. 12.
31. Fox. Used of *false prophets*, Ezek. xiii. 4; of a *wicked ruler*, Luke xiii. 32.

G.

32. Grey Hairs. Hosea vii. 9 Gold tarnished. Lam. iv 1. Grass withered. 2 Kings xix. 26.

33. GRASSHOPPERS. Judges vi. 5.
34. GOATS. Matt. xxv. 32. GRASS. Ps. xcii. 7; xxxvii. 2.
35. GIRDLE. Eph. vi. 14. It is meant to show that we are held up when weak by the power of truth. (Isa. xxii. 21.)
36. HOUSE. *The grave*, Job xxx. 23. *The body*, Job iv. 19, 2 Cor. v. 1. *The church*, 1 Tim. iii. 15. *Heaven*, John xiv. 2.
37. HAMMER. Jer. xxiii. 29. HONEY. Ps. cxix. 103.
38. HEN GATHERING HER CHICKENS UNDER HER WINGS. Matt. xxiii. 37.
39. ISLES. Isa. xlix. 1.
40. INCENSE. Used of *prayer*, Ps. cxli. 2; and of the *merits of Christ*, Rev. viii. 3.
41. JEWELS. Mal. iii. 17.
42. KISS. Used in connection with *love*, Cant. i. 2; *reverence* Exod. xviii. 7, and 1 Sam. x. 1; *submission*, Ps. ii. 12; and *deceit*, Matt. xxvi. 49.
43. KINGS. Rev. i. 5, 6, compared with Rev. xxii. 5.

L.

44. LEAVES. Used of *prosperity*, Ps. i. 3; *eternal life*, Rev. xxii. 2; *mortality*, Isa. lxiv. 6; *timidity*, Lev. xxvi. 36.
45. LILY. Used of *Christ*, Cant. ii. 1; of *believers*, Hos. v. 14. LAMB. Used of *Christ*, John i. 29; of *believers*, Isa. xl. 11.
43. LION. Used for *Christ*, Rev. v. 5; for *believers*, Prov. xxviii. 1; for *Satan*, 1 Peter v. 8; for *wicked men*, 2 Tim. iv. 17, Ezek. xxii. 25.
47. LEAVEN. Used of *sin*, Matt. xvi. 6, 1 Cor. v. 6, 7; of *grace*, Matt. xiii. 33.
48. LIGHT. Of *God's word*, Ps. cxix. 105; of *happiness*, Isa. lviii. 8; of a *good king*, 2 Sam. xxi.
49. LEPROSY. Like *sin;* (1) *defiling*, Lev. xiii. 44, 45; (2) *spreading*, Lev. xiii. 22, 1 Cor. v. 6; (3) *separating*, Numb. v. 2, Rev. xxi. 27; (4) *sometimes incurable*, 2 Kings v. 7, with Jer. xiii. 23.
50. LEANNESS. Put for *temporal calamity*, Isa. x. 16; for *spiritual weakness*, Isa. xxiv. 16, Ps. civ. 15.

M.

51. MILK. Isa. lv. 1; MARROW, Ps. lxiii. 5; MEAT, John iv. 32-34; MANNA, REV. ii. 17.
52. MORNING. Put for *swiftness* in Ps. cxxxix. 9; for *divine truth*, in Isa. viii. 20 (margin); and for the *resurrection*, in Ps. xlix. 14.
53. MEMBERS, in Eph. v. 30; MAN, in Eph. iv. 13; MERCHANTMAN, Matt. xiii. 45.
54. MIRE. Used for *sin*, 2 Peter ii. 22; and for *contempt*, 2 Sam. xxii. 43.
55. NIGHT. Put for *death*, in John ix. 4; for *time of ignorance*, in Rom. xiii. 12; and for *affliction*, in Isa. xxi. 12.
56. NOON. Amos viii. 9.
57. NEST. Hab. ii. 9
58. NURSE. Used of *Christian kings*, in Isa. xlix. 23; and of *Christian ministers*, in 1 Thess. ii. 7.
59. OINTMENT. Descriptive of *Christ's name*, in Cant. i. 3; and of *brotherly unity*, in Ps. cxxxiii. 2.
60. ORPHANS. Lam. v. 3; John xiv. 18 (marg.); and OUTCASTS, in Jer. xxx. 17.
61. OAK. In Isa. vi. 13; Amos ii. 9.

P.

62. PILLARS. Gal. ii. 9, and Jer. i. 18.
63. PALACE. Applied to the *temple of Jerusalem*, 1 Chron. xxix. 1; and to the *church of God*, in Ps. lxxviii. 69; xlviii. 13.
64. PRISON. Of *sin*, Isa. xli. 7; and of *the grave*, liii. 8.
65. PRINCE. Isa. ix. 6.
66. PIT. *Snare*, Ps. vii. 15; *sorrow*, Ps. xl. 2; *grave*, Isa. xxxviii. 17.
67. POISON. Rom. iii. 13; James iii. 8.

Q, R.

68. QUENCH. *Love*, Cant. viii. 7; *life*, Isa. xliii. 17; 2 Sam

xiv. 7; xxi. 17; *temptation*, Eph. vi. 16; *Holy Spirit*, 1 Thes. v 19; *Divine wrath*, Isa. i. 31; 2 Kings xxii. 17.
69. RAZOR. See Ps. lii. 2; Isa. vii. 20.
70. REED. Used for *instability*, Luke, vii. 24; *despondency*, Isa. xlii. 3; and *disappointing hope*, Isa. xxxvi. 6; 2 Kings xviii. 21.
71. REAPING. See John iv. 36-38; Matt. iii. 39.
72. RACE. 1 Cor. ix. 24; Heb. xii. 1

S.

73. SALT. Matt. v. 13. STEWARDS, 1 Pet. iv. 10. SHOWERS, Mic. v. 7. SHEEP, John x. 27. SOLDIERS. 2 Tim. ii. 3. STONES, 1 Pet. ii. 5. STRANGERS, 1 Pet. ii. 11.
74. SHADOW. Used in connection with *death*, Ps. xxiii. 4, *divine care*, Ps. xci. 1: and *the law of Moses*, Heb. x. 1.

T, V.

75. TRAPS. Josh. xxiii. 13. THORNS. 2 Sam. xxiii. 6 THIEVES. John x. 8.
76. TOWER. Ps. lxi. 3.
77. TENT. Used of the *heavens*, Isa. xl. 22; and of the *church*, Isa. liv. 2. TEMPLE. Used of the *heavens*, Ps. xi. 4; and of the *church*, Eph. ii. 21.
78. VIRGINS. Matt. xxv. 1, etc. VESSELS. 2 Tim. ii. 20.
79. VIPERS. Matt. iii. 7.
80. VAPOR. James iv. 13, 14.

W, Y.

81. WATER. John vii. 38, 39. WIND. John iii. 8.
82. WOLVES. Matt. vii. 15. WAVES. Jude 13. WELLS WITHOUT WATER. 2 Pet. ii. 17.
83. YOKE. Describes the *service of Christ*, Matt. xi. 29; *cruel oppression*, 1 Kings xii. 4; *spiritual bondage*, Acts xv. 10.

KEY TO SCRIPTURE ENIGMAS.

KEY TO ENIGMA NO. 1.—DAVID.

KEY TO ENIGMA NO. 2.—"EVE."—Gen. iii. 20.

KEY TO ENIGMA NO. 3.—"GOG."—Rev. xx. 8, 9.

KEY TO ENIGMA NO. 4.—THE RIVER THAT WENT OUT OF EDEN.—Gen. ii. 10.

KEY TO ENIGMA NO. 5.—OG'S IRON BEDSTEAD.—Deut. iii. 11

KEY TO ENIGMA NO. 6.—AARON'S ROD.

KEY TO ENIGMA NO. 7.—THE STONE WHICH SLEW GOLIATH.

KEY TO ENIGMA NO. 8.—SUNDAY.—Ex. xx. 10.

KEY TO ENIGMA NO. 9.—"LORD, SAVE US: WE PERISH" Matt. viii. 25.

1. L-ot . . . . Gen. xiii. 11.
2. O-thniel . . . . Judges iii. 9.
3. R-achel . . . . Gen. xxix. 17.
4. D-eborah . . . . Judges v. 7.

5. S-hishak . . . . 1 Kings xiv. 25.
6. A-hab . . . . 1 Kings xviii. 18.
7. V-ashti . . . . Esther i. 9.
8. E-sther . . . . Esther viii. 3.

9. U-r................Genesis xv. 7.
10. S-myrna............Rev. i. 11.

11. W......... ....
12. E-den..............Gen. ii. 8.

'8. P-hilistines..........1 Sam. xix. 8.
14. E-gyptians...... ..Isaiah xx. 4.
15. R-hegium............Acts xxviii. 11.
16. I-conium   ....Acts xiii. 51.
17. S-eir................Deut. ii. 4.
18. H-oreb ....Deut. i. 6.

KEY TO ENIGMA NO. 10.—ELIMELECH—BETHLEHEM.—
Ruth i. 11.

1. E-lia-b..............Num. xxvi. 8, 9.
2. L-uk-e..............Col. iv. 14.
3. I-scario-t............Matt. x. 4.
4. M-eriba-h...........Num. xx. 13.
5. E-ba-l..............Deut. xi. 29.
6. L-ak-e..............Luke viii. 33.
7. E-la-h.....'.........1 Sam. xvii. 2.
8. C-oloss-e........ ...Col. i. 2.
9. H-ela-m............2 Sam. x. 16

KEY TO ENIGMA NO. 11.—GENESIS—NUMBERS.

1. G-ideo-n... ....Judges vii. 21.
2. E-sa-u..............Gen. xxv. 17
3. N-ahu-m............Nahum i. 1.
5. E-lia-b. ....1 Sam. xvi. 7.
5. S-alom-e............Mark xv. 40.
6. I-zha-r.............1 Chron. vi. 2.
7. S-osthene-s...... ...Acts xviii. 17.

SCRIPTURE ENIGMAS 81

KEY TO ENIGMA NO. 12.—"THE DAYSPRING."—Luke i 78

1. T-urtle-doves.......Luke ii. 24.
2. H-erod............Matthew ii. 7.
3. E-gypt............Matthew ii. 13.
4. D-ream...........Genesis xxviii. 12.
5. A-ser ....Luke ii. 36.
6. Y-oke............Matthew xi. 29.
7. S-tar.............Matthew ii. 9.
8. P-assover.........Exodus xii. 11.
9. R-achel..........Jeremiah xxxi. 15.
10. I-mmanuel........Isaiah vii. 14.
11. N-azareth........Luke ii. 51.
12. G-ethsemane......Matthew xxvi. 36.

KEY TO ENIGMA NO. 13.—"I AM ALPHA AND OMEGA"

(Rev. i. 11, 13; xxii. 12, 13, 16, 20), "the First and the Last" (Isaiah xliv. 6; xlviii. 12; xli. 4.

1. Ishbosheath........2 Sam. iv. 1—12.
2. AM-monites....... { 1 Sam. xi.; xii. 12 ; Judges xi. 4 —6; 2 Sam. x. 6—19.
3. ALPH-æus........ { Matt x. 2, 3 ; Mark iii. 16—19 Luke vi. 13—16.
4. A-mram..........1 Chron. vi. 3 ; Exod. vi. 18, 20.
5. AND-rew.........John i. 40—42.
6. OM-ri............1 Kings xvi. 15—18.
7. E-mmaus.........Luke xiv. 13—31.
8. GA-maliel........Acts xxii. 3 ; v. 34—39.

KEY TO ENIGMA NO 14.—"INCREASE OUR FAITH."—
Luke xvii. v.

1. I-sh-borheth.......2 Samuel iv.
2. N-ethaneel ....2 Chronicles xvii. 7, 9.
3. C-apernaum.......Matthew xi. 23.
4. R-immon.........2 Kings v. 18.
5. E-lymas..........Acts xiii. 8, 12.

CURIOSITIES OF THE BIBLE

   6. A-rk ....Gen. vii. 11—13 ; viii. 13—116.
   7. S-amuel ....1 Samuel iii. ; xii. 2, 23.
   8. E-unice.............2 Timothy i. 5; iii. 15

   9. O-g ....Numbers xxi. 33
10. U-pharsin....... ..Daniel v. 25.
11. R-ehoboam.........1 Kings xii. 13.

12. F-ire..............Jeremiah xxiii. 29.
13. A-ngels............Hebrews i. 14.
14. I-shmael...........Jeremiah xli. 2.
15. T-itus..............2 Corinthians vii. 5, 7.
16. H-orn..............Luke i. 69.

KEY TO ENIGMA NO. 15.—JONATHAN.—2 SAM. XV. 36
ABIATHAR.—2 SAM. XV. 35

   1. J-oshu-*a*............Exodus xvii. 9.
   2 O-re-*b*.............Judges vii. 25.
   3. N-imsh-*i*...........1 Kings xix. 16.
   4. A-mas-*a*..... .....2 Sam. xvii. 25.
   5. T-rumpe-*t*..........Josh. vi. 4, 5.
   6. H-ulda-*h*...........2 Kings xxii. 14—16.
   7. A-rmeni-*a*..........2 Kings xix. 37.
   8. N-ebuchadnezza-*r*....Dan. iv. 25—35.

KEY TO ENIGMA NO. 16.—" COME UNTO ME."—Matthew xi. 28

   1. C-aleb ....Numbers xiv. 24.
   2. O-badiah............1 Kings xviii. 3.
   3. M-ary Magdalene....Mark xvi. 9.
   4. E-lizabeth..........Luke i. 6.

   5. U-r................Neh. ix. 7.
   6. N-ain..............Luke vii. 11.
   7. T-admor............2 Chron. viii. 4.
   8. O-phir.............1 Kings ix. 28.

   9. M-icah.............Micah. i. 1.
10. E-lijah.   .... 1 Kings xvii. 1

SCRIPTURE ENIGMAS.

Art thou weary, art thou languid,
Art thou sore distressed ?
Come to me, saith One ; and, coming,
Be at rest.

KEY TO ENIGMA NO. 17.—DUTY—" IN EVERYTHING GIVE THANKS."—1 Thess. v. 18.—PROMISE—" ALL THINGS WORK TOGETHER FOR GOOD TO THEM THAT LOVE GOD. —Rom. viii. 28.

1. I-scariot............Matt. xxvi. 24.
2. N-athan............2 Sam. xii. 7—10.
3. EVE ....Gen. iii. 4—6.
4. R-abbi............Matt. xxiii. 6—8.
5. Y-ea...............2 Cor. i. 20.
6. TH-yatira..........Acts xvi. 14.
7. I-srael........... .Gen. xxxii. 28.
8. N-ob............ .1 Sam. xxii. 18. 19.
9. G-ad..............2 Sam. xxiv. 11.
10. GI-beon..........Josh. ix. 3—11.
11. V-au.............Psa. cxix. 41.
12. E-THAN..........1 Kings iv. 30, 31
13. K-ish ....1 Sam. ix. 3.
14. S-aul ....1 Sam. x. 1.

KEY TO ENIGMA NO. 18—" PRINCE OF PEACE." Isa. ix. 6

1. P-riest............Heb. v. 6.
2. R-oot........... ..Rev. v. 5.
3. I-mage of God.......2 Cor. iv. 4.
4. N-azarene ....Matt. ii. 23.
5. C-ounsellor.........Isa. ix. 6.
6. E-verlasting Father..Isa. ix. 6.
7. O-ffspring of David ..Rev. xvii. 16.
8. F-ountain......... Zech. xiii. 1.

9. Prophet..............Deut. xviii. 18.
10. E-mmanuel..........Matt. i. 23.
11. A-lpha..............Rev. i. 8.
12. C-hief Corner Stone..1 Peter ii. 6.
13. E-ternal Life.........1 John v. 20.

KEY TO ENIGMA NO 19.—"THE LORD BLESS THEE, AN KEEP THEE." Numbers vi. 24.

1. T-imothy............1 Tim. i. 2.
2. H-iram ....1 Kings v. 10, 11.
3. E-lijah.............Luke ix. 30, 33.

4. L-eah...............Gen. xxix. 16.
5. O-bed ....Ruth iv. 17.
6. R-euben ....Gen. xxxv. 23.
7. D-avid..............1 Sam. xvii. 14.

8. B-arnabas...........Acts xiii. 1.
9. L-ysias..............Acts xxiii. 26.
10. E-lhanan............2 Sam. xxi. 19.
11. S-hebne.............Isa. xxxvii. 2.
12. S-harezer...........2 Kings xix. 37.

13. T-ola ....Judges x. 1.
14. H-ezekiah...........2 Chron. xxxii. 33
15. E-srom..............Luke iii. 33.
16. E-liphaz............Job. ii. 11.

17. A-rba...............Joshua xxi. 11.
18. N-athan.............2 Sam. xii. 1.
19. D-eborah............Judges iv. 4.

20. K-ish...............1 Sam. x. 21
21. E-liezer............Gen. xv. ii.
22. E-unice ....2 Tim. i. 5.
23. P-hilip.............John i. 43

SCRIPTURE ENIGMAS.

24. T-ertullus............Acts xxiv. 1, 2.
25. H-erod. ....Luke iii. 19.
26. E-lymas............Acts xiii. 6-8.
27. E-zekiel............Ezek. i. 3.

KEY TO ENIGMA NO. 20.—"THE LORD REIGNETH."—Psalm xciii. 1 : xcvii. 1 ; xcix. 1.

1. THE-ssalonica........Acts xvii. 1. 6.
2. L-ystra ....Acts xiv. 8, 11, 19.
3. OR-nan.............2 Chron. iii. 1 ; 1 Chron. xxi. 18— 26 ; xxii. 1.
4. D-ionysius...........Acts xvii. 16, 34.
5. RE-hoboam ....1 Kings xii. 1—11.
6. I-shbi-benob.........2 Sam. xxi. 16.
7. G-ilgal.............Joshua iv. 19-23.
8. N-ebo..............Deut. xxxii. 49, 50 ; xxxiv. 5, 6.
9. ETH-baal........... 1 Kings xvi. 31 ; xviii. 13.

KEY TO ENIGMA NO. 21.—ZERUIAH—ABIGAIL—SISTERS OF DAVID.—1 Chron. ii. 16, 17.

1. Z-ib-a..............2 Samuel xvii. 4 ; xix. 24—29
2. E-liashi-b............Nehemiah iii. 1 ; xiii. 4—9.
3. R-abb-i.............Matthew xxiii. 8.
4. U-nbelievin-g........Revelation xxi. 8.
5. I-turæ-a............Luke iii. 1.
6. A-bisha-i............1 Samuel xxvi. 6.
7. H-anamee-l.........Jeremiah xxxii. 6—15.

Zeruiah was mother of Joab, Abishai, and Asahel, who are spoken of as sons of Zeruiah.

KEY TO ENIGMA NO. 22.—JERICHO.—Josh. vi. 25—SAMARIA.—
1 Kings xvi. 24, 28.

1. J-uda-s..............John xii. 6;   Matt. xxvi. 15.
2. E-zr-a ....Ezra vii. 10.
3. R-amathaim Zophi-m 1 Sam. i. 1.
4. I-ndi-a ....Esther i. 1.
5. C-hedorlaom-r .... Gen. xiv. 9, 12.
6. H-agga-i............Ezra v. 1, etc.
7. O-she-a....:........Num. xiii.

KEY TO ENIGMA NO. 23.—" COUNSELLOR."—Isaiah ix. 6.

1. C-edar.... ....1 Kings vi. 15.
2. O-ak ....Genesis xxxv. 4.
3. U-rijah...... ....Jeremiah xxxvi. 23.
4. N-o................Jer. xlvi. 25; Ezek. xxx. 14—16
   Nahum iii. 8.
5. S-ycamore ....Luke xix. 4.
6. E-schol ....Num. xiii. 23.
7. L-uke...............Col. iv. 14.
8. L-ydia..............Acts xvi. 14.
9. O-bed..............Matt. i. 5.
10. R-ebekah...........Genesis xxvii.

KEY TO ENIGMA NO. 24.—"MY PEACE I GIVE UNTO YOU".—
John xiv. 27.

1. M-icah..............Micah v. 2.
2. Y-ea................2 Corinthians i. 20.
3. P-aul...............1 Corinthians ix. 1.
4. E-mmaus...........Luke xxiv. 13—31.
5. A-saph.............2 Chronicles xxix. 30.
6. C-ornelius..........Acts x.
7. E-agle ....Deuteronomy xxxii. 11, 12.
8. I-ttai ....2 Samuel xv. 19—22.

SCRIPTURE ENIGMAS.

9. G-alilee..............Isaiah ix. 1, 2 ; Matt. iv. 12-16.
10. I-saiah..............Isaiah vi. 6-8.
11. V-ine...............John xv. 5.
12. E-benezer..........1 Samuel vii. 12.

13. U-r, of the Chaldees..Genesis xi. 31 ; xii. 1.
14. N-ehemiah ....Nehemiah iv. ; xii. 27.
15. T-erah..............Genesis xi. 27.
16. O-ded ....2 Chronicles xxviii. 9-15.

17. Y-ear of jubilee......Leviticus xxv. 8-17; Isa lxi. 1 2
18. O-badiah...........2 Chronicles xvii. 7-9.
19. U-pharsin..........Daniel v. 5, 25-28.

KEY TO ENIGMA NO. 25.—"LOVE YOUR ENEMIES."—Matt. v. 44

1. L-eah...............Genesis xxix. 16.
2. O-g.................Numbers xxi. 33.
3. V-ashti ....Esther i. 12.
4. E-sther ....Esther ii. 7.

5. Y-oke..............Matthew xi. 29.
6. O-nesimus ....Colossians iv. 9.
7. U-rbane...........Romans xvi. 9.
8. R-uth..............Ruth i. 16.

9. E-liashib...........Nehemiah iii. 1.
10. N-aaman...........2 Kings v. 1.
11. E-liab.............1 Samuel xvii. 28.
12. M-ercurias.........Acts xiv. 12.
13. I-shmael ....Genesis xi. 18-20.
14. E-phraim..........Genesis xlviii. 19.
15. S-hallum..........Nehemiah iii. 12

KEY TO ENIGMA NO. 26.—"Behold, I STAND AT THE DOOR, AND KNOCK: if any man hear My voice, and open the door, I will come in to him, and will sup with him, and he with Me." -Rev. iii. 20.

1. IS-sachar............Gen. xxx. 17, 18.
2. TA-rshish..........Jonah i. 3, 4.
3. N-athaniel..........John i. 47.
4. DAT-han............Numb. xvi. 1, 31–33.
5. THE-udas..........Acts v. 34, 36.
6. DO-than............2 Kings vi. 13.
7. OR-pah............Ruth i. 8, 14–16.
8. AN-nas............John xviii. 13.
9. D-emas............2 Tim. iv. 10.
10. KNOCK.

KEY TO ENIGMA NO. 27.—"ASK, AND YE SHALL RECEIVE."— John xvi. 24.

1. A-thaliah...........2 Kings xi.
2. S-hebna............Isaiah xxii 15–19.
3. K-irjath-arba.......Joshua xx. 7.
4. A-bed-nego.........Daniel iii.
5. N-ehushtan.........Num. xxi. 8, 9; 1 Kings xviii. 4.
6. D-iana.............Acts xix. 35.
7. Y-oke..............Matthew xi. 29, 30.
8. E-lhanan...........1 Chron. xx. 5.
9. S-un...............Malachi iv. 2.
10. H-ur..............Exodus xvii. 10–12.
11. A-dah's...........Genesis iv. 20, 21.
12. L-uz..............Genesis xxviii. 10–22.
13. L-evi.............Luke v. 29.

SCRIPTURE ENIGMAS.

14. Rome...............Luke ii. 1.
15. E-bed-melech........Jeremiah xxxviii. 7—13.
16. C-anaan.............Jer. xii. 5, 7 ; Heb. xi. 13-16.
17. E-d.................Joshua xxii. 34.
18. I-ddo...............Zech. i. 1.
19. V-eil of the Temple..Matt. xxvii. 51 ; Heb. x. 19, 20
20. E-leazar............Joshua iii. 13 ; Deut. x. 6.

KEY TO ENIGMA NO. 28.—"THOU GOD SEEST ME."—
Gen. xvi. 13.

1. T-homa-s............John xx. 27.
2. H-at-e..............1 John iii. 15.
3. O-liv-e.............James iii. 11.
4. U-ria-s.............Matt. i. 6. —
5. G-oa-t..............Psalm civ. 18.
6. O-rna-m(ents).......1 Sam. i. 24.
7. D-ov-e..............Gen. viii. 11.

KEY TO ENIGMA NO. 29.—BABEL.

B-abel...............Gen. xi. 4.
A-bel................Gen. iv. 4.
B-el or Baal.........Judges ii. 13, etc.
El...................Gen. xxiii. 20.

KEY TO ENIGMA NO. 30.—"SIN IS THE TRANSGRESSION OF THE
LAW."—1 John iii. 4.

1. S-alem..............Heb. vii. 2.
2. I-chabod............1 Sam. iv. 21.
3. N-azareth ....John i. 46.
4. Isbosheth...........2 Sam. ii. 10.
5. S-almon.............Ruth iv. 21.
6. T-ertullus..........Acts xxiv. 1.
7. H-azael.............1 Kings xix. 15.
8. E-liab..............1 Sam. xvii. 28.

9. T-ahpenes .... 1 Kings xi. 19.
10. R-amah .... 1 Sam. vii. 17.
11. A-thenians .... Acts xvii. 22, 23.
12. N-aaman .... Luke iv. 27; 2 Kings iii.; ix. 24
13. S-amson .... Judges xvi. 30.
14. G-ilead .... 1 Kings xvii. 1.
15. R-uth .... Matt. i. 3-5.
16. E-bed-melech .... Jer. xxxviii. 7-9.
17. S-eir .... Deut. ii. 5.
18. S-ardis .... Rev. iii. 1.
19. I-ssachar .... Gen. xxx. 17, 18.
20. O-thniel .... Judges iii. 9, 10.
21. N-ehemiah .... Neh. ii. 6; v. 14.

22. O-nesimus .... Phil. 10-15.
23. F-orty .... Acts vii. 23.

24. T-amar .... 2 Sam. xiv. 27.
25. H-agar .... Gen. xvi. 1; xxi. 18
26. E-liam .... 2 Sam. xi. 3

27. L-ahai-roi .... Gen. xxv. 11.
28. A-sher .... Deut. xxxiii. 24, 25.
29. W-atch .... Mark xiii. 37.

KEY TO ENIGMA NO. 31.—"SEEK (ye) FIRST THE KINGDOM OF GOD."—Matt. vi. 33.

1. SE-nnacherib .... 2 Kings xix. 35.
2. EK-ron .... 1 Sam. v. 10; vi. 7, 8.

3. F-estus .... Acts xxv., xxvi.
4. IR-ijah .... Jer. xxxvii. 13.
5. ST-ephen .... Acts vii. 55-60.

6. THE-bez .... Judges ix. 50-54.

SCRIPTURE ENIGMAS.

7. KI-shon............Judges v. 21.
8. N-ineveh...........Jonah iii.
9. G-ezer.............1 Kings ix. 16.
10. D-aniel...........Dan. ii., vii., viii., xi., xii.
11. O-nesimus.........Philemon 10-16.
12. MO-am.............1 Kings xi. 7.
13. F-elix............Acts xxiv. 25-27.
14. GO-liath..........1 Sam. xvii. 49.
15. D-iana............Acts. xix. 27.

KEY TO ENIGMA NO. 32.—"CEASE YE FROM MAN."—Isaiah ii. 22

1. C-orn of wheat.......John xii. 24.
2. E-agle..............Deuteronomy xxxii. 11, 12.
3. A-dder..............Psalm lviii. 4.
4. S-erpent............Genesis iii. 1-6.
5. Ensign..............Isaiah xi. 10.
6. Y-oke...............Matthew xi. 29, 30.
7. E-merald............Rev. xxi 19.
8. F-ig-tree...........Luke xiii. 6-9; Matt. xxi. 18-20.
9. R-ock...............Psalm xviii. 2; 1 Cor. x. 4.
10. O-live.............Genesis viii. 11.
11. M-orning star......Revelations xxii. 16.
12. M-anna.............John vi. 48-51.
13. A-nchor............Hebrews vi. 19.
14. Nest...............Obadiah 3, 4.

KEY TO ENIGMA NO. 33.—"GOD HATH MADE MAN UPRIGHT.'—Eccles. vii. 29.

1. G-ad................2 Sam. xxiv. 11, etc.
2. O-badiah............1 Kings xviii. 3.
3. D-ecapolis..........Matt. viii. 28; Mark v. 20.

4. H-aman............Esther iii. 6.
5. A-biathar..........1 Sam. xxii. 20.
6. T-abor.............Judges iv. 6.
7. H-anani............2 Chron. xvi. 7.

8. M-ahanaim..........Gen. xxxii. 2.
9. A-bner.............2 Sam. iii. 38
10. D-arius............Ezra vi. 6—15.
11. E-lisheba..........Exodus vi. 23.

12. M-ephibosheth......2 Sam. ix. 6, 7.
13. A-gag..............1 Sam. xv. 9, 33.
14. N-ob...............1 Sam. xxii. 19.

15. U-rijah............Jer. xxvi. 24.
16. P-hilip............Luke iii. 1.
17. R-ephidim..........Exodus xvii. 8.
18. I-shmael...........Jer. xli. 2.
19. G-abbatha..........John xix. 13.
20. H-aran.............Genesis xi. 27.
21. T-arshish..........2 Chron. xx. 36.

KEY TO ENIGMA NO. 34.—" CASTING ALL YOUR CARE OB HIM."—1 Peter v. 7.

1. CA-leb.............Numbers xiv. 24, 30.
2. ST-raight..........Acts ix. 11.
3. IN-crease..........1 Cor. iii. 6, 7.
4. GALL-io............Acts xviii. 17.
5. YOUR
6. C-aiaphas..........Mark xiv. 61, 62.
7. ARE-tas............2 Cor. xi. 32.
8. ON.................Gen. xli. 45.
9. HI-ran.............1 Kings v. 1—12.
10. M-alchus..........John xviii. 10.

SCRIPTURE ENIGMAS.

KEY TO ENIGMA NO. 35.—"I GO TO PREPARE A PLACE FOR YOU."—John xiv. 2.

1. I-dume-a .... Isaiah xxxiv. 5.
2. G-ra-p(e) .... Cant. ii. 15.
3. O-thnie-l .... Joshua xv. 17.
4. T-hyatir-a .... Acts xvi. 14.
5. O-lympi-c .... Heb. xii. 1.
6. P-in-e .... Neh. viii. 15.
7. R-eproo-f .... 2 Tim. iii. 16.
8. E-n-o(ch) .... Gen. v. 24.
9. P-eo-r .... Num. xiii. 28.
10. A-llegor-y .... Gal. iv. 24.
11. R-ihp-o .... 1 Kings ix. 28.
12. E-sa-u .... Gen. xxxvi. 1.

KEY TO ENIGMA NO. 36.—JAWBONE.—Judges xv. 15—17

1. Jaw.   2. Bone.

KEY TO ENIGMA NO. 37.—PARADISE.

1. P-hilip .... Acts vi. 5.
2. A-raunah .... 2 Sam. xxiv. 22.
3. R-echabites .... Jer. xxxv.
4. A-chash .... Josh. xv. 16, etc.; Judges i. 12, etc
5. D-an .... Rev. vii.
6. I-mlah .... 1 Kings xxii. 9.
7. S-tephanas .... 1 Cor. xvi. 15
8. E-zekiel ....

CURIOSITIES OF THE BIBLE

KEY TO ENIGMA NO. 38.

Initials, down—CORNELIUS.
Finals, up—CENTURION.

1. C-edro-n............John xviii. 1.
2. O-d-o-urs...........Rev. v. 8.
3. R-abbon-i...........John xx. 16.
4. N-icano-r...........Acts vi. 5.
5. E-sa-u..............Heb. xii. 16.
6. L-o-t...............2 Peter ii. 7.
7. I-talian-n..........Acts x. 1.
8. U-rban-e............Rom. xvi. 9.
9. S-ado-c.............Matt. i. 14.

KEY TO ENIGMA NO. 39.—LAMB.—John i. 29.

L-ion...............Psalm xci. 13.
A-dder..............Psalm xci. 13.
M-ole...............Isaiah ii. 20.
B-at................Isaiah ii. 20.

KEY TO ENIGMA NO. 40.—JESUS WEPT AT BETHANY.

J-ehoiad-a..........2 Cor. xxii. 11; xxiii. 11.
E-gyp-t.............Jer. xxvi. 21.
S-egu-b.............1 Kings xvi. 34.
U-ncl-e.............Acts xxiii. 16.
S-anballa-t.........Neh. ii. 10.

W-rat-h.............Rom. i. 18. 19.
E-lish-a............2 Kings vi. 9, 13
P-hilemo-n..........Phil. 10, 11.
T-imoth-y...........2 Tim. iii. 15.

SCRIPTURE ENIGMAS.

KEY TO ENIGMA NO. 41.—FAITH, HOPE, CHARITY.—
1 Cor. xiii. 13.

1. F-elix............Acts xxiv. 25, 26.
2. A-pollos..........Acts xviii. 24—28.
3. I-saac............Heb. xi. 20.
4. T-imothy..........2 Tim. 1—5.
5. H-erodias.........Matt. xiv. 3—11.
6. H-eli.............Luke iii. 23.
7. O-nesimus.........Phil. 10—12.
8. P-riscilla........Acts xviii. 2, 26.
9. E-unice...........2 Tim. i. 5.
10. C-ornelius.......Acts x. 30—45.
11. H-ermogenes......2 Tim. i. 15.
12. A-nanias.........Acts v. 1—5.
13. R-hoda...........Acts xii. 13, 14.
14. I-scariot........John xiii. 2; xiv. 22.
15. T-ertius.........Rom. xvi. 22.
16. Y-ea.............2 Cor. i. 19, 20.

KEY TO ENIGMA NO. 42.—" LOVE NOT THE WORLD."—
1 John ii. 15.

1. L-evi.............Num. xvi. 1.
2. O-bed.............Ruth iv. 17.
3. V-oice............John x. 4.
4. E-liab............1 Sam. xvii. 28.
5. N-athanael........John i. 45, 46.
6. O-mri.............1 Kings xvi. 28.
7. T-arsus...........Acts xxi. 39.
8. T-heudas..........Acts v. 36.
9. H-ebron...........Josh xiv. 13.
10. E-lijah..........1 Kings xix. 4.

11. W-ages............Exodus ii. 9.
12. O-bed-edom.........2 Sam. vi. 11, 12.
13. R-amah.... ....1 Sam. ii. 11.
14. L-entiles...........Gen. xxv. 34.
15. D-aniel........ .....Dan. x. 11.

KEY TO ENIGMA NO. 43.

First.   Watch......Psalm xc. 4.
Second. Man.........Psalm ciii. 15 ; civ. 23.

Whole. WATCHMAN...Psalm cxxvii. 1.

KEY TO ENIGMA NO. 44.—" THE MOUNT OF OLIVES.".
Luke xxii. 39.

1. T-obiah.... ....Nehemiah vi. 19.
2. H-annah...... .....1 Sam. i. 10.
3. E-zekiel....... .....Ezek. i. 1.

4. M-ordecai...........Esther viii. 15.
5. O-badiah............1 Kings xviii. 4.
6. U-rijah.............Jer. xxvi. 21.
7. N-aomi.............Ruth i. 6, 7.
8. T-iglath-pileser......2 Kings xv. 29

9. O-thniel............Judges i. 13.
10. F-elix.. ....Acts xxiv. 25.

11. O-g..............Num. xxi. 33.
12. L-evi.............Num. iii. 6, 7.
13. I-saac............Genesis xxiv. 63
14 V-ashti.............Esther i. 12.
15. E-liphaz...........Job xvi. 2.
16. S-aul........... ....1 Sam. xxxi 4

SCRIPTURE ENIGMAS.

KEY TO ENIGMA NO. 45.—BE NOT FAITHLESS.—John xx. 27.

B-alaam............2 Peter ii. 15.
E-gypt.............Gen. xxi. 21.

N-aboth............1 Kings xxi. 3.
O-mer..............Exodus xvi. 36.
T-arsus............Acts xi. 25.

F-orty.............Acts vii. 29, 30.
A-bel..............Heb. xi. 4.
I-nterpreter.......Gen. xlii. 23.
T-imothy...........1 Tim. i. 2.
H-ezekiah..........1 Kings xx. 21.
L-aban.............Gen. xxiv. 29, 67.
Elisha.............2 Kings xiii. 14.
S-amaria...........1 Kings xvi. 28.
S-himei............2 Sam. xvi. 5.

KEY TO ENIGMA NO. 46.—HAMAN.—Esther vi. 11.

H-adassa-*h*.......Esther ii. 7.
A-s-*a*............2 Chron. xiv. 9–15.
M-iria-*m*.........Num. xii.
A-mas-*a*..........2 Sam. xx. 10.
N-aama-*n*.........2 Kings v.

KEY TO ENIGMA NO. 47.—JESUS.

J-oseph............Ps. cv. 17–22, Luke i. 68–77.
E-sau..............Gen. xxv. 29–34; Heb xii. 16, 17
S-aul..............1 Sam. x. 1–16; Acts viii. 1; ix. 11
U-zzah.............2 Sam. vi. 6, 7.
S-ardis............Rev. iii. 1–7.

" No voice can sing, no heart can frame,
   Nor can the memory find
 A sweeter sound than Jesu's name,
   The Saviour of mankind.

CURIOSITIES OF THE BIBLE.

KEY TO ENIGMA NO. 48.—CHRISTIAN WORSHIP

Initials—PRAISE. *Finals*—PRAYER.
P-hili-*p*................Matt. x. 3 ; John i. 43, 44.
R-emembe-*r*............Luke xvii. 32.
A-celdam-*a*.............Acts i. 18, 19.
I-tal-*y*.................Acts xviii. 1, 2.
S-alom-*e*...............Mark xvi. 1.
E-leaza-*r* ....Matt. i. 15.

KEY TO ENIGMA NO. 49.—ARAM.—Numb. xxiii. 7.—MARA.— Ruth. i. 29.

A-ntipas................Rev. ii. 13.
R-amah.................1 Sam. vii. 17.
A-bner.................2 Sam. iii. 20.
M-atton................2 Kings xi. 18.

KEY TO ENIGMA NO. 50.

1. Cross. 1 Cor. i. 17, 18, 23, 24.
2. Dross.
3. Loss. Lydia. Acts xvi. 14, 15 ; Phil. iii. 7, 8.

KEY TO ENIGMA NO. 51.—SINAI.—Exod. xx. ; Rom. iii. 20.

1. Sin. Rom. vi. 23. 2. Ai. Josh. vii.

KEY TO ENIGMA NO. 52.

First. Morning. Psa. xxx. 5. *Second.* Star. 1 Cor xv. 41.
Whole. MORNING-STAR. .Rev. xxii. 16.

KEY TO ENIGMA NO. 53.—ESTHER.

Teresh..................Esth. ii. 21 ; vi. 2, etc.
Heres.... ....Judg. i. 35.
Trees....... ......   Isa. lv. 12.
Three ....Josh. xv. 14.
Sheet   .... Acts v. 11, 12

SCRIPTURE ENIGMAS.

Seth..................Gen. iv. 25.
Seer..................1 Sam. ix. 9, 19.
Resh..................Psa. cxix. 153.
Rest. ....Matt. xi. 28.
Thee ....Mark x. 49.

KEY TO ENIGMA NO. 54.—LOVE.

L-ois.. ....2 Tim. 1—5.
O-badiah..............1 Kings xviii. 4.
V-ashti...............Esther i. 10—19.
E-li ....1 Sam. iii. 13.

1 Cor. xiii. 13.—" And now abideth faith, hope, charity these three ; but the greatest of these is charity."

1 John iv. 11.—" Beloved, if God so loved us, we ought also to love one another."

KEY TO ENIGMA NO. 55.—LOVE AS BRETHREN.—1 Peter iii. 8.

L-amech...............Gen. iv. 19, 22.
O-badiah ....1 Kings xviii. 7, 12.
V-anity...............Eccles. i. 1, 14.
E-lah.................1 Sam. xxi. 9.

A-bijam ....1 Kings xiv. 31.
S-abeans..............Job i. 14, 15.

B-lastus ....Acts. xii. 20.
R-amoth Gilead........2 Kings ix. 1, 2.
E-lam.................Gen. xiv. 1.
T-ertius..............Rom. xvi. 22.
H-aggith..............1 Kings i. 5.
R-uth.................Ruth iv. 10.
E-d...................Josh. xxii. 34.
N-aphtali.............Gen. xxx. 8.

CURIOSITIES OF THE BIBLE.

KEY TO ENIGMA NO. 56.—VINE.—John. xv. 5.

1. V-igilance..........1 Peter v. 8.
2. I-nheritance.........1 Peter i. 4.
3. N-egligence..........2 Peter i. 12.
4. E-videuce............Heb. xi. 1.

KEY TO ENIGMA NO. 57.

Key to Threefold Acrostic.

Stanza	1	2	3	4	5	6	7	8	9	10.
	R	e	d	e	m	p	t	i	o	n.
	B	y	p	u	r	c	h	a	s	e.
	A	n	d	b	y	p	o	w	e	r.

KEY TO ENIGMA NO. 58.—ANAMMELECH—2 Kings xvii. 31

1. Heman..............1 Kings iv. 31.
2. Camel...............Lev. xi. 4.

KEY TO ENIGMA NO. 59.—MANOAH.—Judges xiii.

1. Man.   2. O!   3. Ah!

KEY TO ENIGMA NO. 60.—"ABISHAG."—1 Kings i. 4.—' &c BEKAH."—Gen. xxiv. 16.

1. A-sshu-r.............Gen. x. 11.
2. B-ernic-e............Acts xxv. 23.
3. I-shbi-beno-b.... ...2 Sam. xxi. 16, 17.
4. S-hunammit-e........2 Kings iv. 16.
5. H-abakku-k..........Hab. ii. 2.
6. A-s-a ....1 Kings xv. 13.
7. G-oliat-h............1 Sam. xvii. 42—51.

KEY TO ENIGMA NO. 61.—ADRAMMELECH.—2 Kings xix 37

1. Lamech.............Gen. iv. 19—21.
2. Ed ....Joshua xxii. 10, 34.
3. Ram...............Job xxxii. 2, etc

SCRIPTURE ENIGMAS.

KEY TO ENIGMA NO. 62.—WAIT ON THE LORD.—Psalm. xxvii. 14

W-ell..................2 Sam. xvii. 17, 19.
A-mos................Amos i. 1.
I-rad..................Gen. iv. 17, 18.
T-ola..................Judges x. 1.
O-badiah.............Obad. 1-16.
N-ehushtan..........2 Kings xviii. 4.
T-imnath.............Judges xiv. 5, 6.
H-achaliah...........Neh. i. 1.
E-lisheba............Exod. vi. 23.
L-achish.............2 Kings xviii. 17.
O-nesiphorus........2 Tim i. 16.
R-ezin................2 Kings xvi. 5.
D-an..................Rev. vii. 5—8.

KEY TO ENIGMA NO. 63.—SUB-MISSION.—Matt. xviii. 11; Job. i. 11.

KEY TO ENIGMA NO. 64.—JEHOSHAPHAT.—2 Chron. xx 31, 32

1. J-oseph............Gen. xli. 41—43.
2. E-phah............Zech. v. 5—11.
3. H-oshea...........2 Kings xvii. 3, 4.
4. O-shea............Num. xiii. 8, 16.
5. S-haphat..........1 Kings xix. 19; 2 Kings ii. 13.
6. H-eth..............Gen. xlix. 29, 31.
7. A-saph............1 Chron. xxv. 6; Psa. l. and lxxiii to lxxxiii.
8. P-aseah...........Ezra ii. 49; Phascah, Neh. vii 51
9. H-osah............Josh. xix. 19.
10. A-jah.............Gen. xxxvi. 10, 24, 25, and 2.
11. T-oah............1 Chron. vi. 34.

KEY TO ENIGMA NO. 65.—HORSEMAN.—Nahum iii. 3.

Horse.................Deut. xvii. 16
Man...................Psa. cxliv. 3, 4.

KEY TO ENIGMA NO. 66.—EVE.—Gen. iii. 15.

E-lijah .... 1 Kings xix. 4.
V-ine.............. ... John xv. 3.
E-sther............... Esther ii. 7.

KEY TO ENIGMA NO. 67.—"SARGON—TARTAN."—Isa. xx.

S-anballa-t............ Neh. iv. 1.
A-ban-a............... 2 Kings v. 12.
R-ide-r.............. Exodus xv. 1.
G-rea-t.............. Psa. cxxxvi. 4.
O-she-a.............. Num. xiii. 8.
N-u-n................ Num. xiii. 8.

KEY TO ENIGMA NO. 68.—GAMALIEL—Acts xxii. 3.

1. Elim .... Exod. xv. 27.
2. Gaal............... Judges ix. 14.

KEY TO ENIGMA NO. 69.—ARIMATHEA.—Matt. xxvii. 57.

1 Ahira............... Numb. i. 15.
2. Tema.............. Gen. xxv. 15.

KEY TO ENIGMA NO. 70.—SAMUEL.—HANNAH.—1 Sam. i. 20.

S-eraiah............. Jer. li. 59.
A-bora............... 2 Kings v. 12.
M-attan.............. 2 Kings xi. 18.
U-pharsin............ Dan. v. 25.
E-liada.............. 2 Chron. xvii. 17.
L-ibnah.............. Joshua xxi. 13.

KEY TO ENIGMA, NO 71.—THE GOOD SHEPHERD.

1. T-abitha............ Acts ix. 36—39.
2. H-agar .... Gen xxi. 14.
3. E-zekiel............ Ezekiel i. 1.
4. G-ehazi .... 2 Kings v. 25.
5. O-reb .... Judges vii. 25.
6. O-badiah .... 1 Kings xviii. 5.
7. D-aniel............. Daniel vi. 23.

SCRIPTURE ENIGMAS.

8. S-amson........................Judges xv. 15.
9. H-ezekiah......................2 Kings xx. 5.
10. E-lah..........................1 Sam. xvii. 2, 51
11. P-eter.........................Luke xxii. 61, 62.
12. H-oreb.........................Exodus iii. 1.
13. E-sau..........................Gen. xxvii. 41.
14. R-ahab.........................Heb. xi. 31.
15. D-avid.........................1 Sam. xix. 1, 2.

KEY TO ENIGMA NO. 72.—DO GOOD.

D-eborah................Judges iv. 9.
O-badiah................1 Kings xviii. 13.
G-ehazi.................2 Kings v. 20, 22.
O-bededem...............2 Sam. vi. 10.
O-rpah..................Ruth i. 4.
D-avid..................2 Sam. xviii. 13.

KEY TO ENIGMA NO. 73.—MOSES—AARON.

1. M-ammo-n..........Luke xvi. 9-14.
2. O-n-o.............Neh. vi. 2; xi. 35.
3. S-hina-r..........Gen. xi. 1-9.
4. E-phphath-a.......Mark vii. 34.
5. S-heb-a...........1 Kings x. 2, 10; Jer. vi 20; Ezek xxvii. 22.

KEY TO ENIGMA NO. 74.—THE BRANCH.—Zec iii. 8 · vi 12

1. T-eman.............Gen. xxxvi. 15.
2. H-or...............Num. xx. 22, 28.
3. E-lisheba..........Exodus vi. 25.
4. B-arnabas..........Acts xiv. 12.
5. R-ephidim..........Ex. xvii. 1, 3.
6. A-mram.............Ex. vi. 20.
7. N-icodemus.........John iii. 1, 3.
8. C-ephas............John i. 42.
9. H-anani............2 Chron. xvi. 7

CURIOSITIES OF THE BIBLE.

KEY TO ENIGMA NO. 75.—DAGON.—1 Sam. v. 1-7.

1. D-oeg................1 Sam. xxi. 7 ; xxii. 9.
2. A-hithophel..........2 Sam. xvii. 1-3, 23.
3. G-edaliah.... ......2 Kings xxv. 22-26; Jer. xi, 7-12 ; xli. 2-10.
4. O-bed................2 Chron. xxviii, 6-15.
5. N-adal...............1 Sam. xxv. 3, 33.

KEY TO ENIGMA NO. 76.—" HOW MANIFOLD ARE THY WORKS."
—Ps. cix. 24.

1. H-yssop... ....1 Kings iv. 33.
2. O-aks of Bashan.....Isa. ii. 13.
3. W-illow trees........Psa. cxxxvii. 2.

4. M-yrtle tree.........Isa lv. 13.
5. A-lmond tree........Eccles. xii. 5.
6. N-uts................Gen. xliii. 2.
7. I-sraelites...........Exod. xv. 27.
8. F-ig tree............Matt. xxiv. 32.
9. O-il tree............Isa. xii. 19.
10. L-ign aloes.........Num. xxiv. 5, 6.
11. D-ry tree...........Ezek. xvii. 24.

12. A-lmug tree........1 Kings x. 11, 12.
13. R-ose..............Isa. xxxv. 1.
14. E-den..............Gen. ii. 9.

15. T-ree of life........Rev. xxii. 2.
16. H-eath............. .Jer. xvii. 5, 6.
17. Y-ear by year.......Deut. xiv. 22.

18. W-heat.............Exod. ix. 32.
19. O-live tree..........Judges ix. 8, 9
20. R-od...............Num. xvii. 8.
21. K-ernels............Num. vi. 4.
22. S-ycamore tree......Luke xix. 45.

SCRIPTURE ENIGMAS. 105

KEY TO ENIGMA NO. 77.—"EVEN CHRIST PLEASED NOT HIMSELF."—Rom. xv. 3.

1. E-sther..............Esther vii. 3.
2. V-oshni.............1 Chron. vi. 28.
3. E-li................1 Sam. iv. 10, 11.
4. N-ebuchadnezzer.....2 Chron. xxxvi. 20
5. C-esar..............Luke ii. 1.
6. H-ezekiah...........2 Kings xx. 1—7.
7. R-abshakeh..........2 Kings xviii. 19.
8. I-saiah.............2 Kings xix. 5, 6.
9. S-himei.............2 Sam. xvi. 5.
10. T-homas............John xx. 24.
11. P-aul..............Acts ix. 8, 16.
12. L-aban.............Gen. xxxi. 24.
13. E-ve...............Gen. iii.
14. A-sabel............2 Sam. ii. 18.
15. S-amson............Judges xvi.
16. E-sau..............Gen. xxv. 27—34.
17. D-avid.............1 Sam. xvii. 49.
18. N-abal.............1 Sam. xxv. 10.
19. O-badiah...........1 Kings xviii. 1.
20. T-arshish..........2 Chron. ix. 21.
21. H-ushai............2 Sam. xv. 32
22. I-saac.............Gen. xxvi. 7.
23. M-ary..............Mark xvi. 9.
24. S-imeon............Gen. xlii. 24.
25. E-liezer...........Gen. xv. 2; xxiv.
26. L-ebanon...........2 Chron. ii. 8.
27. F-elix.............Acts xxiv. 27.

KEY TO ENIGMA NO. 78.—LOVE YOUR ENEMIES.—Matt v. 44

1 L-uke...............1 Tim. iv. 11 ; Col. iv 14.
2. O-phir..............1 Kings ix. 28; x. 11
3. V-ine...............John xv.
4. E-shcol.............Numbers xiii. 23

5. Y-early..............Heb. ix. 7, etc.
6. O-bed-Edom........5 Sam. vi. 11.
7. U-zzah..............2 Sam. vi. 6, 7.
8. R-hoboam..........1 Kings xii. 8.
9. E-lijah..............2 Kings ii. 11.
10. N-icodemus.........John iii. 1.
11. E-lah...............1 Kings xvi. 10.
12. M-anasseh (55 years).2 Chron. xxxiii. 1.
13. I-saac..............Gen. xxvii.
14. E-zekel ....Ezek. iii. 26; xxiv. 27.
15. S-heba.............2 Sam. xx.

KEY TO ENIGMA NO. 79.—ELIJAH—ELISHA

1. E-unic-e............2 Tim. i. 5.
2. L-emue-l...........Prov. xxx. 1.
3. I-tta-i..............2 Sam. xv. 19–21.
4. J-ebusite-s..........Numbers xiii. 29.
5. A-drammelec-h.......2 Kings xvii. 21.
6. H-ammedath-a.......Esther viii. 5.

KEY TO ENIGMA NO. 80.—REFUGE.—Heb. vi. 18 ; vii. 2!

1. R-izpah.............2 Sam. xxi. 8–10.
2. E-sther.............Esther ii. 17.
3. F-elix..............Acts xxiv. 24, 25.
4. U-nicorn............Numbers xxiii. 22.
5. G-ourd.............Jonah iv. 5, 6.
6. E-uroclydon.........Acts xxvii. 14.

KEY TO ENIGMA NO. 81.—GOD BE WITH YOU.

1. G-ood...... ......Matt. xix. 16, 17.
2. O-nesimus. ....Phil. x. 16.
3. D-orcas.............Acts ix. 36—41
4. B-oaz..............Ruth iv. 13.
5. E-aster............1 Cor. v. 7. 8

SCRIPTURE ENIGMAS.

6. W-hite.. ....Rev. vii. 13, 14
7. I-saac..............Gen. xxi. 4, 6.
8. T-imothy..........2 Tim i.
9. H-ushai...........2 Sam. xvii. 5-14.
10. Y-esterday.........Ps. xc. 4.
11. O-mega............Rev. xxii. 13.
12. U-rim.............Ex. xxviii. 30

KEY TO ENIGMA NO. 82.—PEACE.—John xiv. 27

1. P-hicol... ....Gen. xxi. 22.
2. E-bedmelech........Jer. xxxviii. 7, etc.
3. A-bram............Gen. xiv. 13.
4. C-ephas............John i. 42.
5. E-lim..............Exodus xv. 27.

KEY TO ENIGMA NO. 83.—OMNISCIENCE.

1. O-mri..............1 Kings xvi. 23, 24.
2. M-icaiah...........1 Kings xxii. 26.
3. N-amaan.... ....2 Kings v. 1.
4. I-shbosheth.........2 Sam. iii. 13; iv. 5, 6.
5. S-himei............2 Sam. xvi. 5; xix. 16, 27
6. C-hilion.......... ...Ruth i. 2.
7. I-conium...........Acts xiii. 51.
8. E-mmaus..........Luke xxiv. 13.
9. N-azarite..........Numbers vi.
10. C-leopas...........Luke xxiv. 18.
11. E-lias.............**Matt. xi. 14.**

KEY TO ENIGMA NO. 84.—BETHPHAGE.—Matt. xxi. 1

1. B-ethany............John xi. 1.
2. E-lath...............2 Kings xvi. 6.
3. T-imnath...........Judges xiv. 5, 6.
4. H-amoth...........Jer. xlix. 23.
5. P-adanaram.........Gen. xxviii. 1.
6. H-eshbon..........Num. xxi. 25.
7. A-rimathea........Mark xv. 43.
8. G-alilee............Matt. xxviii. 16, 17.
9. E-gypt.............Gen. xlii 1, 2.

KEY TO ENIGMA NO. 85.—" SEEK YE THE KINGDOM OF GOD"
—Luke xii. 31.

1. S-imeon............Acts xiii. 1.
2. E-lias..............James v. 17.
3. E-lymas............Acts xiii. 8.
4. K-ish...............1 Sam. ix. 1.
5. Y-outh.............Lam. iii. 27.
6. E-penetus..........Rom. xvi. 5.
7. T-urtius...........Rom. xvi. 22.
8. H-achilah..........1 Sam. xxvi.
9. E-thiopia..........Esther i. 1.
10. K-ezia............Job xlii. 14, 15.
11. I-saiah...........Isaiah i. 1.
12. N-aomi............Ruth i. 20.
13. G-ideon..........Judges vi. 11.
14. D-arius...........Dan. ix. 1.
15. O-rpah............Ruth i. 2, 4.
16. M-iriam...........Exodus xv. 20.
17. O-badiah..........Obadiah i. 1.
18. F-elix............Acts xxiii. 33.
19. G-ath.............1 Sam. vi. 17.
20. O-both............Num. xxxiii. 43
21. D-rusilla.........Acts xxiv. 24.

SCRIPTURE ENIGMAS.

KEY TO ENIGMA NO. 86.—"WATCH AND PRAY."—Matt. xxvi. 41.

W-ater............John viii. 37, 38.
A-rimathea........John xix. 38.
T-abitha..........Acts ix. 40.
C-armi............Joshua vii. 1.
H-iddekel.........Daniel x. 4.

A-mos.............Amos i. 1.
N-oadiah..........Neh. vi. 14.
D-emitrius........Acts xix. 24.

P-hinehas.........Num. xxv. 11.
R-ezin............2 Kings xvi. 6.
A-bel.............2 Sam. xx. 28.
Y-oke.............Lam. iii. 27.

KEY TO ENIGMA NO. 87.—ISAIAH—DANIEL.

1. I-chabo-d....,....1 Sam. iv. 21; xiv. 3.
2. S-amari-a.........1 Kings xvi. 24.
3. A-hima-n..........Num. xiii. 22.
4. I-su-i............Gen. xlvi. 17; Num. xxvi. 44
5. A-nis-e...........Matt. xxiii. 23.
6. H-ie-l............1 Kings xvi. 34.

KEY TO ENIGMA NO. 88.—"THE LORD IS MY LIGHT."

1. T-homas..........John xx. 24.
2. H-aman...........Esther v. 11.
3. E-zra............Ezra vii. 6.
4. L-emuel..........Prov. xxxi. 1.
5. O-thniel.........Judges iii. 9.
6. R-ehoboam........1 Kings xii. 8.
7. D-arius..........Dan. vi. 26.
8. I-shbosheth......2 Sam. iv. 5—8
9. S-anballat.......Neh. vi.

10. M-anoah............Judges xiii. 15, 16.
11. Y-oke..............Matt. xi. 30.
12. L-ot...............Gen. xiii. 10.
13. I-shmael...........2 Kings xxv. 25.
14. G-ehazi............2 Kings v. 20-27.
15. H-eber the Kenite..Judges v. 24.
16. T-iglath-pileser...2 Kings xv. 29.

KEY TO ENIGMA NO. 89.—HAGAR.—Genesis xvi. 6-10.

1. H-zael..............2 Kings viii. 12; xiii. 22.
2. A-chan..............Joshua vii.
3. G-ideon.............Judges vii.
4. A-bimelech..........Judges ix. 53, 54.
5. R-abbah.............2 Sam. xi. 1.

KEY TO ENIGMA NO. 90.—FAITH.—1 Peter i. 3; 1 John v. 4

1. F-ire...............Jeremiah xxiii. 29.
2. A-rk................Gen. vii. 1.
3. I-conium............Acts xiv. 1-6.
4. T-hyatira...........Acts xvi. 14.
5. H-eaven.............Hebrews xi. 16.

KEY TO ENIGMA NO. 91.—"GOD IS LOVE."—1 John i. 7

1. G-old (tried in the fire). Zec. xiii. 9; 1 Peter i. 7.
2. O-ath...............Heb. vi. 16, 17.
3. D-eath..............Rom. vi. 23.
4. I-dle soul..........Prov. xix. 15.
5. S-alt...............Matt. v. 13.
6. L-amb...............Rev. v. 6.
7. O-x.................Isaiah i. 3.
8. V-eil...............Matt. xxvii. 51.
9. E-agle..............2 Sam. i. 23.

KEY TO ENIGMA NO. 92.—HEZEKIAH.—Isaiah xxxvii. 15.—
ZEDEKIAH.—2 Kings xxv. 7.

1. H-u-z .... Gen. xxii. 21.
2. E-v-e .... Gen. iii. 20.
3. Z-elopheha-d .... Num. xxvii. 7
4. E-unic-e .... 2 Tim. i. 5.
5. K-insfol-k .... Job xix. 14
6. I-tto-i .... 2 Sam. xv. 19.
7. A-s-a .... 1 Kings xv. 13.
8. H-anania-h .... Daniel i. 7.

KEY TO ENIGMA NO. 94.—"LIVE PEACEABLY."—Rom. xii. 18

L-uke .... Col. iv. 14.
I-srael .... Gen. xxxii. 28.
V-ine .... John xv. 5.
E-lam .... Exodus xv. 27.

P-hillippi .... Phil. iv. 15, 16.
E-zra .... Ezra vii. 6.
A-mos .... Acts xv. 16, 17.
C-ilicia .... Acts xxi. 39.
E-liakim .... 2 Kings xiii. 34.
A-bner .... 2 Sam. ii. 8.
B-athsheba .... 1 Kings i. 11.
L-evi .... 2 Chron. xi. 14.
Y-outh .... Lam. iii. 27.

KEY TO ENIGMA NO. 95.—SIMON PETER.—Matt. x 2
Mark. iii, 16; Luke vi. 14.

1. S-a-p .... Psa. civ. 16.
2. I-c-e .... Psa. cxlvii. 17.
3. M-oun-t .... Matt. v. 1.
4. O-n-e .... 1 John v. 7.
5. N-os .... Psa. cxix. 151

**KEY TO ENIGMA NO. 96.—" YET THERE IS ROOM."—
Luke xiv. 22.**

Y-outh................	1 Sam. xvii. 33.
E-tiam................	2 Sam. xi. 3.
T-hessalonica..........	2 Tim. iv. 10.
T-irzah................	1 Kings xvi. 9.
H-aran................	Gen. xi. 29.
E-thiopia.............	Jer. xxxviii. 7.
R-ahab................	James ii. 25.
E-glah.	2 Sam. iii. 5.
I-ron.	Judges iv. 2, 3.
S-othenes.............	Acts xviii. 17.
R-echab...............	2 Kings x. 15, 16.
O-mri................	1 Kings xvi. 21, 22
O-bed................	Ruth iv. 16, 17.
M-ene	Dan. v. 25.

**KEY TO ENIGMA NO. 97.—JEHOIADA—ATHALIAH.—2 Chron
xxii. 10, 11 ; xxiii. 14 ; xxiv. 22.**

1. J-egar-sahaduth-*a*..... Gen. xxxi. 47.
2. E-as-*t*.............. Judges vii. 12 ; viii. 10.
3. H-achila-*h*.......... 1 Sam. xxvi. 1, 9, 25.
4. O-she-*a*............ Num. xiii. 8, 16.
5. I-shmae-*l*........... Gen. xxi. 16 ; xxv. 12.
6. A-*i*................ Joshua vii. 5, 6.
7. D-ur-*a*............. Dan. iii. 1, 12.
8. A-bia-*h* .... 1 Sam. viii. 2. 3.

SCRIPTURE ENIGMAS.

KEY TO ENIGMA NO. 98.—JERUSALEM.—Psa. xlviii. 2.— BETH-LEHEM.—Matt. ii. 6.

1. J-oa-b.............1 Kings ii. 32—34.
2. E-v-e.............Gen. iii. 6, 20.
3. R-es-t............Heb. iv. 9.
4. U-rija-h..........2 Kings xvi. 10—16.
5. S-helumiei-l......Num. ii. 12.
6. A-gagit-e........Esther iii. 10; 1 Sam. 15, 36.
7. L-ais-h...........Judges xviii. 27—29.
8. E-unic-e..........2 Tim. 1, 5; Acts xvi. 1.
9. M-ahanai-m.......Gen. xxxii. 1, 2.

KEY TO ENIGMA NO. 99.—AMASA.—2 Sam. xvii. 25; xx. 10.—ABNER.—1 Sam. xiv. 50, 51; 2 Sam. iii. 27.

1. A-rabi-a..........Gal. i. 17.
2. M-era-b...........1 Sam. xiv. 49.
2. A-bdo-n...........Judges xii. 13—15.
4. S-almon-e.........Acts xxvii. 7.
5. A-r...............Deut. ii. 9.

ANSWER NO. 100.—" LET THERE BE LIGHT."—Gen. i. 3.

L-achish ....2 Kings xiv. 19.
E-gypt.............Gen. xii. 10; xlii. 1, 2.
T-ibni.............1 Kings xvi. 21.
T-ekel.............Dan. v. 27.
H-aman.............Esther iii. 10.
E-lijah............1 Kings xxi. 19.
R-izpah............2 Sam. xxi. 10.
E-sarhaddon........2 Kings xix. 37.
B-enhadad..........1 Kings xx. 42.
E-glon.............Judges iii. 14.
L-evi..............Deut. x. 8.
I-saiah............2 Kings xix. 20.
G-ilboa............1 Sam. xxxi. 8.
H-anani............1 Kings xvi. 1.
T-iglath-pilesar...2 Chron. xxviii. 20.

CURIOSITIES OF THE BIBLE

KEY TO ENIGMA NO. 101.—"ALL SEEK THEIR OWN."—
Phil. ii. 21.

A-bner..............2 Sam. xvii. 57
L-ebbeus............Matt. x. 3.
L-ystra.............Acts xiv. 8, 13.

S-ihon..............Deut. i. 4.
E-liezar............Gen. xxiv. 33.
E-nos...............Gen. iv. 26.
K-adash-barnea......Num. xxxii. 8.

T-amar..............2 Sam. xiv. 27.
H-annah.............1 Sam. i. 23, 28.
E-lijah.............1 Kings xix. 13, 15.
I-talian............Acts x. 1.
R-abbah.............2 Sam. xii. 27.

O-phir..............1 Kings xxii. 48.
W-ood...............1 Sam. xiv. 26, 27.
N-azareth...........Luke i. 26, 27.

KEY TO ENIGMA NO. 102.—CROSS.

Isaa-c..............Gen. xxvi. 18.
Sei-r...............Gen. xxxvi. 8.
S-o,................2 Kings xvii. 4.
Stephana-s..........1 Cor. i. 16.
Matthia-s...........Acts i. 26.

ANSWER NO. 103.—RUTH—BOAZ.—Matt. i. 5

1. R-aha-b...........John ii. 8 ; Heb. xi. 31.
2. U-nt-o............Matt. xi. 1.
3. T-ol-a............Judges x. 1.
4. H-u-z.............Gen. xxii. 21.

SCRIPTURE ENIGMAS.

KEY TO ENIGMA NO. 104.—*Initials*—DRUSILLA; *Finals*—AND FELIX.

D-almanuth-*a* . . . . . .Mark viii. 9, 10.
R-oma-*n* . . . . .Acts xxii. 25, 29.
U-ncircumcise-*d* . . . .1 Sam. xvii. 36.
S-herif-*f* . . . . .Dan. iii. 2, 3.
I-gnoranc-*e* . . . . .Acts iii. 13-17.
L-emue-*l* . . . . .Prov. xxxi. 1.
L-o-Amm-*i* . . . . .Hosea i. 9.
A-rta-*x*-erxes . . . . . . .Ezra vii. 12.

KEY TO ENIGMA NO. 105.—BARNABAS.—Acts xiv. 11-20

Bar-ley . . . . .Ruth ii. 17.
Na-il . . . . .Judges iv. 21.
Bas-ket . . . . .Acts ix. 25; 2 Chron. xi. 32.

KEY TO ENIGMA NO. 106.—KADESH-BARNEA.—Deut. ix. 23.

K-esi-*a* . . . . .Job xlii. 14.
A-ge-*e* . . . . .2 Sam. xxiii. 11.
D-alpho-*n* . . . . .Esther ix. 7.
E-lieze-*r* . . . . .Gen. xv. 2.
S-hime-*a* . . . . 1 Chron. iii. 5.
H-oba-*b* . . . . .Num. v. 29.

KEY TO ENIGMA NO. 107.—"GOD RESISTETH THE PROUD."— 1 Peter v. 5.

G-era . . . . .2 Sam. xvi. 5.
O-thniel . . . . .Judges i. 13.
D-elilah . . . . .Judges xvi. 18

R-hoda..........Acts xii. 13.
E-aster..........Acts xii. 4.
S-hushan........Neh. i. 1.
I-conium........Acts xiii. 51.
S-in............Exodus xvi. 1
T-arsus.........Acts xxi. 39.
E-noch..........Jude 14, 15
T-heudas........Acts v. 36.
H-ebron.........Numbers xiii. 22.

T-yre...........Isaiah xxiii. 8
H-ezekiah.......2 Kings xviii. 4.
E-phraim........Numbers xiii 8.

P-halti.........1 Sam. xxv. 44.
R-ebekah........Gen. xxvii. 6, 17.
O-badiah........1 Kings xviii. 3.
U-zziah.........2 Chron. xxvi. 19.
D-eborah........Judges v. 7.

KEY TO ENIGMA NO. 108.—NAOMI.—Book of Ruth

Na-hum.
O-badiah.
Mi-cah.

KEY TO ENIGMA NO. 109.—" IT SHALL BE WELL WITH THE RIGHTEOUS."

I-srael..........Num. xi. 10.
T-aberah........Num. xi. 3.

S-eer...........1 Sam. ix. 9.
H-obab..........Num. x. 29.
A-bsalom........2 Sam. xiv. 25.
L-ydia..........Acts xvi. 13, 14
L-uke...........2 Tim. iv. 11.

SCRIPTURE ENIGMAS.

B-ethany............Luke x. 38; John xi.
E-lah...............1 Sam. xvii. 2.

W-isdom.............Prov. viii. 11.
E-zekiel............Ezek. i. 1.
L-evi...............Gen. xxxv. 23.
L-amech.............Gen. v. 28.

W-ise-men...........Matt. ii. 1-11.
I-shmael............Gen. xxi. 9-21.
T-abor..............Psalm lxxxix. 12.
H-oreb..............Deut. v. 1.

T-hyathira..........Acts xvi. 14.
H-ophni.............1 Sam. ii. 34.
E-uphrates..........Gen. ii. 14.

R-achel.............Gen. xxix. 9.
I-saac..............Genesis xxvii.
G-ehozi.............2 Kings v. 20.
H-ezekiah...........2 Kings xx. 8-11.
T-yre...............1 Kings v. 1.
E-limelech..........Ruth i. 1, 2.
O-badiah............Obad. i. 1.
U-rim and Thummim...Exodus xxviii. 30.
S-alvation..........Rev. vii. 9-21.

KEY TO ENIGMA NO. 110.—THOU GOD SEEST ME.—
Gen. xvi. 3.

T-hummim............Exodus xxviii. 30.
H-annah.............1 Sam. ii. 1.
O-bed-edom..........1 Chron. xiii. 14.
U-lai...............Dan. viii. 2.

G-ennesaret.........Mark vi. 52.
O-rnan..............1 Chron xxi. 15
D-elilah............Jud. xvi. 18.

S-apphira..............Acts v. 9, 10.
E-nos..................Gen. iv. 26.
E-noch.................Gen. iv. 17.
S-aul..................1 Sam. xviii. 8.
T-abitha...............Acts ix. 40, 41.
M-idian................Exodus ii. 15.
E-lah..................1 Sam. xvii. 2.

KEY TO ENIGMA NO. 111.—I AM THAT I AM.—Exodus iii. 4

I-shmaelites...........Gen. xxxvii. 28.
A-binadab..............1 Chron. ii. 13.
M-aachah...............1 Kings xv. 10.
T-ekoah................2 Sam. xiv. 2.
H-abakkuk..............Hab. ii. 4.
A-hithophel............2 Sam. xv. 31.
T-hyatira..............Acts xvi. 14.
I-shboseth.............2 Sam. ii. 10.
A-nthoth...............1 Kings ii. 26.
M-alachi...............Luke i. 17.

KEY TO ENIGMA NO. 112.—"HOPE THOU IN GOD."—
Psalm xlii. 11.

H-ebron................1 Sam. ii. 2-4.
O-thniel...............Judges i. 11, 33.
P-adan-aram............Gen. xxviii. 5.
E-lisha................2 Kings iii. 11.
T-erah.................Gen. xi. 31, 32.
H-azael................2 Kings viii. 15.
O-livet................2 Sam. xv. 30
U-ri...................Exodus xxxi. 1, 2
I-sboheth..............2 Sam. iv. 5, 6.
N-achons...............2 Sam. vi. 6.

SCRIPTURE ENIGMAS.

G-ibal..............Josh. v 12.
O-bed..............Ruth iv. 17.
D-emetrius..........Acts xix. 24, 20.

KEY TO ENIGMA NO. 113.—HARDEN NOT YOUR HEARTS -
Psalm xcv. 8.

H-adad.............1 Kings iv. 14.
A-lexandria........Acts xviii. 24.
R-ome..............Acts xix. 21.
D-ura..............Dan. iii. 1.
E-lah..............1 Sam. xxi. 9.
N-adab.............1 Kings xiv. 20.

N-athan............1 Kings i. 10.
O-ded..............2 Chron. xxviii. 9.
Tertius............Rom. xvi. 22.

Y-oke..............Gen. xxvii. 4.
O-zem..............1 Chron. ii. 15.
U-riah.............2 Sam. xii. 9.
R-ephidim..........Exodus xvii. 8.

H-ephzi-bah........2 Kings xxi. 1.
E-phphatha.........Mark vii. 34.
A-senath...........Gen. xli. 45.
R-ahab.............James ii. 15; Heb. xi. 31.
T-yrannas..........Acts xix. 9.
S-abeans...........Job i. 15.

KEY TO ENIGMA, NO. 114.—GLORY TO GOD.—Luke ii. 14.

1. G-ad..............2 Sam. xxiv 11.
2. L-uz..............Gen. xxviii. 19.
3. O-badiah..........2 Kings xviii. 4.
4. R-ezin............2 Kings xv. 42.
" Y-early..........Jud. xi. 41.

6. T-aphanhes..........Jer. xliii. 8, 9.
7. O-bed-Edom.........2 Sam. vi. 11.
8. G-eba................1 Kings.
9. O-nesiphorus........2 Tim. i. 16.
10. D-eborah............Gen. xxxv. 8.

KEY TO EASTER ACROSTIC NO. 115.—NOW IS CHRIST RISEN FROM THE DEAD.—1 Cor. xv. 20.

N-oah...............Gen. ix. 20, 21.
O-badiah............Obadiah i.
W-orship............Matt. iv. 10.
I-bzan..............Judges xii. 8.
S-alem..............Gen. xiv. 18.

C-apernaum..........Matt iv. 13.
H-aggai.............Ezra v. 1.
R-echabites.........Jer. xxxv. 13.
I-ttai..............2 Sam. xv. 19.
S-enacherib.........2 Kings xviii. 3.
T-obiah.............Nem. iv. 8.

R-ephidim...........Exodus xvii. 8
I-shbosheth.........2 Sam. iv.
S-amuel.............1 Sam. xii. 18.
E-benezer...........1 Sam. vii. 12.
N-ehemiah...........Nem. i. 11.

F-elix..............Acts xxiv. 25.
R-amah of Benjamin.1 Sam. xxviii. 3.
O-mri...............1 Kings xvi. 16.
M-attan.............2 Kings xi. 18.

T-ertullus..........Acts xxiv.
H-aman..............Esther vii. 10.
E-bed-meleh the
   eunuch...........Jer. xxxviii. 7

SCRIPTURE ENIGMAS.

D-ungeon..............Jer. xxxviii. 13.
E-l-elohe-Israel......Gen. xxxiii. 20.
A-chan...............Joshua vii. 1.
D-evil...............Eph. vi 11.

KEY TO ENIGMA NO. 116.—ADD TO YOUR FAITH, VIRTUE.—
2 Peter i. 5.

A-pollos.............Acts xviii. 34.
D-amaris.............Acts xvii. 34.
D-agon...............1 Sam. v. 2.

T-atnai..............Ezra v. 3.
O-rnan...............1 Chron. xxi. 18.

Y-arn................1 Kings x. 28.
O-badiah.............Obadiah i.
U-z..................Job i. 1.
R-ehoboth............Gen. xxvi. 22.

F-estus..............Acts xxiv. 27.
A-rchippus...........Phil. ii.
I-shbi-benob.........2 Sam. xxi. 16.
T-ebeth..............Esther ii. 16
H-aggeth.............2 Sam. iii. 4.

V-ine................Isaiah v. 7.
I-dumea..............Ezekiel xxxv. 15
R-aguel..............Num. x. 29.
T-oi.................2 Sam. viii. 10
U-zziah..............Zec. xiv. 5.
E-domites............Gen. xxvi. 9.

**KEY TO ENIGMA NO. 117.—"BE GLAD IN THE LORD."—
Psa. xciv. 34.**

1. B-artimeus..............Mark x. 46.
2. E-lymas................Acts xiii. 4.
3. G-ilgal.................Jud. ii. 1.
4. L-ehi...................Jud. xv. 19
5. A-dam..................Josh. xiii. 16.
6. D-ura..................Dan. iii. 1.
7. I-saac..................Gen. xxvi. 1.
8. N-athan................2 Sam. xii. 13.
9. T-ilgath pileser........2 Chron xxviii. 20.
10. H-iram................1 Kings vii. 45.
11. E-glon................Jud. iii. 14.
12. L-ystra................Acts xiv. 8.
13. O-mri.................1 Kings xvi. 16.
14. R-amah...............1 Sam. ii. 11.
15. D-athan...............2 Kings vi. 13.

**KEY TO ENIGMA NO. 118.—THOU HAST PUT GLADNESS IN MY
HEART.—Psa. iv. 7**

1. T-heshol-d.............Ezek. x. 4.
2. H-ama-n...............Esther vii. 9, 10.
3. O-se-e.................Rom. ix. 25.
4. U-ria-s.................Matt. i. 6.
5. H-erodia-s.............Mark vi. 19.
6. A-bisha-i..............1 Sam. xxvi 8.
7. S-iho-n................Num. xxi. 23
8. T-erapi-m.............Jud. xvii. 5.
9. P-rophec-y............2 Peter i. 21.
10. U-zzia-h..............2 Chron. xxvi. 16.
11. T-yr-e................Isaiah xxiii. 8.
12. G-algoth-a............Matt. xxvii. 38.
13. L-odeba-r.............2 Sam. xvii. 27.
14. A-rara-t...............Gen. viii. 20.

SCRIPTURE ENIGMAS.

KEY TO ENIGMA NO. 119.—JEREMIAH and ANATHOTH.—
Jer. i. 1.

J-oshu-a..............Deut. xxxiv. 9.
E-kro-n..............2 Kings i. 2.
R-eb-a...............Num. xxxi. 8.
E-gyp-t..............1 Kings iv. 30.
M-ephiboshet-h.......2 Sam. ix. 6, 7.
I-dd-o...............1 Chron. xxvii. 21.
A-n-t................Prov. vi. 6.
H-orma-h.............Num. xxi. 16.

KEY TO ENIGMA NO 120.—BARNABAS.—Acts iv. 36, 37

1. B-artimaeus ....Mark xlvi. 52.
2. A-himelech..........1 Sam. xxii. 9.
3. R-echabites.........Jer. xxxv.
4. N-ineveh............Jonah iii.
5. A-ssyria............2 Kings xix. 35.
6. B-ow ....Gen. ix. 12.
7. A-rabia.............Cal. i. 7.
8. S-halmaneser........2 Kings xvii. 3.

KEY TO ENIGMA NO. 121.—DAMASCUS—HANANIAH.—Acts i 9

D-ebora-h ....Gen. xxxx. 8.
A-bana-a..............2 Kings v. 12.
M-atta-n..............2 Kings xi. 18.
A-quil-a..............Acts xviii. 2, 3.
S-almo-n..............Ruth iv. 21.
C-ush-i...............2 Sam. xviii. 21.
U-zz-a................1 Chron. xiii. 10
S-ara-h...............Gen. xvii. 15.

KEY TO ENIGMA NO. 122.—DANIEL.

1. D-orcas .... Acts ix. 36.
2. A-bel .... Gen. iv. 8.
3. N-athan............ 2 Sam. xii. 7.
4. I-srael .... Gen. xxvii. 41.
5. E-gypt............. Ex. xiii. 3.
6. L-emuel........... Prov. xxxi. 1.

KEY TO ENIGMA NO. 123.—WASH AND BE CLEAN.—2 Kings v. 1.

1. W-idow............ Luke xxi. 3.
2. A-binadab.......... 1 Sam. xvii. 13.
3. S-hiloh............. 1 Sam. iii. 21.
4. H-adassah.......... Esther ii. 7.
5. A-malkites......... 1 Sam. xxx. 1
6. N-aamah........... Gen. iv. 22.
7. D-amascus .... Acts ix. 19, 20.
8. B-enhadad......... 2 Kings xx. 31.
9. E-phesus.......... Acts xix. 1—9.
10. C-armel............ 1 Sam. xxv. 2, 3.
11. L-ydia............. Acts xvi. 14, 15.
12. E-gypt............. Gen. xvi. 1.
13. A-bsalom........... 2 Sam. xviii. 18.
14. N-isroch .... 2 Kings xxxvi. 37.

KEY TO ENIGMA NO. 124 —PATIENCE.—Rom. v. 3.

1. P-aul .... 1 Tim. i. 1.
2. A-bel .... Gen. iv. 11.
3. T-imothy.......... 2 Tim. iii. 15.
4. I-sraelites......... Exod. xix. 45.
5. E-sau .... Gen. xxv. 33.
6. N-athaniel......... John. ix. 17—49.
7. C-anaan........... Ex. iii. 8.
8. E-phriam.......... Gen. xlviii. 20.

SCRIPTURE ENIGMAS.

KEY TO ENIGMA No. 125.—CLEANSE THOU ME FROM SECRET FAULTS.—Psa. cxcii.

1. C-ain .... Gen. iv. 12.
2. L-amech .... Gen. v. 28.
3. E-ve .... Gen. iii. 20.
4. A-dam .... Gen. iii. 20.
5. N-ehemiah .... Neh. i. 4.
6. S-aul .... 1 Sam. xv. 17-30.
7. E-paphroditus ..... Phil. ii. 25.

8. T-ertius .... Rom. xvi. 22.
9. H-achilah .... 1 Sam. xxiii. 19.
10. O-ded .... 2 Chron. xxviii. 9.
11. U-rijah .... 2 Kings xvi. 11.

12. M-anoah .... Jud. xiii. 17.
13. E-d .... Josh. xxii. 34.

14. F-elix .... Acts xxiv. 27.
15. R-ehoboam .... 2 Chron. x. 13.
16. O-n .... Gen. xli. 45.
17. M-oab .... 2 Kings iii. 27.

18. S-arah .... Gen. xviii. 11.
19. E-sau .... Gen. xxxiii. 18.
20. C-yrus .... Isa. xlv. 1.
21. R-achab .... Jer. xxxv. 6.
22. E-zek .... Gen. xxvi. 21.
23. T-homas .... John xx. 19.

24. F-estus .... Acts xxv. 9-11.
25. A-chan .... Josh. vii. 20.
26. U-zzah .... 2 Sam. vi. 6.
27. L-azarus .... John xi. 43.
28. T-ertullus .... Acts xxiv. 2.
29. S-amuel .... 1 Sam. xv. 25.

CURIOSITIES OF THE BIBLE.

KEY TO ENIGMA NO. 126.—DRAW NIGH TO GOD.—Jas. iv. 8

1. D-aniel................1 Chron. iii. 1.
2. R-iblah ....2 Kings xxv. 6.
3. A-haziahs...........2 Kings xi. 1.
4. In-a-well ....2 Sam. xvii. 18.
5. N-ob.. ....1 Sam xxii. 19.
6. I-shbi-benob.. ......1 Sam. xxi. 16.
7. G-oliath.... ....1 Sam. xvi. 23.
8. H-anani.............2 Chron. xvi. 7.
9. T-hebez............Jud. ix. 50-54.
10. O-rpah..............Ruth i. 14.
11. G-adara... . .....Mark v. 1-9.
12. O-rnan.............1 Chron. xxi. 18.
13. D-othan............2 Kings xi. 13.

KEY TO ENIGMA NO. 127.—I WILL COME AGAIN.—John xiv 3

1. I-ssachar...........Gen. lix. 14.
2. W-isdom...........Prov. viii. 30.
3. I-saac.............Gen. xxi. 16.
4. L-evites..... ......Num. i. 50.
5. L-evi..............Jud. xv. 9.
6. C-ain .. ..Gen. iv. 16.
7. O-badiah...........1 Kings xviii. 4.
8. M-elchizedec. .....Gen. xv. 19.
9. E-li...............1 Sam. iii. 13.
10. A-hitophells........2 Sam. xvii. 7.
11. G-omorah.......... Gen. xix. 28.
12. A-himaaz..........2 Sam. xvii. 17.
13. I-chabod ....1 Sam. iv. 22.
14. N-ebo...............Deut. xxxiv. 1, 5.

SCRIPTURE ENIGMAS.

KEY TO ENIGMA NO. 128.—JESUS WEPT. John. xi. 35.

1. J-oppa . . . . Acts ix. 39.
2. E-limelech . . . . Ruth i. 2.
3. S-hephariah . . . . 2 Sam. iii. 4.
4. U-zziah . . . . 2 Chron. xxvi.
5. S-tephanas . . . . 2 Cor. xv. 25.

6. W-onderful . . . . Isa. ix. 6.
7. E-liab . . . . 1 Sam. xvii. 28.
8. P-adanaram . . . . Gen. xxviii.
9. T-erah . . . . Gen. xi. 31.

KEY TO ENIGMA NO. 129.—HOREB.—Ex. xvii. 6 ; 1 Cor. x. 4

1. H-ezekiah . . . . 2 Kings xx. 1.
2. O-n . . . . Gen. xli. 45.
3. R-aamses . . . . Ex. i. 2.
4. E-noch . . . . Gen. 22-29.
5. B-abel . . . . Gen. x. 10.

KEY TO ENIGMA NO. 130.—AGABUS.—Acts xi., 27 ; xxi. 10.

1. A-sher . . . . Deut. xxxiii. 25.
2. G-ershom . . . . Ex. ii. 22.
3. A-mmiel . . . . Num. xiii. 12.
4. B-alaam . . . . Num. xxiv. 17.
5. U-r of the Chaldees . . Gen. xi. 27.
6. S-hishak . . . . 2 Chron. xii. 2.

KEY TO ENIGMA NO. 131.—OVERCOME EVIL WITH GOOD.—
Rom. xii. 21.

1. O-phir.. ....2 Chron. viii. 18.
2. V-ine...............Ps. lxxx. 8; Is. v. 1.
3. E-zekiel........ ...Ezekiel i. 1.
4. R-echabites.........Jer. xxxv.
5. C-ain ....Gen. iv. 8.
6. O-thniel............Jud. i. 12, 13.
7. M-ary..............Ex. x. 20; 1 Chron. iv. 17.
8. E-gypt.............Ex. xx. 33.

9. E-sau...............Gen. xxvii. 34.
10. V-ophsis ....Num. xiii. 14.
11. I-srael.............Gen. xlii. 30.
12. L-azarus............Luke xvi. 20.

13. W-omen of Thebez...Jud. ix. 50.
14. I-bzan..............Jud. xii. 8, 9.
15. T-yre ....Ezek. xxvii. 28.
16. H-ananiah. ....Dan. i. 7.

17. G-erizim............Deut. xi. 29.
18. O-badiah............1 Kings xiii. 4.
19. O-wl...............Isa. xiii. 19.
20. D-aniel............Ezek. xiv. 14 ; Dan. xiv. 14

KEY TO ENIGMA NO. 132.—EZRA.—Chap. xii. 6.

1. E-l-beth-el...........Gen. xxxv. 7.
2. Z-ipporah ....Ex. xviii. 1.
3. R-uth...............Ruth i. 16.
4. A-sahel ....2 Sam. ii 18.

SCRIPTURE ENIGMAS.

KEY TO ENIGMA NO. 133.—CAPERNAUM.—Matt. xi. 23.

1. C-horazin.............Luke x. 13.
2. A-ntioch.............Acts xi. 26.
3. P-ergamos...........Rev. ii. 12.
4. E-phesus............Acts xix. 1.
5. R-ome...............Acts xxviii. 30.
6. N-ineveh............Jonah iii. 5.
7. A-thens.............Acts xvii. 23.
8. U-z.................Job i. 1.
9. M-achpel............Gen. xxiii. 17.

KEY TO ENIGMA NO. 134.—"LET NOT YOUR HEART BE TROUBLED."

1. L-aodicean..........Rev. iii. 14.
2. E-phesus............
3. T-hyatira...........Rev. ii. 18-28.

4. N-icodemus..........John iii. 1-21.
5. O-nesiphorus........2 Tim. i. 16-18.
6. T-imothy............

7. Y-oke...............Matt. xi. 18.
8. O-lives, Mount of...Acts i. 12.
9. U-nity..............Ephes iv. 3.
10. R-edeemer..........Psa. xix. 14.

11. H-annah............1 Sam. i. 14.
12. E-li...............1 Sam. i. 17.
13. A-saph.............1 Chron. xxv. 1.
14. R-amoth Gilead.....Deut. iv. 34.
15. T-iberias, Sea of..John xxi. 1.

16. B-ethesda, Pool of..John v. 2.
17. E-utychus..........Acts xx. 9.

18. T-yre.............Isaiah xxiii.
19. R-ezin............2 Kings xv. 34.
20. O-badiah..........1 Kings xviii. 4.
21. U-riah............2 Sam. xi. 15.
22. B-athsheba ....2 Sam. xi. 3
23. L-odebar..........2 Sam. ix. 4, 5.
24. E-sther...........Esther viii.
25. D-avid............Matt. i. 1.

KEY TO ENIGMA NO. 135.—THE TWO COWS THAT DREW THE ARK UPON ITS RETURN TO ISRAEL.—1 Samuel vi. 7—14.

KEY TO ENIGMA NO. 136.—THE WINDOW FROM WHICH EUTYCHUS FELL.—Acts xx. 9.

KEY TO ENIGMA NO. 137.—JOSEPH'S COFFIN.—Gen. l. 26; Exod. xiii 19; Josh. xxiv. 32.

KEY TO ENIGMA NO. 138.—"ABBA."—Mark xiv. 36; Rom. viii. 15; Gal. iv. 6.

KEY TO ENIGMA NO. 139.—GRACE—GLORY.

1. G-odliness...........2 Peter i. 6.
2. R-ighteous...........1 Peter iv. 18.
3. A-ssurance...........Heb. vi. 11.
4. C-onfidence..........1 John v. 14.
5. E-lection............Rom. ix. 11, 12; 2 Peter i. 10.

1. G-ain...............1 Tim. vi. 6.
2. L-ove...............1 Cor. viii. 13.
3. O-mega..............Rev. i. 2; xxii. 13
4. R-est...............2 Thess. i. 7.
5. Y-ea................2 Cor. i. 10.

KEY TO ENIGMA NO. 140.—THE NIGHT COMETH.—John ix. 4

T-heophilus.........Luke i. 3; Acts i. 50.
H-azeroth...........Num. xii. 15, 16.
E-phphatha..........Mark vii. 34.

SCRIPTURE ENIGMAS

N-imrod .... Gen. x. 8, 9.
I-saac ... ...Gen. xxiv. 63.
G-ershom .. ..Exodus ii. 22.
H-iddekel. ... ... .Gen. ii. 14.
T-roas .. ..2 Tim. iv. 3.

C-ana ....John xxi. 2.
O-badiah.. ....1 Kings xviii. 5, 6.
M-anasseh ... . ..2 Kings xx. 21.
E-non ... .John iii. 23.
T-imothy..........Tim. iv. 12.
H-aran ....Gen. xi. 27.

KEY TO ENIGMA NO. 141.—JEZEBEL—OBADIAH.—
2 Kings xviii. 4.

J-ethr-o ....Exodus iii. 1.
E-liashi-b..........Neh. viii. 4, 5.
Z-ib-a ....2 Sam. ix.
E-lda-d ....Num. xi. 26–29.
B-eer-lahai-ro-i.... .Gen. xvi. 6–15.
E-lish-a .... 2 Kings iv. 14. 3.
L-amec-h.. ....Gen. v. 80; vi. 8; xxii. 7, 5.

KEY TO ENIGMA NO. 142.—ABRAHAM—BY FAITH.—Rom iv

1. A-binada-b..........1 Sam. vii. 1.
2. B-ethan-y ....Mark xiv. 3.
3. R-oo-f.... . ...Mark ii. 4.
4. A-dmath-a.. ....Esther i. 14.
5. H-ophn-i ....1 Sam. iv. 11.
6. A-rara-t ....Gen. viii. 4–20.
7. M-oria-h ....Gen. xxii. 2, 9, 10

KEY TO ENIGMA NO. 143.—MELCHIZEDEK.—Gen xiv. 18; Psalm cx. 4.

1 M-ar-*k*..............Acts xii. 12; xv. 37, 39.
2 E-v-*e*..............Gen. iii. 6.
3. L-aha-*d*.............1 Chron. iv. 2.
4 C-hlo-*e*.............1 Cor. i. 4.
5. H-aru-*z*............2 Kings xxi. 19.
6 I.................Personal pronoun.

KEY TO ENIGMA NO. 144.—" REST IN THE LORD."—Psalm xxxvii. 7.

R-abbath..........2 Sam. xi. 1.
E-knon............2 Kings i. 2.
S-amaria..........
T-admor..........1 Kings ix. 18.
I-shmael..........Gen. xvii. 20.
N-ahash..........1 Sam. xi. 1.
T-arshish.........Jonah i. 3.
H-iel.............1 Kings xvi. 34.
E-bedmelech......Jer. xxxviii. 12, 13.
L-emuel..........Prov. xxxi. 1.
O-livet...........3 Sam. xv. 30.
R-ipzah..........2 Sam. xxi. 8.
D-amascus........Gen. xv. 2.

KEY TO ENIGMA NO. 145.—HADASSAH—MORDECAI.—Esther ii. 7.

1. H-ira-*m*...............1 Kings v. 1, 15.
2. A-hi-*o*................1 Sam. vi. 3.
3 D-ebi-*r*...............Josh. x, 3, 27.
4. A-ta-*d*................Gen. i. 10, 11.
5. S-alom-*e*..............Mark xvi. 1.
6. S-ado-*c*...............Matt. i. 14.
7. A-bagth-*a*.............Esther i. 10.
8. H-ega-*i*...............Esther ii. 8.

SCRIPTURE ENIGMAS.

KEY TO ENIGMA NO. 146.—GIDEON—PHURAH.—
Judges ii. 9, 11.

1. G-at-*h* . . . . 2 Sam. xxi. 22.
2. I-r-*a* . . . . 2 Sam. xx. 26.
3. D-eka-*r* . . . . 1 Kings iv. 9.
4. E-lih-*u* . . . . Job xxxii. 1, 6.
5. O-phra-*h* . . . . Judges vi. 11, 14; viii. 32.
6. N-e-*p*-(heg) . . . . Exodus vi. 21; Num. xvi.

KEY TO ENIGMA NO. 147.

1. Rain . . . . Isaiah lv. 10.
2. Bow . . . . Lam. ii. 4.
3. Rainbow . . . . Gen. xii 12, 17.

KEY TO ENIGMA NO. 148.

1. Fig.   2. Tree.
Whole, Fig-tree. Luke xiii. 6; Mark ix. 13, 14, 20, 21.

KEY TO ENIGMA NO 149.—RICHES.

1. R.uby . . . . Prov. xxxi. 10.
2. I-dol . . . . 2 Cor. viii. 4.
3. C-amel . . . . Matt. xix. 24.
4. H-eavens . . . . Psalm viii. 3.
5. E-nd . . . . 1 Peter iv. 7.
6. S-pikenard . . . . John xii. 3.

KEY TO ENIGMA NO. 150.—ASA—EVE.—2 Chron. xv.; Gen iii

1. A-b-*e*-l . . . . 1 Sam. vi. 18.
2. S-e-*v*-an . . . . Esther viii. 9.
3. A-r-*e*-tas . . . . 2 Cor. xi. 31.

KEY TO ENIGMA NO. 151.—SERPENT.—2 Cor. ii. 8

1. S-ight................Luke iv. 18.
2. E-yes................John xi. 15.
3. R-est................Matt. ix. 28.
4. P-erdition............2 Peter iii. 7.
5. E-lements............2 Peter iii. 10.
6. N-ails................John xx. 25.
7. T-hieves.............Matt. xxvii. 38.

KEY TO ENIGMA NO. 152.—SOLOMON

1. Beth-*s*-aida...........Matt. ii. 21.
2. Cr-*o*-b...............2 Sam. xxi. 18, 19.
3. Beth-*l*-ehem..........Mic. v. 2.
4. N-*o*-b...............1 Sam. xxii. 9, 19.
5. Ra-*m*-ah.............Jer. xxxi. 15, 17.
6. Ar-*o*-er.............Deut. ii. 36.
7. Tim-*n*-ath...........Jud. 14.

KEY TO ENIGMA NO. 153.—SENNACHERIB—ADRAMMELECH.-
Isa. xxxvii. 37.

1. S-arept-*a*............Luke iv. 25, 26.
2. E-lda-*d*..............Num. xi. 26, 28.
3. N-ebuchadnezza-*r*.....Daniel iv. 31, 36.
4. N-ehust-*a*............2 Kings xxiv. 8, 15.
5. A-mra-*m*..............1 Chron. vi. 3.
6. C-apernau-*m*..........Matt. xi. 13.
7. H-eg-*e*...............Esther i. 3.
8. E-ge-*l*...............2 Sam. xx. 19.
9. R-om-*e*...............1 Tim. i. 16, 17.
10. I-saa-*c*..............Gen. xvii. 19.
11. B aalbert-*h*   ...... Judges viii. 33.

SCRIPTURE ENIGMAS.

KEY TO ENIGMA NO. 154.—THE BREASTPLATE—URIM AND THUMMIM.

1. T-oh-*u*..............1 Sam. i. 50.
2. H-adadeze-*r*..........2 Sam. viii. 3.
3. E-l-*i*................1 Sam. iv. 19, 18.

4. B-ochi-*m*............Jud. ii. 4, 5.
5. R-eb-*a*..............Josh. xiii. 21.
6. E-tha-*n*.............Psa. 89—title.
7. A-hilu-*d*............2 Sam. viii. 16
8. S-auballa-*t*.........Neh. ii. 10.
9. T-abera-*h*...........Num. xi. 3.

10. P-all-*u*............1 Chron. v. x, 2, 3.
11. L-eshe-*m*...........Josh. xix. 47; Gen xxx 6
12. A-krabbi-*m*.........Num. xxxiv. 4.
13. T-o-*i*..............2 Sam. viii. 9, 10.
14. E-liaki-*m*..........2 Kings xviii. 18.

KEY TO ENIGMA, NO. 155.—DAVID.

1. D-evil...............1 Pet. v. 8.
2. A-quila..............Acts xviii. 2, 3.
3. V-eil................Ruth iii. 15.
4. I-dolatry............Ezek. xx. 16.
5. D-aniel..............Dan. vi. 22.

KEY TO ENIGMA, NO. 156.—GOD IS LOVE.

1. G-oliath.............1 Sam. xvii. 4—10
2. O-badiah.............1 Kings xviii. 4.
3. D-avid...............Psalms.

4. I-shmael.............Gen. xxi. 13.
5. S-aul................1 Sam xv.

6. L-ydia...............Acts xvi. 14.
7. O-mri................1 Kings xvi. 23, 24.
8. V-ashti..............Esther i. 11, 12.
9. E-lijah..............2 Kings ii. 9—15

KEY TO ENIGMA, NO. 157.—"TAKE FAST HOLD OF INSTRUCTION."—Proverbs iv. 13.

1. T-arshish......................Jonah i. 3.
2. A-braham ....Gen. xviii. 7, 8.
3. K-idron............................2 Sam. xv. 23.
4. E-zra...............................Ezra vii. 6.
5. F-elix .. ..Acts xxiv. 25, 26.
6. A-aron............................Exod. xxxii. 22—24.
7. S-himei.........................2 Sam. xvi. 5, 6.
8. T-imothy.......................2 Tim. iv. 13
9. H-iram..........................1 Kings v. 9, 10.
10. O-phir..........................1 Kings ix. 28.
11. L-azarus......................John xi. 43, 44.
12. D-emas........................2 Tim. iv. 10.
13. O-nesimus ....Philemon 10.
14. F-elix..........................Acts xxiii. 23, 24, 31.
15. I-saac..........................Gen. xxii. 9.
16. N-aboth.......................1 Kings xxi. 1—4.
17. S-hiboleth....................Judges xii. 5, 6
18. T-rogyllium...................Acts xx. 15.
19. R-amah........................1 Sam. ii. 11.
20. U-zzah.........................2 Sam. vi. 6, 7.
21. C-ain...........................Gen. iv. 5, 8.
22. T-imothy......................2 Tim. iii. 15.
23. I-shbosheth...................2 Sam. iv. 5, 6.
24. O-nesiphorus.................2 Tim. i. 16.
25. N-icodemus ....John iii. 1, 2.

KEY TO ENIGMA, NO. 158.—"WAIT ON THE LORD."—Psalm xxvii. 14.

1. W-idow of Nain................Luke vii. 12.
2. A-braham.......................Gen. xii. 12, 13.
3. I-shmael........................Gen. xxi. 18.
4. T-imothy........................2 Tim. i. 5 ; iii. 15.

SCRIPTURE ENIGMAS.

5. O-nesimus..................Philemon 10.
6. N-ehemiah..................Neh. i. 3, 4.

7. T-abitha...................Acts ix. 39, 40.
8. H-aggai....................Hag. i. 3, 4.
9. E-lijah....................1 Kings xviii.

10. L-ot......................Gen. xiv. 14.
11. O-badiah..................1 Kings xviii. 7—9.
12. R-amah....................1 Sam. xxv. 1.
13. D-avid....................1 Sam. xiii. 14.

KEY TO ENIGMA, NO. 159.—" NOT SLOTHFUL IN BUSINESS."—
Romans xii. 11.

1. N-athaniel.................John i. 47.
2. O-g........................Numb. xxi. 33.
3. T-abeel....................Ezra. iv. 7.

4. S-olomon...................1 Kings x. 1.
5. L-amech....................Gen. iv. 23.
6. O-nesiphorus...............2 Tim. i. 16.
7. T-erah.....................Gen. xi. 31.
8. H-erod.....................Matt. ii. 3.
9. F-elix.....................Acts xxiv. 1—22.
10. U-riah....................2 Sam. xi. 14—17.
11. L-amentations.............Lam. iii.

12. I-shmael..................2 Kings xxv. 25.
13. N-aboth...................1 Kings xxi. 16.

14. B-artimæus................Mark x. 46—49.
15. U-z.......................Job i. 1.
16. S-isera...................Judges iv. 22.
17. I-mmanuel.................Isa. vii. 14.
18. N-ahash...................1 Sam. xi. 2.
19. E-liezer..................Gen. xv. 2; xxiv 12.
20. S-hadrach.................Dan. iii. 13.
21. S-imeon...................Luke ii 34, 35.

KEY TO ENIGMA, NO. 160.—"GOD IS LOVE."—1 John iv. 8.

1. G-aza's strong gates Samson bore quite away. Judg. xvi 2. 3.
2. O-nesimus' debt Paul said he would pay. Philem. 19.
3. D-agon before the ark fell flatly down. 1 Sam. v. 3, 38.
4. I-chabod's father died beneath God's frown. 1 Sam. iv. 21
5. S-anballat's servant bore a letter forth. Neh. vi. 5, 6
6. L-aban's large flocks were bless'd for Jacob's worth. Gen xxx. 30.
7. O-thniel by brav'ry won his cousin's hand. Jud. i. 13.
8. V-ashti refused t' obey her lord's command. Esth. i. 12.
9. E-gypt for many years the Hebrews fed. (Gen. xlvii. 27.)

Till forth from thence they were by Moses led.
That *God is Love* should cheer each anxious heart,
And from that love nought can his children part.

KEY TO ENIGMA, NO. 161.—"CEASE TO DO EVIL."—Isaiah i. 16.

1. C-rispus ....1 Cor. i. 14; Acts xviii. 8
2. E-lisha........................2 Kings ii. 11, 12.
3. A-bimelech....................Judges ix. 48, 49.
4. S-olomon......................1 Kings iv. 33
5. E-hud.........................Judges iii. 15.
6. T-harshish....................1 Kings x. 22.
7. O-rnan's......................2 Chron. iii. 1.
8. D-avid's......................2 Sam. xxi. 17.
9. O-thniel. ....Judges iii. 9—11.
10. E-glon........................Judges iii. 14.
11. V-ashti.......................Esther i. 9.
12. I-shbosheth...................2 Sam. iii. 15, 16.
13. L-ot..........................Gen xiii. 10, 11.

SCRIPTURE ENIGMAS.

KEY TO ENIGMA, NO. 162.—"PRAY WITHOUT CEASING."—
1 Thessalonians v. 17.

1. P-hilip.........................Acts viii. 31—35.
2. R-ebekah ....Gen. xxiv. 63, 64.
3. A-chan........................Josh. vii. 24, 25.
4. Y-oung pigeon.............Lev. xii. 6.

5. W-indow.....................2 Kings ix. 32, 33.
6. I-shmael.....................Gen. xxv. 12—16.
7. T-ekoah......................2 Sam. xiv. 1—20.
8. H-annah.....................1 Sam. ii. 1.
9. O-mri.........................1 Kings xvi. 23, 24.
10. U-zziah.....................2 Chron. xxvi. 9, 10.
11. T-aberah...................Numb. xi. 2, 3.

12. C-aleb......................{ Josh. xv. 14 (See Numb. xiii. 33).
13. E-sau.......................Gen. xxv. 27, 28.
14. A-maziah..................2 Chron. xxv. 6, 11.
15. S-aul........................1 Sam. xxxi. 4.
16. I-saac.......................Gen. xxiv. 2, 3.
17. N-athaniel................John i. 47.
18. G-ibeon....................Josh. x. 12.

KEY TO ENIGMA, NO. 163.—MIZPAH.—Genesis xxxi. 48, 49

1. M-nason (Calmet)..............Acts xxi. 16.
2. I-chabod.........................1 Sam. iv. 21.
3. Z-iklag...........................1 Sam. xxvii. 6.
4. P-aul.............................Acts ix. 15.
5. A-gag............................1 Sam. xv. 33.
6. H-aman.........................Esther vii. 10.

KEY TO ENIGMA, 164.—"PRINCE OF PEACE."—Isaiah ix. 6

1. P-isgah....................Num. xxiii. 14.
2. R-ebekah..................Gen. xxvii. 41—46.
3. I-conium...................Acts xiv. 1—6.
4. N-athaniel.................John i. 48.
5. C-ushi.....................2 Sam. xviii. 31, 32.
6. E-lhanan...................2 Sam. xxi. 19.
7. O-thniel...................Judges i. 12, 13.
8. F-elix.....................Acts xxiv. 25.
9. P-haraoh...................Gen. xii. 18—20.
10. E-zra.....................Ezra vii. 6.
11. A-haziah..................2 Kings ix. 27.
12. C-apernaum................Matt. iv. 13.
13. E-noch....................Gen. v. 24.

KEY TO ENIGMA NO.165.—"SEARCH THE SCRIPTURES."—*John* v.3b

1. S-hibboleth................Judges xii. 5, 6.
2. E-vening...................Gen. i. 5.
3. A-lmighty..................{ Job xxxvii. 23; Jer xxxii. 17.
4. R-od (Aaron's).............Numb. xvii. 8.
5. C-ountless.................Rev. vii. 9.
6. H-o, every one that thirsteth......Isa. lv. 1.
7. T-urn ye, turn ye..........Ezek. xxxiii. 11.
8. H-ead......................Eph. v. 23.
9. E-ternity..................Isa. lvii. 15.
10. S-pirit...................John iv. 23, 24
11. C-ome.....................Rev. xxii. 17.
12. R-eady....................Matt. xxiv. 44.
13. I-mage....................Gen i. 26.
14. P-eace....................John xx. 26.
15. T-oil.....................Matt. vi. 28, 29.
16. U-rim.....................Numb. xxvii. 21.
17. R-eed.....................Matt. xi. 7.
18. E-mpty....................Luke i. 53.
19. S-aved....................1 Cor. v. 5.

SCRIPTURE ENIGMAS.

KEY TO ENIGMA NO. 166.—"CONSIDER THE LILIES."—
Matt. vi. 28.

1. C-hedorlaomer.................Gen. xiv. 17.
2. O-mri.......................1 Kings xvi. 28.
3. N-ebuchadnezzar..............Dan. iv. 33.
4. S-aul........................1 Sam. xxviii. 8
5. I-shobosheth.................2 Sam. iv. 7.
6. D-avid.......................2 Sam. i. 17.
7. E-vil-merodach...............Jer. lii. 31-34.
8. R-enoboam....................1 Kings xii. 8.

9. T-iglath-pileser.............2 Kings xvi. 7.
10. H-ezekiah...................2 Kings xix. 15-19.
11. E-glon......................Judges iii. 21, 25.

12. L-emuel.....................Prov. xxxi. 1.
13. I-nner court................Esther v. 1.
14. L-achish....................2 Chron. xi. 9 ; xxv. 27
15. I-saiah.....................2 Kings xx. 5-7.
16. E-sarhaddon.................2 Kings xxi. 37.
17. S-olomon. ....2 Chron. i. 12.

KEY TO ENIGMA NO. 167.—"BE COURTEOUS."—1 *Peter* iii. 8.

1. B-arzillai ....2 Sam. xvii. 27-29.
2. E-li ....1 Sam. iv. 17, 18.
3. C-ain........................Gen. iv. 9, 10.
4. O-bed........................2 Chron. xxvii. 9.
5. U-riah.......................2 Sam. xi. 15-17.
6. R-euben ....Gen. xxxviii. 26.
7. T-obiah. ....Neh. iv. 3.
8. E-hud........................Judges iii. 15, 16.
9. O-bed........................Ruth iv. 14-17.
10. U-zzah.....................2 Sam. vi. 6, 7.
11. S-amson....................Judges xvi. 17-20 and 30

KEY TO ENIGMA NO. 168.—STEPHEN.—*Acts* vii. 59. ANTIPAS.—*Rev.* ii. 13.

1. S-arept-a.......................Luke iv. 26.
2. T-ribulatio-n.... ....John xvi. 33.
3. E-gyp-t.................. ....Deut. vii. 8.
4. P-hilipp-i......................Acts xvi. 12, 25.
5. H-el-p....... . ...Ps. lx. 11.
6. E-zr-a..........................Ezra vii. 6, 10.
7. N-icodemu-s...................John iii. 1, 2; xix. 39.

KEY TO ENIGMA NO. 169.—GERSHOM.—*Exodus* xviii. 3; 1 *Chron.* vi. 2 3; *Numb.* iv. 15. ELEAZAR.—*Exodus* xxxviii. 1.

1. G-alile-e........... ....Luke iii. 1.
2. E-ba-l.......................Deut. xi. 29.
3. R-om-e.......................Acts xviii. 2; Luke ii. 1
4. S-amari-a................ ....1 Kings xvi. 24.
5. H-u-z........................Gen. xxii. 20, 21.
6. O-she-a......................Numbers xiii 8
7. M-achi-r................ ....{ 2. Sam. ix. 4, and xvii 27, etc.

KEY TO ENIGMA NO. 170.—IMMANUEL.—*Isaiah* vii. 14.

I-saiah............... ....Isaiah ix. 6, 7.
M-artha............... ....Luke x. 40, 41.
M-ary........................Luke x. 39.
A-nna.......................Luke ii. 36-38.
N-icodemus............... ......John xix. 39, 40.
U-r..... ....Gen. xi. 28, 31.
E-mmaus.......................Luke xxiv. 13-35.
L-azarus. ....John xi. 43, 44

SCRIPTURE ENIGMAS.

KEY TO NEW YEARS ENIGMA NO. 171.—"LOOKING UNTO JESUS."—*Heb.* xii. 2.

1. L-ydia .... Acts xvi. 14, 15.
2. O-nesiphorus .... 2 Tim. i. 16-18.
3. O-nesimus .... Philemon, ver. 10, 11
4. K-orah .... Numb. xvi. 32, 33.
5. I-saiah .... Isaiah. ix. 6.
6. N-icodemus .... John iii. 1.
7. G-aius .... 3 John, ver. 1.

8. U-zziah .... 2 Chron. xxvi. 19, 20
9. N-athanael .... John i. 45-49.
10. T-ychicus .... Ephesians vi. 21.
11. O-badiah .... 1. Kings xviii. 3, 4.

12. J-udas .... Matt. xxv. 47.
13. E-lisha .... 2. Kings v. 10-14.
14. S-tephen .... Acts vii. 59, 60.
15. U-r .... Genesis xi. 31.
16. S-imon .... Luke xxii 31-34

KEY TO ANAGRAM NO. 1.

Nos. 6, 5, 1, 2, 3, Haman..Esther vii. 10.
" 3, 4, 5, 6,   Noah....Gen. x. 1.
" 6, 2, 1,   Ham....Gen. x. 6.
" 1, 2, 3,   Man....Gen. iii. 24.
" 1, 2, 4, 3,   Moon...Josh. xv. 55.
" 3, 2, 5, 1,   Naam...1 Chron. iv. 15.
" 3, 4,   No......Jer. lvi. 25.
" 4, 3,   On.....Gen. xli. 45.

KEY TO ANAGRAM NO. 2. —NEBUCHADNEZZAR —Dan ii. 28

1. N-adab............... Levit. x. 1-2.
2. E-zra ....Ezra vii. 6.
3. B-arcah .... Jer. xxxvi. 4—31.
4. U-zzah ....1 Sam. vi. 6, 7.
5. C-herub....... .....Exod. xxxvii. 8.
6. H-eber·····..........Jud. iv. 17.
7. A-bner ... .1 Sam. xiv. 50.
8. D-ura...............Dan. iii. 1.
9. N-eah..............Josh. xix. 13.
10. E-den.............Gen. ii. 8.
11. Z-ered ....Deut. ii. 14, 13.
12. Z-abud............1 Kings iv. 5.
13. A-zzah ....Deut. ii. 13.
14. R-eu...... ....Gen. xi. 18.

ANSWERS TO SCRIPTURE ANAGRAMS.

KEY TO ANAGRAM NO. 3.

NEBUCHADNEZZAR.

N-er	1 Sam. xiv. 50.
E-zra	Ezra vii. 11.
B-ezer	Deut. iv. 43.
U-z	Job i. 1.
C-ana	John ii. 1.
H-ur	Exod. xvii. 12.
A-bana	2 Kings v. 12.
D-an	Gen. xlix. 16.
N-un	Numbers xxvii. 18.
E-hud	Judges iii. 15.
Z-eeb	Judges vii. 25.
Z-ebah	Judges viii. 5.
A-bner	2 Sam. ii. 8.
R-euben	Deut. xxxiii. 6.

KEY TO ANAGRAM NO. 4.

JERUSALEM.

J-ael	Judges v. 24.
E-lam	Gen. x. 22.
Ram	1 Chron. ii. 9.
U-r	Gen. xv. 7.
S-amuel	1 Sam. vii. 6.
A-r	Numb. xxi. 28.
L-emuel	Prov. xxxi. 1.
E-sau	Gen. xxxvi. 9.
M-ars Hill	Acts xvii. 22.

CURIOSITIES OF THE BIBLE.

KEY TO BIBLE CHARACTERS, NO. 1. — GAMALIEL. —
Acts v. 34.

1. G-alilee..........................Acts ii. 7.
2. A-nna............................Luke ii. 36.
3. M-nason.........................Acts xxi 16.
4. A-nanias........................Acts v. 5.
5. L-uke...........................2 Tim. iv. 11.
6. I-conium........................Acts xiv. 19.
7. E-mmaus.........................Luke xxiv. 13.
8. L-ydda..........................Acts ix. 32

KEY TO BIBLE CHARACTERS, NO. 2. — AHASUERUS. —
Esther vi. 1.

1. A-bigail........................1 Sam. xxv. 3, 39.
2. H-or............................Numb. xx, 27, 28.
3. A-bner..........................1 Sam. xiv. 50.
4. S-anballat......................Neh. iv. 7.
5. U-zza...........................1 Chron. xiii. 10.
6. E-liezer........................Gen. xv. 2.
7. R-amoth.........................Josh. xx. 8.
8. U-r.............................Gen. xi. 31.
9. S-hiloh.........................Gen. xlix. 10.

KEY TO BIBLE CHARACTERS, NO. 3.—ADULLAM.—1 Samuel
xxii. 1, 2.

1. A-bed-nego......................Dan. iii. 27, 28.
2. D-othan.........................{ Gen. xxxvii. 17; 2 Kings vi. 13—20.
3. U-zziah.........................2 Chron. xxvi. 19, 20.
4. L-aban..........................Gen. xxvii. 43.
5. L-uz............................Gen. xxviii 19.
6. A-chan..........................Josh. vii. 24, 25
7. M-anoah.........................Judges xiii. 2

BIBLE CHARACTERS.   147

KEY TO BIBLE CHARACTERS, NO. 4.—PHILADELPHIA.—Rev. i. 11

1. P-hilemon................Philemon 1, 2.
2. H-erodion................Rom. xvi. 11.
3. I-turæa..................Luke iii 1.
4. L-ystra..................Acts xiv. 19.
5. A-pollos.................Acts xviii. 24.
6. D-amascus................2 Cor. xi. 32, 33
7. E-penetus................Rom. xvi. 5.
8. L-ebbæus.................Matt. x. 3.
9. P-hebe...................Rom. xvi. i. 2.
10. II-erodians.............Matt. xxii. 16.
11. I-talian Band...........Acts x. 1.
22. A-gabus.................Acts xxi. 10.

KEY TO BIBLE CHARACTERS, NO. 5.—ELIMELECH.—Ruth i. 2

1. E-liab...................1 Sam. xvi. 6, 7.
2. L-aish...................Judges xviii. 29
3. I-ssachar ....Gen. xlix. 14.
4. M-achpelah...............Gen. xxiii. 17.
5. E-bed-melech.............Jer. xxxviii. 7—11.
6. L-ebanon................. Deut. iii. 25.
7. E-zion-geber.............1 Kings xxii. 48.
8. C-yrus...................Isa. xliv. 28.
9. II-iel...................1 Kings xvi. 34.

KEY TO BIBLE CHARACTERS, NO. 6.—AHITHOPHEL.—2 Samuel xvii. 1—23.

1. A-bijah ....1 Kings xiv. 13.
2. II-uldah ....2 Chron. xxxiv. 22.
3. I-shmael.................Gen. xvi. 12.
4. T-imnath-heres...........Judges ii. 9
5. H-aman...................Esther vi. 6 ; vii. 10.
6. O-rnan...... .... { 1 Chron. xxi. 23; 2 Sam xxiv. 23.
7. P-i-Hahiroth.............Exod. xiv. 9, 28.
8. H-ebron..................2 Sam. iii. 2, 3.
9. E-ben-ezer...............1 Sam. vii. 12
10. L-amech.................Gen. v. 28, 29

KEY TO BIBLE CHARACTERS, NO. 7.—OBADIAH.—1 Kings xviii. 3.

1. O-rpah.....................Ruth i. 14, 15
2. B-aalah, or Kirjath-jearim........ { 1 Sam. vii. 2; 1 Chron xiii. 6.
3. A-mos......................Amos i. 1; vii. 14, 15.
4. D-aniel....................Daniel vi. 3; v. 29.
5. I-shbi-benob................2 Sam. xxi. 16, 17.
6. A-chsah....................Judges i. 12, 13.
7. H-iel...................... { Josh. vi. 26; 1 Kings xvi. 34.

KEY TO BIBLE CHARACTERS, NO. 8.—REBEKAH.—Genesis xxvii. 6—46.

1. R-ehoboam................1 Kings xii. 13, 19.
2. E-leazar....................Numb. iv. 16.
3. B-alaam....................Numb. xxxi. 8.
4. E-lijah.....................1 Kings xviii. 22; xix. 2, 3
5. K-eilah....................1 Sam. xxiii. v. 12.
6. A-i........................Josh. vii. 5.
7. Hiram.....................1 Kings ix. 27, 28

KEY TO BIBLE CHARACTERS, NO. 9.—BARZILLAI.—1 Sam. xvii. 27—29.

1. B-eersheba................Gen. xxvi. 26—33
2. A-bsolom..................2 Sam. xv. 10.
3. R-echabites................Jer. xxxv. 18, 19.
4. Z-elophehad...............Numb. xxvii. 7.
5. I-chabod...................1 Sam. xiv. 3.
6. L-achish..................2 Kings xiv. 19.
7. L-evites...................Deut. xviii. 1.
8. A-bner....................2 Sam. iii. 30, 38.
9. I-saac.....................Gen. xxii. 7, 8.

BIBLE CHARACTERS. 149

KEY TO BIBLE CHARACTERS, NO. 10.—JEROBOAM.—1 Kings xii. 26—33.

1. J-esse.........................1 Sam. xvii. 58.
2. E-uphrates....................Josh. i. 4.
3. R-amah........................1 Sam. vii. 15—17.
4. O-thniel......................Judges iii. 9, 10.
5. B-athsheba....................1 Kings ii. 13.
6. O-g...........................Numb. xxi. 33—35.
7. A-hio.........................2 Sam. vi. 3.
8. M-ordecai.....................Esther ix. 4.

KEY TO BIBLE CHARACTERS, NO. 11.—GEHAZI.—2 Kings v. 25—27.

1. G-ilgal.......................Josh iv. 20.
2. E-ndor........................1 Sam. xxviii. 7, 9.
3. H-ur..........................Exod. xvii. 12.
4. A-biathar.....................1 Sam. xxii. 20.
5. Z-arephath....................1 Kings xvii. 9, 15, 16.
6. I-ndia........................Esther i. 1.

KEY TO BIBLE CHARACTERS, NO. 12.—CORNELIUS.—Acts x. 1, 2

1. C-laudius Lysias..............Acts xxii. 28; xxiii. 26
2. O-nesiphorus..................2 Tim. i. 16, 17.
3. R-ome.........................Acts xviii. 2.
4. N-ain.........................Luke vii. 11—15.
5. E-uroclydon...................Acts xxvii. 14.
6. L-aodiceans...................Rev. iii. 14—19.
7. I-llyricum....................Rom. xv. 19.
8. U-rbane.......................Rom. xvi. 9.
9. S-usanna......................Luke viii. 3.

KEY TO BIBLE CHARACTERS, NO. 13.—EVIL-MERODACH.— 2 Kings xxv. 27.

1. E-xorcists....................Acts xix. 13.
2. V-eil.........................Ruth iii. 15.
3. I-mage........................1 Sam. xix. 13.
4. L-oaves.......................Lev. xxiii. 17.

5. M-urrain..................Exod. ix. 3.
6. E-gypt....................... { Gen. xxxvii. 28; Matt ii. 13.
7. R-ue........................Luke xi. 42.
8. O-nion.....................Numb. xi. 5.
9. D-oeg......................1 Sam. xxii. 9.
10. A-rgument.................Job. xxiii. 4.
11. C-oat......................Gen. xxxvii. 33.
12. H-usband..................Prov. xii. 4.

KEY TO BIBLE CHARACTERS, NO. 14.—ISHMAEL, ABRAHAM.—
Genesis xxi. 16; xvi. 16

1. I-r-a........................2 Sam. xx. 26.
2. S-egu-b....................1 Kings xvi. 34.
3. H-amo-r....................Gen. xxxiii. 19
4. M-ar-a.....................Ruth i. 20.
5. A-rauna-h..................2 Sam. xxiv. 22.
6. E-thiopi-a..................Acts viii. 27.
7. L-ukewar-m.................Rev. iii. 16.

KEY TO BIBLE CHARACTERS, NO. 15.

The earliest, the deepest, and the most lasting impressions the mind receives are those which the mother imparts. The piety of *Isaac* may in some degree be traced to the faith and prayerfulness of *Sarah* (Heb. ix. 11; Gen. xvii. 15, 16; Gen. xxi. 6). The eminence of Jacob was possibly to some extent to be ascribed to the home influence and special affection of *Rebekah* While Esau was much engaged in the chase, Jacob was under the tuition of his mother. (Gen. xxv. 27, 28). **Moses** and **Aaron** were examples of the holy influence the eminent piety of their mother *Jochebed* had upon them (Exod. ii. 3; Heb. xi. 23). Though **Samson** is an affecting illustration of backsliding from the ways of the Lord, yet his early devotedness to the service of God was doubtlessly owing to the influence of his mother, the prayerful and believing *wife of Manoah* (Judges xiii.) Samuel was born in the atmosphere of *Hannah's* devotion, and his childhood spent under her pious care (1 Sam. i. 27, 28). Other Old Testament worthies might be selected to show the beneficial influence the maternal relation directly or indirectly exerts. The most remarkable proof in the New Testament of the salutary influence of maternal piety is that of *Eunice* and *Lois* on the mind, character, and usefulness of Timothy (2 Tim. i. 5).

Maternal influence, so often used for good, possesses also great power for mischief to the interests of those on whom it is exercised. "As is the mother, so is the daughter." (Ezek. xvi. 44). The wickedness of **Ahaziah** is accounted for on this principle: "His mother *Athaliah* was his counsellor to do wickedly" (2 Chron. xxii. 3). The inspired historian does not leave on record the fact of a YOUNG WOMAN committing such an atrocious deed as to ask that a good and faithful man should be beheaded, without telling the reader she was instructed of *Herodias* her mother to do this thing (Matt. xiv. 6—8).

KEY TO BIBLE CHARACTERS, NO. 16.

Samson, though the strongest man, was so weak when trusting in himself that he was twice ensnared by Philistine women. His strength was not in his hair, but in the Lord; and while his locks were unshorn he retained the outward sign of his devotedness to the Lord. When he parted with his locks he resigned the last sign of his being a Nazarite, his apostasy was complete, and he was the easy victim of his enemies (Judges xvi. 17—20).

Goliath of Gath, the mighty Philistine giant, trusted in the height of his form and the strength of his arm; but he fell before the sling and stone of the shepherd youth who assailed him in the strength of the Lord, and not relying on his own skill strength, or weapons (1 Sam. xvii. 40—45).

Hazael, the king of Syria, relying upon his own moral strength, shrunk from the scenes of infamy which Elisha the prophet predicted he would enact. His self-confidence induced him to exclaim, "But what, is thy servant a dog, that he should do this great thing?" (2 Kings viii. 13.) His subsequent history shows that he exceeded in his doings the wickedness which in his words he deprecated and deemed impossible.

Nebuchadnezzar, trusting in himself and in his vast resources, in the spirit of self-vaunting, walked in his palace, and said "Is not this great Babylon, that I have built for the house of the kingdom by the might of my power, and for the honor of my majesty?" (Dan. iv. 30.) While he was yet boastfully speaking, even in the same hour, he is deprived of his reason, and sent to herd with the beasts of the field. And afterwards he acknowledges his sin, adores the righteousness of God, and leaves on record his testimony, "I, Nebuchadnezzar, praise and extol and honor the King of heaven, all whose works are truth, and his ways judgment: and those that walk in pride he is able to abase" (Dan. iv. 47). The original document containing this testimony Sir Henry Rawlinson has discovered and brought to this country.

Peter the apostle trusted to himself when he said to his Lord, "Though all should be offended, yet will not I" (Mark xiv. 29); and, "Lord, I am ready to go with thee both into prison and to death" (Luke xxii. 33). He failed, and he denied the heavenly Master to whom he had expressed the strongest attachment.

KEY TO BIBLE CHARACTERS, NO. 17.

Nadab and **Abihu**, the sons of Aaron, recklessly entered on the service of the Lord, and "offered strange fire before the Lord, which he commanded them not. And there went out fire from the Lord, and devoured them, and they died before the Lord" (Lev. x. 1, 2).

Miriam treated her brother Moses irreverently, and spake against him, and she was smitten with leprosy, and she was shut out of the camp seven days (Numb. xii. 1—8; 10, 14, 15).

Korah, Dathan, and Abiram formed a conspiracy, and treated Moses with irreverence, and attempted to take upon themselves to offer incense. The earth swallowed up some, and "fire from the Lord consumed the two hundred and fifty men that offered incense" (Numb. xvi. 31—35).

Uzzah irreverently put forth his hand and touched the ark when the oxen shook it. And the anger of the Lord was kindled against Uzzah; and God smote him there for his error, and there he died by the ark of God (2 Sam. vi. 6).

Eutychus, a young man attending the preaching of Paul, fell into a deep sleep. He sunk down with sleep, and "fell down from the third loft, and was taken up dead" (Acts xx. 9).

These are some of the solemn warnings against indifference and irreverence towards holy things and persons; and there are others which may be searched out.

KEY TO BIBLE CHARACTERS, NO. 18.

Enoch walked with God in the exercises of devotion, and he had the testimony that he pleased God, and was translated, that he should not see death (Gen. v. 24; Heb. xi. 5).

Isaac was eminent for his solitary meditation and devotional spirit, and God blessed him, and gave him the desire of his heart (Gen. xxiv. 63, 67).

Jacob lived in the habit of prayer, so that his very dreams were of heaven and God; see the account of the vision of Bethel. But the highest honor on his devotion was reserved for the more extraordinary scene at Peniel, when his name was changed from Jacob to that of Israel, as a memorial that he had power with God" (Gen. xxxii. 28).

God put honor on the devotion of **Elijah**, when he stayed the clouds that they rained not upon the earth for the space of six months, and when he miraculously fed him during that period. Again, in answer to the prayer of Elijah, God caused rain to fall and abundance to appear on the earth (James v. 17. 18).

Hezekiah in his trouble prayed unto the Lord, and the Lord honored him by granting his request, and saying unto him, "I have heard thy prayer, I have seen thy tears: behold I will add unto thy days fifteen years" (Isa. xxxviii. 5).

Daniel maintained his habit of devotion, though death was the sentence which he incurred by calling upon his God. The Lord honored him by shutting the mouths of the lions, to which he had been cast to be devoured (Dan. vi. 27).

The disciples in the upper room at Jerusalem, continuing in devotion for ten days, were honored with the gifts and graces of the Holy Spirit, and endowed with miraculous power (Acts i. 14; ii 4)

KEY TO BIBLE CHARACTERS, NO. 19.

We might answer this question by quoting the greater part of the eleventh chapter of the Epistle to the Hebrews. In addition to the worthies there named, we may notice—**the shepherds**, who showed their faith in the message of the angel by immediately leaving their flocks and going to Bethlehem to see the young child. **Simeon** and **Anna**, watching in the temple, by faith waited for "the consolation of Israel." **The Syrophenician woman**, whose faith sustained her importunity amidst discouragements, until the boon she sought for her daughter was granted. **The woman** who touched the hem of Christ's garment and was healed. Many others of this class may be cited; but the most striking illustration of the power of faith is **the dying thief**, who addressed Christ as "Lord," though in the depth of his humiliation; whose faith saw him entering "paradise," though dying in the greatest ignominy; and who begged an interest in his remembrance as the richest blessing, though he appeared in the extreme of destitution. He realized a living Saviour, though that Saviour was in the agonies of death.

KEY TO BIBLE CHARACTERS, NO. 20.

Isaac is the most remarkable instance of early consecration to God in his voluntary concurrence with the purpose of his father who bound him on the altar to offer him up as a living sacrifice. He was abundantly blessed in his wife Rebekah, in the renewal of the Abrahamic covenant, and in his prosperity in the land of Gerar.

Moses was a child of faith and prayer, and displayed remarkable decision in his youthful days; so that while he was educated by Egyptian tutors in every department of science, he resisted the idolatrous influences, and adhered most firmly to the religion of his pious mother. He was honored of God by being chosen to lead the tribes of Israel, and was favored with more intimate communion with God than any other of the Lord's servants.

Samuel was born in an atmosphere of piety, and when but a child was called of God to the prophetic office. He was blessed and honored of God to the end of his days on earth. He anointed Saul and David, the first and second kings of Israel, and was the medium of communication between God and his people.

David "was but a youth" when he gave himself to the Lord, and he was raised to the throne of Israel.

Josiah, though only a child of eight years when he ascended the throne, yet continued during thirty-one years to reign and to do that which was right in the sight of the Lord (2 Kings xxii. 1, 2).

Jeremiah, though we have no definite data by which we can tell his age when called to be a prophet, yet he must have been very young to justify him in saying, "Ah, Lord God! behold, I cannot speak, for I am a child." He was for many years favored with Divine manifestations, and blessed with holy courage in the performance of his arduous work.

Timothy, from his childhood, was a possessor of eminent piety, and was honored of God as a faithful preacher of the gospel and a recipient of two epistles, which have been documents of reference to the church of Christ in general, and to young ministers in particular.

These and many others illustrate the truth recorded by Samuel, "Them that honor me I will honor; and they that despise me shall be lightly esteemed" (1 Sam. ii. 30).

WHAT CHRISTIANS SHOULD BE

ACCORDING TO THE BIBLE.

Abhorring that which is evil .... Rom. xii. 9
Abstaining from all appearance of evil ...... 1 Thess. v. 22
Always abounding in the work of the Lord ... 1 Cor. xv. 58.
Always confident .... 2 Cor. v. 6.
Approving things that are excellent .... Phil. i. 10.
Asking and receiving........................ 1 Jno. iii. 22.
Avenging not themselves .... Rom. xii. 19.
Avoiding profane and vain babblings .... 1 Tim. vi. 10.
Awaking to righteousness.................... 1 Cor. xv. 34.
Bearing one another's burdens .... Gal. vi. 2.
Believing to the saving of the soul .... Heb. x. 30.
Bewaring of covetousness .... Lu. xii. 15.
Blameless and harmless, the Sons of God....... Phil. ii. 15.
Blessing them which persecute us............ Rom. xii. 14
Boldly saying the Lord is my helper........... He xiii. 6.
Bringing forth fruit unto God................ Rom. vii. 4.
Calling upon the name of Jesus Christ our Lord.. 1 Cor. i. 2.
Careful for nothing.......................... Phil. iv 6.
Careful [only] to maintain good works.......... Tit. iii 3.
Casting all our care upon Him................ 1 Pe. v. 7.
Circumcised without hands .... Col. ii. 11
Cleansed from all filthiness.................. 1 Cor. vii. 1.
Cleansed with the blood of Christ from all sin ... 1 Jno. i. 9

Note. The Key or answers are numbered separately, which accounts for the lapse in paging.

Cleaving to that which is good. .... Rom. xii. 9
Clothed with humility........... .... 1 Pe. v. 5
Coming continually unto Christ............... 1 Pe. ii. 4
Considering Christ Jesus..................... Heb. iii. 1.
Content with such things as we have.... ...... Heb. xiii. 5
Continuing constant in prayer........ .. ....Rom. xii. 12.
Crucified by the cross unto the world......... ..Gal. vi. 14.
Dead to sin... .... Rom. vi. 2
Dead to the law.............................. Rom. vii. 4.
Declaring plainly that we seek a country........ Heb. xi. 14.
Delivered from the power of darkness........... Col. i. 13
Denying self, or the old nature............. . Mat. xvi. 14.
Discerning both good and evil.............. ... Heb. v. 14.
Distributing to the necessity of saints... ......Rom. xii 13.
Dwelling in love and in God................. 1 Jno. iv. 16.
Earnestly contending for the faith ...'............ Jude 3.
Earnestly desiring our house from heaven.......2 Cor. v. 2.
Edifying one another....................... 1 Thes. v. 11.
Endeavoring to keep the unity of the Spirit......Eph. iv. 3.
Enduring hardness........................... 2 Tim. ii. 3.
Entering with boldness into the holiest ....Heb. x. 19.
Espoused to one husband..................... 2 Cor. xi. 2.
Excelling to the edifying of the Church...... 1 Cor. xiv. 12.
Exhorting one another as the day approaches.....Heb. x. 25.
Faithful stewards........................... 1 Cor. iv. 2.
Fearing God...... ....1 Pe. ii. 17.
Fervent in spirit..................... ...Rom. xii. 11.
Fervently loving one another with a pure heart...1 Pe i. 22.
Filled with all the fulness of God.......... . Eph. iii. 19.
Filled with the Spirit........................ Eph. v. 18.
Filled with the fruits of righteousness........... Phil. i. 11.
Following peace with all men, and holiness..... Heb. xii. 14
Following the steps of Jesus................... 1 Pe. ii. 21.
Forbearing one another in love....... .... Eph. iv. 2.
Forgiving one another................... ...... Col. iii. 13.
Fruitful in every good work..................... Col. i. 10.
Gentle unto all men.... .. .. 2 Tim ii. 24

WHAT CHRISTIANS SHOULD BE.

Glorifying God in body and in spirit.......... 1 Cor. vi. 20.
Given to hospitality......................... Rom. xii. 13
Giving diligence to make our calling and election sure ....2 Pe. i. 20.
Giving thanks always for all things... . ...Eph. v. 20
Giving not grudgingly, or of necessity ....2 Cor. ix. 7
Grieving not the Holy Spirit of God ....Eph. iv. 30
Growing in grace and knowledge of Christ.....2 Pe. iii. 18
Happy in bearing reproach for Christ.......... 1 Pe. iv. 14.
Hastening the coming of the day of God ......2 Pe. iii. 12
Having promise of the life that now is and that to come................................1 Tim. iv. 8.
Holding fast that which is good..............1 Thes. v. 21.
Holding fast the form of sound words......... 2 Tim. i. 12.
Holding fast the faithful word....................Tit. i. 9.
Holy in all manner of conversation............. 1 Pe. i. 15.
Hoping to the end...........................1 Pe. i. 13
Humbling self under the mighty hand of God....1 Pe. v. 6.
Hungering and thirsting after righteousness.......Mat. v. 6.
Illuminated............................. .... Heb. 1. 32.
Increasing in the knowledge of God.............Col. i. 10.
Inheriting all things......................... Rev. xxi. 7.
Instant in season, out of season...............2 Tim. iv. 2.
Joined unto the Lord........................1 Cor. vi. 17.
Joying in God through our Lord Jesus Christ....Rom. v. 11.
Judging one another no more................Rom. xiv. 13.
Keeping the commandments of Christ.........Jno. xiv. 21.
Keeping that which is committed to our trust..1 Tim. vi. 20.
Keeping ourselves unspotted from the world ....James i. 27.
Keeping ourselves from idols.................. 1 Jno. v. 21.
Keeping ourselves in the love of God............Jude xxi.
Kind one to another, tenderhearted....... .....Eph. iv. 32.
Kindly affectioned one to another. .... Rom. xii. 10.
Knit together in love........................... Col. ii. 2.
Knowing that we have eternal life.............1 Jno. v. 13.
Laboring to enter into that rest................Heb. iv. 11.
Laying aside all malice and all guile.... ....1 Pe. ii. 1

Laying up for ourselves treasures in Heaven.....Mat. vi. 20
Led by the Spirit of God..................Rom. viii. 14.
Letting no corrupt communication proceed out
    of the mouth............................ Eph. iv. 29
Like minded, having the same love............ Phil. ii. 2.
Living henceforth not unto ourselves, but unto
    Him.................................... 2 Cor. v. 15.
Looking not at the things which are seen......2 Cor. iv. 18.
Looking for the Saviour..................... Phil. iii. 20.
Looking for that blessed hope..................Tit. ii. 13.
Looking for Him that shall appear........ .....Heb. ix. 28.
Looking off unto Jesus...................... Heb. xii. 2.
Loving God because He first loved us......... 1 Jno. iv. 19.
Loving Christ whom we have not seen............1 Pe. i. 8.
Loving one another, and thus showing that we
    are His................................Jno. xiii. 35.
Made meet to be partakers of the saints' inher-
    itance................................... Col. i. 12.
Meek, and inheriting the earth................. Mat. v. 5.
Merciful, and obtaining mercy.................. Mat. v. 7.
Mindful of the words recorded in the Scriptures..2 Pe. iii. 2.
Mortifying our members which are on the earth.. Col. iii. 5.
Not pleasing ourselves.......................Rom. xv. 1.
Not resisting evil............................. Mat. v. 39.
Not taking anxious thought about our life...... Mat. vi. 25.
Not judging, that we be not judged............ Mat. vii. 1.
Not fearing them which kill the body........... Mat. x. 28.
Not of the world.................... ....Jno. xvii. 16
Not conformed to this world....................Rom. xii. 2
Not wise in our own conceits....?............. Rom. xii. 16
Not our own.................................1 Cor. vi. 19
Not children in understanding.............. 1 Cor. xiv. 20.
Not unequally yoked together with unbelievers..2 Cor. vi. 14.
Not entangled again with the law......... .... . Gal. v. 1.
Not weary in well doing...................... . Gal. vi. 9
Not sleeping, as do others.................. . 1 Thes. v. 6
Not self-willed, not soon angry................ . Tit. i. 7

WHAT CHRISTIANS SHOULD BE.

Not forsaking the assembling of ourselves together .... Heb. x. 25.
Not despising the chastening of the Lord .... Heb. xii. 5
Not carried about with diverse and strange doctrines.... .... Heb. xiii. 9.
Not rendering evil for evil .... 1 Pe. iii. 9
Now past all condemnation .... Rom. viii. 1.
Now made nigh by the blood of Christ .... Eph. ii. 13.
Now the Sons of God .... 1 Jno. iii. 2.
Obedient children .... 1 Pe. i. 14.
Occupying till Christ comes.................. Lu. xix. 13.
Ordained unto eternal life................. Acts. xiii. 48
Overcoming by the blood of the Lamb......... Rev. xii. 11.
Passed from death unto life................... Jno. v. 24
Patient in tribulation........................ Rom. xii. 12.
Patient toward all men...................... 1 Thes. v. 14
Patiently waiting for Christ................ 2 Thes. iii. 5
Peacemakers .... Mat. v. 9
Perfectly joined together in the same mind..... 1 Cor. i. 10.
Pitiful and courteous .... 1 Pe. iii. 8.
Praying without ceasing..................... 1 Thes. v. 1.
Praying always in the spirit, for all saints ...... Eph. vi. 18.
Proving what is acceptable unto the Lord ...... Eph. v. 10.
Purchased with blood........................ Acts xx. 28.
Purifying ourselves even as He is pure.. ...... 1 Jno. v. 3.
Putting away all bitterness and wrath.. ...... Eph. iv. 31.
Putting on the new man..................... Eph. iv. 24.
Putting on the whole armour of God........... Eph. vi. 11.
Putting on love above all these things........... Col. iii. 14
Quenching not the spirit.................... 1 Thes. v. 19.
Reaching forth unto those things that are before..Phil. iii. 13.
Ready to every good work..................... Tit. iii. 1.
Receiving a kingdom........................ Heb. xii. 28.
Receiving the promise of the Spirit........... Gal. iii. 14.
Reckoning ourselves dead unto sin............ Rom. vi. 11.
Redeeming the time......................... Eph. v. 15.
Refraining the tongue from evil............... 1 Pet. iii. 10

Rejoicing in the Lord always................... Phil. iv. 4
Returned unto the Shepherd and Bishop of our
   Souls .... 1 Pet. ii. 25.
Running with patience the race set before us... Heb. xii. 1.
Sanctified through the offering of Christ........ Heb x. 10.
Saved by grace through faith................. Eph ii. 9
Sealed with that Holy Spirit of promise....... Eph. i. 13.
Searching the Scriptures..................... Jno. v 39
Seeking not our own, but the welfare of others.. 1 Cor. x. 24.
Separated from the world ....2 Cor. vi. 17.
Serving one another by love................... Gal. v. 13.
Sincere and without offence till the day of Christ..Phil. i. 10.
Sounding out the word of the Lord............1 Thes. i. 8.
Speaking the truth in love.................... Eph. iv. 55.
Speaking not evil one of another............. James iv. 11.
Stablished in the faith.......................... Col. ii. 7.
Striving together for the faith of the gospel......Phil. i. 27.
Taking heed to an evil heart of unbelief....... Heb. iii. 12.
Taught of God to love one another........... 1 Thes. iv. 9.
Teaching and admonishing one another......... Col. iii. 16.
Thankful..................................... Col. iii. 15.
Thinking no evil............................. 1 Cor. xiii. 5.
Transformed by the renewing of the mind...... Rom. xii. 2.
Trusting in the living God...................1 Tim. iv. 10.
Using this world as not abusing it.............1 Cor. vii. 31
Victorious through faith .... 1 Jno. v. 4.
Vigilant against our adversary the devil.... .....1 Pe. v. 8
Waiting for the Son of God from heaven ..... 1 Thes. i. 10.
Walking in the light, as He is in the light....... 1 Jno. i. 7
Wanting nothing.............................James i. 4.
Watching and standing fast in the faith....... 1 Cor. xvi. 13.
Weeping with them that weep... .... Rom. xii. 15.
Wise unto that which is good................ Rom. xvi. 19
Working out our own salvation .... Phil. ii. 12.
Worshipping God by the Spirit. ... . Phil. iii. 3
Yielding ourselves unto God.... ....Rom. vi. 13.
Zealous of good works........................ Tit. ii. 14.

CURIOUS FACTS ABOUT THE BIBLE.

These curious facts about the Bible were ascertained, it is stated, by a convict sentenced to a long term of solitary confinement: The Bible contains 3,586,489 letters, 773,692 words, 31,173 verses, 1,189 chapters, and 66 books. The word *and* occurs 46,277 times. The word *Lord* occurs 1,855 times. The word *reverend* occurs but once, which is in the 9th verse of the 111th Psalm. The middle verse is the 8th verse of the 118th Psalm. The 21st verse of the 7th chapter of Ezra contains all the letters of the alphabet except the letter J. The finest chapter to read is the 26th chapter of the Acts of the Apostles. The 19th chapter of 2 Kings and the 37th chapter of Isaiah are alike. The longest verse is the 9th verse of the 8th chapter of Esther. The shortest verse is the 35th of the 11th chapter of St. John. The 8th, 15th, 21st, and 31st verses of the 107th Psalm are alike. Each verse of the 136th Psalm ends alike. There are no words or names of more than six syllables.

CHRONOLOGICAL INDEX

TO

THE BIBLE.

PERIOD I.

FROM THE CREATION TO THE DELUGE, CONTAINING 1,656 YEARS.

A. M.	B. C.		
1	4004	The creation of the world............................	Genesis 1:2.
	"	Fall of our first parents, Adam and Eve, from holiness and happiness, by disobeying God. Promise of a Saviour...	" 3.
2	4002	Cain born..	" 4:1.
3	4001	Abel born..	" 4:2.
129	3875	Abel murdered by his brother Cain	" 4:8.
130	3874	Seth born, his father, Adam, being 130 years old...	" 5:3.
622	3382	Enoch born...	" 5:18, 19.
687	3317	Methuselah born.......................................	" 5:21.
930	3074	Adam dies, aged 930 years	" 5:5.
987	3017	Enoch translated, aged 365 years...................	" 5:24.
1042	2962	Seth dies, aged 912 years.............................	" 5:8.
1056	2948	Noah born..	" 5:28, 29.
			" 6:3–22.
1536	2468	The Deluge threatened, and Noah commissioned to preach repentance during 120 years..........	1 Pet. 3:20. 2 Pet. 2:5.
1656	2348	Methuselah dies, aged 969 years	Genesis 5:27.
		In the same year Noah enters into the ark, being 600 years old...	" 7:6, 7.

PERIOD II.

FROM THE DELUGE TO THE CALL OF ABRAHAM, CONTAINING 427 YEARS.

A. M.	B. C.		
1657	2347	Noah, with his family, leaves the ark after the deluge, and offering sacrifices, he receives the covenant of safety, of which the rainbow was the token...	Genesis 8:18, 20. " 9:8, 17.
1770	2234	Babel built..	" 11.
1770	2234	The confusion of languages, and dispersion of mankind...	" 11.
1771	2233	Nimrod lays the first foundation of the Babylonian or Assyrian monarchy.................................	" 10:8–11.
1816	2188	Mizraim lays the foundation of the Egyptian monarchy..	" 10:13.
2006	1998	Noah dies, aged 950 years...........................	" 9:29.
2008	1996	Abram or Abraham born.............................	" 11:26.

450

CHRONOLOGICAL INDEX. 451

PERIOD III.
FROM THE CALL OF ABRAHAM TO THE EXODUS OF ISRAEL FROM EGYPT, 430 YEARS.

A.M.	B.C.		
2068	1936	Abram called from Chaldean idolatry, at 60 years of age..	Genesis 11:31.
2083	1921	Abram's second call to Canaan	" 12:1-4.
2091	1913	Abram's victory over the kings, and rescue of Lot..	" 14:1-24.
2094	1910	Ishmael born, Abram being 86 years old..........	" 16.
2107	1997	God's covenant with Abram, changing his name to *Abraham;* circumcision instituted—Lot delivered, and Sodom, Gomorrah, Admah, and Zeboiim destroyed by fire on account of their abominations..	" 17-19.
2108	1896	Isaac born, Abraham being 100 years old	" 21.
			" 22.
2133	1871	Abraham offers Isaac as a burnt sacrifice to God.. }	Heb. 11:17-19. Jas. 2:21.
2145	1859	Sarah, Abraham wife, dies, aged 127 years........	Genesis 23:1.
2148	1856	Isaac marries Rebecca	" 24.
2168	1836	Jacob and Esau born, Isaac being 60 years old....	" 25:26.
2183	1821	Abraham dies, aged 175 years....................	" 25:7, 8.
2245	1759	Jacob goes to his uncle Laban in Syria, and marries his daughters, Leah and Rachel	" 28.
2258	1746	Joseph born, Jacob being 90 years old............	" 30:23, 24.
2265	1739	Jacob returns to Canaan	" 31; 32.
2275	1729	Joseph sold as a slave by his brethren.............	" 37.
2288	1716	He explains Pharaoh's dreams, and is made governor of Egypt...................................	" 41.
2298	1706	Joseph's brethren settle in Egypt..................	" 43; 44.
2315	1689	Jacob foretells the advent of Messiah, and dies in Egypt, aged 147 years	" 49.
2368	1636	Joseph dies, aged 110 years.......................	" 50:26.
2430	1574	Aaron born	Exod. 6:20; 7:7.
2433	1571	Moses born	" 2:1-10.
2473	1531	Moses flees into Midian...........................	" 2:11-13.
2513	1491	Moses commissioned by God to deliver Israel......	" 3:2.

PERIOD IV.
FROM THE EXODUS OF ISRAEL FROM EGYPT TO THE BUILDING OF SOLOMON'S TEMPLE, 487 YEARS.

A.M.	B.C.		
2513	1491	Miraculous passage of the Red sea by the Israelites	Exod. 14:15.
2514	1490	The law delivered on Sinai	" 19-40.
2552	1452	Miriam, sister of Moses, dies, aged 130 years......	Num. 20:1.
"	"	Aaron dies, aged 123 years	" 20:28, 39.
2553	1451	Moses dies, aged 120 years, Joshua being ordained his successor	Deut. 34.
"	"	The Israelites pass the river Jordan, the manna ceases, and Jericho taken........................	Josh. 1-6.
2561	1443	Joshua dies, aged 110 years	" 24.
2849	1155	Samuel born	1 Sam. 1:19.
2888	1116	Eli, the high-priest, dies. Ark of God taken by the Philistines......................................	" 4:1.
2909	1095	Saul anointed king of Israel	" 10; 11:12
2919	1085	David born	
2941	1063	David anointed to be king, and slays Goliath ...... {	" 16:13. " 17:4; 9.
2949	1055	Saul is defeated in battle, and in despair kills himself. David acknowledged king by Judah	" 31.
2956	1048	Ishbosheth, king of Israel, assassinated, and the whole kingdom united under David	2 Sam. 1.

452   CURIOSITIES OF THE BIBLE.

PERIOD IV.—Continued.

A.M.	B. C.		
2957	1047	Jerusalem taken from the Jebusites by David, and made the royal city	2 Sam. 5.
2969	1035	David commits adultery with Bathsheba, and contrives the death of her husband Uriah	" 11.
2970	1034	David brought to repentance for his sin by Nathan the prophet, sent to him by the LORD	" 12.
2971	1033	Solomon is born	" 12:24.
2981	1023	Absalom rebels against his father, and is slain by Joab	" 15; 18
2989	1015	David causes Solomon to be proclaimed king, defeating the rebellion of Adonijah	1 Kings 1.
2990	1014	David dies, aged 70 years	" 2.
3000	1004	Solomon's temple finished, after seven years building	" 6; 7.

PERIOD V.

FROM THE BUILDING OF SOLOMON'S TEMPLE TO THE DESTRUCTION OF JERUSALEM AND CAPTIVITY OF THE JEWS IN BABYLON, 412 YEARS.

B. C.	KINGS OF JUDAH BEGAN TO REIGN.	KINGS OF ISRAEL BEGAN TO REIGN.	PROPHETS.
975	Rehoboam	Jereboam I.	Abijah, Shemaiah.
958	Abijah, or Abijam	"	
955	Asa	Nadab (954)	Azariah.
953	"	Baasha	Hanani.
930	"	Elah	Jehu.
929	"	Zimri.	
"	"	Omri.	
918	"	Ahab	Elijah, 910–896.
914	Jehoshaphat	"	Micaiah.
897	"	Ahaziah	Elisha, 896–838.
896	"	Jehoram, or Joram	Jahaziel.
892	Jehoram	"	
885	Ahaziah	"	
884	Athaliah	Jehu	Jehoiada.
878	Joash, or Jehoahaz	"	
857	"	Jehoahaz	Jonah, 856–784.
839	Amaziah	Jehoash.	
825	"	Jeroboam II.	
810	Uzziah or Azariah	"	Amos, 810–785.
784	"	Anarchy, 11 years	Hosea, 810–725.
773	"	Zechariah	Joel, 810–660.
772	"	Shallum; Menahem.	
761	"	Pekahiah	Isaiah, 810–698.
759	"	Pekah.	
758	Jotham	"	Micah, 758–699.
742	Ahaz	"	Oded.
730	"	Hoshea.	
726	Hezekiah	(Captivity, 721)	Nahum, 720–698.
698	Manasseh	"	
643	Amon	"	Zephaniah, 640–609.
641	Josiah	"	Jeremiah, 628–586.
610	Jehoahaz, or Shallum	"	Habakkuk, 612–598.
"	Jehoiakim	"	Daniel, 606–534.
599	Jehoiachin, or Coniah	"	
"	Zedekiah.		
588	Babylonian captivity		Obadiah, 588–582.

FROM THE DESTRUCTION OF JERUSALEM BY NEBUCHADNEZZAR, TO THE BIRTH OF CHRIST, 588 YEARS.

B. C.	HISTORICAL EVENTS.	PROPHETS.
588	Destruction of Jerusalem by the Chaldeans, and captivity of the Jews.	
538	Babylon taken by Cyrus..........................	Ezekiel, 595-556.
536	Proclamation of Cyrus; Zerubbabel and Joshua.	
534	Foundation of the temple.	
529	Artaxerxes (Cambyses) forbids the work.	
520	Favorable decree of Ahasuerus (Darius Hystaspes.)	Haggai, 520-518.
518	Esther made queen	Zechariah, 520-518.
515	The second temple finished.	
510	Haman's plot frustrated.	
484	Xerxes, king of Persia.	
464	Artaxerxes Longimanus.	
457	Ezra sent to govern Jerusalem.	
445	Nehemiah sent as governor.	
423	Darius Nothus	Malachi, 436-420.
335	Alexander the Great invades Persia, and establishes the Macedonian or Grecian empire.	
332	Jaddus high-priest.	
323	Alexander dies.	
320	Ptolemæus Lagus surprises Jerusalem.	
277	Septuagint version made by order of Ptolemæus Philadelphus.	
170	Antiochus Epiphanes takes Jerusalem.	
167	His persecution.	
166	Judas Maccabæus governor.	
161	Jonathan governor.	
152	He becomes high-priest.	
143	Simon: treaty with the Romans and Lacedemonians.	
135	John Hyrcanus.	
107	Judas (Aristobulus) high-priest and king.	
88	Anna the prophetess born.	
63	Jerusalem taken by Pompey, and Judea made a Roman province.	
40	Herod made king.	
28	Augustus Cæsar emperor of Rome.	
19	The poet Virgil dies.	
18	Herod begins to rebuilt the temple.	
4	John the Baptist born.	
4	Christ born, 4 years before the era known as A. D.	

PERIOD VII.

FROM THE BIRTH OF JESUS CHRIST TO THE END OF THE FIRST CENTURY.

A. D.		
	Nativity of Jesus Christ, four years before A. D. 1.....	Luke 2:1-16.
8	Jesus visits Jerusalem	" 2:41-52
22	Pilate sent from Rome as governor of Judea	" 3:1.
25	John Baptist begins his ministry......................	Matt. 3:1.
26	Jesus baptized by John	" 3:1.
29	Jesus Christ crucified, and rose from the dead	" 27; 28.

CURIOSITIES OF THE BIBLE.

PERIOD VII.—Continued.

A. D.		
36	Saul converted....................................	Acts 9; 13:19.
38	Conversion of the Gentiles	" 10.
44	James beheaded by Herod: Peter liberated by an angel..	" 12:1-19.
63	Paul sent a prisoner to Rome	" 26:28.
65	The Jewish war begins.	
66	Paul suffers martyrdom at Rome by order of Nero......	2 Tim. 4:6, 7.
67	The Roman general raises the siege of Jerusalem, by which an opportunity is afforded for the Christians to retire to Pella beyond Jordan, as admonished by Christ........	Matt. 24:16-20.
70	Jerusalem besieged and taken by Titus Vespasian, according to the predictions of Christ; when 1,100,000 Jews perished, by famine, sword, fire, and crucifixion; besides 97,000 who were sold as slaves, and vast multitudes who perished in other parts of Judea	Luke 19:41-44.
71	Jerusalem and its temple razed to their foundations......	Matt. 24:2.
95	John banished to the isle of Patmos, by Domitian.......	Rev. 1:9.
96	John writes the Revelation.	
97	John liberated from exile, and writes his gospel.	
100	John, the last surviving apostle, dies, about 100 years old.	

PROMINENT EVENTS IN
Ecclesiastical History

FROM THE DEATH OF JOHN TO THE FALL OF THE WESTERN EMPIRE.

A.D. 101 to 476.

101. Death of Clement Bishop of Rome.
106. Death of Ignatius Bishop of Antioch, by wild beasts.
107. Symeon, Bishop of Jerusalem crucified.
119. Fourth general Persecution under Adrian.
135. 580,000 Jews destroyed by Romans.
136. Adrian builds Ælia Capitalina on the right of Jerusalem.
147. Justin Martyr writes his first apology for Christianity.
152. The Council of Pergamos, the first on record.
167. Persecution of the Christians at Smyrna.
174. Polycarp and Pionices martyred.
177. Persecution at Lyons and Vienne. Bishop Pothinus martyred.
185. Death of Origen, the eminent Commentator.
189. The Saracens first appear defeat the Romans.
194. The Scriptures translated into Syriac.
195. The Scriptures translated unto Latin.
196. Tertullian writes his Apology for Christianity.
197. Fifth General Persecution under Severus.
202. Severus issues an Edict prohibiting Christians from disseminating their doctrines.
203. Death of Irenæus, Bishop of Lyons.
204. Origen, expounder of the Scriptures at Alexandria.
218. Death of Clement of Alexandria.
235. Sixth general persecution, under Maximinus.
242. Churches first used by Christians.
249. Seventh general persecution, under Decius.
259. Eight general persecution under Valerian.
257. Martyrdom of Cyprian and Sixtus II, Bishop of Rome.
260. Temple of Diana at Ephesus burnt.
270. Birth of Eusebius, Bishop of Cæsarea.
272. The ninth general persecution, under Aurelian.
286. The North men attack the Roman Empire in the West and the Persians in the East.
302. The tenth persecution, under Diocletian.
306. Constantine Emperor, in the West; Licinus in the East.
312. Constantine the Great embraces Christianity.
321. Constantine commands the Observance of Sunday on all his subjects.
325. Council of Nice condemns Arianism.
335. Death of Constantine the Great.
361. Julian the Apostate becomes Emperor.
385. Jerome translates the Hebrew Scripture in Latin.
397. Death of Ambrose, Archbishop of Milan.
407. Death of Chrysostom, Patriarch of Constantinople.
410. Rome sacked and burned by Alaric, King of the Visigoths.
415. Cyril becomes Bishop of Alexandria.
430. Death of Augustine.
461. Leo, the great Pope of Rome, claims to be vicar of Christ.
476. Extinction of the Western Empire by Goths.
476. The sacking of Rome by Odoacer was the great event which preceded the Middle or Dark ages.

CHRONOLOGICAL TABLE OF THE PATRIARCHS, FROM ADAM TO MOSES, 2500 YEARS.

This table exhibits the years of the birth and death of the patriarchs; the comparative length of their lives; who of them were alive at the same period; and the rapid decrease in the length of life after the deluge. Thus, Lamech the father of Noah was born A. M. 874, and died A. M. 1651; he was contemporary with Adam 56 years, and he died but five years before the flood. Shem was born nearly 100 years before the flood, and lived many years after both Abraham and Isaac were born.

YEARS FROM THE CREATION.	100	200	300	400	500	600	700	800	900	1000	1100	1200	1300	1400	1500	1600	1700	1800	1900	2000	2100	2200	2300	2400	2500
Adam									930																
Seth	130									1042															
Enos		235									1140														
Cainan			325									1235													
Mahalaleel			395									1290													
Jared				460										1422											
Enoch						622			987																
Methuselah							687									1656									
Lamech								874								1651									
Noah										1056								2006							
Shem																1558			2158						
Arphaxad																	1658		2096						
Salah																	1693		2126						
Eber																		1723		2187					
Peleg																		1757	1996						
Reu																		1787	2026						
Serug																			1819	2049					
Nahor																			1849	1997					
Terah																			1878	2083					
Abraham																				2008	2183				
Isaac																				2108	2288				
Jacob																				2168	2315				
Levi																					2255	2371			
Kohath																					2288	2421			
Amram																						2367	2504		
Moses																						2433	2553		
YEARS BEFORE CHRIST.	4000	3900	3800	3700	3600	3500	3400	3300	3200	3100	3000	2900	2800	2700	2600	2500	2400	2300	2200	2100	2000	1900	1800	1700	1600	1500

Deluge A. M. 1656.

Deluge B. C. 2348.

Special Prayers

RECORDED IN THE
BIBLE.

By Whom.	Subjects.	Recorded.
Abraham's Servant	Success in his mission	Gen. 24.
Jacob	Protection against Esau	" 23.
Moses	Forgiveness for Idolatrous Israel	Ex. 32.
Moses	For the Divine presence	" 33.
Moses	For Miriam when smitten with Leprosy	Num. 12.
Moses	To enter Canaan	Deut. 3.
Sampson	To be avenged on his Enemies	Jud. 16.
Hannah	For a man child	1 Sam. 1.
David	Prayer and Thanksgiving after Nathans message	2 Sam. 7.
Solomon	Dedication of the temple	1 Kings 8.
Hezekiah	Protection against Sennacherib	2 " 19.
"	When dangerously ill	" 20.
Jabez	For Divine blessing	1 Chron. 4.
Asa	When going to battle with Zerah the Ethiopian	2 " 6.
Jehoshaphat	For protection against invading armies	" 20.
Hezekiah	For the unprepared for keeping the passover	" 30.
Ezra	Confession of the peoples sin	Ezra. 9.
Nehemiah	For the remnant in Captivity	Neh. 1.
"	For protection against Sanballat and Tobiah	" 4.
Levites	Confession of Gods good and their sins	" 9.
Agur	For moderation in his desires	Prov. 29.
Hezekiah	See above (2 Kings 19, 20.)	Isa. 37, 38
Jeremiah	In a great famine	Jer. 14.
Daniels	For restoration of Jerusalem	Dan. 9.
Habakkuk	For revival of Gods work	Heb. 3.
Lords Prayer	The model Prayer	Matt. 6.
Jesus	Under suffering in Gethsemane	" 26.
Jesus	Suspension of Divine consolation	" 27.
Lords Prayer	St. Lukes account	Luke. 2.
Publicans "	For Divine mercy	" 18.
Jesus	See above (Matt. 26.)	" 22.
Dying Thief	To be remembered by Jesus	" 23.
Jesus	Imploring his Fathers aid	John. 12.
Jesus	For himself, his apostles and all believers	" 17.
Apostles	On choosing an apostle	Acts. 1.
Primitive Church	For support under persecution	" 4.

THE MIRACLES RECORDED IN THE OLD TESTAMENT.

Miracles	Where wrought.	Recorded in.
Aaron's rod changed	Egypt	Exod. vii. 10-12.
Waters made blood	Egypt	20-25.
Frogs produced	Egypt	viii. 5-14.
Lice	Egypt	16-18.
Flies	Egypt	20-24.
Murrain	Egypt	ix. 3-6.
Boils	Egypt	8-11.
Thunder, etc	Egypt	22-26.
Locusts	Egypt	x. 15-19.
Darkness	Egypt	21-23.
Death of the first-born	Egypt	xii. 29, 30
Red Sea	Egypt	xiv. 21-31.
Marah's waters sweetened	Marah	xv. 23-25.
Manna sent	In wilderness	xvi. 14-35.
Water from the rock Rephidim	Rephidim	xvii. 5-7.
Aaron's rod budded	Kadesh	Num. xvii. 1, etc.
Nadab and Abihu consumed	Sinai	Lev. x. 1, 2.
The burning of Taberah	Taberah	Num. xi 1-2.
Earthquake and fire		xvi. 31-35.
Water flowing from the rock	Desert of Zin	xx. 7-11.
Serpent, healing the Israelites	Desert of Zin	xxi. 8, 9.
Balaam's ass speaking	Pethor	xxii. 21-35.
The river Jordan divided	River Jordan	Josh. iii. 14-19.
Walls of Jericho fall down	Jericho	vi. 6-20.
Sun and moon stand still	Gibeon	x. 12-14.
Water flowing from the rock	En-hakkore	Judg. xv. 19.
Philistines slain before the ark	Ashded	1 Sam v. 1-12.
Men of Beth-shemesh smitten	Beth-shemesh	vi. 19.
Thunder destroys Philistines	Ebenezer	vii. 10-12.
Thunder and rain in harvest	Gilgal	xii. 18.
Sound in the mulberry trees	Rephaim	2 Sam. v. 23-25.
Uzzah struck dead	Perez-uzzah	vi. 7.
Jeroboam's hand withered	Beth-el	1 Kings xiii. 4, 6.
Widow of Zarepath's meal	Zarepath	xvii. 14-16.
Widow's son raised	Zarepath	17-24.
Sacrifice consumed	Mount Carmel	xviii. 30-38.
Rain obtained	Land of Israel	41-45
Ahaziah's captains consumed	Near Samaria	2 Kings i. 10-12.
River Jordan divided	River Jordan	ii. 7, 8, 14.
Waters of Jericho healed	Jericho	21, 22
Water for Jehoshaphat's army	Land of Moab	iii. 16-20.
The widow's oil multiplied		iv. 2-7.
Shunammite's son raised	Shunem	32-37.
The deadly pottage cured	Gilgal	38-41.
Hundred men fed with twenty loaves	Gilgal	42-44.
Naaman cured of his leprosy	Samaria	v. 10-14
Leprosy inflicted on Gehazi	Samaria	20-27.
Iron swims	River Jordan	vi. 5-7.
King of Syria's army smitten	Dotham	18-20.
Elisha's bones revive the dead		xiii. 21.
Sennacherib's army destroyed	Jerusalem	xix. 35.
Sun goeth back	Jerusalem	xx. 9-11.
Uzziah struck with leprosy	Jerusalem	2 Ch. xxvi. 16-21.
Shadrach, Meshach, etc., delivered	Babylon	Dan. iii. 19-27.
Daniel in the den of lions	Babylon	vi. 16-23.
Jonah in the whale's belly		Jonah ii. 1-10.

THE MIRACLES OF CHRIST.
ARRANGED IN CHRONOLOGICAL ORDER.

Miracles.	Places.	References.
Turns water into wine	Cana	John ii. 1-11.
Cures the nobleman's son of Capernaum	"	iv. 46-64.
Causes a miraculous draught of fishes	Sea of Galilee	Luke v. 1-11.
Cures a demoniac	Capernaum	Mark i. 23-28.
Heals Peter's wife's mother of a fever.	"	30, 31.
Heals a leper	"	40-45.
Heals the centurion's servant	"	Matt. viii. 5-13.
Raises the widow's son	Nain	Luke vii. 11-17.
Calms the tempest	Sea of Galilee	Matt. viii. 23-27.
Cures the demoniacs of Gadara	Gadara	28-34.
Cures a man of the palsy	Capernaum	ix. 1-8.
Restores to life the daughter of Jairus	"	18, 19, 28-26
Cures a woman diseased with a flux of blood	"	Luke viii. 43-48.
Restores to sight two blind men	"	Matt. ix. 27-31.
Heals one possessed with a dumb spirit	"	32, 33.
Cures an infirm man at Bethesda	Jerusalem	John v. 1-9.
Cures a man with withered hand	Judea	Matt. xii. 10-13.
Cures a demoniac	Capernaum	22, 23.
Feeds miraculously five thousand	Decapolis	xiv.; xv. 21.
Heals the woman of Canaan's daughter	Near Tyre	xv. 22-28.
Heals a man who was dumb and deaf	Decapolis	Mark vii. 31-37.
Feeds miraculously four thousand	"	Matt. xv. 32-39.
Gives sight to a blind man	Bethsaida	Mark xiii. 22-26.
Cures a boy possessed of a devil	Tabor	Matt. xvii. 14-21.
Restores to sight a man born blind	Jerusalem	John ix.
Heals a woman under an infirmity eighteen years	Galilee	Luke xiii. 11-17.
Cures a dropsy	"	xiv. 1-6.
Cleanses ten lepers	Samaria	xvii. 11-19.
Raises Lazarus from the dead	Bethany	John xi.
Restores to sight two blind men	Jericho	Matt. xx. 30-34.
Blasts the fig-tree	Olivet	xxi. 18-22.
Heals the ear of Malchus	Gethsemane	Luke xxii. 50, 51.
Causes the miraculous draught of fishes	Sea of Galilee	John xxi. 1-14.

THE MIRACLES RECORDED IN THE ACTS OF THE APOSTLES.

Miracles.	Where wrought.	Recorded in.
Peter heals a lame man	Jerusalem	
Ananias and Sapphira struck dead	Jerusalem	Acts iii. 1-11.
Apostles perform many wonders	Jerusalem	v. 1-10
Peter and John communicate the Holy Ghost	Samaria	v. 12-16
Peter healeth Eneas of a palsy	Lydda	viii. 14-17.
—raiseth Tabitha, or Dorcas, to life	Joppa	ix. 33, 34.
—delivered out of prison by an angel	Jerusalem	ix. 37-41.
God smites Herod, so that he dies	Jerusalem	xii. 7-17.
Elymas, the sorcerer, smitten with blindness	Paphos	xii. 21-23. xiii. 7-11.
Paul Converted	Road to Damascus	ix. 1-9.
—heals a cripple	Lystra	xiv. 8-10.
—casts out a spirit of divination	Phillippi	xvi. 17-18.
—and Silas's prison doors opened by an earthquake	Phillippi	xvi. 25, 27.
—communicates the Holy Ghost	Corinth	xix. 1-7.
—heals multitudes	Corinth	xix. 11, 12.
—restores Eutychus to life	Troas	xx. 9-12.
—shakes off the viper	Melita	xxviii. 3-7.
—heals the father of Publius, and others	Melita	xxviii. 7-9.

THE PARABLES RECORDED IN THE OLD TESTAMENT

Parables.	Spoken at	Recorded in.
OF BALAAM.—Concerning the Moabites and Israelites	Mount Pisgah	Num. xxiii. 24
JOTHAM.—Trees making a king	Mount Gerizim	Judg. ix. 7 15.
SAMSON.—Strong bringing forth sweetness	Timnath	Judg. xiv. 14.
NATHAN.—Poor man's ewe lamb	Jerusalem	2 Sam. xii. 1-4.
WOMAN OF TEKOAH.—Two brothers striving	Jerusalem	2 Sam. xiv. 1.
THE SMITTEN PROPHET.—The escaped prisoner	Near Samaria	1 Kings xx. 35 43
JEHOASH, KING OF ISRAEL.—The thistle and cedar	Jerusalem	2 Kings xiv. 9.
ISAIAH.—Vineyard yielding wild grapes	Jerusalem	Isa. v. 1-6.
EZEKIEL.—Lions' whelps	Babylon	
The boiling pot	Babylon	Ezek. xix. 2-9.
The great eagles and the vine	Babylon	Ezek. xxiv. 3-5. Ezek. xvii. 3-10.

THE PARABLES OF JESUS.
ARRANGED IN CHRONOLOGICAL ORDER.

Parables.	Places.	References.
PARABLE OF THE		
Sower	Capernaum	Matt. xiii. 1-23.
Tares	"	24-30-36-43.
Seed springing up imperfectly	"	Mark iv. 26-29.
Grain of mustard-seed	"	Matt. xii. 31, 32.
Leaven	"	xiii. 33.
Found treasure	"	44.
Precious pearl	"	45, 46.
Net	"	47-50.
Two debtors	"	Luke vii. 36-50.
Unmerciful servant	"	Matt. xviii. 23-35
Samaritan	Near Jericho	Luke x. 25-37
Rich fool	Galilee	xii. 16-21.
Servants who waited for their Lord	"	xii. 35-48.
Barren fig-tree	"	xiii. 6-9.
Lost sheep	"	xv. 3-7.
Lost piece of money	"	8-10.
Prodigal son	"	11-32.
Dishonest steward	"	xvi. 1-12.
Rich man and Lazarus	"	19-31.
Unjust Judge	Peræa	xviii. 1-
Pharisee and Publican	"	9-14.
Laborers in the vineyard	"	Matt. xx. 1-16
Pounds	Jericho	Luke xix. 12-2
Two sons	Jerusalem	Matt. xxi. 28-3.
Vineyard	"	33-46.
Marriage feast	"	xxii. 1-14.
The virgins	"	xxv. 1-13.
Talents	"	14-30.
Sheep and the goats	"	31

THE DISCOURSES OF JESUS.
ARRANGED IN CHRONOLOGICAL ORDER.

Discourses.	Places.	References.
Conversation with Nicodemus	Jerusalem	John iii. 1-21.
Conversation with woman of Samaria	Sychar	iv. 1-42.
Discourse in the Synagogue of Nazareth	Nazareth	Luke iv. 16-31.
Sermon upon the mount	"	Matt. v.; vii.
Instruction to the Apostles	Galilee	x.
Denunciations against Chorazin, etc.	"	xi. 20-21
Discourse on occasion of healing the infirm man	Jerusalem	John v.
Discourse concerning the disciples plucking of corn on the Sabbath	Judea	Matt. xii. 1-8
Reputation of his working miracles by the agency of Beelzebub	Capernaum	22-37
Discourse on the bread of life	"	John vii.
Discourse about internal purity	"	Matt. xv. 1-20.
Discourse against giving or taking offence, and concerning forgiveness of injuries	"	xvii*.
Discourse at the feast of tabernacles	Jerusalem	John vii.
Discourse on occasion of woman taken in adultery	"	viii.; i. 1L
Discourse concerning the sheep	"	x.
Denunciations against the Scribes and Pharisees	Parœa	Luke xi. 29-36
Discourse concerning humility and prudence	Galilee	xiv. 7-14
Directions how to attain heaven	Parœa	Matt. xix. 16-30.
Discourse concerning his sufferings	Jerusalem	xx. 17-19.
Denunciation against the Pharisees	"	xxiii.
Prediction of the destruction of Jerusalem	"	xxiv.
The consolatory discourse	"	John xv.; xvii.
Discourse as he went to Gethsemane	"	Matt. xxvi. 31-36.
Discourse to the disciples before his ascension	"	xxviii. 16 20

TABLES

OF

WEIGHTS, MEASURES, AND MONEY,

MENTIONED IN THE BIBLE.

1. JEWISH WEIGHTS, REDUCED TO ENGLISH TROY WEIGHT.

	lbs.	oz.	pen.	gr.
The gerah, one-twentieth of a shekel	0	0	0	12
The bekah, half a shekel	0	0	5	0
The shekel	0	0	10	0
The maneh, 60 shekels	2	6	0	0
The talent, 50 manehs, or 3,000 shekels	125	0	0	0

2. SCRIPTURE MEASURES OF LENGTH, REDUCED TO ENGLISH MEASURE.

	Eng. feet.	Inches.
A digit	0	0.912
4 = A Palm	0	3.648
12 = 3 = A span	0	10.944
24 = 6 = 3 = A cubit	1	9.888
96 = 24 = 6 = 2 = A fathom	7	3.552
144 = 36 = 12 = 6 = 1.5 = Ezekiel's reed	10	11.328
192 = 48 = 16 = 8 = 2 = 1.3 = An Arabian pole	14	7.104
1920 = 480 = 160 = 80 = 20 = 13.3 = 10 = A measuring line	145	11.04

3. THE LONG SCRIPTURE MEASURES.

	Eng. miles.	paces.	feet.
A cubit	0	0	1.824
400 = A stadium or furlong	0	145	4.6
2000 = 5 = A sabbath-day's journey	0	729	3.
4000 = 10 = 2 = An eastern mile	1	403	1.
12000 = 30 = 6 = 3 = A parasang	4	153	3.
96000 = 240 = 48 = 24 = 8 = A day's journey	33	172	4.

NOTE.—6 feet = 1 pace ; 1,056 paces = 1 mile.

4. SCRIPTURE MEASURES OF CAPACITY FOR LIQUIDS, REDUCED TO ENGLISH WINE MEASURE.

					Gal.	pints
A caph					0	0.625
1.3 = A log					0	0.833
5.3 = 4 = A cab					0	3.333
16 = 12 = 3 = A hin					1	2.
32 = 24 = 6 = 2 = A seah					2	4.
96 = 72 = 18 = 6 = 3 = A bath, ephah, or firkin					7	4.50
960 = 720 = 180 = 60 = 20 = 10 = A kor, choros, or homer					75	5.15

---

5. SCRIPTURE MEASURES OF CAPACITY FOR THINGS DRY, REDUCED TO ENGLISH CORN MEASURE.

						Bush.	pks.	gal.	pints
A gachal						0	0	0	0.14
20 = A cab						0	0	0	2.833
36 = 1.8 = An omer or gomer						0	0	0	5.1
120 = 6 = 3.3 = A seah						0	1	0	1.
360 = 18 = 10 = 3 = An ephah						0	3	0	3.
1800 = 90 = 50 = 15 = 5 = A letech						4	0	0	0.
3600 = 180 = 100 = 30 = 10 = A homer or kor						8	0	0	1.

---

6. JEWISH MONEY, REDUCED TO THE ENGLISH AND AMERICAN STANDARDS.

	£.	s.	d.	$	cts.
A gerah	0	0	1.3687	0	02.5
10 = A bekah	0	1	1.6875	0	25.09
20 = 2 = A shekel	0	2	3.375	0	50.187
1200 = 120 = 50 = A maneh, or mina Hebr.	5	14	0.75	25	09.35
60000 = 6000 = 3000 = 60 = A talent	342	3	9.	1505	62.5
A solidus aureus, or sextula, was worth	0	12	0.5	2	64.09
A siclus aureus, or gold shekel, was worth	1	16	6.	8	03.
A talent of gold was worth	5475	0	0.	24309	00.

In the preceding table, silver is valued at 5s. and gold at £4 per ounce.

---

7. ROMAN MONEY, MENTIONED IN THE NEW TESTAMENT, REDUCED TO THE ENGLISH AND AMERICAN STANDARD.

	£	s.	d.	far.	$	cts.
A mite	0	0	0	0.75	0	00.343
A farthing, about	0	0	0	1.50	0	00.687
A penny, or denarius	0	0	7	2.	0	13.75
A pound, or mina	3	2	6	0.	13	75.

NAMES AND TITLES

APPLIED TO OUR

OUR LORD AND SAVIOUR JESUS CHRIST,

IN THE HOLY SCRIPTURES.

The following Names or Titles of our Lord and Saviour Jesus Christ, are to be found in the Scriptures of the Old and New Testament:

Adam, 1 Cor. 15: 45.
Advocate, 1 John 2: 1.
Almighty, Rev. 1: 8.
Alpha and Omega, Rev. I: 8.
Amen, Rev 3: 14.
Angel of the Lord, Gen. 16: 7–11.
Anointed, Psalm 2: 2
Apostle, Heb. 3: 1.
Arm of the Lord, Isa. 51: 9, 10.
Author of Eternal Salvation, Heb. 5: 9.
Author of Faith, Heb. 12 2.

Beginning and End, Rev. 22. 13.
Beginning of Creation of God, Rev. 3: 14.
Beloved, Matt. 12: 18.
Beloved Son, Matt. 3: 17; Luke 3 22.
Blessed and only Potentate, 1 Tim. 6: 15.
Branch, Zech. 6: 12.
Branch of Righteousness, Jer. 33. 15.
Bread, John 6: 41.
Bread from Heaven, John 6: 51.
Bread of God, John 6. 33.
Bread of Life, John 6: 35.
Bright and Morning Star, Rev. 22: 16.
Brightness of Father's Glory, Heb. 1 : 3.

Captain of Salvation, Heb. 2: 10.
Carpenter, Mark 6: 3.
Carpenter's Son, Matt. 13: 55.
Chief Corner-Stone, 1 Peter 2· 6.
Chiefest among Ten Thousand, Song 5 :10.
Child, Isa. 9: 6.
Child Jesus, Luke 2: 27, 43.
Chosen of God, 1 Peter 2: 4.
Christ, John 6: 69.

Christ, a King. Luke 23:2.
Christ Jesus, Heb. 3: 1.
Christ Jesus our Lord, 1 Tim. 1 : 12.
Christ of God, Luke 9: 20.
Christ, the Chosen of God, Luke 23: 35.
Christ the Lord, Luke 2: 11.
Christ, the Son of God, Acts 9: 20.
Christ. Son of the Blessed, Mark 14: 61.
Commander, Isa 55: 4.
Consolation of Israel, Luke 2. 25.
Corner Stone Isa. 28: 16.
Counsellor, Isa 9: 6.
Covenant, Isa, 42:6.

David, their King, Jer. 30:9.
Day-Spring Luke 1: 78.
Deliverer. Rom. 11:26.
Desire of All Nations, Hag. 2: 6.
Door, John 10: 9.
Door of the Sheep, John 10: 7.

Elect, Isa. 42: 1.
Emmanuel, Matt. 1: 23.
Ensign, Isa. 11: 10.
Everlasting Father, Isa. 9: 6.

Faithful, and True, Rev. 19; 11.
Faithful Witness, Rev. 1: 5.
Faithful and True Witness, Rev. 3: 14.
Finisher of Faith. Heb. 12: 2.
First and Last, Rev. 22: 13, 1: 17.
First Begotten, Heb. 1: 6.
First Begotten of the dead, Rev. 1· 5.
First-born among brethren, Rom 8: 29.
First-born from the dead, Col. 1: 18.
First born of every creature, Col. 1: 15.

TITLES OF CHRIST.

First Fruits, 1 Cor. 15: 20.
Forerunner, Heb. 6: 20.
Foundation, 1 Cor. 3: 11.
Fountain opened, Zech. 13: 1.
Friend of Sinners, Matt. 11: 19.

Gift of God, John 4: 10.
Glory of Israel, Luke 2: 32.
God blessed for ever, Rom. 9: 5.
God manifest in the flesh, 1 Tim. 3: 16.
God of Israel, the Saviour, Isa. 45: 15.
God of the whole earth, Isa. 54: 5.
God our Saviour, 1 Tim. 2; 3.
God's dear Son, Col. 1: 13.
God with us, Matt. 1: 23.
Good Master. Matt. 19: 16.
Governor, Matt. 2: 6.
Great Shepherd of the Sheep, Heb. 13: 20.

Head of every man, 1 Cor. 11: 3.
Head of the Church, Col. 1: 18.
Head of the Corner, Matt. 21: 42.
Heir of all things, Heb. 1: 1, 2.
High Priest, Heb. 3: 1.
High Priest of good things to come, Heb. 9: 11.
Holy Child Jesus, Acts 4: 30.
Holy One, Psa. 16: 10.
Holy One of God, Mark 1: 24.
Holy One of Israel, Isa. 41: 14; 54: 5.
Holy Thing, Luke 1: 35.
Hope, Our, 1 Tim. 1: 1.
Horn of Salvation, Luke 1: 69.

I AM, John 8: 58.
Image, express, of God's person, Heb. 1: 3.
Image of God, 2 Cor. 4: 4.
Immanuel, Isa. 7: 14.

Jesus, Matt. 1: 21.
Jesus Christ, Matt. 1: 1.
Jesus Christ, our Saviour, Tit. 3: 6.
Jesus of Nazareth, Mark 1: 24.
Jesus of Nazareth, the King of the Jews, John 19: 19.
Jesus, the King of the Jews, Matt. 27: 37.
Jesus, the Son of God, Heb. 4; 14.
Jesus, the Son of Joseph, John 6: 42.
Judge, Acts 10: 42.
Just, Acts 3: 14.
Just Man, Matt. 27: 19.
Just One, Acts 7: 52.
Just Person, Matt. 27: 24.

King, Luke 19: 38.
King of Glory, Psa. 24: 7-10.
King of Israel, John 1: 49.
King of kings, 1 Tim. 6: 15.
King of the Jews, Matt. 2: 2.
King of Zion, Matt. 21: 5.
King over all the earth, Zech. 14: 9.

Lamb, Rev. 5: 6.
Lamb of God, John 1: 29, 36.

Lamb that was slain, Rev. 5: 12.
Leader, Isa. 55: 4.
Life, John 14: 6.
Life, Our, Col. 3: 4.
Light, Everlasting, Isa. 60: 20.
Light of the world, John 8: 12.
Light to the Gentiles, Isa. 42: 6.
Light, True, John 1: 9.
Lion of the tribe of Judah, Rev. 5: 8.
Living Bread, John 6: 51.
Living Stone, 1 Pet. 2: 4.
Lord, Matt. 22: 43.
Lord and Saviour Jesus Christ, 2 Pe. 1: 11
Lord Christ, Col. 3: 24.
Lord from Heaven, 1 Cor. 15: 47
Lord Jesus, Acts 7: 59.
Lord Jesus Christ, 2 Thess. 3: 6.
Lord Jesus Christ, our Saviour, Tit. 1: 4.
Lord of All, Acts 10: 36.
Lord of Glory, Jas. 2: 1.
Lord of Hosts, Isa. 44: 6.
Lord of Lords, Rev. 19: 16.
Lord, Mighty in Battle, Psa. 24: 8.
Lord of the dead and living, Rom. 14: 9.
Lord of the Sabbath, Mark 2: 28.
Lord over All, Rom. 10: 12.
Lord's Christ, Luke 2: 26.
Lord, Strong and Mighty, Psa. 24: 8.
Lord, The, our Righteousness, Jer. 23: 6
Lord, your Holy One, Isa. 43: 15.
Lord, your Redeemer. Isa. 43: 14.

Man, Mark 15: 39.
Man Christ Jesus, 1 Tim. 2: 5.
Man of Sorrows, Isa. 53: 3.
Master, Matt. 23: 10.
Mediator, 1 Tim. 2: 5.
Mediator of the New Covenant, Heb 12: 24.
Messenger of the Covenant, Mal. 3: 1.
Messiah, the Prince, Dan. 9: 25.
Messias, John 1: 41.
Mighty God, Isa. 9: 6.
Mighty One of Israel, Isa. 30: 29.
Mighty One of Jacob, Isa. 49: 26.
Mighty to save, Isa. 63: 1.
Morning Star, Rev. 22: 16.
Most Holy, Dan. 9: 24.
Most Mighty, Psa. 45: 3.

Nazarene, Matt. 2: 23.

Offspring of David, Rev. 22: 16.
Only-Begotten of the Father, John 1: 14
Only-Begotten Son, John 1: 18.

Passover, 1 Cor. 5: 7.
Plant of Renown, Ezek. 34: 29.
Potentate (only), 1 Tim. 6: 15.
Power of God, 1 Cor. 1: 24.
Precious Corner-Stone, Isa. 28: 16.
Priest, Heb. 7: 17.
Prince, Acts 5: 31.
Prince of Life, Acts 3: 15

Prince of Peace, Isa. 9:6.
Prince of the kings of the Earth, Rev. 1:5.
Prophet, John 6.14.
Propitiation, 1 John 2:2.

Rabbi, John 1:49.
Rabboni, John 20:16.
Redeemer, Job 19:25.
Redemption, 1 Cor. 1:30.
Resurrection, John 11.25.
Righteous Branch, Jer. 23:5.
Righteous Judge, 2 Tim. 4:8.
Righteous Servant, Isa. 53:11.
Righteousness, 1 Cor. 1.30.
Rock, 1 Cor. 10.4.
Rock of Offence, 1 Pet. 2:8.
Root of David, Rev. 5.5.
Root of Jesse, Rom. 15:12.
Rose of Sharon, Sol. Song 2:1.
Ruler in Israel, Micah 5:2.

Sanctification, 1 Cor. 1:30.
Saviour, Luke 2.11.
Saviour of the body, Eph. 5:23.
Saviour of the world, 1 John 4:14.
Sceptre, Numb. 24:17.
Second man, 1 Cor. 15:47.
Seed of David, 2 Tim. 2:8.
Seed of the woman, Gen. 3:15.
Servant, Matt. 12:18.
Servant of Rulers, Isa. 49:7.
Shepherd and Bishop of Souls, 1 Peter 2:25.
Shepherd, Chief, 1 Pet. 5:4.
Shepherd, Good, John 10:11.
Shepherd, Great, Heb. 13:20.
Shepherd of Israel, Psa. 80:1.
Shiloh, Gen. 49:10.
Son Jesus Christ, 1 John 3:23.
Son of David, Matt. 21:9.
Son of God, Rev. 2:18.

Son of Joseph, Luke 3:23.
Son of man, John 3:13.
Son of Mary, Mark 6:3.
Son of the Blessed, Mark 14:61.
Son of the Father, 2 John 1:3.
Son of the Highest, Luke 1:32.
Son of the Living God, Matt. 16:16.
Son of the Most High God, Mark 5:7.
Stone, Matt. 21:42.
Stone of Stumbling, 1 Pet. 2:8.
Sun of Righteousness, Mal. 4:2.
Sure Foundation, Isa. 28:16.
Surety of a better testament, Heb. 7:22

Teacher, John 3:2.
The Beloved, Eph. 1:6.
The Man, John 19:5.
The Only Wise God, our Saviour, Jude 25.
Tried Stone, Isa. 28:16.
True, Rev 19:11.
True God, 1 John 5:20.
True Vine, John 15:1.
Truth, John 14:6.

Unspeakable Gift, 2 Cor. 9:15.

Very Christ, Acts 9:22.
Vine, John 15:5.

Way, John 14:6.
Which is, which was, which is to come, Rev. 1:4.
Wisdom of God, 1 Cor. 1:24.
Wisdom, Our, 1 Cor. 1:30.
Witness to the People, John 18:37.
Wonderful, Isa. 9:6.
Word, John 1:1.
Word of God, Rev. 19:13.
Word of Life, 1 John 1:1.

Young Child, Matt. 2:8, 13.

www.ingramcontent.com/pod-product-compliance
Lightning Source LLC
Chambersburg PA
CBHW031953300426
44117CB00008B/742